Hands-On Turbo Pascal

An Introduction to Object-Oriented Programming

Larry Joel Goldstein

Brady

New York London Toronto Sydney Tokyo Singapore

BRADY

Simon & Schuster, Inc.
15 Columbus Circle
New York, NY 10023

Manufactured in the United States of America

10 9 8 7 6 5 4 3 2 1

Library of Congress Cataloging in Publication Data

Goldstein, Larry Joel.
Hands-on Turbo Pascal : an introduction to object oriented programming / Larry Joel Goldstein.
p. cm.
Includes index.

1. Pascal (Computer program language) 2. Turbo Pascal (Computer program) 3. Object-oriented programming. I. Title.
QA76.73.P2G56 1991
005.265–dc20 91-8407
CIP

ISBN 0-13-629635-1

Contents

Limits of Liability and Disclaimer of Warranty

Trademarks

1 Introduction

As computers have become more powerful, the programs they run have become proportionately longer and more complex. In the 1950s a program of 20,000 lines was extremely ambitious. Today, many of the more complex programs demanded by the scientific and military community consist of more than one million lines! As the length of a program grows, it becomes more difficult to plan, code, and debug. To confront the difficulties inherent in building today's programs, it is necessary to plan and organize carefully. To aid in these efforts, computer scientists have developed *structured programming*, which is a set of programming rules that, if followed, avoid many sorts of programming errors and make debugging and program maintenance easier.

Object-oriented programming is another recent development from the computer scientists. It allows the programmer to reuse code that was previously developed, usually by another programmer. By making use of "objects," you can recycle old code even if you know very little of the details of how the code works. Moreover, you can even modify the effect of the code to suit your purposes! And you do this using only the compiled code, not the source code.

The Purpose of This Book

In this book, we discuss object-oriented programming using Turbo Pascal 6.0. This book teaches Pascal programming from the beginning. However, the emphasis is on using modern program design and debugging, especially structured and object-oriented techniques.

The main goals of this book are:

- **To teach programming in the Pascal language.** Pascal is a standard language for developing programs, both in the academic and commercial worlds. In this book, we teach you to program in the Turbo Pascal dialect of the Pascal programming language.

- **To discuss structured programming and object-oriented programming.** Turbo Pascal is an example of a "structured programming language." We will discuss exactly what this means, as well as how to structure your programs for clarity, efficiency, and maintainability. Turbo Pascal version 5.5 introduced object-oriented structures which increase your capability to structure your programs. We will discuss in a fair amount of detail how you can use objects in your programs.
- **To introduce general techniques of programming.** These techniques include program planning, testing, and debugging.
- **To introduce you to some significant applications of programming.** We will build a number of interesting applications programs. These programs will illustrate the tremendous range which computer applications can cover. They will also illustrate valuable programming techniques.
- **To prepare you to create Turbo Pascal application programs of your own.** By the end of this course you will be able to combine your knowledge of Turbo Pascal, general programming techniques, and knowledge of applications to build and debug your own applications programs.
- **To learn the operation of the various components of the Turbo Pascal programming environment.** Turbo Pascal is more than just a programming language. It is an integrated environment for program development, including an editor, compiler, and debugger. In this book we will teach you to operate the various elements of this programming environment.
- **To prepare you to learn to use the Turbo Vision object-oriented programming system.** Turbo Pascal 6.0 introduces Turbo Vision, a sophisticated program applications framework that minimizes many of the coding and design tasks common to most programs, tasks such as menu display and item selection, dialog boxes, mouse use, and so forth. To use Turbo Vision, it is necessary for you to understand the fundamentals of Turbo Pascal programming as well as the elements of object-oriented design. You'll acquire experience with both of these in this book. You may then go on to read the Turbo Vision manual.

Many of you will undoubtedly have some experience in programming, possibly in one of the versions of BASIC. That's fine. You may need to unlearn some bad habits you picked up, but your experience in programming will easily be adapted to Pascal.

For those of you with no experience in programming, don't worry! The book will proceed leisurely enough for you not to feel lost.

What You Need

This book discusses Turbo Pascal, versions 6.0 or later that run on an IBM PC or compatible. If you have a version earlier than 6.0, that version does not include the object-oriented structures we will be discussing. In addition, the earlier programming environment is somewhat different from the one introduced in version 6.0. So if you have a version of Turbo Pascal earlier than 6.0, you will need to upgrade it. (Call Borland International. They will tell you how to accomplish this.)

Turbo Pascal Installation

Before we begin our discussion of programming in Turbo Pascal, let's explore the Turbo Pascal programming environment. We assume that you have followed the installation instructions which came with your copy of the program. Turbo Pascal must be installed on either your hard disk or on a set of floppy disks. Note that the distribution disks may not be used to run Turbo Pascal directly, but only for the installation process.[1]

For simplicity throughout this book, we will assume that you have installed the program on a hard disk. (If you are using the program on a floppy disk, some obvious alterations from the discussion will be required.)

Borland has automated the installation process in a program INSTALL.EXE on the disk labeled **Install/Compiler**. To run this program:

1. Insert the disk containing the program INSTALL.EXE in either drive A: or B:.
2. Make the drive containing the disk the current drive.
3. Type **Install** and press Enter.
4. Follow the instructions on the screen.

You will be asked for the name of the drive containing the installation program. Enter the name of the drive (A or B) without the colon.

You are then given the choice of either installing Turbo Pascal for the first time on your hard disk, updating Turbo Pascal from a previous release, or installing Turbo Pascal on floppy disks. Let's assume that you make the first choice, first-time installation on your hard disk.

[1] Floppy disk installation does not allow the user to make use of Turbo Vision or the Turbo Help system. This is due to the limited space on a disk.

Turbo Pascal contains fairly many files. These must be organized into directories. You are asked for your choice of these directories. Until you get used to the system, you should probably not alter the default choices of directories, which are: C:\TP for all Turbo Pascal files, except C:\TP\DOC for documentation and C:\TP\TURBO3 for Turbo Pascal version 3 compatibility files. After you become more expert, you can make your own directory structure.

Now select **Start Installation**. The Turbo Pascal files will be copied to the directories specified. You will be prompted when it is necessary to change disks.

After installation is complete, you may run Turbo Pascal by making C:\TP the current directory and typing **TURBO** followed by pressing (Enter).

Starting Turbo Pascal

To start Turbo Pascal, choose as the current directory the hard disk directory which contains your Turbo Pascal program files. For instance, if you installed these files in the directory C:\TP, then you may make this the current directory using the DOS command:

CD C:\TP (Enter)

You may now start Turbo Pascal by giving the command:

TURBO (Enter)

The Turbo Pascal environment will be initialized and you will see a title screen.[2] Press any key or click on the OK box with the mouse. You will then see the Turbo Pascal environment display shown in Figure 1.1.

The Turbo Pascal Integrated Development Environment

Before we can do any programming, we must learn to operate the environment. Let's cover the basics. The *Integrated Development Environment* (IDE) has four components: the *menu bar*, the *desktop*, the *status* area, and the *output screen*. The first three are visible in Figure 1.1, so let's describe them first.

[2] The title screen is displayed only the first time you start Turbo Pascal.

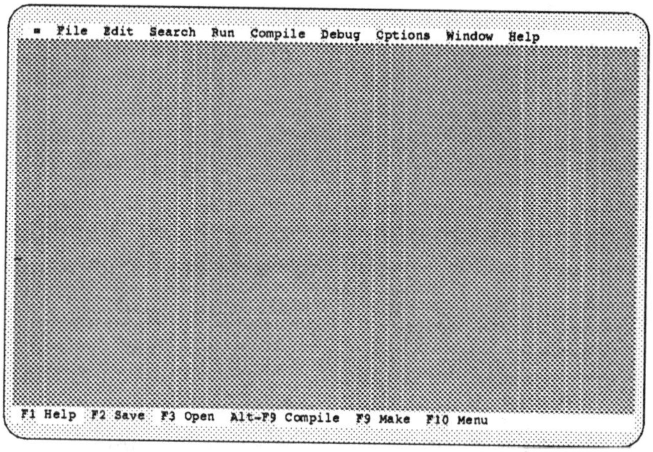

Figure 1.1.
Turbo Pascal environment display.

The menu bar is the area at the top of the screen containing a list of menus (e.g., File, Edit, Compile). You activate menus by selecting them from the menu bar.

The desktop is the area in the middle of the screen. In this area you may place one or more *windows*. There are several different types of windows. An **Edit** window is used to enter and edit program code. A **Watch** window is used to observe the values of variables and machine information while a program is running. (This is useful in debugging programs.) The desktop area can contain several windows. You can specify the precise arrangement of the desktop. You can specify the size and position of windows and you may alter the arrangement of the desktop at any time. For instance, it may be useful to have several editing windows open at once to facilitate writing one section of a program while examining the impact on another section. We will discuss manipulation of windows below.

The *status* area consists of the area at the bottom of the screen. This area is used for several purposes. First, it shows a list of any shortcut keys which are operative. The keys available will change depending on exactly what you are doing.

The status area also serves as a source of user help. As you select a command, the status area provides a description of what the command accomplishes. By referring to this area, you may preview the action of a command before you select it.

The status area also informs you of the current activities of the program. This is especially valuable during commands which last a while.

Not yet visible is the *user screen.* This screen shows program output produced when a program is run. To see the user screen, press the key combination Alt - F5. To return to the main Turbo Pascal screen, press this same key combination again. We'll see how the user screen works shortly.

The Menu Bar

Each command on the menu bar (e.g., File or Run) has a submenu of commands. You may select commands from the menu bar using either the keyboard or the mouse. There are, in fact, several ways to select a command.

Method 1

1. Press F10 to activate the menu bar.
2. Use the arrow keys to select the command you wish to execute.
3. Press Enter. The submenu associated with the command is displayed.
4. Use the arrow keys to select a command from the submenu.
5. Press Enter.

Method 2

In steps 2 and 4, you may use the highlighted letter of the command or subcommand. For example, once the menu bar is activated, you may select the **File** command by pressing the key **F**. (This is the letter which is highlighted in the menu bar entry. On some screens, the method of "highlighting" is underlining.)

Method 3

To select a menu bar command directly, use the combination Alt and the key highlighted in the command desired. For instance, to select the **File** command, you could press the key combination Alt - **F**. Note that with this method, it is not necessary to activate the menu bar first. After selecting a menu bar command, you use either the arrow keys or the highlighted letter to select a submenu command.

Method 4

Click on the command with the left mouse button. This method may be used both for commands on the Menu Bar or on a submenu.

Using one of the above four methods to select the **File** command, you will see a display like the one shown in Figure 1.2. Note the highlighted command on the submenu and the help information contained in the status

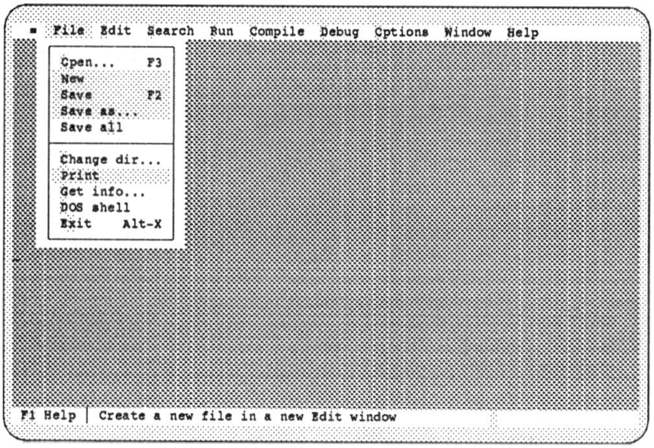

Figure 1.2.
The File submenu.

area. You may change the highlighted command using the arrow keys. As you do so, the help information changes.

The (Esc) key is used to cancel a command. By pressing (Esc), you are returned to the previous menu and any selection in a submenu is cancelled. By pressing (Esc) a number of times, you may "backtrack" through a sequence of selections, cancelling them as you go. For example, pressing (Esc) in the previous situation will cancel the File submenu and return you to the desktop.

Some submenu commands have an arrow at the end of their menu entry. Selecting such a command results in display of another menu (a sub-submenu—see Figure 1.3). You select commands from the sub-submenu just as you would from the submenu.

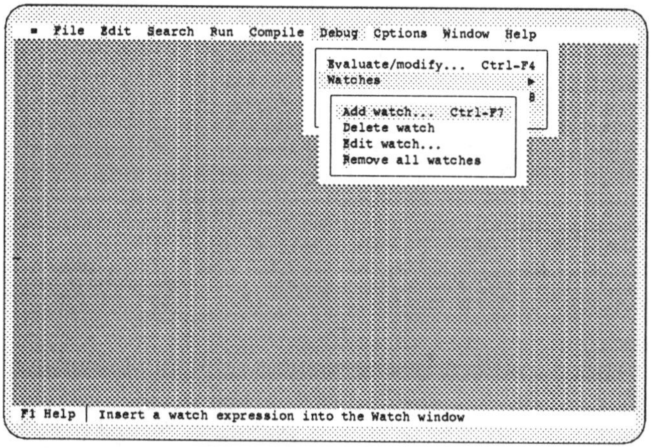

Figure 1.3.
A sub-submenu.

Some submenu commands have three dots at the end of their menu entry. Selecting such a command results in display of a *dialog box.* (See Figure 1.4.) Such a box allows you to supply information either by filling in fields or "pressing buttons." We will discuss the operation of dialog boxes shortly.

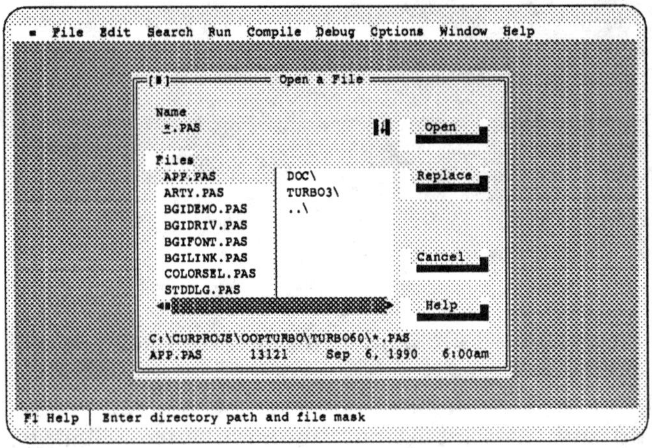

Figure 1.4.
A dialog box.

Windows

There are several different types of windows used by Turbo Pascal. However, all of these windows have the following common characteristics: a window number, a title bar, a close box, scroll bars, a resize corner, and a zoom box. Let's learn to do window manipulations using these elements.

In order to have a concrete window to work with, start Turbo Pascal and obtain the screen showing the initial (blank) desktop. Select the menu command **Help** and select the subcommand **Help on Help** to display the Help window shown in Figure 1.5.

The window has a border, the *frame.* Look along the top of the frame. In the center is a title bar which identifies the window. In this case, the title bar tells you that the window is a Help window. Later, we will introduce Edit windows which can be used to enter or edit programs. For these windows, the title bar gives the name of the file you are editing.

At the top right corner of the frame is a digit, an identifying number of the window. Windows are numbered consecutively, in the order in which they are opened.

At the top left corner of the frame is a square, called the *close box* of the window. By clicking on the close box with the mouse, you can close the window. That is, you can eliminate the window from the screen.

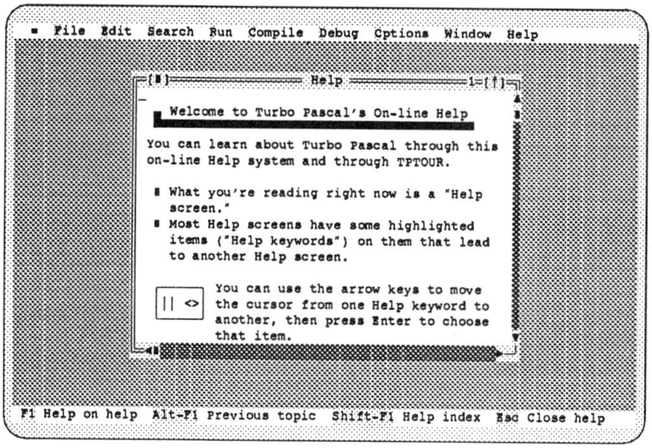

Figure 1.5.
A Help window.

The bottom right corner of the frame is the *resize corner.* It is used to change the size of the window. To do so, select the resize corner with the mouse and drag the mouse until the bottom right corner corresponds to the size window you want. For example, Figure 1.6 shows the result of changing the size of the Help window.

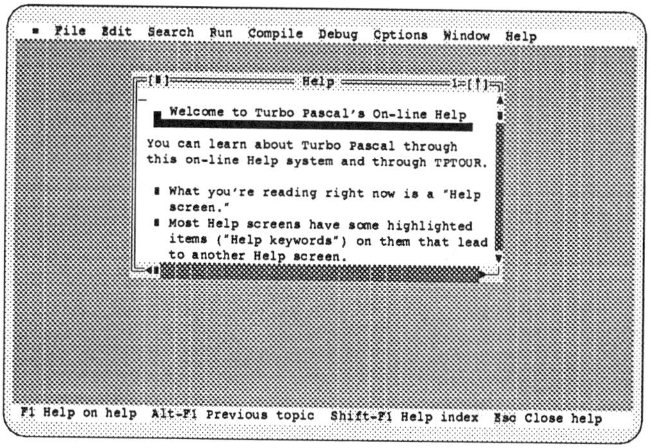

Figure 1.6.
Changing the size of the Help window.

Along the right and bottom sides of the frame are *scroll bars,* which allow you to scroll the contents of the window horizontally or vertically. To do this, drag with the mouse along the appropriate scroll bar or click on the arrows at either end. The window will scroll in the direction you drag. The size of the scroll is proportional to the length of the drag or click. You should practice scrolling the Help window in all directions.

At the right end of the top of the frame is a single or double arrow. This symbol is the *zoom box.* By clicking on this box with the mouse, you can zoom the window to full screen. (See Figure 1.7.) By clicking on it again, you can zoom the window to its original size. When zoomed to full screen, the symbol is a double arrow; when zoomed to original size, the symbol is a single arrow.

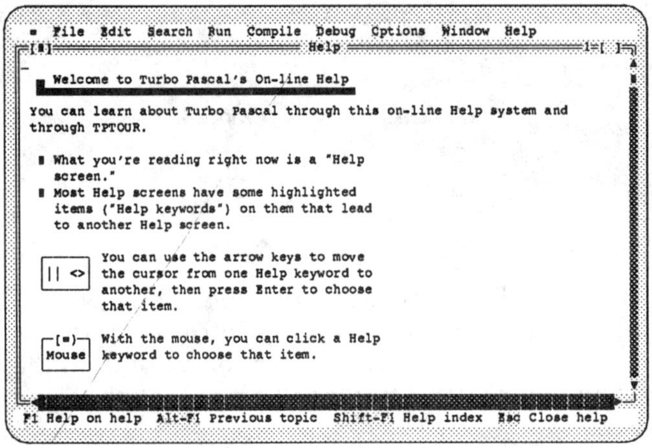

Figure 1.7.
Zooming the Help window to full screen.

It is typical to have several windows open at once. Let's create an Edit window by giving the command **File|New**. This creates a window with a title bar NONAME00.PAS, as shown in Figure 1.8. Let's give this command again to create another window, as shown in Figure 1.9.

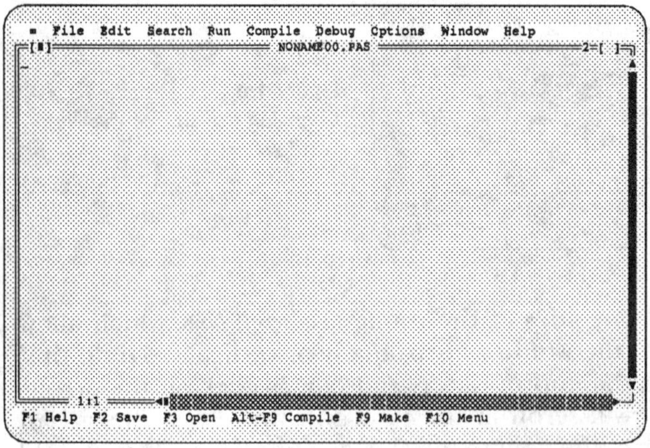

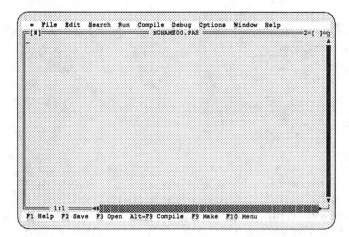

Figure 1.8.
Adding an Edit window.

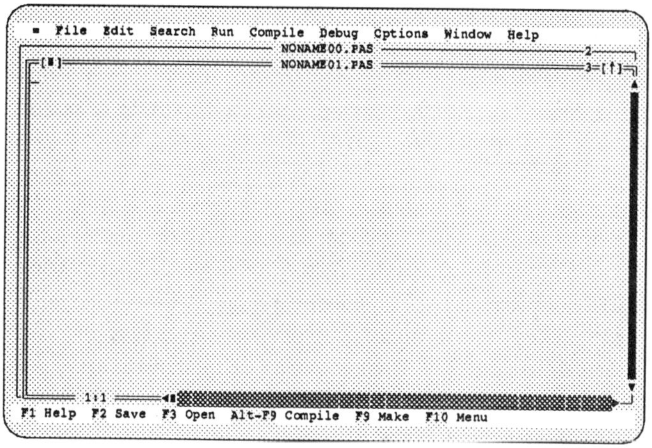

Figure 1.9.
Adding another Edit window.

Note that the two Edit windows cover up the Help window created earlier. This is because they are both full-screen windows. You may resize them so that all three windows are visible. This is done by using the resize corner of each window. Moreover, you may reposition a window on the screen by dragging on the top of the frame. It is a good exercise to use these operations to duplicate the window arrangement shown in Figure 1.10.

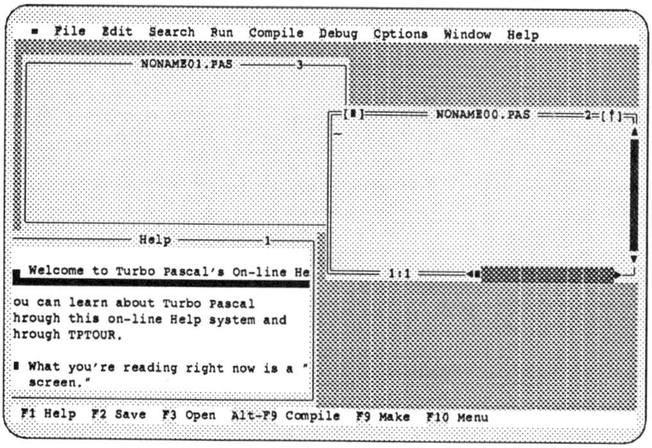

Figure 1.10.
Arranging the windows.

At any given moment, one window is designated as the *active window*. This window has a highlighted frame. For example, in Figure 1.10, window 2 is active. You may change the active window by clicking the mouse anywhere in the new active window. Alternatively, you may give a command with the form: Alt -#

Here, # denotes the number of the window to be made active. This command not only activates the window but also displays the window if it is not visible. By pressing the key F6, you may cycle through the various windows, making each window active in turn.

We have described various window operations using the mouse. There are keyboard analogues for each of these operations. Most can be accessed using the **Window** command on the Menu Bar. For instance, there are submenu commands under Window which allow you to zoom, resize, and close windows. There are also function-key equivalent commands. However, for purposes of this text, let's stick to either mouse or menu operations. As you become more proficient, you may want to substitute some keyboard shortcuts for these. Refer to your *Turbo Pascal 6.0 User's Guide* for tables of keyboard shortcuts.

Dialog Boxes

Let's now learn to manipulate dialog boxes. The typical dialog box asks you to provide a number of pieces of information. You can provide the information in any order and may change the data as many times as you wish. Each dialog box has three standard action buttons: **Cancel** closes the dialog box and ignores all its current settings; **OK** causes all the current settings to be read; **Help** opens a Help window which provides help in filling out the dialog box.

You may move around a dialog box using the mouse or the keys Tab and Shift - Tab (which move forward and backward, respectively, through the fields of the dialog box).

In addition to the action buttons, there are four types of fields which are used in dialog boxes: check boxes, radio buttons, input boxes, and list boxes.

A *check box* is a choice for which you specify YES or NO by checking the box or not. You may use a mouse click or the spacebar to toggle a check box between its two options. A YES choice is indicated by placing an X next to the option.

A set of *radio buttons*—as its name implies—is a set of options, out of which you must pick one. To select your choice from a set of radio buttons, you use either a mouse click or the arrow keys. The selected option is then indicated by a dot placed before the option.

An *input box* allows you to type text. For instance, in the dialog box associated with the File|Open command, there is an input box into which you type the name of the file to be opened. Input boxes may be edited using the Del, Backspace, and arrow keys.

A *list box* displays a list (such as a list of files or directories) from which you may make a choice. Often, the list is too large to fit in a list box. To view a different section of such a list, you may use the scroll bars on the right side of the list box to move up to down in the list. You may select an item from a list using the arrow keys or a mouse click.

Entering and Editing Program Source Code

To create a program in Turbo Pascal, you must first enter the instructions you wish the program to perform. You do this by typing the instructions in the edit window. The process of entering and correcting program instructions is called *editing* and is performed in an Edit window.

To open a new Edit window, give the command **File|New**. A new window named NONAME00.PAS will be displayed as shown in Figure 1.11.

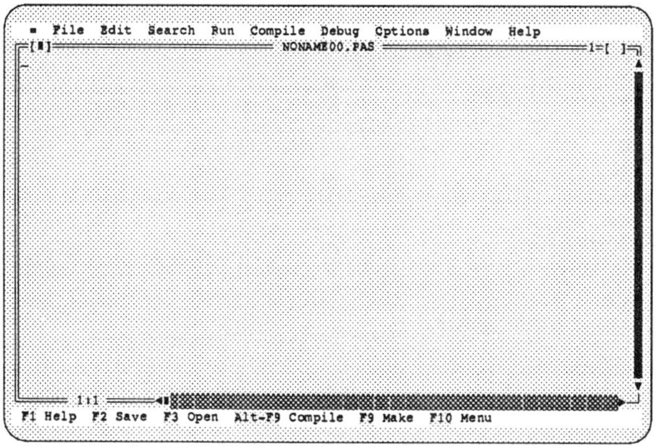

Figure 1.11.
A new Edit window.

To use the Edit window, just make it active. (Either click inside the window with the mouse or give the command Alt -#, where # is the number of the Edit window.) Once the Edit window is active, you may enter text into the window.

```
  ▪  File  Edit  Search  Run  Compile  Debug  Options  Window  Help
┌─[▪]──────────────────── NONAME00.PAS ─────────────────── 1=[↑]═╕
│program Greeting;                                                ▲│
│                                                                 ▪│
│var                                                              ▪│
│  Name : string[25];                                             ▪│
│                                                                  │
│begin                                                             │
│  writeln('Hello. What is your name?');                           │
│  readln(Name);                                                   │
│  writeln('Nice to meet you, ', Name, '. Greetings!');            │
│  writeln('Learning Pascal is fun.')                              │
│end._                                                             │
│                                                                  │
│                                                                 ▼│
├─── 11:5 ═══◄█▒▒▒▒▒▒▒▒▒▒▒▒▒▒▒▒▒▒▒▒▒▒▒▒▒▒▒▒▒▒▒▒▒▒▒▒▒▒▒▒▒▒▒▒▒▒▒█─►─┘
│ F1 Help  F2 Save  F3 Open  Alt-F9 Compile  F9 Make  F10 Menu
```

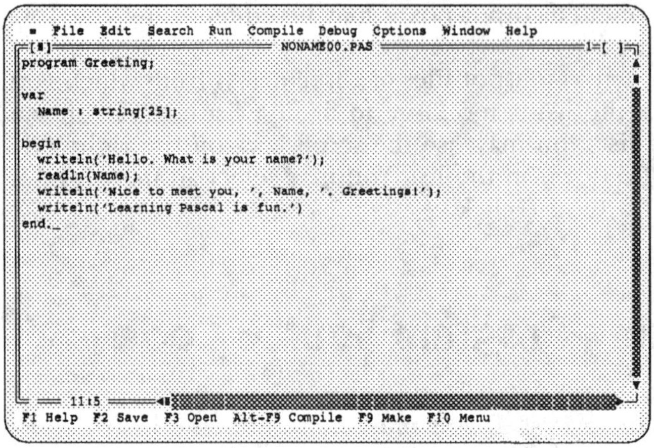

Figure 1.12.
A short Pascal program.

In Figure 1.12, we show a short program you can use to practice on. Type in this program exactly as you see it. Be especially careful to type in the punctuation exactly as you see it. As we will learn shortly, punctuation is very important in Pascal.

Correcting Errors

The Turbo Pascal editor provides a number of methods for correcting errors. The simplest method is to use the backspace key or the Del (= Delete) key.

Pressing the backspace key moves the cursor to the left one space and erases the character in that space. Text to the right of the cursor moves left to fill the space that was occupied by the deleted character.

Pressing the Del key deletes the character at the cursor position. Text to the right of the cursor moves left to fill the space that was occupied by the deleted character.

Moving the Cursor

Typed letters are always inserted at the current cursor position. You may move the cursor within the document by using the arrow keys provided on the numeric keypad, usually on the right side of the keyboard. Using these keys, you may move the cursor up, down, right, and left a line or character at a time, but for more extensive moves within a file, you may use the PgDn and PgUp keys which move the cursor down or up, respectively, a screen at a time.

Note, however, that the keys of the numeric keypad may be used for cursor movement only when the NumLock key is *not* engaged (the default state). If the cursor motion keys don't seem to be working, try pressing the NumLock key.

Overtype Mode versus Insert Mode

There are two typing modes provided by the Turbo Pascal editor. In overtype mode, characters you type replace characters already typed. This is similar to typing on a typewriter. In insert mode, characters you type are inserted. Any text to the right of the cursor is moved over to make room for the characters you type. The default mode is the insert mode.

Note that in insert mode the cursor appears as an underscore character (_), whereas in overtype mode it appears as a solid block.

You may switch between insert and overtype mode using the command Ctrl - **V**. (Hold down Ctrl and type **V**.) This can also be done by pressing the Ins key.

For beginners, the insert mode may seem clumsy since it violates what may be the expectations you've gained from using a typewriter. However, after using it, you will become accustomed to insert mode, which for most work is more useful than overtype mode.

Inserting a Line

You may insert a group of lines anywhere within the program text as follows:

1. Position the cursor at the beginning of the line following the location of the inserting.
2. Press Enter . This inserts a blank line above the cursor.
3. Move the cursor up to the beginning of the blank line just created.
4. Enter the desired lines.

Deleting a Line

Here are two methods to delete a whole line:

1. Position the cursor at the beginning of the line and repeatedly press the Del key to delete all characters on the line. Then press the Del key one more time. This will delete the blank line.
2. Position the cursor anywhere in the line, hold down Ctrl and press **Y**.

Auto-Indentation

Note that the sample program is formatted like an outline, with some lines indented. Such formatting makes programs more readable. In order to simplify entry of programs in formatted form, the Turbo Pascal editor automatically indents each line the same amount as the previous line. If you don't like this indentation, use the space bar or tab key to move further to the right or the backspace key to move to the left.

You may turn the auto-indentation feature on and off using the command F10|**Options**|**Environment**|**Autoindent Mode**.

The Edit Menu

The Edit menu is shown in Figure 1.13. This menu contains a number of extremely useful and powerful editing commands.

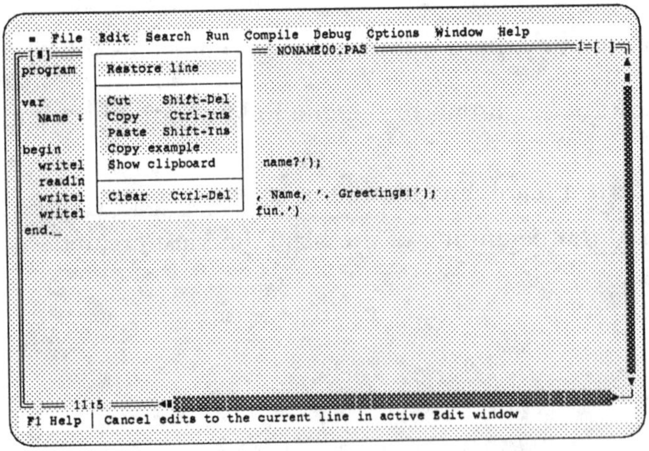

Figure 1.13.
The Edit menu.

The Restore line command is an "undo" feature that reverses the last command that modified or deleted a line. If a line was modified, the modification is undone; if a line was deleted, it is replaced. This command provides "oops" insurance.

To copy, delete, or move a block of text, you must first select the block. To do this, you may use either the mouse or the keyboard. Using the mouse, position the cursor at the first character of the block and drag to the last character. The block will be highlighted. To unselect a block, click the mouse anywhere in the Edit window. To select a block using the keyboard, position the cursor at the first character and press Ctrl-**K-B**; then position the cursor just after the last character of the block and press Ctrl-**K-K**. The selected block will be highlighted. To deselect a selected block from the keyboard, use the command Ctrl-**K-H**.

Once a block is selected, you may copy it to another portion of the document by first positioning the cursor at the desired point of insertion and giving the command Ctrl-**K-C**. This original block becomes deselected and the copy is selected. (This is to facilitate making multiple copies.)

Once a block is selected, you may move it to another portion of the document by first positioning the cursor at the desired new location and giving the command Ctrl-**K-V**.

Once a block is selected, you may erase it by giving the command Ctrl-**K-X**.

You may also manipulate blocks using a special area of memory called the *clipboard,* which is used to hold the most recently copied or deleted text. Commands that use the clipboard are found in the Edit menu (see Figure 1.13).

The Cut command deletes a selected block of text and stores it on the clipboard. From the keyboard, the Cut command may be given by the key combination Shift - Del.

The Copy command copies a selected block to the clipboard without deleting the block. From the keyboard, the Copy command may be given by the key combination Ctrl - Ins.

The Paste command retrieves the contents of the clipboard and inserts them at the current cursor position. From the keyboard, the Paste command may be given by the key combination Shift - Ins.

Using the combination of Cut and Paste, you may move a block of text from one location to the other. You may even cut text from one window and paste it to another. Using Copy and Paste, you may make copies of a block of text.

The command Show clipboard shows you the current contents of the clipboard. The command Clear deletes a selected block, but does not store it on the clipboard. From the keyboard, the Clear command may be given by the key combination Ctrl - Del.

Other Editor Features

The Turbo Pascal editor has many of the features commonly found on word processors, including search and replace operations. Furthermore, it includes a number of cursor movement operations and text delete options which we have not discussed. For more information about the editor commands, see the *Turbo Pascal 6.0 User's Guide.* However, we recommend that you postpone learning any more about the editor until you have learned something about the language part of the system. The above brief discussion is more than enough to get you started.

Deactivating the Edit Window

To deactivate the Edit window you are working in, just activate some other window or the Menu Bar. The text entered in the Edit window remains in RAM. You may reactivate the window and do further editing. Note, however, that deactivating the Edit window does not cause the current program to be saved. This must be done by giving the **File|Save** command (keyboard equivalent F2). (See below.)

The File Command

The File command keyboard equivalent Alt-**F** provides a number of subcommands which allow you to save and recall files. (Figure 1.14 shows the submenu associated to the File command.)

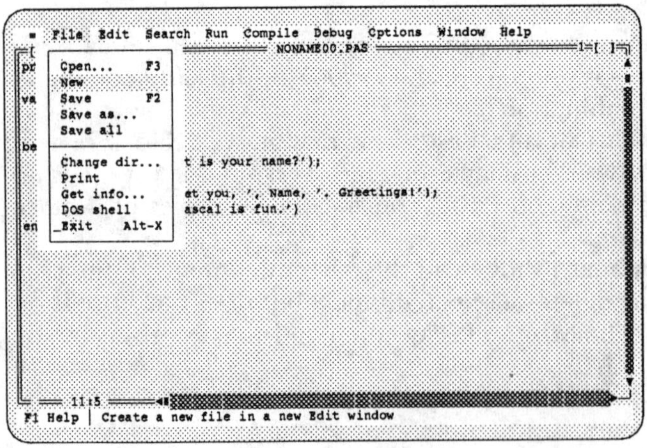

Figure 1.14.
The File submenu.

Activate the window containing the program previously shown in Figure 1.12. Now select the command **File|Save.** Since you have not yet specified a name for the file to contain the program, you are presented with the dialog box shown in Figure 1.15.

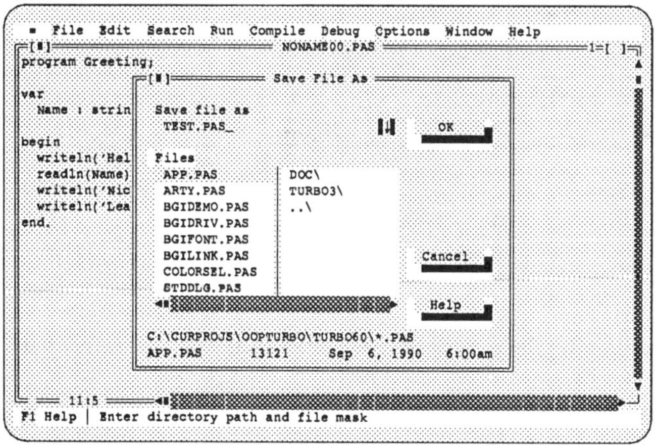

Figure 1.15.
The Save Dialog box.

In the top field, enter the name of the file in which you want to save the current edit window contents (TEST.PAS). You may specify the directory either by typing a complete file specification or by building up the path to the desired directory by choosing subdirectories from the File list at the bottom of the dialog box. When you have specified the file name you wish, select **OK** in the dialog box and the file will be saved as specified.

You should save your program as you are writing it, say every 10 minutes or so. The keyboard shortcut F2 may be used to save the current file you are editing. If you are simultaneously editing in several windows at once, the command File|Save all may be used to save all edit windows at once.

Turbo Pascal maintains a current directory which is used to save and recall files for which no path is specifically given. You may set the current directory using the command File|Change dir... . In the example above, we used the default directory, which is the directory from which *Turbo Pascal* was run.

Once you have saved a file under a given file name, the File|Save command will automatically save the file under the previously given name. If you wish to change the file name or path, you may use the File|Save As... command.

To recall a file, use the **File|Open** (keyboard equivalent F3). The program then displays the dialog box shown in Figure 1.16. You may type in the file to load it or you may choose it from the list at the bottom of the dialog box. Once you specify the file to load, select Open. The file will be loaded

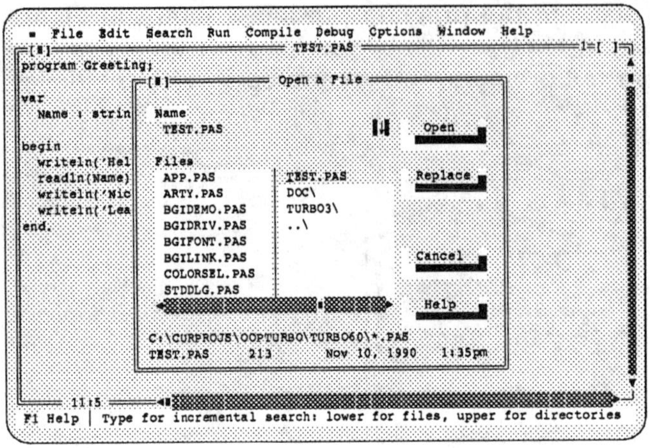

Figure 1.16.
The Open Dialog box.

into a new window. Selecting Replace will load the file into the currently activated Edit window.

The command File|New opens a new Edit window with a file name NONAMEXX.PAS. You may assign your own name when saving the file.

Compiling a Program

The program TEST.PAS which we have just saved is still stored in RAM. However, it is not in a form that the computer may execute. To convert it into such a form, you must compile it using the Compile command on the menu bar. When you give this command, you will see the submenu shown in Figure 1.17.

Select the **Compile** option from this submenu. The program will then be *compiled* (converted into machine language instructions). If Turbo Pascal encounters no errors in your program, you will see a report of successful compilation as shown in Figure 1.18.

A shortcut for executing the Compile command is the Alt-F9 key combination.

There are two types of compilation. In the first, you compile the program to memory. In this case, the machine instructions are stored in RAM and may be executed as described below. However, when you exit Turbo Pascal, the executable version of the program is erased.

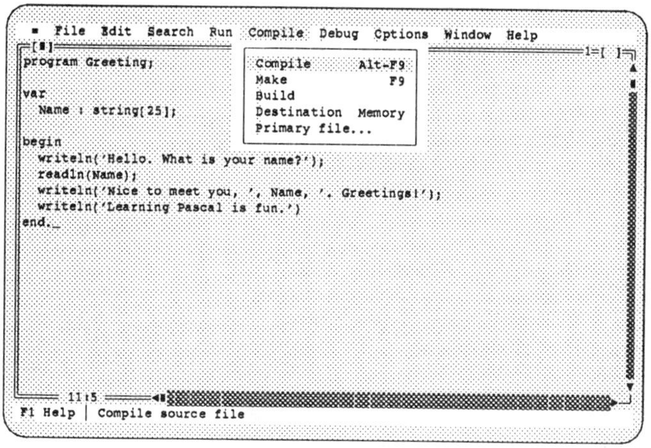

Figure 1.17.
The Compile submenu.

A second method is to compile the program to disk. In this case, Turbo Pascal stores the executable instructions in a file on disk. The file name is the same as you have assigned to the program, but an extension EXE is assigned. The file so created is a stand-alone program which can be run outside of Turbo Pascal. To run such a program, just type the program name (without the EXE extension) and press Enter at the DOS prompt.

The choice among the two methods of compilation is made using the Destination option on the Compile menu. To change this entry, select the desired method of compilation and press Enter. The method of compilation alternates between the choices Memory and Disk.

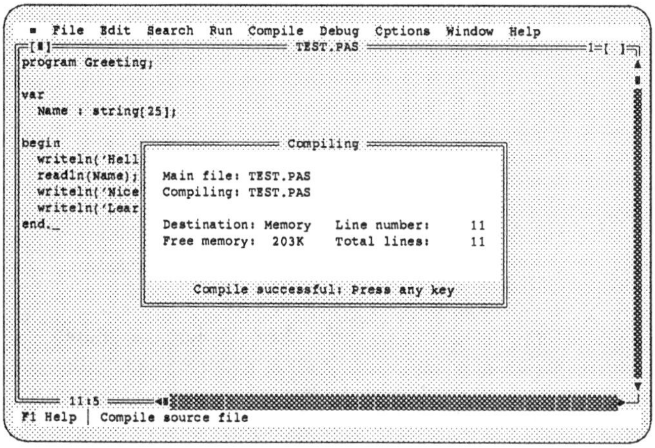

Figure 1.18.
Report of successful compilation.

Running a Program

We now assume that you have successfully entered and compiled the example program. Let's now run it. This can be done by selecting the command Run from the Menu Bar. You will see a submenu as shown in Figure 1.19.

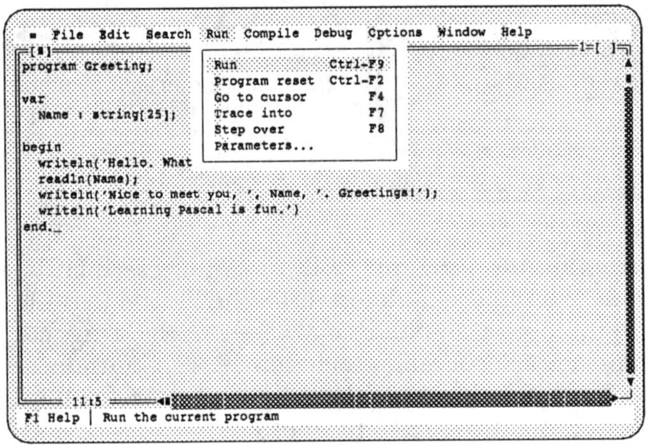

Figure 1.19.
Run submenu.

Select the **Run** entry (keyboard equivalent Ctrl - F9). The program will now be run. The display switches to the user window, which displays the program output and the user input. (See Figure 1.20.)

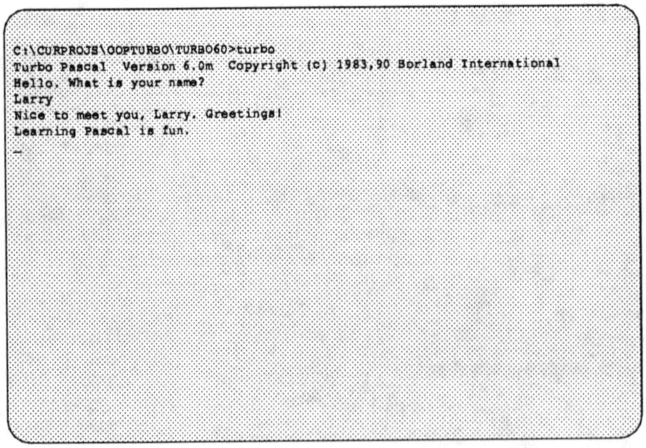

Figure 1.20.
Window displaying program output and user input.

Note that the program asks for the user's name and greets the user. As soon as the program completes execution, the display switches back to the main screen (the one with the Edit window and Menu Bar). In most cases, you will note that the user window disappears too fast for you to examine it in detail. You may switch back to the user window by using the key combination Alt - F5. Using this key combination a second time returns the display to the main screen.

You may rerun the program as many times as you wish, possibly using different sets of input data for each run. For each run, the user window is updated to include any new input and output.

Errors in Compilation

Let's return to the main screen and activate the Edit window containing our program. Delete the line of the program in the `var` section which defines the variable `Name`. The program should now appear as shown in Figure 1.21.

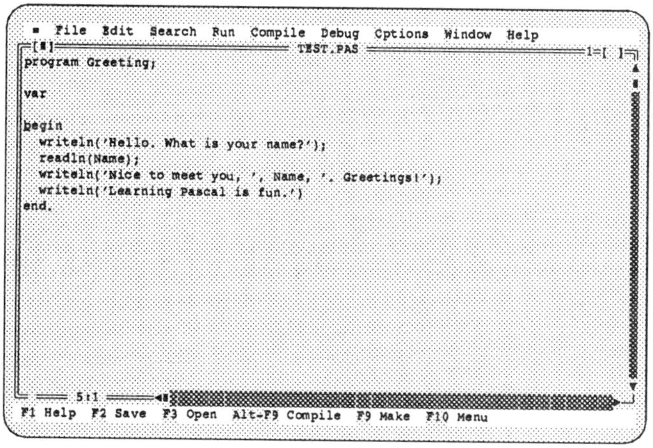
File Edit Search Run Compile Debug Options Window Help
TEST.PAS
program Greeting;
var
begin
writeln('Hello. What is your name?');
readln(Name);
writeln('Nice to meet you, ', Name, '. Greetings!');
writeln('Learning Pascal is fun.')
end.
5:1
F1 Help F2 Save F3 Open Alt-F9 Compile F9 Make F10 Menu

Figure 1.21.
Program after deleting line in the var section which defines the variable Name.

Now try to compile the program. Note that the program gives a message indicating that an error was found. Moreover, the cursor points to the place in the program at which the error was found. (See Figure 1.22.) A compilation error occurs when Turbo Pascal is unable to understand the program as it is written. In this case, the variable `Name` is not defined. In response to the error message, press Esc. You are returned to the Edit window, where you may correct the mistake. Once you do this, recompile the program to check that the mistake was, indeed, corrected.

Errors are found in the order in which they appear. Turbo Pascal indicates the first error that it finds. To find subsequent errors in order, use the command **Search|Find error**.

```
  ▪  File  Edit  Search  Run  Compile  Debug  Options  Window  Help
┌[▪]══════════════════════ TEST.PAS ══════════════════════1═[ ]═┐
│ Error 2: Identifier expected.                                  ▲
│
│var
│
│begin
│  writeln('Hello. What is your name?');
│  readln(Name);
│  writeln('Nice to meet you, ', Name, '. Greetings!');
│  writeln('Learning Pascal is fun.')
│end.
│
│
│
│
│
│
│
│
│ ── 5:1 ───── ◀▪                                                ▼
F1 Help  F2 Save  F3 Open  Alt-F9 Compile  F9 Make  F10 Menu
```

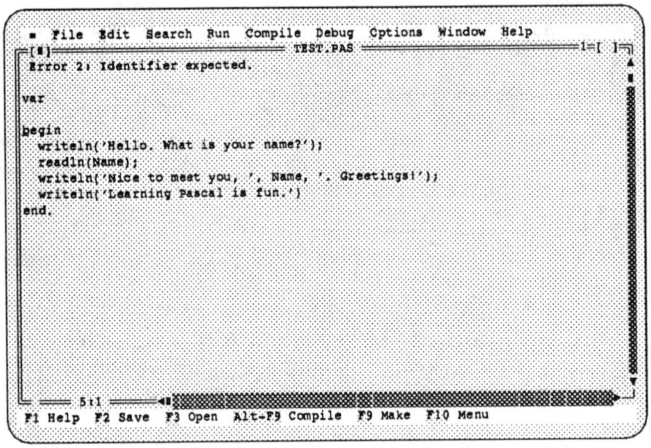

Figure 1.22.
Cursor pointing to the place in the program where the error was found.

Quitting Turbo Pascal

To leave Turbo Pascal, use the command **File|Exit**. An alternate method is to use the key combination Alt-**F-X** or just Alt **X**. In either case, the Turbo Pascal program is terminated and you are returned to the DOS prompt. If you have a file which has not been saved, you are asked whether you wish to save it.

Place First Class
Postage Here
Post Office
Will Not Deliver
Without Postage

College Marketing Group
50 Cross Street
Winchester, MA 01890

ATT: **Cheryl Read**

2 Structured Programming and Top-Down Design

With a view to learning about object-oriented programming later in the book, let's begin by discussing the fundamentals of program planning and program design in Pascal. This will enable us to write our first Pascal programs and introduce us to procedures which are an important ingredient in defining objects.

Pascal was originally designed in the early 1970s as a language to teach the principles of what were then the most recent precepts in program design. Over the last two decades, it has become one of the most widely used programming languages, used both for teaching programming and for development of applications programs. Let's start our discussion of Pascal by giving a brief overview of the program development process and where Pascal fits in. This chapter will lay out the design principles which we will follow in the remainder of the book.

The Program Development Process

In order to construct a house, you must follow an organized sequence of steps: design, permits, excavation, foundation, framing, and so forth. Each step in the building process prepares the way for the next. Moreover, by pursuing an organized approach to building, you minimize the amount of time it takes and cut down on the number of errors.

Constructing a program is very similar to building a house. In order to carry out a programming task in the minimum amount of time and with the fewest possible errors, you must follow an organized program development process that should consist of all of the following steps:

1. *Program planning.* Decide what the program is to do.
2. *Program design.* Plan how the program will work.
3. *Coding.* Write the program code in an appropriate computer language.
4. *Debugging.* Correct any errors in the program.
5. *Documentation.* Write a detailed description of how the program works and how it may be used.
6. *Maintenance.* Correct errors as users point them out. Modify the program in response to user suggestions and needs.

Let's discuss in further detail what is involved in each of these steps.

Program Planning

One of the principal defects of the classic BASIC programming language is that it allows you to sit down and start writing a program without much thought or planning. (And I'll bet many of you thought that was an advantage!) You may be able to get away without planning if you are writing a small program. But as soon as the program becomes the slightest bit complex, program planning becomes a necessity. Your planning must include the following:

- **A clear statement of what the program is supposed to accomplish.** Unless you are clear about the goals of the program, it is highly unlikely that you will be able to successfully write a program to accomplish those goals.
- **A list of the inputs to the program.** This list must include all data the program requires to accomplish its goals and the sources for these data. Potential sources include user input from the keyboard, data files on disk, and communications input, as well as input from a mouse, a digitizer, or any of the many other devices that can be connected to a PC.
- **A list of the outputs from the program.** This list must contain all data that result from running the program and the form in which the data is output: screen, printer, disk file, plotter, and so forth.
- **An analysis of the data manipulation to be accomplished within the program.** That is, what operations must the program perform on the data in order to transform inputs into the required outputs?

- **A plan for the user interface to the program.** That is, you just decide on how the user will interact with the program and how this interaction will take place so as to make it as "user-friendly" as possible.

Program Design

The second step in program development is transforming your program plan into a design, which can be used as the basis for coding and debugging. In this step, you describe the operation of your program using either *flow charts* or *pseudocode.* Flow charts are useful in providing a visual description of a program's parts and how they interrelate to one another. On the other hand, pseudocode consists of a description of a program in English-like shorthand. Flow charts are useful for visualizing the interrelationship of the various sections of a program and the corresponding necessary divisions of labor if several programmers are required simultaneously to work on it. On the other hand, the pseudocode resembles the actual program code. If you do a careful job of describing the program in pseudocode, the coding process can be significantly shortened.

Both flow charts and pseudocode are in common use. In fact, for some complex programming tasks, you may want to describe the program using both of them. We will discuss pseudocode and flow charts further in the next section.

Your program design should include a description of any data organization that the program requires. Some data may be stored in individual variables, whereas other data may be organized into arrays of one or more dimensions.

Furthermore, the program design should include a description of any required algorithms for manipulating the data. (An *algorithm* is a sequence of computer instructions that accomplishes a specific task.) That is, the program design should include a detailed description of how you expect the program to handle the required calculations, data searching, data sorting, data input, and data output.

Finally, the program design should incorporate a description of the user interface. That is, it should include the design of any required input and output screens, and the technique to be used for user interaction with the program.

Coding

The third step in developing a program consists of writing the program code. (This is the step that novices like to jump right into.) In this step, you write computer instructions that carry out the tasks described in the program design. The computer instructions are written in a computer language that allows you to describe the program in a language close to English. For the purposes of this book, we assume that the computer language is Turbo Pascal. However, there are hundreds of languages available. The language you use could just as well be assembly language, BASIC, C, FORTRAN, or Ada.

You write the program code using Turbo Pascal's built-in editor. The program as you enter it is called *source code.* To run the program, your source code must be translated into instructions which the computer can directly interpret. These instructions are called *object code* and are created by compiling the source code.

Testing and Debugging

Testing is the process of checking that a program actually does what you planned it to do. *Debugging* is the process of correcting programming errors. Testing and debugging are related operations carried out at various stages during coding (to test sections of a program) and after coding is complete (to test the operation of the entire program). Throughout the book, we will give tips on testing and debugging procedures.

Documentation

Documentation is written material used to describe a program. Generally speaking, documentation is divided into two categories: user documentation and technical documentation.

User documentation is a description, in nontechnical terms, of how to use the program. This description tells the user what the program does, how to install it for a particular installation, how to respond to the various requests for user interaction, and how to interpret output and error messages provided by the program.

Technical documentation describes, in technical terms, how the program is organized and how it operates. This documentation is principally addressed to programmers who may be called on later to correct bugs and to modify the program. The technical documentation consists of two parts: documented source code and a reference manual. The documented source code consists of the program code with remarks that describe how each section of the program functions and the reasons for the various design decisions made by the original programmer. The reference manual consists of a detailed description of the action of the program in response to each of its user commands.

Maintenance

Maintenance involves repairing bugs that are spotted by program users and making alterations of the program, often in response to user requests for improved operation or additional program features. Program maintenance often must be carried out by a programmer other than the one who did the original programming. Accordingly, maintenance is vitally dependent on the quality of the documentation created in the original program development.

Even if the original programmer must do the maintenance, good documentation is still the key. Imagine trying to remember how a program works several years after you wrote it! Moral: Create detailed documentation. The best idea is to generate your document as you proceed with the program development process. Write your documentation as you develop the code. In that way, the rationale for the code will be fresh in your mind and you won't need to remember just why you handled coding in a particular fashion.

The program development process is summarized in Figure 2.1.

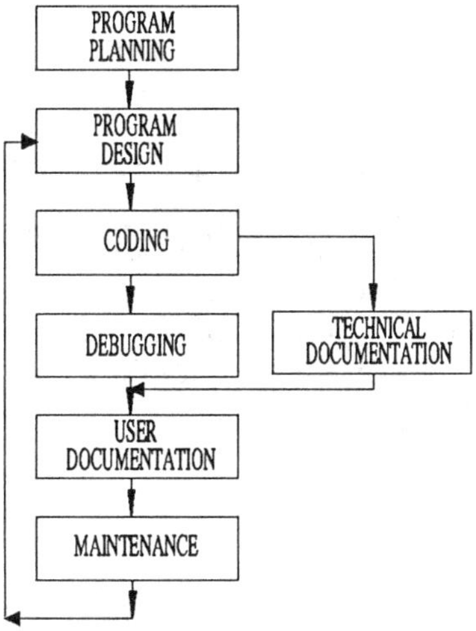

Figure 2.1. The program development process.

Top-Down Design

Complex problems typically have solutions composed of a number of parts. In order to solve the problem, it is therefore useful to break it down into smaller problems and solve each of these component problems. A similar approach works in planning complex programs: Break the program down into a sequence of subprograms. Plan each of the subprograms as if it were a program in its own right. In planning each of the subprograms, it may be necessary to break them down further into subprograms. And so on, using as many levels of refinement as proves necessary to completely plan all details of the program.

The process we have just described is called *top-down design,* since it proceeds from the "top" (the main program) "down" (toward a more detailed description of program components). This process is the one used by most professional programmers in designing their programs. It is a good idea for you to learn how to apply it in designing your programs.

To illustrate the process of top-down design, it is best to give a particular example. Let's use top-down design to create a program to calculate a user's age in days. This program, which we will call AgeInDays, consists of several parts, which can be described by the following outline:

```
Program AgeInDays

  Initial Setup
  Get User's Birth Date
  Compute Age In Days
  Display result
```

The above outline uses English phrases to describe the steps the program requires. Such a description of a program is called *pseudocode.* Note that each descriptive phrase corresponds to a section of program code, which may consist of one or many instructions. The details describing each phrase are not given. Rather, the outline describes the logical structure of the program. Of course, in order to code the program, further details are necessary. Each of the steps that are not completely detailed must be fleshed out. Here is the next level of detail in the program.

```
Program AgeInDays

  Initial Setup
    Get today's date
    Set up table of month lengths
  Get User's Birth Date
    Get date in form mm/dd/yyyy
    Convert input into month, day, and year
  Compute Age In Days
  Display result
```

This last level of description is not yet complete. You must still give the details of how the calculation of the age is done. This involves determining which years are leap years, the number of days in each of the complete years, the number of days in each of the months, and the calculation of the number of days in a fractional part of a month. We'll discuss these details later, as we learn more about Pascal. However, for now, just note that in order to plan a program via top-down design, it is necessary to successively refine the program details through a number of levels. You continue the refinement process until the level of detail is sufficient to write Pascal instructions implementing each detail.

A program developed in this fashion very closely resembles an outline. The main steps of the program provide the first level of detail, the next level of detail corresponds to the second level of the outline, the next level of detail to the third level, and so forth. The idea of writing a program in such an outline form is to make clear the logical structure of the program. At each level of program design (i.e., at each outline level), you are worrying only about program details of a particular level of specificity. This allows you to plan a program and develop it in a sequence of orderly steps, progressively pinning down details as you address higher levels of the outline.

The final outline of the program should allow you to write the code with little additional thought.

The English-language outline for a program, as illustrated above, is called pseudocode, as stated earlier. Use of pseudocode is a common technique for implementing top-down design in preparation for coding in a program language (not only Pascal).

Structured Programming

In the preceding section, we described the top-down procedure for designing programs. This procedure allows you to design programs that have a structure to them. This structure is conferred by the outline you use to organize the program. Actually, in your design and implementation of a program, there is much you can do to make the program structure work for you in making the program easier to design, debug, and maintain. There are a few rules you should follow in designing your program structure:

1. The program design should be stated (in pseudocode) so that you may easily trace the sequence of tasks to be performed.
2. Each task should correspond to a subprogram.
3. Carefully plan the exchange of data between sections of a program. Specifically, state the input data that each section receives and the output data that it must supply.
4. Each subprogram should perform its task independently of the other modules. That is, given the appropriate input data, a module should carry out its task and supply the required data to the main program

without interfering with the other modules. In particular, the only variables of the main program that a module should change are those that represent data the module is asked to supply.

If you don't adhere to rule 4, you can create what are known as side effects. A *side effect* of a subprogram is a program statement that has an unintended effect in the main program. For example, suppose that the main program uses the variable J. Suppose that within a subprogram, you use J as a variable in a loop. If you don't plan your program carefully, on exiting the subprogram, J has the final value it achieved within the loop. In particular, the original value of J in the main program has been lost. This loss of J's value is a side effect of the subprogram. Side effects create bugs that are often very difficult to track down. One of the fundamental goals of structured programming is to avoid side effects.

As we shall soon see, Pascal is a language expressly designed for structured programming. In the chapters that follow, we will learn how to organize Turbo Pascal programs in a structured fashion as well as to make use of the object-oriented features of Turbo Pascal. (More about objects later.)

The Elements of a Pascal Program

By way of a preview, the program AgeInDays is shown in Listing 2.1, below. This listing might seem a bit formidable at this point, but it illustrates most of the features to be found in Pascal programs. So let's call attention to some of the most important.

The program begins with a *program header:*

```
program AgeInDays;
```

This line gives the program a name (AgeInDays). Note that the program is arranged like an outline, exhibiting its top-down design. The further indented a line is, the lower level of detail it describes.

The program begins with sections labeled "uses," "type," "var," and a number of sections labeled "procedure." These sections of the program are called *declarations,* since they declare (that is, define) the various components of the program. The uses section defines what external files the program will be requiring. The type section defines user-created data structures. The var section defines variables. The procedure sections define specific tasks to be performed within the program.

Finally, at the end of the listing is the program itself.

```
begin
  InitVariables (MonthLen, CurrentDate);
  GetInput (BirthDay, MonthLen);
  DetermineAge (Age, BirthDay, CurrentDate, MonthLen);
  PrintOutput (Age)
end.
```

Note that the program consists of a list of tasks which correspond to the first level of the top-down design. These steps are implemented as procedures. Note that you can understand the general idea of the program without even understanding Pascal or how procedures work. The first task of the program is to execute the procedure `InitVariables` using the parameters `MonthLen`, and `CurrentDate`. `MonthLen` is a table of lengths of the various months which is set up by the procedure `InitVariables` and passed back to the main program for its use. `CurrentDate` is a variable which stores the current date. This variable is set from the DOS current date value.

After `InitVariables` is done, the program then performs the procedure GetInput, which asks the user for his or her birth date. This procedure is passed by the table of month lengths `MonthLen` so that it can test the date given to see if it is a valid date. GetInput passes the value of `BirthDay` back to the main program.

Next, the program executes `DetermineAge`, a procedure which computes the person's age in days.

Finally, the program displays the age determined.

To get an idea of how this program works, you should type it in and run it to calculate your own age in days.

It will take us quite a while to explain all the details required to write a Pascal program such as this one. For now, however, just remember the following facts:

1. A Pascal program must begin with a program header.
2. The main portion of the program, called the *body*, starts with the word "begin" and finishes with the word "end" followed by a period.
3. Between the words "begin" and "end" are inserted the lines of the program.
4. Lines are separated by semicolons. (If Pascal can tell from context where the end of a line is, such as a line followed by the word "end," you may omit the semicolon.)

Listing 2.1. Computing user's age in days

```
program AgeInDays;

  uses
    crt,
    dos;

  type
    TypeMonthArray = array [1..12] of integer;
    TypeDate       = record
                       Year  : word;
                       Month : word;
                       Day   : word
                     end;

var
  MonthLen     : TypeMonthArray;
  BirthDay,
  CurrentDate  : TypeDate;
  Age          : word;

procedure InitVariables (var MonthLenType  : MonthArray;
                         var CurrentDate   : TypeDate);
  procedure InitDate (var CurrentDate : TypeDate);
    var
      DummyVar : word;
    begin
      with CurrentDate do
        GetDate (Year, Month, Day, DummyVar)
    end;

  procedure InitMonthVar (var MonthLen      : TypeMonthArray);
    begin
      MonthLen [1]  := 31;
      MonthLen [2]  := 28;
      MonthLen [3]  := 31;
      MonthLen [4]  := 30;
      MonthLen [5]  := 31;
      MonthLen [6]  := 30;
      MonthLen [7]  := 31;
      MonthLen [8]  := 31;
      MonthLen [9]  := 30;
      MonthLen [10]  := 31;
      MonthLen [11]  := 30;
      MonthLen [12]  := 31
    end;
  begin
    InitMonthVar (MonthLen);
    InitDate (CurrentDate);
  end;

function LeapYear (YearToTest : word) : boolean;
  begin
```

```
    LeapYear := (YearToTest mod 4 = 0) and
                ((YearToTest mod 100 <> 0) or
                 (YearToTest mod 400 = 0))
  end;

procedure GetInput (var BirthDay : TypeDate;
                        MonthLen : TypeMonthArray);
  type
    TypeDateStr = string [10];
  var
    DateEntered : TypeDateStr;
    ValidDate   : boolean;
  function NextPart (var DateEntered : TypeDateStr) : word;
    var
      NumString : TypeDateStr;
      ErrorCode,
      ActualNum : integer;
    begin
      NumString := '';
      repeat
        NumString := concat (NumString,
                             copy (DateEntered, 1, 1));
        DateEntered := copy (DateEntered, 2,
                             length (DateEntered) - 1)
      until (DateEntered [1] = '/') or
            (length (DateEntered) = 0);
      DateEntered := copy (DateEntered, 2,
                           length (DateEntered) - 1);
      val (NumString, ActualNum, ErrorCode);
      NextPart := ActualNum;
      if ErrorCode <> 0
        then
          NextPart := 0
  end;
begin
  repeat
    clrscr;
    write ('Enter birth date in --/--/---- form: ');
    readln (DateEntered);
    BirthDay.Month := NextPart (DateEntered);
    BirthDay.Day   := NextPart (DateEntered);
    BirthDay.Year  := NextPart (DateEntered);
    ValidDate := ((BirthDay.Month < 13) and
                  (BirthDay.Month > 0)) and
                 (((BirthDay.Day <= MonthLen
                    [BirthDay.Month]) and
                   (BirthDay.Day > 0)) or
                   (LeapYear (BirthDay.Year) and
                   (BirthDay.Month = 2) and
                   (BirthDay.Day = 29))) and
                   (BirthDay.Year <> 0);
    until ValidDate
  end;
```

```
procedure DetermineAge (var Age          : word;
                            BirthDay     : TypeDate;
                            CurrentDate  : TypeDate;
                            MonthLen     : TypeMonthArray);
  var
    YearCounter : word;
  function NumDaysPastInYr (DateToDo : TypeDate;
                            MonthLen : TypeMonthArray) : word;
    var
      TempValue,
      MonthCounter : word;

  begin
    TempValue := 0;
    for MonthCounter := 1 to (DateToDo.Month - 1) do
      TempValue := TempValue + MonthLen [MonthCounter];
    TempValue := TempValue + DateToDo.Day;
    if LeapYear (DateToDo.Year) and (DateToDo.Month   2)
      then
        TempValue := TempValue + 1;
    NumDaysPastInYr := TempValue
  end;
 function NumDaysInYr (YearToDetermine : word) : word;
  begin
    if LeapYear (YearToDetermine)
      then
        NumDaysInYr := 366
      else
        NumDaysInYr := 365
  end;
 begin
  Age := NumDaysInYr (BirthDay.Year) -
           NumDaysPastInYr (BirthDay, MonthLen);
  for YearCounter := (BirthDay.Year + 1) to
                       (CurrentDate.Year - 1) do
    Age := Age + NumDaysInYr (YearCounter);
  if (BirthDay.Year = CurrentDate.Year)
    then
      Age := Age + NumDaysPastInYr (CurrentDate, MonthLen) -
                                   NumDaysInYr (CurrentDate.Year)
    else
      Age := Age + NumDaysPastInYr (CurrentDate, MonthLen)
 end;

 procedure PrintOutput (    Age : word);
  begin
    writeln ('You are ', Age, ' days old.');
    readln
  end;

 begin
  InitVariables (MonthLen, CurrentDate);
  GetInput (BirthDay, MonthLen);
  DetermineAge (Age, BirthDay, CurrentDate, MonthLen);
  PrintOutput (Age)
 end.
```

3 The Elements of Turbo Pascal

A Few Simple Pascal Programs

Let's establish a few elementary ideas by writing a few simple programs. We begin by writing a program which prints out the message: `Hello there. Welcome to Turbo Pascal.`

The Pascal statement for writing a line of output to the screen is **writeln**. To output the expression desired, we use the statement:

```
writeln('Hello there. Welcome to Turbo Pascal.');
```

Note that we have enclosed the text we wish to output in single quotes. We now build a program around this single statement. We add a statement

```
readln
```

at the end of the program. This just pauses the output screen until you press Enter, after which you are returned to the Turbo Pascal output screen. We will add this statement to all programs in this book where we need a pause to see the output.

Listing 3.1. A greeting program.

```
program Greeting;
begin
  writeln('Hello there. Welcome to Turbo Pascal.');
  readln
end.
```

Why not type in the program in Listing 3.1 in an Edit window? Then choose the **Compile** command to compile the program. If you typed in the program without error, you will be able to successfully compile the program. Now give the **Run** command to actually execute the program. You will see the program execute. (The message will be displayed.) When you wish to return to the desktop, press any key.

That was easy. Let's now try something more complicated. Let's write a program to add two numbers you specify. Let the two numbers be stored in the variables Number1 and Number2, respectively. Since we wish to allow numbers with decimal parts, we will declare these two variables to be of type real. (Pascal forces you to worry in advance about details like this!) We do this with a declaration of the form:

```
var
  Number1, Number2 : real;
```

The Pascal statement for reading a line of text typed in at the keyboard is readln. For instance, to ask the reader for the first number and then to read it from the keyboard, we use the statements:

```
writeln('What is the first number?');
readln(Number1);
```

In response to these statements, Turbo Pascal first asks for the first number. Type the first number and press Enter when you are done.

A similar pair of statements is used to input the second number. To calculate and display the sum, we use the statement:

```
writeln('The sum is ', Number1+Number2);
```

Note that the statement causes the display of two pieces of data: the text "The sum is ", and the value of the sum Number1 + Number2. The two data items are separated by a comma. Note also that we have left a space after the word 'is'. This is done to force a space before the sum. Here is the complete program which inputs the two numbers and calculates their sum.

Listing 3.2. Addition

```
program Addition;
var
  Number1, Number2 : real;
begin
  writeln('This program adds two numbers');
  writeln('What is the first number?');
  readln(Number1);
  writeln('What is the second number?');
  readln(Number2);
  writeln('The sum is ', Number1+Number2);
  readln
end.
```

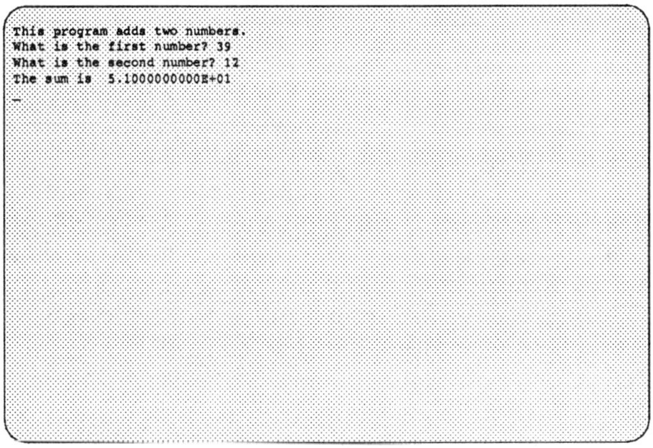
This program adds two numbers.
What is the first number? 39
What is the second number? 12
The sum is 5.1000000000E+01

Figure 3.1.
Output of sum displayed in scientific notation

Figure 3.1 shows the output of a typical run of this program. Note that the output is not quite what you might have expected. The sum of 39 and 12 is displayed in scientific notation! Indeed, unless you specify otherwise, Pascal displays real numbers in scientific notation. (We'll discuss scientific notation shortly.)

To obtain output in a more traditional form, you must specify the total number of characters to be displayed and the number of digits past the decimal point. For instance, to display at least 10 characters of output and 5 digits past the decimal point, you would replace the next to last line of the program with the statement:

```
writeln('The sum is ', Number1+Number2 :10:5);
```

With this line in place, the output of the program is as shown in Figure 3.2.

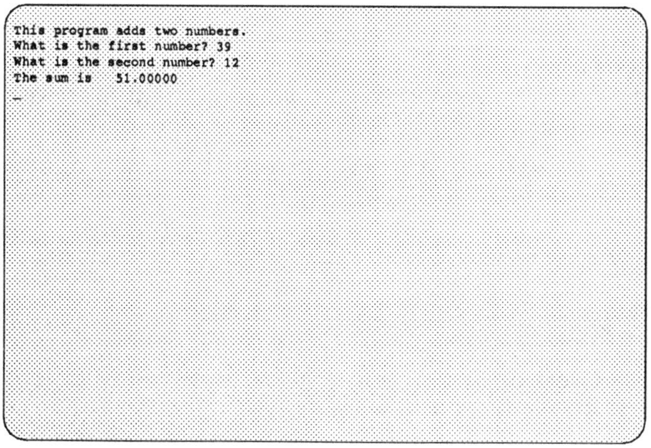
This program adds two numbers.
What is the first number? 39
What is the second number? 12
The sum is 51.00000

Figure 3.2.
Output of sum displayed in scientific notation

Simple Data Types

The Notion of a Data Type

A computer program can perform various manipulations of data. For example, a program can perform arithmetic operations using numerical data items. Or, it can perform text manipulations such as arranging words in alphabetical order. The manipulations a program can perform very much depend on the particular data being manipulated. For example, you can't multiply letters of the alphabet and you can't alphabetize a list of decimal numbers. In order for a program to function properly, not only must it be given data to work with, but each piece of data must be classified according to the sort of manipulations it can be subjected to.

In Pascal, each piece of data is assigned a *type*. We have already met the notion of a type in the program Addition (see Listing 3.2), where we specified that the variables `Number1` and `Number2` were of type real. This is a very important restriction on the variables, since it tells the program that the variables can only be assigned certain values. In turn, this specifies the sort of data manipulations in which the variables may be used. (We'll shortly learn the operations which can be performed using real numbers.)

Pascal can be very unforgiving if you ignore a variable's type. For instance, if you entered a letter when asked for `Number1` in the program Addition, the program will be halted since you have generated a *run-time error* (in this case, attempting to assign an illegal value to a variable).

Pascal has a rich list of predefined data types and corresponding data manipulations. In problem solving, using Pascal, part of the process involves analyzing your data and deciding what types to assign to them. If you do this skillfully, you can use Pascal's many built-in data manipulation facilities and solve your problem in a very succinct way. Pascal's predefined data types include integers, characters, real numbers, arrays, sets, and files, to mention only a few. With each data type comes a set of data manipulations built into Pascal. Pascal even allows you to define data types of your own.

In Pascal, there are eight elementary data types: integer, shortint, longint, real, char, boolean, word, byte, and string. Let's now describe each of these data types in some detail.

The integer Data Type

An integer is a whole number consisting of an optional sign (+ or −) followed by a sequence of digits. Here are some examples of integers.

12, –238, 0, +5823

Note that if the sign is omitted, then a + sign is understood. An integer can contain no decimal point or fractional part. Moreover, an integer cannot contain commas. (That is: 5,742 is not a legal way to write an integer.)

Integers are the simplest sorts of numbers and are suitable for many calculations in which exact answers are required, such as keeping a count of the number of times an operation is performed.

For each version of Pascal, there is a number called *maxint* which is the largest positive integer allowed. In Turbo Pascal, maxint is equal to 32767 (which equals $2^{15} - 1$) so that an integer is a whole number between –32768 and +32767.

If you attempt to assign an integer value larger than maxint, you will generate a run-time error, resulting in a halt of your Turbo Pascal program.

Note that the constant maxint does not need to be declared. It is predeclared and may be used freely in a program without any declaration.

The shortint Data Type

A shortint is an integer in the range –128 to +127. This data type is especially useful for storing signed bytes. (Beginners can safely ignore this type.)

The byte Data Type

In many microcomputer applications, it is necessary to work with integers which are restricted to lie in the range 0 to 255. Such integers are called *bytes,* since they may be stored within a microcomputer's memory using a single byte (eight bits) of storage. Because manipulations of bytes is so common, Turbo Pascal includes a byte data type as one of its scalar data types. A variable of the byte type may be assigned only integers between 0 and 255, inclusive.

The word Data Type

A variable of the type word may be assigned integers in the range 0 to 65535 (0 to $2^{16} - 1$).

The longint Data Type

A longint is a number in the range –2147483648 to 2147483647 ($-2^{31} - 1$ to 2^{31}). These longint numbers are used for making calculations where many digits of integer precision are required, as in accounting. Calculation with longints is exact: no round-off error is present as can be the case with reals.

The real Data Type

A real number in Pascal is a number which can be written as a finite decimal, such as 5.0, –0.785, or 157.2. A real number consists of an optional sign (+ or –), followed by one or more digits, a decimal point, and one or more further digits. In addition, a real number can include an optional exponent. (See discussion of scientific notation below.)

The real numbers with 0 fractional part, such as 5.0, –12.0, 125.0 correspond to certain integers (5, –12, and 125, respectively). If you wish, you may write such reals using the corresponding integers. That is, you may write 5 instead of 5.0, –12 instead of –12.0 and 125 instead of 125.0. Pascal stores integers in a very different way from reals. If you use an integer where Pascal expects a real, it will automatically convert from integer to real form. However, this conversion takes program time and reals require more memory than integers. Therefore, you should develop the habit of using reals only where necessary.

It may seem strange to include both real and integer as distinct data types. After all, every integer has a corresponding real number. However, there is a good reason for this distinction. A computer stores an integer using much less memory than required for a real. Moreover, arithmetic among integers can be performed much more rapidly than the corresponding arithmetic among real numbers. The savings in memory and program operating time more than justify making the distinction between real and integer.

A real number in Turbo Pascal lies in the range 2.9×10^{-39} to 1.7×10^{38}.

Scientific Notation

Unless you specify otherwise, Pascal expresses real numbers in *floating point notation* (also called *scientific notation*). In this notation, Pascal expresses a number as a number times a power of 10. The power of 10 is denoted using the letter E followed by a sign and a digit. For example, the number

9.23E+3 stands for
9.23 times 10 to the power +3, or
$9.23 \times 1000 = 9230.0$

–5.1E–02 stands for
–5.1 times 10 to the power –2, or
$-5.1 \times 0.01 = -0.051$

–.017E–14 stands for
–.017 times 10 to the power –14, or
–.017 times 0.0000000000001 = 0.0000000000000017

12.15E+10 stands for
12.15 times 10 to the power 10, or
12.15 × 10000000000 = 121500000000.0

Pascal requires that a real number have a digit on either side of its decimal point. Thus, for instance, the decimal value of the fraction 1/4 can be expressed as 0.25 or 2.5E–1, but .25 is not acceptable. Nor is 15. (with the decimal point only). This is not a legal way to write the number 15.0.

As with integers, a Pascal real cannot contain any commas. Moreover, the initial + sign is optional in the case of a positive real number. So, for example, both +0.05 and 0.05 are legal real numbers.

Other real Data Types

Turbo Pascal supports single, double, extended, and comp data types. These allow for extensive selectivity in calculating with decimal numbers in various ranges and with varying degrees of accuracy. For purposes of this text, we will discuss only the real data type. See your reference manual for the details about the other types.

The char Data Type

A char is a single letter, digit, punctuation mark, or control symbol recognized by the computer. Here are some examples of chars:

```
'a',   'B',   '7',   ',',   '@',   '%',   ' '
```

(The last character is a space.) A character is written enclosed within single quotation marks. Note that a space is a character just like any letter or digit. This space character is written ' ' (quotation marks around a blank space).

Many programs make use of chars. For example, a program may ask the user to respond to a question with "Y" or "N" for Yes or No. Furthermore, many manipulations of text can be accomplished by handling a single character at a time.

The boolean Data Type

A boolean variable has one of two possible values: true or false. Boolean variables are used to keep track of conditions which currently exist within a program. (Has a certain event occurred? Is a particular routine complete?)

One of the most important features which make computer programs useful is their ability to respond to varying conditions during program execution: For example, if the value of X equals 0, then the program will execute one statement; otherwise, the program will execute a different statement. In order to make such a logical decision, the program must be able to decide whether the logical expression `X = 0` is currently true or false. Pascal provides the boolean data type to express the truth value (true or false) of such an expression. Note that the equals sign used in this expression is a comparison operator. You should contrast it with the operator := used to assign a value to a variable.

The string Data Type

We will discuss the string data type later in this chapter.

Identifiers, Constants, and Variables

Identifiers

An *identifier* is the name given to an entity within a Pascal program. In Turbo Pascal, identifiers can consist of as many as 64 characters and must begin with either a letter or an underscore (_).

Identifiers are used as variable and constant names, procedure and function names, and names of user-defined data types.

Literal Constants

A Pascal program may include explicit data items of any data type. Such data items are called *literal constants.* Here are some examples of literal integer constants:

```
-100, 2553, 20481
```

Some examples of literal real constants are:

```
1.89, -2.83E+4, 45.887
```

Here are some literal char constants:

```
'a', '#', 'T', '('
```

There are just two literal constants of boolean type, namely the two predefined constants:

```
false, true
```

Be careful. Here "false" is not the sequence of letters "F," "A," "L," "S," "E." Rather, it is the predefined constant indicating one of the truth values for a logical expression.

In addition to the above literal constants which correspond to the simple data types, Pascal allows use of literal string constants. Such constants consist of a phrase contained within single quotes. Here are some string constants:

```
'This is a Pascal program.'
'Error in input. Repeat input.'
'Insert diskette containing data.'
```

String constants are used in `write` and `writeln` statements to introduce text messages into a program.

Declared Constants

Literal constants, such as 14, 17.85, or 'c', may be written explicitly in Pascal statements. However, it is often convenient to assign a constant a name which reflects its meaning. Constants which are assigned a name are called *declared constants.*

Actually, the idea of a declared constant should not be a new idea for you. In geometry, the constant 3.14159... is used so frequently that it is assigned the name "Pi." Similarly, in mathematics, the base of natural logarithms, 2.718281..., occurs in so many formulas that it is given the name "e." Many of the constants in physics are given specific names. For example, the universal gravitational constant is named "G."

In programming, using declared constants can improve the intelligibility of expressions and programs. For example, consider the formula for the area of a circle. From geometry, the area of a circle is given by the formula:

```
Area = Pi * Radius2
```

where Pi is the geometrical constant given approximately as 3.14159... . We could write this formula using a literal constant in the form:

```
Area = 3.14159 * Radius * Radius
```

In this formula, the use of 3.14159 obscures the meaning of the constant. For one thing, the given number does not suggest its geometric origin. Second, 3.14159 is only an approximation to the real value of Pi to six significant figures. It is better to denote the constant as Pi and assign the value 3.14159 to this constant, so that the formula has the more familiar form:

```
Area = Pi * Radius * Radius
```

The meaning of the formula is clearer when labeling the number as Pi. Moreover, if you later wish to substitute an approximation for Pi which has more or fewer significant digits, you may do so by merely changing the value of Pi rather than changing numbers throughout the program.

Declared constants are defined using a `const` declaration at the beginning of a program. This declaration is introduced by the word "const" followed by a list of constant names and their values. For example, in the case of our real number Pi, we would have the declaration:

```
const Pi = 3.14159;
```

The semicolon separates the constant definition from the next element in the program.

A `const` declaration may be used to declare any number of constants of any data types. For example, here is a const declaration in which a number of constants are declared.

```
const A = 5.37;
      B = 10.11;
      Ch = 'f';
      Ch1 = 'g';
      X = 15;
      Y = 100;
      Maxim = true;
      Prompt1 = 'Input Error';
```

The definitions of consecutive constants are separated from one another by semicolons.

Note that it is not necessary to tell Turbo Pascal the type of a declared constant. Pascal determines the data type from the assigned value. Thus, for example, in the above declaration, A and B are real constants, since 5.37 and 10.11 are real. Similarly, Ch and Ch1 are char constants and X and Y are integer constants.

Constant names are Pascal identifiers. So, in choosing constant names, all of the rules for Pascal identifiers apply. That is, a constant name must start with a letter and consist only of digits and letters (and other characters depending on the implementation). Any length restriction on Pascal identifiers applies to constant names.

Variables

A *variable* is an identifier which can be assigned a value within a program. For example, in the program Addition, we used the variables `Number1` and `Number2` to represent the two numbers input by the user.

Every variable has a type indicating the type of data which can be assigned. For example, the variable `Number1` was a variable of type integer, which means that it can only be assigned integer values. Similarly, if `Alpha` is a variable of type char, then `Alpha` may be assigned any value of type char.

Within the computer, each variable is assigned a memory location to hold its currently assigned value. The name of the variable (e.g., `Number1` or `Alpha`) can be thought of as the name of the memory location.

It is very important not to confuse the name of a variable (e.g., `Number1`) with its current value (e.g., 13000). The name of the variable is the name of the memory location belonging to the variable. The current value is the data stored in that memory location.

All variables must be declared before you use them in a program. In a `var` declaration, the declaration consists of specifying an identifier and a data type.

Here is a typical `var` declaration.

```
var
      X,Y,Z : integer;
      A,B,Alpha : char;
      EndFile : boolean;
```

It declares the variables `X`, `Y` and `Z` to be of type integer; `A`, `B`, and `Alpha` to be of type char; and `EndFile` to be of type boolean. Note the use of colons after the lists of variable names and the use of semicolons separating the various types of declarations.

Pascal allows considerable flexibility in `var` declarations. For example, the above declaration could just as well have been written:

```
var
      X,Z : integer;
      EndFile : boolean;
      Y : integer;
      A : char:
      B,Alpha : char;
```

Note that the order of the variables within a declaration is immaterial, as is the order of the declarations. Moreover, there may be any number of declarations corresponding to each data type.

It is easy to forget to include a variable in a declaration. I do it all the time! But don't worry too much about this. Your Pascal compiler will not let you get away with it. It will respond with an error message which indicates that there is an undeclared identifier in the source code. You must correct the error before successful compilation of your program can occur.

In Turbo Pascal, the `const` and `var` declarations may occur in any order with respect to each other.

During program operation, the value of a variable may be set using an assignment statement. For example, you may assign the value 5.38 to the variable `Number1` by using a statement of the form:

```
Number1 := 5.38;
```

You should read this statement: "`Number1` is assigned the value 5.38." In response to this statement, the computer stores the value 5.38 in the memory location corresponding to `Number1`. Any previous value of `Number1` is erased and is no longer available to the program.

The symbol := is Pascal's assignment operator. It directs Pascal to assign to the variable on the left (`Number1`) the value on the right (5.38). Don't confuse this symbol with the identity symbol =. Your compiler will reject an assignment statement of the form

```
Number1 = 5.38;
```

The assignment statement may be used to assign values to variables of any type. For example, you can assign the character 'A' to the char variable `Ch1` using the statement:

```
Ch1 := 'A';
```

Similarly, you can assign the value false to the boolean variable `ProgDone` using the statement:

```
ProgDone := false;
```

In response to a variable reference within a statement, the program looks into memory and retrieves the current value of that variable. The value retrieved is then used in place of the variable reference in carrying out the statement. Viewing variable manipulation in this way is often helpful in understanding the operation of Pascal statements. For example, consider the following statement:

```
X := X + 1;
```

Let's see what Pascal does on encountering this statement.

1. Compute the value of X+1. (In any assignment statement, Pascal first computes the value on the right side of the assignment operator. We assume that X has previously been initialized.)
2. Look up the value of X in memory.
3. Add 1 to this value.
4. Assign the value of X+1 to X.
5. Store the value of X+1 in the memory location reserved for X.

For example, suppose that X currently has the value 8. Pascal will compute the value 8 + 1 = 9 and assign the value 9 to X. The effect of the statement, then, is to increase the value of X by 1.

Note that in an assignment statement, you may have any expression (e.g., X+1) on the right side of the assignment := . However, on the left side, you are allowed to use only a variable and not an expression. That is, you may not make assignments of the form:

```
X+1  := X;
```

A Pascal program begins by setting up memory locations corresponding to the variables declared in the program. However, the program does not automatically assign any initial values to these variables. The process of assigning starting values to the variables is called *variable initialization.* It is your responsibility to initialize all variables before they are used.

There are several ways to initialize a variable. One method is to use an assignment statement. For example, the statement:

```
X := -1;
```

initializes the variable X with the value −1. Another method of initializing a variable is to use a procedure (like readln) which assigns the variable a value. For example, the statement:

```
readln(X);
```

accepts a value from the user and assigns the value to X.

As a program begins, the variables are assigned whatever values happen to be in their respective memory locations at that moment. And usually these values are nonsense, at least as far as the program is concerned. Using uninitialized variables may cause a program crash. Even if they do not cause a crash, your program will produce unpredictable results. In any case, you should recall the following important maxim of programming:

```
garbage in = garbage out
```

(If you input garbage values to your program, then your output will also be garbage.) So remember:

Remember to initialize your variables before they are used. One approach to initialization is to set variables equal to the first value they will assume within the program. In many programs, it is hard to determine in advance what this value will be. For such programs, you can initialize all integers and reals with 0, char variables with a space, and all boolean variables with false. This can be done at the beginning of the program so that you can be assured that whatever other errors may have crept into your program, there are no initialization errors.

Strings

The string Data Types

Earlier in the chapter, we introduced *literal string constants,* which are used to represent constant strings of text. Turbo Pascal includes a string data type which can be used in declaring variables to store literal string constants. Actually, there is a sequence of string data types, designated

```
string[n]
```

where n is the maximum length of the literal string constant which can be stored. The value of n must be an integer in the range 1 to 255. In addition, there is the string data type which allows strings of length up to 255.

For example, consider the following declaration:

```
var
  Choice : string[1];
  Name1, Name2 : string[10];
  Response : string[20]
```

Choice can store a literal string constant having length at most 1; Name1 and Name2 can store literal string constants of length at most 10; Response can store a literal string constant of length at most 20.

Assigning Values to string Variables

You can assign a value to Response using a statement of the form:

```
Response := 'Alice'
```

In this example, Response is assigned as its value the literal string constant 'Alice'. You may assign any literal string constant to a variable of type string[n]. However, all characters after the nth are truncated. Thus, for example, consider the following assignment statement:

```
Response := 'This is the twenty-third day of June'
```

The literal string constant on the right has 36 characters. The value assigned to Response by the above statement consists of the first 20 characters, namely:

```
'This is the twenty-t'
```

You may assign the value of one string variable to another, as in the statement:

```
Name1 := Name2;
```

which assigns the value of Name2 to Name1.

In all string assignments, excess characters are truncated. For example, consider the statements:

```
Response := 'This is a test';
Name1 := Response;
```

Name1 is assigned the string consisting of the first 10 characters of the value of Response, namely 'This is a '.

Input and Output of strings

You may use readln and writeln with variables of string type. For example, consider the following program:

Listing 3.3. Introduction

```
program Introduction;
var
  Name : string[10];

begin
  writeln('What is your name?');
  readln(Name);
  writeln('Hello, ',Name,'. 'Nice to meet you.');
  readln
end.
```

The second statement in the program requests the user's name. The third line prints the name in a greeting. Here is a sample run of this program.

```
What is your name?
Janet (Enter)
Hello, Janet. Nice to meet you.
```

Note that the underlined text denotes input supplied from the keyboard.

Strings versus Characters

Turbo Pascal allows you to assign character values to string variables. For example, suppose that `Ch` is a variable of the type char and `Choice` is of the type string. Then the following statement is valid:

```
Choice := Ch
```

It assigns to `Choice` a string consisting of a single character, namely the value of `Ch`.

Note, however, that you may NOT assign a string of any length to a character value. For example, suppose that the value of `Response` is a string of length 1. Then the following statement will lead to a compiler error:

```
Ch := Response
```

Accessing the Individual Characters of a String

You may access the rth character of a string `Str` as:

```
Str[r]
```

For example, suppose that `Name` has the value '`Janet`'. Then

```
Janet[3]
```

is the character '`n`'.

If you attempt to reference a nonexistent character, say the −1st, then Turbo Pascal will report an error (a compiler error, if you reference the character literally, or a run-time error if a variable is assigned a nonexistent character during program execution).

Later in the book, we will show how to manipulate individual characters of strings in order to perform various kinds of text processing.

String Concatenation

In the preceding section, we discussed arithmetic operators and arithmetic expressions. Analogously, there are string operators and string expressions. More precisely, there is a single operator among strings, namely +, which is used to denote the operation called *string concatenation* (or *concatenation,* for short). The concatenation of strings is obtained by juxtaposing the strings one after another. For example, the expression:

```
'ABC' + 'DEF'
```

stands for the concatenation of 'ABC' and 'DEF', which is just the string:

```
'ABCDEF'
```

The above example involves literal string constants. However, you can also concatenate values stored in string variables. For instance, consider the following statement:

```
Response := Response + Ch
```

It assigns to the string variable Response the current value of Response concatenated with the value of Ch. For instance, if Response currently equals 'ABC' and Ch is equal to 'E', then the statement assigns Response the value

```
'ABCE'
```

A *string expression* is a string formed from strings and the string operator +. Here is an example of a string expression:

```
Str1+Str2+Str3
```

You may use string expressions in writeln, as in the example:

```
writeln(Str1+Str2+Str3)
```

On encountering such a statement, Turbo Pascal first evaluates the string expression and then carries out the writeln using the resulting string.

Note, however, that string expressions may not be used within a readln statement. That is, a statement of the form:

```
readln(Str1+Str2)
```

is syntactically incorrect and will be rejected by the compiler.

Arithmetic

In solving problems, we must be able to manipulate the data stored in variables. The most familiar form of data manipulation is arithmetic using real numbers and integers. Arithmetic calculations are used to solve problems ranging from tax planning to the design of airplanes. In this section, we lay the foundations for solving such problems by learning how Turbo Pascal handles arithmetic.

Real Arithmetic

Real numbers are used to solve scientific, business, and other problems which involve decimal arithmetic. Let's now discuss how to use real numbers for problem solving in Pascal.

Standard arithmetic operations. Pascal includes the four basic arithmetic operations among real numbers, namely addition, subtraction, multiplication, and division. Addition and subtraction are denoted, as usual, by the operators + and −.

Multiplication is denoted by the operator *. For example, 8.0 times 4.3 is written in the form:

```
8.0 * 4.3
```

The product of `Alpha` and `Beta` is written in the form:

```
Alpha * Beta
```

Division is denoted by the /. Thus, for example, the quotient 3.0 divided by 4.0 is written as:

```
3.0/4.0
```

The quotient of `Alpha` divided by `Beta` is written:

```
Alpha/Beta
```

Two Important Points About Real Arithmetic

The result of a calculation involving real numbers is always a real number. An integer may be used in place of a real number in calculations. If necessary, Pascal will automatically convert an integer to the corresponding real number.

Of course, Pascal incorporates the mathematical requirement that in a quotient `Alpha/Beta`, the denominator, `Beta`, must be non-zero. That is, you may not perform operations which require division by 0, such as:

```
12.0/0 or -1.3/0
```

Division by zero will cause a run-time error and so must be avoided. Turbo Pascal will print out an error message telling you that division by zero has been attempted.

In spite of your best efforts, division by zero may creep into a program unexpectedly. For example, you may evaluate `Beta` by using a calculation. It is possible that the calculation yields 0. Any subsequent attempt to divide by `Beta` will result in division by 0.

A second related hazard results from attempting to divide by a real number which is "too small." Pascal has a minimum positive real number which it will recognize as non-zero. This number is quite small in most versions of Pascal. For example, in Turbo Pascal, it equals

```
1E-38 = .00000000000000000000000000000000000001.
```

Any number whose absolute value (that is, the number ignoring its leading + and – sign) is less than this minimum will automatically be set equal to zero. This can result in an error which is particularly difficult to detect since the error message simply says that division by zero has occurred. And in looking at the program you cannot find any values of 0 which could have been used in a division! Indeed, you could calculate `Beta` and be guaranteed (from mathematical considerations) that `Beta` is not equal to zero. However, if `Beta` is too small, Pascal will set `Beta` equal to 0 and division by 0 could result.

There is a largest real number which Pascal will recognize. This number is also system dependent and is usually quite large. In Turbo Pascal, it is 1.7E38. An operation yielding a result which is larger than the maximum real number is called an *overflow* and will cause a run-time error.

Raising to Powers

You should note that standard Pascal has no exponentiation operator. That is, Pascal has no built-in mechanism for computing powers such as:

$\texttt{Alpha}^{\texttt{Beta}}$

Simple Pascal statements can be written to calculate these powers. Later, we will discuss how to raise numbers to powers in Pascal.

Integer Arithmetic

You may add, subtract, and multiply integers, just as you would real numbers, using the same operators. Here are some examples of integer arithmetic operations:

128 + 34, 15 – 368, 38 * 255

Integer Division

Division among integers is somewhat different from division between real numbers. The differences are caused by the fact that the quotient of two integers is not necessarily an integer. For example, the quotient 3/4 of the two integers 3 and 4 equals the real number 0.75, which is not an integer. (It has a fractional part.)

In some applications, a real quotient is acceptable. However, in other applications, you require a form of division of integers which allows you to divide one integer by another and get an integer answer. For such applications, Pascal provides the division operation, div.

To understand the operation of div, recall your grade school days when you first learned long division. You were taught to divide one integer by another and produce a quotient and a remainder. Here are some examples using this method of division.

5 divided by 3 has quotient 1 and remainder 2

147 divided by 20 has quotient 7 and remainder 7

–34 divided by 3 has quotient –11 and remainder –1

–80 divided by 11 has quotient –7 and remainder –3

5 divided by –2 has quotient –2 and remainder 1

In Pascal integer arithmetic, the above quotients may be obtained using the div operator. For example:

```
5 div 3 is equal to 1

147 div 20 is equal to 7

-34 div 3 is equal to -11

-80 div 11 is equal to -7

5 div -2 is equal to -2
```

In Pascal integer arithmetic, the remainder in a division problem may be obtained using the mod operator. For example:

```
5 mod 3 is equal to 2
147 mod 20 is equal to 7
-34 mod 3 is equal to -1
-80 mod 11 is equal to -3
5 mod -2 is equal to 1
```

Note that both `mod 0` and `div 0` involve division by 0 and so must be avoided. If used, they will lead to a run-time error.

It may seem that `div` and `mod` have no apparent uses. However, there are problems in which they are extremely useful, as the next examples show.

Example 1. A box is designed to hold 3 pounds of candy. Write a program which accepts as input the number of pounds of candy produced on a particular day (fractional pounds are ignored). The program should calculate the number of boxes the candy can fill on that day. (The program should ignore fractional boxes of candy.)

Solution. Let the number of pounds of candy be denoted by the variable `Candy`. Then the corresponding number of boxes of candy equals `Candy` div 3. (Any remainder in the division process corresponds to a fractional box of candy, which is ignored.) Here is the program:

Listing 3.4. CandyPro

```
program CandyPro;
{Calculating the number of boxes of candy produced}

  var
    Candy : integer;{number of pounds of candy}

  begin {CandyPro}
    writeln('Production (in pounds)?');
    readln(Candy);
    writeln('Number of boxes:');
    writeln(Candy div 3);
    readln
  end. {CandyPro}
```

Note that we have included comments within the program. In Turbo Pascal, text included within braces {. . .} or between (* . . . *) is ignored by the compiler. It is always a good idea to include comments in your programs to tell the reader what each program section is supposed to do.

Sample Run. CandyPro

```
Production (in pounds)?
12380
Number of boxes:
4126
```

Example 2. A supermarket clerk has run out of change, except for quarters. Write a program which asks for the amount of a purchase. The program should calculate the number of quarters to be given as change and the amount of change still due.

Solution. This problem is ready-made for using div and mod. However, in order to use integer-integer arithmetic (which div and mod require) let's input the amount of the purchase in pennies. So a $10.00 purchase would require an input of 1000, a $2.58 purchase an input of 258, and so forth. Let's store the input in the integer variable `Purchase`. Let's store the amount of money given in the variable `Amount`. The number of quarters to give as change is then equal to:

```
(Amount-Purchase) div 25
```

and the amount of change still to be given is equal to:

```
(Amount-Purchase) mod 25
```

Here is the program:

Listing 3.5. Change

```
program Change;
{Compute change in quarters}
```

```
var
  Purchase, Amount: integer; {cost, amount in pennies}

begin {Change}
  writeln('Purchase (in pennies; omit $).');
  readln(Purchase);
  writeln('Amount Given (in pennies; omit $).');
  readln(Amount);
  write('Quarters: ');
  writeln((Amount-Purchase) div 25);
  write('Additional Change: ');
  writeln((Amount-Purchase) mod 25);
  readln
end. {Change}
```

Sample Run. Change

```
Purchase (in pennies; omit $).
962
Amount Given (in pennies; omit $).
2000
Quarters: 41
Additional Change: 13
```

Operators and Expressions

An *operator* is a symbol which represents an operation to be performed. In our discussion of real and integer arithmetic, we have introduced the following operators:

+ (addition)

– (subtraction)

* (multiplication)

/ (real division)

div (integer division)

mod (integer remainder)

Unary Plus and Unary Minus

In both real and integer arithmetic, numbers, variables, or expressions can be preceded by a sign, namely + or −. Here are some examples:

```
+X, -Alpha, -(X+Y)
```

These initial signs are operators called, respectively, *unary plus* and *unary minus.* The unary plus operator causes no change to the quantity which follows. The unary minus operator causes the sign of the following quantity to be changed.

Pascal allows you to include both the unary plus and unary minus operators in arithmetic calculations.

Binary versus Unary Operators

An operator represents an operation to be performed on one or more pieces of data. The data items are called *operands.* For example, in the addition X+Y, both X and Y are operands. Some operators, like + (addition) and * (multiplication) require two operands. Such operators are called *binary operators.* Others, like unary plus and unary minus require only a single operand and thus are called *unary operators.*

Arithmetic Expressions

In applied problems, it usually is necessary to perform a sequence of calculations to arrive at an answer. Such a sequence of calculations may be described using an *arithmetic expression,* which is a sequence of variables and constants separated by arithmetic operators. Here are some examples of arithmetic expressions:

```
1 + 2 + 3

2 * Alpha + Beta * Gamma

1 * 2 + 2 * 3 + 3 * 4 + 4 * 5

18 mod 5 * 30 + 1

Alpha * Beta div 5
```

The Value of an Arithmetic Expression

An arithmetic expression has a value which is determined by first substituting the current value for any variables in the expression and performing any required arithmetic.

For example, suppose that `Alpha` has the value 8, `Beta` has the value 3, `Gamma` the value 5. To evaluate the second expression above, we first substitute the values of the variables into the expression to obtain:

2 * 8 + 3 * 5

We next perform the above multiplications to obtain:

16 + 15

Finally, we perform the operation + to obtain:

31

So the value of the given arithmetic expression is 31.

If an expression has an integer value, then we say that the expression is of integer type; if an expression has a real value, then we say that the expression is of real type.

Expressions may be used in assignment statements. For example, the statement:

```
Y := 2 * Alpha + Beta * Gamma;
```

assigns to `Y` the value of the expression on the right of the assignment operator. If `Alpha` has the value 8, `Beta` the value 3, `Gamma` the value 5, then our calculations above show that `Y` is assigned the value 31.

You can assign the value of an integer expression to either an integer variable or a real variable. In the latter case, Pascal compiler will automatically convert the integer value to its corresponding real number. In the above example, if `Y` were real, then the above assignment statement would assign it the value 31.0.

Note, however, that you may assign the value of a real expression only to a real variable.

Operator Precedence

In evaluating the expression:

```
2 * Alpha + Beta * Gamma
```

the multiplications were performed first, since the multiplication operator has a higher precedence than the addition operator. This means that multiplication is performed before addition. Arithmetic operations have a "pecking order," or operator precedence, which specifies the order in which to perform operations. Here is a listing of the precedence of the various arithmetic operators we have introduced. Operators on the same line have equal precedence. The closer to the top of the list, the higher the precedence.

Highest Precedence

Unary +, Unary –

/, * div, mod

Binary +, Binary –

Lowest Precedence

According to this precedence table, all unary plus and unary minus operations are performed first (proceeding in left-to-right order). Next, any of the operations /, *, div, and mod are performed (proceeding in left-to-right order). Finally, the operations of addition and subtraction are performed (proceeding in left-to-right order).

The following example gives some practice in applying the precedence table in evaluating various expressions.

Example 3. Evaluate the following expressions.

(a) 2 * 5 + 5 * 3 + 4 * 10

(b) –8 * 5 div 3 * 2

(c) 4 mod 2 + 3 –4 * 5

(d) X * Y – Z/2, where X equals 5, Y equals 4, Z equals 12.

Solution.

(a) The highest precedence operator is * . Performing the operations at this level first, proceeding from left to right gives:

10 + 15 + 40

Now the operations at the next lowest precedence are performed to yield:

65

(b) First, the unary minus changes the sign of 8 to –8 to give:

(–8) * 5 div 3 * 2

At the next precedence level, (* / div mod), we perform the operations from left to right. The first operation is (–8) * 5 which gives:

–40 div 3 * 2

The next operation is –40 div 3, which gives:

–13 * 2

Finally, there is only one operation left to perform and it gives the value of the expression, –26.

(c) The highest level operators in the expression are mod and * . We perform these operations first, from left to right:

4 mod 2 + 3 – 4 * 5 = 0 + 3 – 4 * 5 (mod)
= 0 + 3 – 20 (*0)
= –17 (+ and –)

(d) We first substitute the values of the variables into the expression to obtain:

5 * 4 – 12/2

The highest precedence operators are * and /. We perform these operations first:

5 * 4 – 12/2 = 20 – 12/2 (*)
= 20 – 6 (/)
= 14 (–)

Parentheses

As you can see from the above example, Pascal evaluates expressions in a very strict order. In some applications, you may want to deviate from this order and evaluate some expressions before others. By using parentheses, you may force a deviation from the order decreed by precedence. Portions of an expression within parentheses are evaluated first. For example, consider the following expression:

5 + 3 * (4+2)

Before attempting to evaluate the entire expression, Pascal first evaluates the expression inside the parentheses. That is, it replaces the 4+2 with 6 and then evaluates the expression:

5 + 3 * 6

which equals 23. Note that without the parentheses, the expression:

5 + 3 * 4 + 2

has the value 19. (Check this!) The parentheses force the compiler to consider the 4 + 2 as a unit before considering the remainder of the expression. Therefore, with the parenthesis, the expression has the value 23.

Example 4. Evaluate the following expressions.
(a) 5 * 4 div 3
(b) 5 * (4 div 3)

Solution.

(a) 5 * 4 div 3 = 20 div 3 (*)
= 6 (div)

(b) 5 * (4 div 3) = 5 * 1 (div in parentheses)
= 5 (*)

Nested Parentheses

It is possible to use a set of parentheses within a set of parentheses. In this case, we say that the sets of parentheses are *nested.* For example, here is an expression with a set of nested parentheses:

(1 + 7 * (3+8)) * (5–3)

In the case of nested parentheses, the innermost set is evaluated first. In this case (3+8) is evaluated first.

(1 + 7 * (3+8)) * (5–3) - (1 + 7 * 11) * (5–3)

We are left with two pairs of unnested parentheses. These are evaluated in left-to-right order:

= 78 * (5–3) (first parentheses)
= 78 * 2 (second parentheses)
= 156

The Procedures write and writeln

We have been using the procedures writeln and readln for outputting and inputting. Let's provide some further details about these procedures.

More About writeln

The general form of the procedure writeln is:

```
writeln(expression1, expression2,...);
```

Here the expressions listed are any valid expressions which evaluate to one of Turbo Pascal's simple data types. (We will later define some other data types to which writeln does not apply.) In response to this instruction, the program evaluates each of the expressions listed and displays the results contiguously with no spaces between consecutive expression values.

As a variation, an integer expression may include the formatting clause `:m`, which tells the program to display the value of the expression in a field which is m characters wide. If the field is too large, any empty spaces are put on the left. If the field is too small, the field is enlarged to accommodate the value of the expression.

In the case of a real expression, you may include a formatting clause of the form `:m`, as above, or a formatting clause of the form `:m:n`, which tells the program to display the value of the expression in a field `m` characters wide and to use `n` digits to the right of the decimal point.

The Procedure write

The procedure write works exactly like writeln, except that it omits an end of line sequence (carriage return followed by line feed) at the end of the output. Thus, after a write is executed, the cursor remains at the next character position on the same line.

For example, consider the following instructions:

```
write('ABCD');
writeln('EFG');
writeln('HIJK')
```

They produce the following output:

```
ABCDEFG
HIJK
```

One-Dimensional Arrays

Examples of One-Dimensional Arrays

An *array* (or *one-dimensional array*) is a list of variables of the same type. However, before we go into the technicalities of arrays, let's look at some examples of data lists that arrays will allow us to store and manipulate.

Illustration 1. A freshman chemistry laboratory has 10 students. Each laboratory assignment is graded on a scale of 0 to 100. The grades achieved by the class in a single experiment can be organized in a list of the following sort:

100

90

80

58

90

95

75

60

73

90

Each grade in the list is identified, via its position, with a particular student. The first grade belongs to student 1, the second to student 2, and so forth. Another laboratory assignment would give rise to another such list. The numbers would, in all probability, be different, but the structure of the list would remain the same: a list of 10 integers, each lying between 0 and 100.

Illustration 2. A supermarket has five departments. It uses an accounting program to keep track of sales and inventory. At the end of each day, the program calculates the sales from each department and stores them in a list. Here is a typical list:

1081.75

780.30

4538.20

2127.80

977.01

The first item gives the daily sales of department 1, the second the daily sales of department 2, and so forth.

The accounting program does considerable processing using the data items in the list. It calculates the sum of all the entries to compute total daily sales, compares each department's sales with the corresponding number for yesterday, the same day last week, and the same date last year, and so forth.

Illustration 3. A government agency uses a survey of 1,000 women to assess the need for day care facilities. It uses a computer program to analyze the survey data. Corresponding to each survey question, it compiles a list of all responses. For instance, consider the answers to the question: Do you work? The answers would be compiled in a list of the form:

Yes

Yes

Yes

No

No

.

.

.

The list contains 1,000 responses. The first response corresponds to survey respondent 1, the second to survey respondent 2, and so forth. This list, along with corresponding lists for the other survey questions are used by the analysis program to answer questions like: What percentage of women who work have more than three dependents? What is the median family income of families having a woman its sole source of support?

The Notion of an Array

To deal with data lists like those in Illustrations 1 through 3, Pascal provides the array data type. An *array* is a collection of a fixed number of variables of the same data type. The variables of an array have a common name and are distinguished by means of *subscripts* (also called *indexes*). For example, here is an array containing four integer variables:

```
Table[1]
Table[2]
Table[3]
Table[4]
```

The four variables `Table[1]`, `Table[2]`, `Table[3]`, `Table[4]` share the common name Table. They are distinguished by means of the subscripts 1, 2, 3, 4. The common name of the variables is used as the name of the array.

Each of the four variables may be assigned a value. Each set of values for the variables gives a value for the array Table. Here are three values for Table.

Value 1 of Table	Value 2 of Table	Value 3 of Table
11	10	–1
1	78	347
17	–2	0
–412	5	18

For example, corresponding to the value 1 of Table, `Table[1]` is assigned the value 11, `Table[2]` is assigned the value 1, `Table[3]` is assigned the value 17, `Table[4]` is assigned the value –412.

Array Components and Base Type

The variables in an array are called its *components* or *elements*. So, for example, in the array `Table`, the components are the variables `Table[1]`, `Table[2]`, `Table[3]`, `Table[4]`. The data type of the components is called the *base type* of the array.

An array can be visualized as a sequence of memory locations, one for each array component. Note that `Table[1], ... , Table[4]` are the names of the memory locations. The contents of the locations are the current values of the variables.

1. We can store the grade data of Illustration 1 in an array with data type integer.
2. The departmental sales data of Illustration 2 could be stored in an array with data type real.
3. The YES-NO survey answers in Illustration 3 can be stored in an array with data type boolean (Yes = true, No = false).

Array Subscripts

An array component (element) is identified by the array name and the appropriate subscript (index) contained within brackets. For example, let's give the name `Grades` to the array corresponding to Illustration 1. Then `Grades` contains 10 components, which we can identify with the subscripts 1..10. The components are then the variables:

```
Grades[1]
Grades[2]
   .
   .
   .
Grades[10]
```

The subscript in this example serves as a student ID. That is, `Grades[1]` corresponds to the grade of student 1, `Grades[2]` corresponds to the grade of student 2, and so forth. Note that we could just as well defined the subscripts to be the characters "A".."J". In this case, the components would be the variables:

```
Grades['A']
Grades['B']
   .
   .
   .
Grades['J']
```

Declaring an Array

Arrays must be declared within a var declaration. For example, the declaration for the array

```
Grades[1]
Grades[2]
   .
   .
   .
Grades[10]
```

goes as follows:

```
var
  Grades  :  array[1..10]  of  integer;
```

Here is how this declaration breaks down syntactically. The declaration begins with the array name `Grades` followed by a colon. Then follows the reserved word array followed by the subscript range within brackets. Then comes the reserved word `of` followed by the data type of the array, `integer`.

To get some practice in writing array declarations, let's write declarations for the arrays in Illustrations 2 and 3.

Illustration 2. In Illustration 2, there are five components which must store real values. So we make the data type of the array real. Let's identify the departments by the letters A to E. Correspondingly, let's use as subscripts the characters "A" . . . "E". Let's name the array Stores. Then a proper declaration would be:

```
var
  Stores : array['A'..'E'] of real;
```

The components of this array are the variables:

```
Stores['A']
Stores['B']
Stores['C']
Stores['D']
Stores['E']
```

Illustration 3. In Illustration 3, there are 1,000 components, one corresponding to each survey respondent. This suggests that we use as subscripts the integers 1..1000. Since the component variables are to store one of the two values true or false, we make the data type boolean. Here is the declaration:

```
var
  Work : array[1..1000] of boolean;
```

Here are the components of this array:

```
Work[1]
Work[2]
.
.
.
Work[1000]
```

In all of the above examples, the array components were identified by a single subscript, that is, by a single list of subscript values. Later in this book, we will introduce more general arrays, whose components can be identified by two (or more) subscripts. The number of subscripts required to describe an array is called the *dimension* of the array. The arrays of this chapter are all one-dimensional arrays. However, in order to make our discussion less clumsy, throughout we will use "array" to mean "one-dimensional array."

In declaring the subscript range for an array, you cannot use the value of a variable. That means that the following sort of declaration is illegal.

```
var
  XYZ : array[1..N] of integer;
```

Pascal sets aside memory space for an array when the program is compiled. A statement such as this one confuses the compiler, since it doesn't know the value of N and so doesn't know how much memory to reserve for the array.

Note, however, that you may use constants in an array definition. For instance, in the above example, if N were declared as an integer constant, say 5, then the above declaration of XYZ would be perfectly acceptable.

The Data in an Array

So far, we have been concerned with defining arrays. Let's now turn our attention to the data contained in an array and the operations which can be performed on this data.

Assigning a Value to an Array

The components of an array may be assigned values just like any other variables. For example, here are some statements which assign values to components of some of the arrays introduced above:

```
Grades[1]  := 94;
Works[296]  := true;
```

The subscript can be given as the value of an expression. For example, if J is equal to 5, then

```
Number[J]  := 9;
```

assigns `Number[5]` the value 9. Furthermore,

```
Works[100*J-1]  := false
```

assigns `Work[499]` the value false. (Note that `100*J-1` is equal to 100 * 5 – 1 = 499.)

The idea of giving the subscript in terms of a variable can be used to advantage in assigning many component values at a time, as we shall see in the next chapter.

Don't refer to an array component that doesn't exist! For example, you can't refer to `Works[2000]`, since the declaration for `Works` allows subscripts only in the range 1..1000. If you refer to a subscript outside the allowed range, the compiler will treat your reference as an undeclared variable and give an Out of Range error.

Be especially careful in computing your subscripts as values of expressions, as we did in the last example. Doing so is a powerful tool. However, in using this tool, you should carefully check that the expressions you use will always produce values within the allowed subscript range. The compiler can't tell whether an expression (such as `100*J-1` above) will produce proper subscripts. (If `J` equals 1, then the value 99 for the subscript is all right; if `J` equals 50, then the value is 4999, and is out of bounds.) If evaluating the subscript produces an illegal value, then a run-time error will result. This sort of error may be quite nasty to track down. You may have the compiler check ranges by inserting the compiler directive {$R+} in your source code before the ranges you wish checked. This may add to the compiled length of your program and increase running time somewhat, but is an invaluable debugging aid.

Just like any other variables, the components of an array are not assigned any initial values. If you refer to an array component before it has been assigned a value, then most Pascal compilers will use whatever value happens to be lying around in memory. This will generally create weird program effects. For this reason, it is a good idea to initialize your arrays as one of the first steps in a program. At the very least, your program design should guarantee that a component is assigned a value before it is used (`for...do` loops are convenient for doing this).

The type assignment rule for variables also applies to components of an array: You may only assign to components values which are of the same type as the components—that is, of thc data type of the array. Your compiler will refuse to compile a program in which a value of a different type is assigned.

Accessing Data in Array Components

A program may use the current values stored in an array's components just as it would use any variables. Here are some examples of statements referring to components of the arrays defined above.

```
Number[5] := 4*Number[5] + 3; {Assign 4 times the
                               present value of
                               Number[5] plus 3 to
                               Number[5]}

Grades[1] := Grades[1] + 10; {Adding a 10 point curve
                                 class grades.}
```

4 Turbo Pascal's Control Structures

In the preceding chapter, we introduced the most elementary data types of Turbo Pascal. Of course, data types and data by itself are not of much value. You need to manipulate data in order to make programming worthwhile. In this chapter, we introduce the basic control structures you can use with Turbo Pascal in order to build programs.

Loops

Introduction

A computer can execute instructions with lightning speeds ranging from tens of thousands of instructions per second (for the smaller personal computers) to hundreds of millions of instructions per second for the fastest mainframes. Such incredible speed would not mean much if it were necessary to write the instructions individually. Imagine writing 100 million instructions to keep a computer working for only one second! Fortunately, most algorithms to perform useful tasks can be described in terms of groups of instructions which are executed repeatedly. Such a group of instructions is called a *loop*. Loops allow us to express long, and often complex, programs using very few instructions. For example, a 100 instruction loop repeated 10,000 times executes a million instructions.

Pascal has several instructions for managing loops. In this section, we will present the simplest, the `for...do` statement. Consider the statement:

```
writeln('Pascal')
```

which displays the message:

```
Pascal
```

To repeat this statement 5 times, we may use the statement:

```
for Count := 1 to 5 do
  writeln('Pascal')
```

The effect of this statement is to produce the display:

```
Pascal
Pascal
Pascal
Pascal
Pascal
```

Here is how the `for...do` statement accomplishes this task. The statement after `do` (namely, `writeln('Pascal');`) is to be repeated. This statement is called the *body* of the loop. When Pascal starts to execute the `for...do` statement, it sets the value of `Count` equal to 1. It then executes the body of the loop. Next, Pascal increases `Count` to 2 and executes the body of the loop again. And so on, with `Count` equal to 3, 4, and 5. Each repetition of the body of the loop displays 'Pascal' and starts a new line. After the repetition with `Count` equal to 5, Pascal moves on to the next program statement (the one after `for...do`).

Example 1. Write a program to display the word TITLE centered in a rectangular box 7 characters high and 15 characters wide. (See the Sample Run shown on page 76.)

Solution. In looking at the display we must generate, we notice that it is composed of several distinct parts: the top and bottom of the box, the sides, and the word 'TITLE'. The top and bottom may be generated by displaying a sequence of 15 hyphens (-). The sides may be drawn using the character (|).

Let's create the display from the top down, writing a single line at a time. There are three different types of lines we must create:

1. The top and bottom are rows of 15 hyphens each:

   ```
   ---------------
   ```

2. There are six lines of the form:

   ```
   |             |
   ```

   These lines consist of the character |, followed by 13 blanks, followed by the character |. The blanks form the area where the word TITLE will be placed. Let's call these lines the sides.

3. The line with the word TITLE has the form:

   | TITLE |

   That is, the character |, followed by 4 spaces, followed by the word TITLE, followed by 4 spaces, followed by the character |. Call this line the title line. Then our program can be described by the following pseudocode:

```
program Title.
  Draw top.
  Draw sides 3 times.
  Draw title line.
  Draw sides 3 times.
  Draw bottom.
```

Let's now proceed with a stepwise refinement for steps 1 and 5. We can use a loop to draw the top and bottom:

```
Draw top.
  Write 15 hyphens.

Draw bottom.
  Write 15 hyphens.
```

From the program design, it is now relatively simple to code the program. Note that the loop variable `count` must be declared as an integer variable.

Listing 4.1. Title

```
program Title;
{This program prints the word TITLE in a box
7 characters high and 15 characters wide.}
var
  Count : integer;

begin {Title}
  for Count := 1 to 15 do                {Draw top}
      write('-');
  writeln;    {End line}
  for Count := 1 to 3 do                 {Draw sides}
      writeln('|             |');
  writeln('|    TITLE    |');              {Write Title}
  for Count := 1 to 3 do                 {Draw sides}
      writeln('|             |');
  for Count := 1 to 15 do                {Draw bottom}
      write('-');
  writeln;                               {End line}
  readln
end. {Title}
```

Sample Run. Title

```
---------------
|             |
|             |
|             |
|    TITLE    |
|             |
|             |
|             |
---------------
```

Pascal's `for...do` statement is quite flexible. For instance, it allows for variations like:

```
for J := 'A' to 'E' do
  write(J)
```

In this statement, `J` must be declared as a char variable. The loop body (namely `write(J)`) is repeated as `J` assumes each of the values "A," "B," "C," "D," "E." The loop rcsults in the display:

```
ABCDE
```

The loop variable should not be changed within the body of a loop. There is no rule of syntax which prevents you from assigning a new value to the loop variable within the body of a loop, and Pascal will allow you to do it. However, it is considered very bad programming style to do so and will likely make your program do some strange things.

In a `for...do` statement, the loop variable increases with each repetition of the loop. In many applications, you will want the loop variable to count backwards. This can be done with the downto variation of the statement. For example, the loop

```
for J := 100 downto 1 do
  writeln(J)
```

produces the display:

```
100
99
98
97
 .
 .
 .
 2
 1
```

The loop variable counts backwards 100, 99, 98, 97, ..., and so forth.

Syntax of the for...do Statement

The general form of the for...do statement is:

```
for <variable> := <start> (down)to <finish> do
  <statement>;
```

Here <variable> is a variable which must appear in a var declaration, <start> is the starting value of <variable>, <finish> is the final value of <variable> and <statement> is the body of the loop which is repeated for each value of <variable> between <start> and <finish> inclusive. "Variable" is called the *loop variable* or *loop counter.*

If the word "down" is omitted, then the loop variable is increased to the next value at the end of each repetition of the loop. If the word "down" is included, then the loop variable is decreased to the preceding value at the end of each repetition of the loop.

The type of <variable> may be integer, char, boolean, or any of the other ordinal data types we will consider later. However, note that <variable> may not be of type real. Here is the reason why. For each of the non-real data types, each value has a distinct "next" value. The value after 1 is 2; the value after "A" is "B"; the value after false is true. A real number has no "next" value. In a for...do statement, <variable> goes from one value to the "next". This works fine with integer, char, or boolean variables, but not with a real variable.

In a for...do statement, one or both of <start> and <finish> may be expressions, as in the following example:

```
for J := X+1 to 2*Y do
  readln(C);
```

In executing this loop, Pascal first calculates the values of the expressions X+1 and 2*Y (using the current values of X and Y) and uses these as <start> and <finish>, respectively.

Deciding When to End a Loop

A loop involves the repetition of a set of program statements. It is very important that you understand how Pascal decides to stop the repetition. In the case of for...do, Pascal starts the loop by determining whether <start> is greater than <finish>. If so, the loop ends without the body being executed even once! For example, the following loop:

```
for J := 100 to 1 do
  writeln('This is a test.');
```

will result in no output since <start> (100) is greater than <finish> (1).

Assuming <start> is less than or equal to <finish>, here is how a for...do loop works:

1. Sets the loop counter equal to <start>.
2. Executes the body of the loop.
3. Increases the loop counter by 1.
4. If the new value of the loop counter is less than or equal to <finish>, Pascal starts again with step 2. Otherwise, Pascal exits the loop.
5. The value of the loop variable is undefined after the loop is exited. That is, the loop variable is defined only within the body of the loop.

A loop using downto works similarly. At the end of a loop repetition, the loop counter is decreased to the preceding value. If this value is less than <finish> then the loop is exited. Otherwise, the body of the loop is repeated using the new value of the loop counter.

Using the Loop Variable Within the Loop

The loop counter may be used within the body of the loop so that the task performed varies with the value of the loop counter. For example, consider this loop:

```
for J := 10 downto 1 do
  writeln('*':J);
```

Here, the body of the loop depends on the loop counter J; namely, the body displays "*" in a field J characters wide. Executing this loop results in the display:

```
         *
        *
       *
      *
     *
    *
   *
  *
 *
*
```

As we shall see, many applications involve using the loop variable within the body of a loop, often in a clever way.

The loop counter is a variable just like any other. However, you should take some care in how you use a loop counter. In particular, you should observe the following cautions:

1. Don't modify the loop counter within the loop. If you do, you may create a loop which goes on forever (an infinite loop) or other strange effects. For example, consider the following loop.

```
for J := 1 to 100 do
  J := 1
```

   Here, the loop counter is modified within the loop with the assignment `J := 1`. In each loop repetition, the loop counter is tested to determine whether the loop should be exited. In each case, the value of `J` is 1, so the loop is repeated. In other words, the loop never ends!

2. Don't use the loop counter outside the loop. After a loop is exited, the loop counter has the value last assigned to it within the loop. You could use the loop counter outside the loop. However, it is considered bad programming form to do so.

As mentioned above, `<start>` and `<finish>` may be given as expressions. However, when this is the case, you should be careful not to make an assignment which will modify the value of `<start>` or `<finish>` within the loop. This can easily create an infinite loop, as in the following example.

```
for Count := X to 3*X do
  X := X+1;
```

Example 2. Write a program to calculate the sum:

```
1+2+3+...+100
```

Solution. Since we are asked to add 100 numbers, it is clear that we must somehow employ a loop to manage the addition. Doing so requires that we introduce a new idea. Let's store the sum in the variable `Sum`. Rather than attempt to add the 100 numbers in a single operation, let's form the sum in 100 steps, at each step adding a single number. We start out by setting `Sum` equal to 0. Then we add 1 to `Sum`, then 2, then 3, and so forth. After 100 steps, `Sum` will contain the desired sum.

The above calculations are described in the following pseudocode.

```
program Addition.
  Sum := 0.
  for Num :=1 to 100
    Add Num to Sum.
  Display Sum.
```

Note that on the Numth repetition of the loop, the number Num is added to Sum. So after the first repetition, Sum is equal to 0+1; after two repetitions, Sum is equal to 0+1+2; and after 100 repetitions, Sum is equal to 0+1+2+...+100. That is, Sum has the value we desire to calculate. In this example, the variable Sum is used as an *accumulator.* That is, it is used to accumulate a sum.

Based on the above program design, we arrive at the following program coding.

Listing 4.2. Addition

```
program Addition;
{This program adds all the integers from 1
to 100, stores the sum in the variable Sum, and
prints out the sum.}

  var
    Num, Sum : integer;

  begin {Addition}
    Sum := 0;
      for Num := 1 to 100 do
        Sum := Sum + Num;
  write('The sum equals ');
  writeln(Sum);
  readln
end. {Addition}
```

Sample Run. Addition

```
The sum equals 5050
```

Example 3. Write a program to calculate the sum:

```
1 + 1/2 + 1/3 + ... + 1/Terms
```

where Terms, the number of terms, is specified by the user. This sum is called the *harmonic series.*

Solution. This example presents several new wrinkles. First of all, we must ask the user for the value of Terms. Second, we must accumulate the given sum. Let's use the variable Sum to contain the desired sum and let Num be the loop variable. In accumulating the value of Sum, we must use Terms as the final value of our loop. Third, we must perform arithmetic with the loop variable: For each value of Num, we must add to Sum the value 1/Num. That is, on the first repetition of the loop, we add 1/1, on the second repetition 1/2, on the third 1/3, and so on.

Here is the pseudocode for our program.

```
program Harmonic.
  Sum := 0.
  Obtain value of Terms.
  for Num := 1 to Terms do
    Add 1/Num to Sum.
  Display value of Sum.
```

Based on our program design, we arrive at the following program coding. In this example, Sum must be a real variable since it will clearly have a decimal part (except in the single case Terms=1). Also note that we have requested a display of Sum to 5 decimal places.

Listing 4.3. Harmonic

```
program Harmonic;
{This program sums the first Terms terms of the harmonic
series:
1 + 1/2 + 1/3 + ... + 1/Terms.
Here Terms is specified by the user.}

  var
    Terms, Num : integer;
    Sum : real;

  begin {Harmonic}
    Sum := 0;
    writeln('How many terms to sum?');
    readln(Terms);
    for Num := 1 to Terms do
      Sum := Sum + 1/Num;
    write('The sum of the first ',Terms,' terms is: ');
    writeln(Sum:10:5);
    readln
  end. {Harmonic}
```

Sample Run. Harmonic

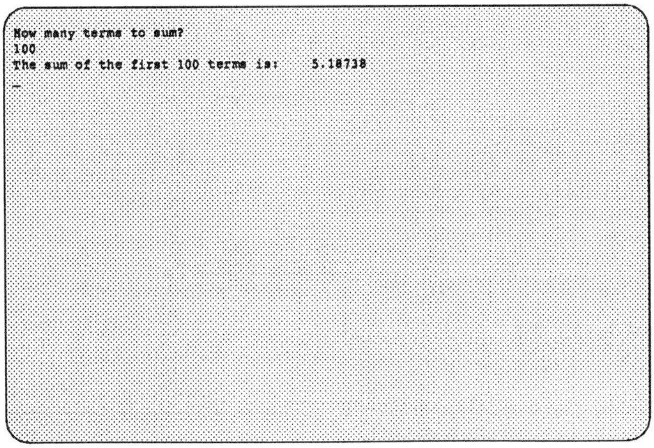

How many terms to sum?
100
The sum of the first 100 terms is: 5.18738

Compound Statements

Up to this point, our Pascal statements consisted of a single action. Such statements are called *simple statements.* Pascal allows more general statements, called compound statements, which specify multiple actions. As we shall see, such statements are of particular use in decision-making statements.

A *compound statement* is a sequence of Pascal statements which are grouped together. A compound statement is introduced by the keyword begin and is terminated with the keyword end. Here is an example of a compound statement:

```
begin
  write('Your tax is ');
  writeln(tax);
  write('This is ');
  write(100*Tax/income);
  writeln(' percent of your income.')
end;
```

The use of compound statements is governed by the following rule: A compound statement may be used anywhere a statement is legal.

Example 4. Write a program which accepts five numbers from the user and calculates their average.

Solution. To calculate the average, we must add the numbers and then divide by 5. Since the user is to supply the numbers as the program is running, we can accept the numbers and accumulate their sum in the variable Sum, in much the same fashion as we did in the last two examples. To do so, we employ a loop with 5 repetitions. Let's store the average in the variable Average.

Here is the pseudocode for the program. Note that each repetition of the loop involves several tasks. This will translate into the body of the loop being a compound statement.

```
program Average
  Sum := 0;
  for J := 1 to 5 do
    Request Jth Number.
    Add Jth Number to Sum.
  Average := Sum/5;
  Display value of Average.
```

Note that in the pseudocode we denote a compound statement by indentation. This is a useful convention which we will follow throughout the book.

Going from the pseudocode to the program coding is straightforward, with one curve ball.

In requesting the value of the Jth number, we could do things on the cheap and print a prompt of the form: "What is the number?" However, in order to help the user keep the input straight (we must start thinking like software engineers!), our prompt should tell the user which number to put in. This necessitates using the loop counter in the prompt that requests a number. This is easily done, once we have come up with the idea. The prompt is:

```
writeln('What is number ',J,'?')
```

Here J is the loop counter. So on the first repetition of the loop, the prompt reads:

```
What is number 1?
```

On the second, the prompt reads:

```
What is number 2?
```

And so forth.

Here is the source code for our program.

Listing 4.4. Average

```
program Average;
{This program inputs five numbers from the user
and computes the average.}

  var
    Sum, Number, Avg : real;
    J : integer;

  begin {Average}
    Sum := 0;
    for J := 1 to 5 do
      begin
        writeln('What is number ',J,'?');
        readln(Number);
        Sum := Sum + Number
      end;
    Avg := Sum/5;
    writeln('The average is ', Avg:5:2);
    readln
  end. {Average}
```

Sample Run. Average

```
What is number 1?
17.3
What is number 2?
25.1
What is number 3?
12.9
What is number 4?
15.5
What is number 5?
27.4
The average is 19.64
_
```

One of the most important applications of computers is in the area of business calculations. In the next example, we design a program to perform a set of typical business calculations in connection with a mortgage.

Example 5. Write a program which accepts the present balance, annual interest rate (as a percentage), and the monthly mortgage payment. The program should compute for each of the next 12 months, the amount of interest for the month and the balance of the mortgage.

Solution. Let's begin by describing the mathematics of a mortgage. At the end of each month, there is a certain `Balance` owed on the mortgage. To this `Balance` we add the monthly Interest and subtract the monthly Payment. This produces the `Balance` for the next month. We may describe the calculation of next month's balance from this month's via the statement:

```
Balance := Balance + Interest - Payment
```

The amount of `Interest` for the month may be calculated from the formula:

```
Interest = Rate*Balance
```

Here `Rate` is the monthly rate of interest, obtained by dividing the annual rate of interest by 12. For example, if the annual rate of interest is 12 percent, then we compute the monthly `Rate` by first converting 12 percent to the decimal 0.12 and then dividing by 12 to obtain the value of `Rate`, namely 0.01.

In our program, we must request three pieces of information from the user: the initial value of `Balance`, the annual percentage rate of interest, and the monthly `Payment`. The program must calculate the value of `Rate`. Then, for each of the next 12 months, the program must compute the monthly `Interest`, calculate the new `Balance`, and display the values in a table.

The program design is straightforward, but there are a number of details to attend to. We organize the program to first obtain the required values from the user. The program then displays a heading for the table of numerical values to be displayed:

```
Month Interest  Balance
```

The program then uses a loop to calculate the entries of the table for month 1, 2, ..., 12.

Here is the pseudocode for the program.

```
program Mortgage
  Obtain current mortgage balance.
  Obtain the annual interest rate.
  Obtain monthly payment.
  Compute the monthly interest Rate.
  Display heading of table.
  for Month := 1 to 12 do
    Interest := Rate*Balance;
    Balance := Balance + Interest - Payment;
    Display Month, Interest, Balance
```

From the pseudocode, we may code the program. As usual, a number of details are determined during the implementation. For example, at this stage we design the prompts, and decide on the detailed layout of the table. For example, you should note that we introduced the table with the line: "The next 12 months:" followed by a line of space. We also decided to make each of the three columns of the table 10 characters wide. Since the program deals with money, the output is displayed with two decimal places.

Listing 4.5. Mortgage

```
program Mortgage;
{This program calculates the monthly balances of a mortgage.
The user is asked to specify the current balance, the
monthly payment, and the annual interest rate. The program
calculates the mortgage balances for each of the next
12 months.}

  var
    AnnualRate, Balance, Interest,
    Payment, MonthlyRate : real;
    J, Month : integer;
```

```
begin {Mortgage}
  write('What is the current mortgage balance (omit "$")? ');
  readln(Balance);
  write('What is the annual interest rate (omit "%")? ');
  readln(AnnualRate);
  write('What is the monthly payment (omit "$")? ');
  readln(Payment);
  MonthlyRate := AnnualRate / 12;
  MonthlyRate := 0.01 * MonthlyRate;  {Express as decimal}
  writeln('The next 12 months: ');
  writeln;  {Blank line before table}
  writeln('Month':10,'Interest':10,'Balance':10);
  for J := 1 to 30 do  {Draw a line under the heading}
    write('_');
  writeln;  {Move to beginning of next line}
  writeln;  {Leave a blank line}
  for Month := 1 to 12 do
    begin
      Interest := MonthlyRate * Balance;
      Balance := Balance + Interest - Payment;
      write (Month:10);
      write (Interest:10:2);
      writeln (Balance:10:2)
    end;
  readln
end. {Mortgage}
```

Sample Run. Mortgage

```
What is the current mortgage balance (omit "$")? 100000
What is the annual interest rate (omit "%")? 12
What is the monthly payment (omit "$")? 1200
The next 12 months:

     Month  Interest   Balance
______________________________

         1   1000.00  99800.00
         2    998.00  99598.00
         3    995.98  99393.98
         4    993.94  99187.92
         5    991.88  98979.80
         6    989.80  98769.60
         7    987.70  98557.29
         8    985.57  98342.87
         9    983.43  98126.29
        10    981.26  97907.56
        11    979.08  97686.63
        12    976.87  97463.50
_
```

Nested Loops

The body of a loop may include a loop. In this case, the loops are said to be *nested.* Here is an example of a set of nested loops:

```
for Outer := 1 to 5 do
  begin
    for Inner := 1 to 4 do
      write(10*Outer+Inner, ' ');
    writeln
  end;
```

The loop counter for the outer loop is called `Outer` and the loop counter for the inner loop is called `Inner`. Each repetition of the outer loop results in executing the inner loop:

```
for Inner := 1 to 4 do
  write(10*Outer+Inner,' ');
 writeln;
```

For example, the first repetition (`Outer` equals 1) of the outer loop results in the output:

```
11 12 13 14
```

Moreover, the next output will appear on the following line because of the `writeln`. The second repetition (`Outer` equals 2) results in the output:

```
21 22 23 24
```

And so forth. The output from the four repetitions of the outer loop yields the output:

```
11 12 13 14
21 22 23 24
31 32 33 34
41 42 43 44
51 52 53 54
```

In the above example, the loops were nested two layers deep. You may nest loops three, four, or more layers deep. There is a limit to the amount of nesting allowed, but it is unlikely that you will ever run up against this limit in any practical program you will write.

Boolean Expressions

One of the most important capabilities of a computer is its ability to "make decisions" while a program is running. In making decisions, the computer decides, on the basis of current conditions within the computer, which of several sets of statements to execute.

For example, consider a program to assist a teacher in calculating student grades at the end of the semester. To do this, the teacher must first input the grades for a particular student. From these grades, the program must calculate the student's semester average. Finally, based on the numerical average, the program must assign a grade, based on the scale:

```
Range              Grade
>= 90                A
>= 80 and < 90       B
>= 70 and < 80       C
>= 60 and < 70       D
< 60                 F
```

That is, after calculating a student's average, the program must "decide" which of the above ranges the grade falls into. Based on the result of this decision, the program must print out the appropriate grade.

In this section, we will learn to incorporate such decision making into Pascal programs.

To understand how to program decision-making in Pascal, let's return to the grade-determination problem described above. Suppose that each student has five test grades, all of which count equally in computing the semester average. Suppose that the semester average is stored in the real variable `Average`. After the program calculates the value of `Average`, the program must decide which grade to assign. The decision-making process may be broken down into the following sequence of actions:

1. If `Average` is greater than or equal to 90, then assign the grade A.
2. If not, if `Average` is greater than or equal to 80, then assign the grade B.
3. If not, if `Average` is greater than or equal to 70, then assign the grade C.
4. If not, if `Average` is greater than or equal to 60, then assign the grade D.
5. If not, assign the grade F.

Each of these actions involves a decision whose outcome is based on the truth or falsity of a particular expression. For example, the outcome of the decision in action 1 is based on the truth or falsity of the expression:

```
Average is greater than or equal to 90
```

If this expression is true, then the program assigns the grade "A." If this expression is false, the program goes on to the next statement.

The above expression can be written using programming notation in the form:

```
Average >= 90                                                     (*)
```

The notation >= means "greater than or equal to" and the expression is read "Average is greater than or equal to 90."

The expression (*) is an example of a *boolean expression,* an expression which has a value of true or false.

A boolean expression generally involves one or more program variables whose values determine the truth or falsity of the expression. For example, the value of the boolean expression (*) depends on the value of the variable `Average`: If the value of `Average` is 93.0, then `Average` is greater than or equal to 90 and the value of the boolean expression is true. On the other hand, if the valuc of `Average` is 89.99, then `Average` is not greater than or equal to 90, so that the value of the boolean expression is false. In the first case, the program will assign the grade "A," whereas in the second it won't. (Teachers are cruel!)

Of course, assigning the "A" grades is only part of the task. We will give the complete grade assignment later in the chapter, after we have developed some experience with boolean expressions.

Each of the actions 1–5 involves a decision based on the value of a different boolean expression. Thus, we can see that decision making within a program is intimately tied up with the notion of boolean expressions and their truth or falsity. So before we go any further with a discussion of decision making per se, let's take a closer look at boolean expressions.

Value of a Boolean Expression

A boolean expression is an expression which has a value true or false. Some boolean expressions are quite simple; others are quite complex. However, all boolean expressions, no matter how complex, arise in one of three ways:

1. *A boolean variable.* Recall that a boolean variable is a variable which can assume only the values true and false. A boolean variable then constitutes a boolean expression. The value of the expression is the same as that of the boolean variable.

2. *A relational boolean expression.* A relational boolean expression is one which states a relationship, as in the expression:

   Average >= 90

   In this example, the expression states a relationship (which may or may not be true) between Average and 90. The symbol >= is called a

relational operator. Here is a list of all the relational operators recognized by Pascal:

>	Greater than
<	Less than
>=	Greater than or equal to
<=	Less than or equal to
=	Equal to
<>	Not equal to

We will discuss the meaning and use of each of these operators shortly.

3. *A complex boolean expression.* A complex boolean expression is formed by combining boolean expressions using the logical operators and, or, and not. An example is the expression:

```
(Average < 90) and (Average >= 80)
```

formed from the two expressions

```
(Average < 90)
(Average >= 80)
```

and the logical operator *and.*

We don't have much new to say about boolean variables at this point. However, there is quite a bit to say about relational boolean expressions and complex boolean expressions. We discuss relational boolean expressions below and reserve the discussion of complex boolean expressions until later in the chapter.

Relational Boolean Expressions

A relational boolean expression represents a relationship between two expressions. The relationship is identified by a relational operator which is placed between the two expressions.

You may use the following relational operators to compare values of variables A and B, which may be of any scalar data type:

Relational Operator	Meaning	Example
=	equals	A = B
<>	not equal to	A <> B
>	greater than	A > B
<	less than	A < B
>=	greater than or equal to	A >= B
<=	less than or equal to	A <= B

Example 1. Suppose that `A` and `B` are integer variables and `Letter1` and `Letter2` are char variables. Determine whether the following relational boolean expressions are true or false.

1. A < B (A equals 1, B equals –3)
2. A <> B (A equals 2, B equals 3)
3. A <= B (A equals –1, B equals 2)
4. Letter1 <> Letter2 (Letter1 equals 'A', Letter2 equals '#')

Solution.

1. false. 1 is not less than –3.
2. true. 2 is not equal to 3.
3. true. –1 is less than or equal to 2.
4. true. 'A' is not equal to '#'.

Example 2. Write a boolean expression corresponding to each of the following.

1. X+Y is less than or equal to Z
2. 3*Beta is greater than (Beta+Alpha)*Beta

3. Continue has the value true
4. X has the same value as Y

Solution.

1. X+Y <= Z
2. 3*Beta > (Beta+Alpha)*Beta
3. Continue = true
4. X = Y

Be careful not to confuse the equality operator = with the assignment operator := . The equality operator is used in boolean expressions (and also in constant declarations) to indicate that the values of two expressions are equal. The assignment operator is used to assign a value to a variable. For example,

```
X = Y
```

is a boolean expression which is true if the value of `X` equals the value of `Y` and is false otherwise. On the other hand,

```
X := Y;
```

is a statement which assigns the value of `Y` to the variable `X`.

Boolean Relational Operators Involving Strings

In our discussion above, we have discussed boolean relational operators and boolean relational expressions involving real, integer, and char variables. Turbo Pascal also includes several boolean relational operators which can be used in connection with strings, namely <, >, <=, >=, =, and <>.

Suppose that `Str1` and `Str2` are string variables of any type. Then we can form the following string boolean relational expressions:

- `Str1` = `Str2` is true if `Str1` and `Str2` agree in all their characters.
- `Str1` < `Str2` is true provided that `Str1` precedes `Str2` in alphabetical order. In case `Str1` and `Str2` are of different lengths and the shorter one agrees with the initial segment of the longer, then the shorter string is regarded as coming first.
- `Str1` > `Str2` is true provided that `Str1` succeeds `Str2` in alphabetical order. In case `Str1` and `Str2` are of different lengths and the shorter

one agrees with the initial segment of the longer, then the shorter string is regarded as coming first.

- Str1 <= Str2 is true provided that either Str1 < Str2 or Str1 = Str2.
- Str1 >= Str2 is true provided that either Str1 > Str2 or Str1 = Str2.

For example, here are some string boolean relational expressions and their respective truth values:

```
'ABCD' < 'ABFGE' is true
'ABCD' > 'A' is true
'ABCD' <= 'BCD' is true
'ABCD' = 'ABCD' is true
```

String boolean relational expressions may be used in conditional statements in exactly the same way as the boolean relational expressions we introduced earlier in the section.

Assignment of the Values of Boolean Expressions

As we have seen above, a boolean expression has a value which is either true or false. The value of a boolean expression may be assigned to a boolean variable. For example, if GradeA is a boolean variable, then the assignment:

```
GradeA := (A >= 90)
```

assigns to GradeA the value of the relational expression (A >= 90). That is, if A is greater than or equal to 90, then GradeA is assigned the value true; if A is less than 90, then GradeA is assigned the value false. The variable GradeA thus indicates whether or not a grade of A is merited.

More generally, the value of a boolean expression may be assigned to a boolean variable using a statement of the form:

```
<bvariable> := <bexpression>
```

Here <bvariable> denotes a boolean variable and <bexpression> denotes a boolean expression. Such a statement assigns to <bvariable> the value (true or false) of <bexpression>.

As another example, suppose that X and Y are integer variables, Equal is a boolean variable and that X has the value 1, Y has the value 2. Then the statement

```
Equal := (X=Y)
```

assigns to the boolean variable `Equal` the value of the boolean expression `(X=Y)`. For the given assignment of the values of `X` and `Y`, `Equal` is assigned the value false.

The parentheses in the above boolean expressions are actually unnecessary. For example, we could just as well write the statement of the second example in the form

```
Equal   :=   X=Y
```

This is because the relational operators, like `=`, have higher precedence than the assignment operator. This means that the expression `X=Y` is evaluated before the assignment. However, the parentheses do no harm and make the statement easier to read. As a result, I prefer the parenthesized version of the statement.

Complex Boolean Expressions

In many applications, it is necessary to use boolean expressions which express more complicated logical conditions than those already discussed. For example, consider the problem of assigning grades to students based on the value of the semester `Average`. A grade of B is assigned, provided that `Average` is less than 90 and greater than or equal to 80. Thus, assignment of a B is governed by the truth or falsity of the boolean expression:

```
(Average < 90) and (Average >= 80)
```

This boolean expression is an example of a complex boolean expression built out of the two boolean expressions:

```
(Average < 90)
(Average >= 80)
```

These two relational boolean expressions are connected by the operator `and`. In addition to the operator `and`, we may construct complex boolean expressions using the operators `or`, `xor`, and `not`. In this section, we will examine such complex boolean expressions in detail.

The Operator and

The logical operator `and` is used to create boolean expressions which are true provided that each of two boolean expressions is true. The operator and can be used in complex boolean expressions of the form:

```
expression1 and expression2
```

Here `expression1` and `expression2` are boolean expressions. Such a complex boolean expression is true, provided that both boolean expressions `expression1` and `expression2` are true; if one or both of the boolean expressions are false, then the complex expression is false.

For example, consider the boolean expression:

```
(Average < 90) and (Average >= 80)
```

This statement is true only if both of the statements

```
Average < 90
Average >= 80
```

are true. The statement is false otherwise. That is, the complex expression is true provided that `Average` is both less than 90 and greater than or equal to 80. Thus, for example, if `Average` is equal to 82.3, then the complex statement is true; if `Average` is equal to 74.1, then the complex statement is false.

Several *and* operators may be used within a single expression. For example, the expression:

```
Continue and (X=1) and (Alpha <> 'C')
```

is true, provided that `Continue` is true and `X` is equal to 1 and `Alpha` is not equal to '`C`.'

The Operator or

The logical operator `or` is used to create boolean expressions which are true provided that one or the other (or both) of two boolean expressions is true.

The operator `or` can be used in complex boolean expressions of the form:

```
expression1 or expression2
```

Here `expression1` and `expression2` are boolean expressions. Such a complex boolean expression is true provided that either `expression1` or `expression2` is true; if both of the boolean expressions are false, then the complex expression is false.

For example, consider the boolean expression:

```
(X > 1 ) or (X < -1)
```

This statement is true if at least one of the statements

```
(X > 1)
(X < -1)
```

is true and it is false otherwise. That is, the complex expression is true provided that either X is greater than 1 or X is less than –1. Thus, for example, if X is equal to 3 or to –2, then the complex expression is true; if X is equal to 0, then the complex expression is false.

Several or operators may be used in a single expression. For example, the expression:

```
(Ch = 'A') or (Ch = 'B') or (Ch = 'C')
```

is true provided that Ch has one of the values 'A', 'B,' or 'C'; if Ch has some other value, then the expression is false.

Example 2. Write an expression which is true if Alpha is equal to 'A' and either Beta is equal to 'B' or X is equal to 1.

Solution. The logical condition expressed above involves three conditions and may be written as follows:

```
(Alpha = 'A') and ((Beta = 'B') or (X = 1))
```

The parentheses indicate that the expression after and is the complex expression:

```
(Beta = 'B') or (X = 1)
```

The Operator not

The operator not is used to form the negation or logical opposite of a boolean expression. For example, the negation of the boolean expression:

```
X = 1
```

is the boolean expression:

```
not (X = 1)
```

The first expression is true if X is equal to 1 and false otherwise; the negation is true if X = 1 is false and false if X = 1 is true. That is, the negation is true if X is not equal to 1 and is false if X is equal to 1. In other words:

```
not (X=1)
```

is equivalent to:

```
(X <> 1)
```

The general use of the `not` operator has the syntax:

```
not expression
```

The `not` operator may be used to form the negation of any boolean expression, simple or complex. For example, the negation of the expression:

```
(Ch = 'Y') or (Ch = 'N')
```

is the expression:

```
not ((Ch = 'Y') or (Ch = 'N'))
```

This expression has the value:

```
true     if Ch has a value other than 'Y' or 'N';
false    otherwise.
```

Such expressions are useful in responding to user input, as the following example shows.

Example 3. A user must respond to a program prompt by typing either **Y** for yes or **N** for no. Write a statement which responds to an input other than "Y" or "N" by asking the user to repeat the input.

Solution. Let's assume that the input character is stored in the char variable `Ch`. Then the value of `Ch` is something other than 'Y' or 'N' precisely when the following expression is true:

```
not ((Ch = 'Y') or (Ch = 'N'))
```

Therefore, the desired statement is:

```
if not ((Ch = 'Y') or (Ch = 'N')) then
  writeln('Input Error. Repeat Input.');
```

Evaluating Boolean Expressions

In Chapter 3, we introduced the notion of an algebraic expression and discussed the rules for evaluating such expressions. As you will recall, an algebraic expression has a numerical value. There are rules for evaluating boolean expressions similar to those for evaluating algebraic expressions, based on the precedence of the various boolean operators `and`, `or`, `not` and the various relational operators (<, >, =, <>, etc.).

Parentheses are used, just as with algebraic expressions, to change the normal precedence rules in effect for evaluating boolean expressions. Extra pairs of parentheses are ignored by Turbo Pascal. For example, the following two statements are interpreted as the same:

```
if X > 1 then writeln('X is greater than 1.');
if (X > 1) then writeln('X is greater than 1.');
```

Turbo Pascal's precedence rules enable it to pick out the boolean expression X > 1 without the aid of parentheses. But the parentheses in the second statement causes no harm.

While parentheses can be used to make expressions more legible, there is considerable latitude in exactly how to do this. For example, the following statements are interpreted as the same.

```
if (X > 1) and (X < 5) then
  writeln('X is within range.');

if ((X > 1) and (X < 5)) then
  writeln('X is within range.');
```

It is up to you to select the version which is most intelligible to you.

A Detailed Example

Let's now return to the grade assignment problem which we posed at the beginning of the chapter. Let's begin by stating the problem in a precise form.

Example 4. Students in Sally Smith's chemistry class accumulate five equally weighted grades per semester. Write a Turbo Pascal program which accepts these five grades as input and determines the student's semester average and assigns grades based on the scale:

Range	Grade
>= 90	A
>= 80 and < 90	B
>= 70 and < 80	C
>= 60 and < 70	D
< 60	F

Solution. Let's begin with an analysis of the algorithms required. A student has five grades. Let's denote these by:

```
Grade[1], Grade[2], Grade[3], Grade[4], Grade[5]
```

Inputting the grades is a simple task of the sort we have done many times. Let `Average` denote the semester average corresponding to the five grades. Then `Average` may be calculated using the formula:

```
Average = (Grade[1] + Grade[2] + Grade[3] + Grade[4] + Grade[5])/5
```

Let's now design the program. The program neatly breaks down into three steps: obtaining the grades, computing the average, and assigning the grade. Accordingly, we have the following pseudocode.

```
program GradeAssignment.
  Input grades.
  Compute average.
  Assign grade and report result.
```

Let's assume that the various grades (`Grade[1]-Grade[5]`) are reals. This allows for fractional points. Since `Average` is computed using division, it will, in general, result in another real. So let's make `Average` a real variable.

Assigning the grade can be done using a set of if...then statements, one for each possible grade. For example, the statement corresponding to the grade '`B`' is:

```
if (Average < 90.0) and (Average >= 80.0) then
  writeln('Grade: B');
```

Similar statements may be used to assign the other grades.

With the program design worked out, we can proceed to the coding. Here is the listing of the program.

Listing 4.6. Grades

```
program Grades;
{This program assigns a semester grade and calculates the semester
average based on five grades input by the user.}

  var
    Grade : array[1..5] of real;
    Average : real ;
    J : integer;

  begin {Grades}
    for J := 1 to 5 do
      begin
        write('What is grade # ', J,'? ');
        readln(Grade[J])
      end;
    Average :=
      (Grade[1] + Grade[2] + Grade[3] + Grade[4] + Grade[5])/5;
    writeln('Average: ', Average:5:1);
    if Average >= 90.0 then
      writeln('Grade: A');
    if (Average < 90.0) and (Average >= 80.0) then
      writeln('Grade: B');
```

```
    if (Average < 80.0) and (Average >= 70.0) then
      writeln('Grade: C');
    if (Average < 70.0) and (Average >= 60.0) then
      writeln('Grade: D');
    if Average < 60.0 then
      writeln('Grade: F');
    readln
  end. {Grades}
```

Sample Run. Grades

```
What is grade # 1? 90
What is grade # 2? 85
What is grade # 3? 95
What is grade # 4? 90
What is grade # 5? 70
Average: 86.0
Grade: B
_
```

The if...then and if...then...else Statements

In the preceding section, we introduced the notion of a boolean expression, which is used in decision-making statements. In this section, we discuss two such statements, `if...then` and `if...then...else`.

The if...then Statement

The `if...then` statement allows you to make a decision within a program. As an example, let's go back to the grade assignment program discussed in the preceding section. Assignment of the grade "A" can be accomplished with the statement:

```
if Average >= 90 then
  writeln('Grade:A.');
```

In response to this statement, Pascal determines the value of the boolean expression:

```
Average >= 90
```

If the value of the expression is true (that is, if `Average` is greater than or equal to 90), then Pascal executes the statement following `then`. That is, it displays the string constant:

```
'Grade:A'
```

If the value of the boolean expression is false, then Pascal skips the remainder of the statement.

Syntax of the if...then Statement

An `if...then` statement has the form:

```
if <boolean expression> then <statement>;
```

In response to this statement:

1. Pascal determines the value (true or false) of `<boolean expression>`.
2. If the value is true, then Pascal executes `<statement>` and then exits the `if...then` statement and goes on to the next statement in the program.
3. If the value of `<boolean expression>` is false, then Pascal ignores the remainder of the `if...then` statement.

Applications of the if...then Statement

The next few examples provide some practice in the use of the `if...then` structure.

Example 1. Write a program which determines the larger of two real numbers supplied by the user.

Solution. Let's store the two numbers supplied by the user in the real variables `Num1` and `Num2`. Our program will store the larger of the two numbers in the variable `Larger`. We will determine which is greater using two if...then statements:

```
if Num1 >= Num2 then Larger := Num1;
if Num1 < Num2 then Larger := Num2;
```

Note that implicit in the above statements is our arbitrary design decision that if `Num1` is equal to `Num2`, then `Larger` will be set equal to `Num1` (rather than to `Num2`).

The program consists of three steps, as described in the following pseudocode.

```
program Maximum.
  Get real numbers Num1,Num2 from user.
  Determine the larger of Num1 and Num2.
  Display original numbers and the larger number.
```

The first and third steps are similar to tasks we have coded previously. The second step consists of the two if...then statements given above. Modifying these Pascal statements, we can code the program as follows.

Listing 4.7. Maximum

```
program Maximum;
{Find the larger of two numbers input by user}

  var
    Num1, Num2, Larger : real;

  begin {Maximum}
    writeln('Choose two real numbers.');
    write('First number? ');
    readln(Num1);
    write('Second number? ');
    readln(Num2);
    if (Num1 >= Num2)
      then
        Larger := Num1;
    if (Num1 < Num2)
      then
        Larger := Num2;
    write('The larger of');
    write(Num1:5:1,' and',Num2:5:1,' is');
    writeln(Larger:5:1);
    readln
  end. {Maximum}
```

Sample Run. Maximum

```
Choose two real numbers.
First number? 47.1
Second number? 18.2
The larger of 47.1 and 18.2 is 47.1
_
```

Example 2. Jones and Smith are candidates for election to the local school board. Write a program which accepts from the user the number of votes each received and the number of abstentions. The program should compute the percent of votes in each category and should determine the majority winner.

Solution. In this example, it is convenient to combine the analysis and design phases. The main module consists of the following steps.

```
program election.
  Input election results.
  Compute statistics.
  Determine Winner.
```

Stepwise refinements are needed for each step in our solutions. Here are the second-level designs for the steps in the main module.

```
Input election results.
  Input number of votes for Smith.
  Input number of votes for Jones.
  Input number of abstentions.

Compute statistics.
  Compute total votes cast.
  Compute percent for Smith.
  Compute percent for Jones.
  Compute percent abstentions.
```

```
Determine Winner
  Display percentages.
  Display winner.
```

Based on the above designs, we introduce the variables:

```
Smith = the number of votes for Smith
Jones = the number of votes for Jones
Abstentions = the number of abstentions
Total = the total number of votes cast
PercentSmith = percent for Smith
PercentJones = percent for Jones
PercentAbs = percent abstentions
```

Then using these variables, we will incorporate the following formulas in our solution.

```
Total := Smith + Jones + Abstentions
PercentSmith := 100*Smith/Total
PercentJones := 100*Jones/Total
PercentAbs := 100*Abstentions/Total
```

Now that we have values for each candidate, the winner can be determined using several `if...then` statements comparing Smith and Jones, as follows:

```
if PercentSmith > PercentJones then
  writeln('Smith Wins');
if PercentSmith < PercentJones then
  writeln('Jones Wins')
if PercentSmith = PercentJones then
  writeln('Smith and Jones are tied');
```

We may now code the program, based on our design.

Listing 4.8. Election

```
program Election;
{This program decides the victor in an election
between Smith and Jones. It also calculates the
percentages that each achieved.}

  var
    Smith, Jones, Abstentions, Total,
    PercentSmith, PercentJones, PercentAbs : real;

  begin {Election}
    {Input election results}
    write('Number of votes for Smith: ');
    readln(Smith);
    write('Number of votes for Jones: ');
    readln(Jones);
```

```
    write('Number of abstentions: ');
    readln(Abstentions);
    {Compute statistics}
    Total := Smith + Jones + Abstentions;
    PercentSmith := 100*Smith/Total;
    PercentJones := 100*Jones/Total;
    PercentAbs := 100*Abstentions/Total;
    {Determine winner}
    writeln('Smith ',PercentSmith:3:0,'%');
    writeln('Jones ',PercentJones:3:0,'%');
    writeln('Abstentions ',PercentAbs:3:0,'%');
    if (PercentSmith > PercentJones)
      then
        writeln('Smith Wins');
    if (PercentSmith < PercentJones)
      then
        writeln('Jones Wins');
    if (PercentSmith = PercentJones)
      then
        writeln('Smith and Jones are tied');
    readln
  end. {Election}
```

Sample Run. Election

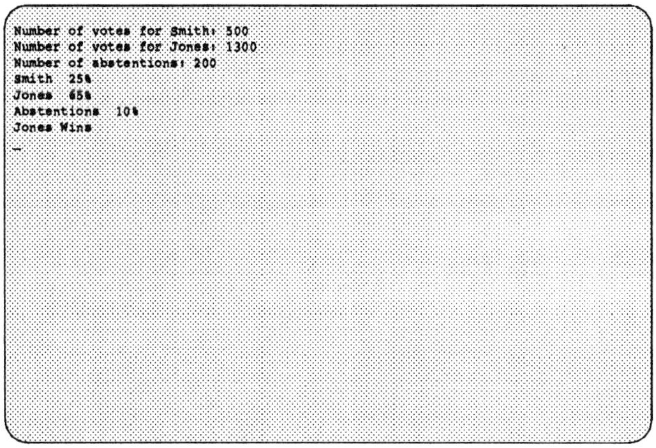

Nested if...then Statements

An `if...then` statement has the form:

```
if <boolean expression> then <statement>
```

Here <statement> may be any Pascal statement (simple or compound). In particular, <statement> may be another if...then statement. For example, consider the following statement:

```
if X > 5 then if X < 10 then writeln('X is ok');
```

In interpreting this statement, Pascal first determines whether X is greater than 5. If so, it executes the statement after the first then. That is, Pascal determines whether X is less than 10. If so, it displays the message:

```
X is ok
```

If X is not greater than 5 or X is not less than 10, Pascal exits the statement without any action.

In the above example, one if...then statement is used within another. Such if...then statements are said to be *nested*. Pascal allows nesting of if...then statements to any level. (An if...then inside an if...then inside an if...then, and so forth.)

Nested if...then statements can be hard to read. So it is wise to use an indentation format to make them intelligible. For example, the above statement is best written in the form:

```
if X > 5 then
    if X < 10 then
      writeln('X is Ok');
```

In this format, it is clear that the second line is executed only if X is greater than 5 and the third line is executed only if X is less than 10.

The if...then...else Statement

The if...then statement has the form:

```
if <boolean expression> then <statement>;
```

If <boolean expression> is true, then <statement> is executed. However, if <boolean expression> is false, then no action is taken. In many applications, however, you will wish to take one action if <boolean expression> is true and another if <boolean expression> is false. This can be done using the if...then...else statement, which has the format:

```
if <boolean expression> then
    <statement 1>
else
    <statement 2>;
```

For example, consider the statement:

```
if X <> 0 then
    writeln('X is non-zero')
else
    writeln('X is zero');
```

In executing this statement, Pascal first determines whether the value of X is non-zero. If so, then it displays the message:

```
X is non-zero
```

Otherwise (that is, if X is equal to 0), it displays the message:

```
X is zero
```

You should note the format used with the if...then...else statement. This format enhances the readability of the statement.

Here is how the if...then...else statement works in general.

1. Pascal determines whether <boolean expression> is true or false.
2. If <boolean expression> is true then <statement 1> is executed.
3. If <boolean expression> is false then <statement 2> is executed.
4. Pascal exits the if...then...else statement.

Use of Compound Statements With if...then...else

One or both of the statements in if...then...else may be compound statements. Here is an example of this usage:

```
if Alpha = 'A' then
  begin
    write('The value of Alpha is ');
    writeln(Alpha)
  end
else
  begin
    writeln('The value of Alpha is not ''A''');
    writeln('It is ', Alpha)
  end;
```

Note that the end in the first compound statement is not followed by a semicolon. This is correct, since there should not be a semicolon following the statement preceding else.

Nested if...then...else Statements

You may nest if...then...else statements, thereby succinctly expressing very complex logic. For example, consider the following statement which we will find useful in the next example:

```
if Income > 4000.0 then
    if Income < 29000.0 then
      Tax1 := 0.15*(Income-4000.0)
    else
    Tax1 := 0.15*(29000.0-4000.0)
else
  Tax := 0.0;
```

Here, the outside if...then...else statement uses another if...then...else statement as its own <statement 1>. To interpret this statement, use the indentation as a guide: If Income is greater than 4000.0, then the statement

```
if Income < 29000.0 then
  Tax1 := 0.15*(Income-4000)
else
  Tax1 := 0.15*(29000.0-4000.0)
```

is executed. If Income is not greater than 4000.0 then the statement

```
Tax1 := 0.0;
```

is executed.

Nested if...then...else statements have the potential for ambiguity which Pascal will automatically resolve for you, but perhaps not in the way you were expecting. For example, consider the following statement:

```
if Income > 4000.0 then
  if Income < 29000.0
    then
      Tax1 := 0.15*(Income-4000)
    else
      Tax1 := 0.15*(29000.0-4000.0);
```

As it is written, it is an if...then...else statement nested within an if...then statement. However, if you write it in the form

```
if Income > 4000.0 then
  if Income < 29000.0
    then
      Tax1 := 0.15*(Income-4000)else
  Tax1 := 0.15*(29000.0-4000.0);
```

it appears to be an if...then statement nested within an if...then...else statement.

Be careful. Pascal always associates an `else` with the nearest preceding `then`. In the case of these examples, Pascal will associate the `else` with the second `then` and interpret the statement in the first form.

Don't let your formatting mislead you into misinterpreting what a statement does. An incorrect formatting of the code as in the second statement above will create a logical error that can be extremely difficult to track down. From the source code, it will look as if the logic is correct. However, Pascal does not interpret the source code in the same way that you have formatted it!

The next example provides some practice in problem solving using the `if...then...else` statement.

Example 3. In May 1985, President Reagan proposed an overhaul of the Federal income tax law. He proposed the following tax schedule:

0% on Income from $0 to $4,000;

15% on Income from $4,000 to $29,000;

25% on Income from $29,000 to $70,000;

35% on Income over $70,000.

Write a program to calculate the tax on an amount of income supplied by the user.

Solution. The first level of detail of the program consists of the following three steps.

```
program ComputeTax.
  Get income amount from user.
  Compute amount of tax.
  Display amount of tax.
```

The first and third steps don't require further elaboration. The second step is the key one and requires that we design an algorithm.

Let `Income` denote the amount of income input by the user and let `Tax` denote the tax on this amount of income. Let's compute `Tax` as a sum of `Tax1`, `Tax2`, and `Tax3`, the amounts of tax on incomes in the last three ranges (from $4,000 to $29,000, from $29,000 to $70,000, over $70,000).

Computing `Tax1`, `Tax2`, and `Tax3` involves a rather complex set of decisions, as expressed in the following algorithm:

1. Let's start at the bottom of the total income and compute `Tax1` first.

   a. If `Income` is greater than $4,000, then:

      (1) If `Income` is less than $29,000, then `Tax1` is equal to 0.15*(`Income`–4000.0).

(2) If `Income` is greater than $29,000 then `Tax1` is equal to 0.15*(29000–4000.0)

b. If `Income` is not greater than $4,000, then `Tax1` is equal to 0.0.

2. Let's next compute `Tax2`.

a. If `Income` is greater than $29,000, then:

(1) If `Income` is less than $70,000, then `Tax2` is equal to 0.25*(`Income`–29000.0).

(2) If `Income` is greater than or equal to $70,000, then `Tax2` is equal to 0.25*(70000.0–29000.0).

b. If `Income` is not greater than $29000.0, then `Tax2` is equal to 0.0.

3. Finally, we compute `Tax3`.

a. If `Income` is greater than $70,000, then `Tax3` is equal to 0.35*(`Income`–70000.0).

b. If `Income` is not greater than $70,000, then `Tax3` is equal to 0.0.

This completes the design of the algorithm corresponding to the second step in the design. Our algorithm is somewhat complex, but there can be no apology for this. Indeed, if you attempt to calculate the tax on a particular amount of income, you would go through, more or less, the same set of decisions reflected in the above algorithm.

The indentations in the above algorithm description give the precise nesting for the required `if...then...else` statements. For example, step 1 of the algorithm corresponds to the Pascal statement:

```
{Calculate Tax1}
if Income > 4000.0 then
  if Income < 29000.0 then
    Tax1 := 0.15*(income-4000.0)
  else
    Tax1 := 0.15*(29000.0-4000.0)
else
  Tax := 0.0;
```

Here is the coding for the program.

Listing 4-9. ComputeTax

```
program ComputeTax;
{This program computes the tax corresponding to an amount of income input
by the user.}
```

```
var
  Income, Tax, Tax1, Tax2, Tax3 : real;

begin {ComputeTax}
  writeln('What is the income amount?');
  readln(Income);
  {Calculate Tax1}
  if (Income > 4000.0) then
    if (Income < 29000.0) then
      Tax1 := 0.15*(Income-4000.0)
    else
      Tax1 := 0.15*(29000.0-4000.0)
  else
    Tax1 := 0.0;
  {Calculate Tax2}
  if (Income > 29000.0) then
    if (Income < 70000.0) then
      Tax2 := 0.25*(Income-29000.0)
    else
      Tax2 := 0.25*(70000.0-29000.0)
  else
    Tax2 := 0.0;
  {Calculate Tax3}
  if (Income > 70000.0) then
    Tax3 := 0.35*(Income-70000.0)
  else
    Tax3 := 0.0;
  {Calculate Tax}
  Tax := Tax1 + Tax2 + Tax3;
  write('The tax is $');
  writeln(Tax:10:2);
  readln
end. {ComputeTax}
```

Sample Run. ComputeTax

```
What is the income amount?
170000
The tax is $  49000.00
_
```

The while...do and repeat...until Statements

Earlier in the chapter, we introduced the notion of a loop in connection with our discussion of the `for...do` statement. Actually, `for...do` is just one of Pascal's loop control statements. In this section and the next, we will introduce the others, `while...do` and `repeat...until.`

A loop consists of two parts: a body and a continuation condition.

- The *body* of a loop is a group of statements which is repeated a number of times.
- The *continuation condition* controls how many times the body is repeated. During each repetition, the continuation condition is tested to determine whether to repeat the body another time.

A Review of for...do Loops

The `for...do` statement implements the simplest type of loop. It has the form

```
for loop counter := begin to end do
  body;
```

To better understand `while...do` and `repeat...until` loops, it is useful to have a firm grasp of `for...do` loops. So let's briefly review their operation.

The body of a `for...do` loop may be either a simple or compound statement. The number of repetitions of the body is controlled by the values `begin` and `end` and the variable loop counter. Initially, loop counter is set equal to `begin`. Before each repetition of the body, Pascal asks the question:

```
Is loop counter less than or equal to end?
```

If the answer to the question is '`No`,' then Pascal ends the `for...do` loop and goes to the next program statement. If the answer to the question is '`Yes`,' Pascal continues with the `for...do` loop: It executes the body and increases loop counter by 1. Pascal then repeats the entire process.

In the case of a `for...do` loop, the continuation condition is the boolean expression:

```
loop counter is less than or equal to end
```

When this boolean statement is false, `for...do` ends; when it is true, `for...do` continues with another repetition of body.

while...do Loops

In a `for...do` loop, the continuation condition is given by a particular boolean expression. A `while...do` loop affords considerably more flexibility since it allows you to use any boolean expression as a continuation condition. As an example, consider the following statements:

```
Counter := 1;
while Counter < 100 do
  begin
    writeln(Counter);
    Counter := Counter+1
  end;
```

The first statement sets `Counter` equal to 1. The second statement is a `while...do` loop. The body of the loop is the compound statement:

```
begin
  writeln(Counter);
  Counter := Counter+1
end;
```

The continuation condition is the boolean expression:

```
Counter < 100
```

The body is repeated as long as the continuation condition is `true`. Initially, `Counter` equals 1, so the continuation condition is `true`. The body is executed and results in the display:

```
1
```

Moreover, the variable `Counter` is increased to 2. The continuation condition is still `true`. (2 is less than 100) So the body is executed again. This time, the number 2 is displayed and `Counter` is increased to 3. And so forth. The body of the loop is repeated 99 times. The cumulative display is:

```
1
2
3
4
.
.
.
99
```

During the 99th repetition, `Counter` is increased to 100. The continuation condition then becomes `false`. (100 is not less than 100.) So the loop ends.

The continuation condition of a while...do loop may consist of any boolean expression. The body is repeated as long as the boolean expression is true. The next few examples provide some applications of while...do loops using assorted boolean expressions as continuation conditions.

Example 1. Write a while...do loop which repeatedly inputs integers from the user until the number 0 is received.

Solution. We wish to repeat the statement:

```
readln(Number);
```

where Number is an integer variable. The continuation condition is:

```
Number <> 0
```

That is, as long as Number <> 0 is true the loop continues; if Number <> 0 is false (that is, Number is equal to 0), the loop ends. The desired loop is:

```
while Number <> 0 do
  readln(Number);
```

Note that it is not possible to predict in advance how many times the body of this loop will be repeated. The number of repetitions is controlled by the program user. This is in sharp contrast to for...do loops, in which the body is executed a predictable number of times.

It is especially important to initialize variables used in the continuing condition of a while...do loop. For example, consider the loop of Example 1. If we forget to initialize Number, Pascal will start the loop with Number equal to whatever garbage happens to be lying in the memory location for Number. It may be that Number is set equal to 0. In this case, the continuing condition is false right from the start and the body of the loop will not be executed even once. To prevent this, you should initialize Number with some non-zero value (say, Number equals 1) before the loop begins.

Example 2. Modify the loop of Example 1 so that it counts the number of negative numbers which are entered.

Solution. Let's use an integer variable NegCount to count the Numbers which are negative. Within the body of the loop, we determine if an entry Number is negative; if so, we increase the count NegCount by 1. Here is the loop and the statements initializing Number and NegCount.

```
Number := 1;
NegCount := 0;
while Number <> 0 do
  begin
    readln(Number);
    if Number < 0 then
      NegCount := NegCount+1
  end;
```

Example 3. Modify the loop of Example 2 so that the loop ends either when the number 0 is entered or after 20 numbers.

Solution. Now we must keep track of how many numbers have been entered. Let's do this using the variable `NumEntered`. We initialize `NumEntered` to 0. In the body of the loop, we increase `NumEntered` by 1. The continuation condition is the complex boolean expression:

```
(Number <> 0) or (NumEntered <= 20)
```

That is, when this expression is true (either `Number` is non-zero or `NumEntered` is less than or equal to 20), the loop continues. However, when either `Number` is 0 or `NumEntered` is greater than 20, the loop ends. Here is the required code.

```
Number := 1;
NegCount := 0;
NumEntered := 0;
while (Number <> 0) or (NumEntered <= 20) do
  begin
    readln(Number);
    if Number  0 then
      NegCount := NegCount+1;
    NumEntered := NumEntered + 1;
  end;
```

for...do versus while...do

Any `for...do` statement can be written as a `while...do` loop. The next example shows how to do this.

Example 4. Write the following statement in terms of a `while...do` loop:

```
for Lcv := 1 to 100 do
  Sum := Sum+Lcv;
```

Solution. The given statement adds to `Sum` the various values of `Lcv`, namely 1, 2, 3, ... , 100. This may also be done using the statements:

```
Sum := 0;
Lcv := 1;
while Lcv <= 100 do
  begin
    Sum := Sum + Lcv;
    Lcv := Lcv + 1
  end;
```

Note that we must initialize `Lcv` to 1. In the `for...do` version, this is taken care of automatically. Note, also that the body of the `while...do` loop must contain a statement to increase `Lcv` by 1. In the `for...do` version, this is also taken care of automatically.

In the last example, we illustrated how a `for...do` loop may be written using `while...do`. The example showed how the `for...do` version is typically shorter. However, the `while...do` statement has versatility on its side, as the next example shows.

Example 5. Write a Pascal program to calculate the sum:

```
1 + 4 + 7 + ... + 100
```

Solution. Let's accumulate the sum in the variable `Sum`. We initialize `Sum` at 0. A `while...do` loop can be used to add `Lcv` to `Sum` for `Lcv = 100`, where the `Lcv` is increased by 3 with each repetition of the loop. The first value of `Lcv` is 1, so we initialize `Lcv` with this value. Here is the program.

Listing 4.10. SumBy3

```
program SumBy3;
{Compute the sum 1 + 4 + 7 + ... + 100}

var
  Sum, Lcv : integer;

begin {SumBy3}
  Sum := 0;
  Lcv := 1;
  while (Lcv <= 100) do
    begin
      Sum := Sum + Lcv;
      Lcv := Lcv + 3
    end;
  writeln('The sum is ', Sum);
  readln
end. {SumBy3}
```

Sample Run. SumBy3

```
The sum is 1717
```

The last program could just as well have been written using a `for...do` loop. To do so, we note that the numbers to be summed are of the form

```
3*K+1, where K := 0, 1, ..., 33.
```

(This takes some figuring to come up with.) The program can then be written in the form:

Listing 4.11. SumBy3

```
program SumBy3;

  var
    Sum,Lcv : integer;

  begin
    Sum := 0;
    for Lcv := 0 to 33 do
      Sum := Sum + 3*Lcv + 1;
    writeln('The sum is ', Sum);
    readln
  end.
```

This version is shorter, but requires you to think harder to come up with the correct `for...do` loop.

The repeat Statement

In the discussion above, we introduced the `while...do` statement. One of the significant features of this statement is that the continuation condition is tested at the beginning of each repetition. In particular, if the continuation condition is false when the statement begins, then the loop is never executed. In this section, we discuss the `repeat...until` statement in which the continuation condition is tested after each repetition.

To introduce the `repeat...until` statement, let's begin with an example. Consider the statements:

```
Number := 1;
repeat
  writeln(Number);
  Number := Number + 1
until Number = 100;
```

The variable Number is initially assigned the value 1. The `repeat...until` statement repeats the loop body:

```
writeln(Number);
Number := Number + 1
```

until `Number` has the value 100. In more detail, here is what happens:

1. When `repeat...until` is first called, `Number` has the value 1.
2. The loop body is executed: The value of `Number` (1) is displayed. Moreover, `Number` is assigned the value `Number + 1`, or 2.
3. The boolean expression `Number = 100` is the continuation condition.
   a. If `Number = 100` is true (that is, if `Number` is equal to 100), the `repeat...until` statement is over.
   b. If `Number = 100` is false, then the loop body (as described in Step 2) is repeated.
4. With each repetition of the body, `Number` is increased by 1. After 100 repetitions, `Number = 100` becomes true and the `repeat...until` statement is over.
5. The result of the above statements is to create the display:

```
1
2
3
4
.
.
.
99
```

General Form of the repeat...until Statement

The general `repeat...until` statement has the syntax:

```
repeat
  statement;
  statement;
  .
  .
  .
  statement
until expression
```

Here `statement` is either a simple or compound statement and `expression` is a boolean expression. Note that the last statement before the keyword `until` has no semicolon. A semicolon here is unnecessary since the reserved word `until` acts as a separator between the end of the last statement and the expression.

In words, the semantics of the `repeat...until` statement are as follows:

1. Execute the statements.
2. Evaluate expression.
   a. If the value is false, go back to 1.
   b. If the value is true, exit `repeat...until`.

Comparison of while...do and repeat...until

Both the `while...do` and the `repeat...until` statements allow you to repeatedly execute a loop, with continuation dependent on the value (true or false) of a boolean expression. However, there are some significant differences between the statements.

The most significant difference is in the placement of the test which controls loop continuation. In the `while...do` statement, the test occurs before the loop body is executed. In the `repeat...until` statement, the test occurs after. The placement of the test has an important consequence: In a `while...do` loop, the test may fail at the outset; in this case, the loop body will never be executed. However, in a `repeat...until` statement, the test occurs after the body is executed. In particular, the first test occurs after the first repetition. A consequence of this observation is the following:

In a `repeat...until` statement, the body is always executed at least once.

A `while...do` loop uses its test to decide whether to execute the statements within the loop; a `repeat...until` loop uses its test to decide whether to repeat the statements within the loop. In the above example, we used the expression `Number = 100` to decide when to stop the loop; as soon as `Number` was equal to 100, the loop was over. Here is the same loop, written using a `while...do` statement:

```
Number := 1;
while Number < 100 do
  begin
    writeln(Number);
    Number := Number + 1
  end;
```

Here the expression `Number < 100` is used to decide whether to continue the loop.

Note that the statements comprising the body of a `repeat...until` loop need not be surrounded by the words `begin` and `end`. This is because the words `repeat` and `until` provide a built-in mechanism for Turbo Pascal to determine the beginning and end of the statement list.

Selection Using the case Statement

Many applications programs use a menu system for command selection. For example, here is the main menu of a hypothetical word processing program.

```
Choose from the following menu:
       A: EditNewFile;
       B: EditOldFile;
       C: PrintFile;
       D: EraseFile;
       E: RenameFile;
       F: CopyFile
```

The menu allows the user to select from among six options, labeled A to F. To choose an option, the user types the appropriate letter. The program then performs the action corresponding to the selection.

It is possible to make the selection from such a menu using a sequence of nested `if...then...else` statements. For example, the choice from the above menu can be made using a statement like this. The user's response is assumed to be contained in the variable `Choice`.

```
if Choice = 'A'
  then
    EditNewFile
  else
    if Choice = 'B'
      then
        EditOldFile
      else
        if Choice = 'C'
          then
            PrintFile
          else
            if Choice = 'D'
              then
                EraseFile
              else
                if Choice = 'E'
                  then
                    RenameFile
                  else
                      if Choice = 'F'
                        then
                          CopyFile;
```

This is a very complex sequence of nested `if...then...else` statements, to be sure. And at first glance, it is difficult to see what the statement is meant to do. Fortunately, there is a much more transparent method of accomplishing the same goal, using the `case` statement.

The `case` statement allows the program to choose among a series of actions based on the value of an expression. For example, the above response to the user's request can be accomplished with the statement:

```
case Choice of
  'A': EditNewFile;
  'B': EditOldFile;
  'C': PrintFile;
  'D': EraseFile;
  'E': RenameFile;
  'F': CopyFile
end;
```

Let's analyze how this statement works. The statement begins with the keyword `case` followed by the expression `Choice`. This expression is called the *case expression* and its value determines which action is to be taken. Following is the word "of" and a list of constants, called the *case list.* Following each constant is an action to be taken. When Turbo Pascal encounters this statement, it determines the value of `Choice`. It then locates the value in the case list and performs the designated action. For example, if the value of `Choice` is 'A', then the procedure `EditOldFile` is performed.

Anatomy of the case Statement

Case Expression

The case expression may be any expression which evaluates to an integer, boolean, or char value. Note, however, that a case expression cannot evaluate to a real value.

Case List

The case list must consist of constants whose type matches that of the case expression. Note, however, that the case list cannot include variables or expressions.

Note that each case constant is followed by a colon and a statement (which can be simple or compound). Each statement, except for the last, is followed by a semicolon. The case statement is terminated with the keyword `end`.

In Turbo Pascal, if the case expression evaluates to a value not specified in the case list, then the program exits the case statement with no action.

Note the optional case constant `else`. This case constant can be used to specify an action to be taken if the value of the case expression does not match any of the listed values.

The order of the constants in the constant list is immaterial. For example, the above statement could just as well have been written:

```
case Choice of
  'D': EraseFile;
  'A': EditNewFile;
  'C': PrintFile;
  'B': EditOldFile;
  'E': RenameFile;
  'F': CopyFile
end;
```

Moreover, several constants may correspond to the same action. For example, here is a statement which assigns a letter grade based on the numerical score (0–10) on a quiz.

```
case Quiz of
  10, 9 : writeln('A');
  8 : writeln('B');
  7 : writeln('C');
  6 : writeln('D');
  5,4,3,2,1,0 : writeln('F')
end;
```

Here the scores 10 and 9 both give a grade "A" and scores 5, 4, 3, 2, 1, and 0 all correspond to a grade "F."

It is even possible that no action is taken in the case of some items in the constant list. For example, in the statement:

```
case Accident of
  1 : CarStats;
  2 : ;
  3 : AirStats;
  4 : HomeStats
end;
```

A value of 2 for `Accident` results in no action.

Applications of the case Statement

Example 1. Write a case statement which is equivalent to the statement:

```
if (Uncurved >= 1) and (Uncurved <= 8)
  then
    Curved := Uncurved
  else
    if (Uncurved >= 9) and (Uncurved <= 10)
      then
        Curved := Uncurved+1
      else
        if Uncurved = 11
          then
            Curved := Uncurved+2;
```

Here `Uncurved` and `Curved` are integer variables.

Solution. The possible values of `Uncurved` considered by the statement are 1, 2, 3, 4, 5, 6, 7, 8, 9, 10, 11. We group the various values of `Uncurved` according to the action called for in the statement. Here is the resulting case statement.

```
case Uncurved of
  1,2,3,
  4,5,6,
  7,8    : Curved := Uncurved;
  9,10   : Curved := Uncurved+1;
  11     : Curved := Uncurved+2
end;
```

Our next example develops a simple game in which the computer appears to display reasoning powers.

Example 2. Write a program to play a guessing game. The user is to choose a single-digit number. The program is to ask whether the number is even or odd, and the remainder when the number is divided by 5. From this information, the program is to determine the number.

Solution. The pseudocode for the main module is straightforward:

```
program Guess.
  Obtain digit from user.
  Ask if the digit is even or odd.
  Ask for the remainder on dividing by 5.
  Guess the digit.
```

The only challenge is the design of the guessing procedure. We have tabulated the various combinations of parity (odd or even) with the possible remainders on division by 5 in the following table.

digit	**parity**	**remainder mod 5**
0	even	0
2	even	2
4	even	4
6	even	1
8	even	3
1	odd	1
3	odd	3
5	odd	0
7	odd	2
9	odd	4

From the table, we see that a digit can, in fact, be identified from its parity and the remainder on division mod 5. This is what allows the guessing game to work.

The parity of a number can be determined by computing the value of the number mod 2. A result of 0 corresponds to an even number and a result of 1 corresponds to an odd number. The remainder on division by 5 may be determined by computing the value of the number mod 5. We may then code the above table using a pair of case statements. In the first, the case expression is Digit mod 2; in the second, it is Digit mod 5.

Here is the listing of our game.

Listing 4.12. Guess

```
program Guess;
{This program guesses the digit chosen by the user from its
parity and its remainder divided by 5.}

const
  Even = 0;
  Odd  = 1;
```

```
var
  Digit, Parity, Mod5 : integer;

begin {Guess}
  writeln('Choose a digit (0-9).');
  writeln('Is the digit even or odd?');
  writeln('Type 0 if even and 1 if odd.');
  readln(Parity);
  writeln('What is the remainder when');
  writeln('the digit is divided by 5?');
  readln(Mod5);
  case Parity of
    Even : case Mod5 of
            0 : Digit := 0;
            1 : Digit := 6;
            2 : Digit := 2;
            3 : Digit := 8;
            4 : Digit := 4;
            else : writeln('Invalid input')
          end; {case}
    Odd : case Mod5 of
            0 : Digit := 5;
            1 : Digit := 1;
            2 : Digit := 7;
            3 : Digit := 3;
            4 : Digit := 9;
            else writeln('Invalid input')
          end; {case}
    else writeln('Invalid input')
  end; {case}
  writeln('Your digit is ', Digit);
  readln
end. {Guess}
```

5 Modular Programming, Procedures, and Functions

In the preceding chapters, we discussed the rudiments of Turbo Pascal programming. Our discussions centered around the simple data types available in Turbo Pascal and around the control structures available for building programs. For the most part, our programs were of a fairly simple sort. However, in solving real applications problems, it will be necessary for you to build complex programs, consisting of hundreds or even thousands of lines of code. In order to design and code such programs, it is necessary to pay close attention to how you structure your program.

The key to building complex programs is to *modularize*. That is, you must break the program into parts, with each part performing a single task. In the program planning process, this is exactly what is accomplished by top-down design. In order to implement top-down designs, Pascal provides *procedures* and *functions*, program elements for performing tasks and calculations within the main program. In this chapter, we will discuss how to use procedures and functions in order to implement modular program designs.

Procedures

A *procedure* is a section of a program which performs a specific task. The task assigned to a procedure is performed whenever Pascal encounters the procedure name.

For example, here is a procedure, named `Stars`, which prints 20 asterisks. (Such a procedure can be used in making displayed material look attractive.)

```
procedure Stars;
{Display 20 asterisks}

  begin {Stars}
    write('********************')
  end; {Stars}
```

A procedure is actually a subprogram. That is, a procedure performs a task within a program and is written in a form similar to a Pascal program. Note, however, that a procedure ends with a semicolon rather than a period. You may use the procedure name `Stars` as a Pascal statement. When the program encounters the name `Stars` in a program, it performs the task specified by the procedure. That is, the program displays 20 asterisks.

Here is an example of a program which incorporates the procedure `Stars`.

Listing 5.1. Heading

```
program Heading;

  procedure Stars;
  {Display 20 asterisks}
    begin {Stars}
      write('********************')
    end; {Stars}

  begin {Heading}
    Stars;
    write('Pascal');
    Stars;
    readln
  end. {Heading}
```

Note that the definition of the procedure `Stars` is included within the source code, before the body of the program. The program makes reference to the procedure twice. Corresponding to each reference, the program displays 20 asterisks. Note, however, that because `write` is used, the output of the program is all on a single line.

```
********************Pascal********************
```

Of course, the program could have been written without using the procedure `Stars`. We could have incorporated the code for `Stars` directly within the body of the program, but that would mean writing the complete code twice. However, once a procedure is written, it can be used in many different contexts. For example, here is a program which uses `Stars` to produce a different display.

Listing 5.2. Heading2

```
program Heading2;
{Write the word 'Pascal' with lines of asterisks above and
below it.}

  procedure Stars;
  {Display 20 asterisks}
    begin {Stars}
      write('********************')
    end; {Stars}

  begin {Heading2}
    Stars;     {First 20 asterisks of line above}
    Stars;     {Next 20 asterisks of line above}
    writeln;   {This writeln ends the line of 40 asterisks}
    writeln('Pascal');
    Stars;     {First 20 asterisks of line below}
    Stars;     {Next 20 asterisks of line below}
    writeln;   {This ends a second line of asterisks}
    readln
  end. {Heading2}
```

Using `Stars` twice in succession produces a row of 40 asterisks. The program then uses a writeln statement to end this line. The next line contains the word 'Pascal.' The third line contains a row of 40 asterisks. Here is what the output looks like:

```
****************************************
Pascal
****************************************
```

When Pascal carries out the task specified by the procedure, we say that the program invokes the procedure or that the program calls the procedure. For example, the first program invokes the procedure `Stars` twice. The second program calls the procedure `Stars` four times.

The Syntax of a Procedure

A procedure consists of:

- A procedure heading
- A declaration section
- A body, consisting of:

  the reserved word, `begin`
  the procedure's statements
  the reserved word, `end`
  a semicolon

In Listing 5.1, the procedure heading consists of the reserved word `procedure` and the procedure name `Stars`.

The declaration section is similar to the declaration section of a program. It contains the definitions of any variables or constants used within the procedure. In the case of `Stars`, no such variables are necessary. The format of a procedure declaration section is the same as that of a program.

The body of the procedure contains the statements which are executed when the procedure is called. The body of the procedure starts with the reserved word `begin` and finishes with the reserved word `end` followed by a semicolon.

Note that the procedure comes after the declaration section of the main program and before the body of the main program. In this position, the procedure name `Stars` is defined before it is used within the body of the program.

Both a procedure and a program have similar organizations. Both consist of a declaration section (consisting of definitions of constants and variables), a body (consisting of statements to be executed), and the reserved word `end`. Such a structure is called a *block*.

Our procedure `Stars` provides us with an example of a program header. As we shall see later in the chapter, a program header can be somewhat more complex than this one. For example, a program header can contain information which can be used as a means of communication between the procedure and the calling program. Since we will be considering more general headers later on, we will refrain from giving a syntax diagram of a procedure header until then.

Pascal determines the end of a procedure by the semicolon placed after the keyword `end`. If you use a period instead of a semicolon, then the compiler will interpret the end of the procedure as the end of the program. In most cases, since the compiler will not yet have encountered the program beginning (indicated by the keyword `begin`), this will result in a syntax error message.

Comments and Procedures

You should note the comment {Stars} used after both `begin` and `end`. As we will shortly see, the reserved words `begin` and `end` are typically used many times within a program. Documentation helps to keep straight what is beginning or ending. In this case, the first comment indicates the beginning of the body for the procedure `Stars`. The second comment indicates the end of the procedure body. We will use this form of commenting throughout the book.

The Advantages of Using Procedures

It may seem that procedures add a layer of complication to writing a Pascal program. However, you will find programs organized around procedures to be much clearer, easier to write, and much easier to debug. Here are some of the advantages of using procedures.

1. Using procedures fits naturally with a top-down design approach. The program organization developed in this section fits in neatly with the concepts of modular programming and top-down design. You can start your coding by writing the main module. This much of the program can then be tested. Next, you can code all procedures mentioned in the main module. In coding these procedures, you may require other procedures to be written later. Use of procedures helps to streamline the design of a program and prevents small details from obscuring the program logic.

2. Procedures can often be used more than once in a program and in several different programs, thereby saving programming time. A procedure can be viewed as a black box which performs a particular task within a program. It accepts inputs and produces certain outputs. When programming with procedures, you are plugging various black boxes into your program to accomplish various necessary tasks.

   Certain common tasks appear regularly in totally unrelated programs. In such cases, the same procedures can be used repeatedly. In fact, most Pascal programmers make use of libraries of standard procedures which accomplish often-used tasks. Such libraries can save you from reinventing the wheel every time you write a program.

3. Using procedures provides a natural method for dividing a programming task among a team of programmers. By defining a procedure as a black box which accepts certain inputs and produces certain outputs, the procedure can be programmed as an independent entity. Assigning separate programmers to independent procedures allows a program to be developed by a programming team rather than by a single programmer.

4. Procedures can be tested individually. By testing procedures one at a time, the process of debugging an entire program is organized and simplified.

Design of Procedures

Using procedures can help to break up a complex program into manageable pieces. However, it is important to design the procedures so that they contribute to making the program understandable and more manageable. This goal requires that the source code for procedures be neither too short nor too long.

Generally, you should attempt to make the source code for your procedures fit within one or two screens of text (i.e., about 25–50 lines) If your source code is much longer, the procedure is probably too complicated to be easily understood and should be further broken down using other procedures.

On the other hand, you shouldn't have so many short procedures that they obscure how your program works. This doesn't mean that short procedures should be avoided. If you can clarify your code by introducing a procedure which is only a few lines, by all means do so. In creating a program design, your goal should be, above all else, to clearly expose the logic and organization of your program. An aid in this direction is to use self-documenting procedure names. By just knowing the name of a procedure, you should be able to get an idea of what it does.

Passing Data to Procedures: Value Parameters

In the preceding section, we learned how to modularize programming tasks using procedures. However, our procedures were of a very simple sort: They performed tasks which used no data from the rest of the program. In this section, we will learn about procedures which use data values supplied when the procedure is called.

As a simple example, let's return to the procedure `Stars`, which displayed a row of 20 asterisks. We already employed a number of applications of this procedure. However, as it stands, we cannot use this procedure to display any number of asterisks other than 20. A more useful procedure would be one in which the procedure call provided the number of asterisks to display. Then one procedure call could display 10 asterisks, another call 5 asterisks, and yet another call 12 asterisks. To accomplish this, we need a generalized procedure which displays `N` asterisks, where `N` is an integer to be specified as part of the procedure call. Here is such a procedure:

```
procedure NewStars(    N : integer);
{Write a line of N asterisks}

  var
    J : integer;
```

```
begin {NewStars}
  for J := 1 to N do
    write('*')
end; {NewStars}
```

The header of this procedure indicates that the variable N is to be specified in the procedure call and that the value of N must be an integer. The body of the procedure consists of a loop which displays N asterisks. Note that the procedure does not start a new line after displaying the asterisks.

The procedure call:

```
NewStars(2);
```

assigns a value of 2 to N and causes the procedure to be executed with this value of N. In this case, 2 asterisks are displayed:

```
**
```

The procedure call:

```
NewStars(8);
```

assigns N a value of 8 and causes 8 asterisks to be displayed:

```
********
```

The procedure call:

```
NewStars(-1);
```

assigns N a value of –1. In this case, the upper value of the loop (–1) is less than the lower value (1), so that the body of the loop is never executed. In this case, no asterisks are displayed. This is not an error. This is the way Pascal interprets what you told it to do. If you wish it to take some other action in response to N = -1, you must tell it exactly what you wish it to do.

The number of asterisks displayed by NewStars may even be given as an expression. For example, suppose that the calling program includes the integer variable Z and that when Stars is called, we have Z equal to 5. Then the procedure call:

```
NewStars(2*Z-3);
```

causes the expression 2*Z-3 to be evaluated and its value assigned to N. In this case 2*Z-3 is equal to 2*5 - 3 = 7, so N is assigned the value 7 and the procedure displays 7 asterisks:

```
*******
```

The procedure header of NewStars specifies that N must be an integer. If you attempt to pass a real number to the procedure, then a run-time error will be generated.

As an application of NewStars, consider the following program:

Listing 5.3. Fancy

```
program Fancy;
{Write the word 'Pascal' in a box of asterisks}

  procedure NewStars(     N : integer);
    var
      J : integer;
    begin {NewStars}
      for J := 1 to N do
        write('*')
    end; {NewStars}

  begin {Fancy}
     NewStars(14);
     writeln;  {End the line of asterisks}
     NewStars(4);
     write('Pascal');
     NewStars(4);
     writeln;  {End the line}
     NewStars(14);
     writeln;  {End of the line of asterisks}
     readln
  end. {Fancy}
```

This program creates the display:

```
**************
****Pascal****
**************
```

Value Parameters

In the procedure NewStars, the variable N, defined in the procedure header, is called a *value parameter*. A value parameter is very much like a variable in algebra. It is really a placeholder for a value. When the procedure is called, its parameters are assigned values from the main program. For example, in the first reference to NewStars, we assigned N the value 8. In this case, we say that N (in the procedure) is a *formal* (value) parameter and 8 (in the main program) is an *actual* (value) parameter. A formal parameter is used in the procedure header and acts as a placeholder for the actual parameter, which is specified when the procedure is called.

A procedure may have any number of value parameters. For example, here is a procedure `Multichr(N,Ch)`, which has two value parameters, `N` of type integer and `Ch` of type char. The procedure displays `N` copies of the character specified by `Ch`.

```
procedure Multichr( N : integer;
        Ch : char);
{Write N copies of character Ch}

  var
    J : integer;

  begin {Multichr}
    for J := 1 to N do
      write(Ch)
  end; {Multichr}
```

Here `N` and `Ch` are formal parameters. Here is a procedure call in which they are replaced by the actual parameters 5 and '.', respectively:

```
Multichr(5,'.');
```

This procedure call displays a sequence of 5 periods:

```
.....
```

When a program calls a procedure, it assigns a value to each parameter. This process is called *parameter passing* and we say that the values of the actual parameters are passed to the procedure. You may think of the process of parameter passing as a kind of communication between the calling statement and the procedure called. It is as if there is a one-way telephone line connecting the calling statement and the procedure. When a statement calls a procedure, the values corresponding to the procedure's parameters are determined and sent to the procedure over the telephone wire. Later, we will see how procedures can send values back to the main program.

Syntax of Procedures with Value Parameters

Value parameters of a procedure are defined in the procedure header. They are defined within a pair of parentheses following the procedure name. Value parameters are defined using phrases of the form:

```
var1, var2, ..., varn : type
```

Such a phrase defines one or more variables var1, var2, . . . , varn, all of the specified type. A value parameter definition can contain any number of such phrases, separated by semicolons. Here are some examples of procedure headings in which value parameters are defined:

```
procedure Test1(      X,Y,Z:real;
                           Over : boolean;
                           I : integer);

procedure Test2(      X : real; Y : real);

procedure Test3(      Y : real;
                           Over : boolean;
                           X : real);
```

In defining value parameters, it does not matter how the parameters are grouped or ordered in the procedure header. For a particular data type, there may be one or many lists defining parameters of that type. The order of the lists or of parameters within the lists does not matter.

How Value Parameters Work

A value parameter is a copy of a variable which is private to the procedure. The procedure is given a copy of the actual parameter to manipulate. However, the manipulations do not affect any of the variables in the calling program. For example, suppose that MainVar is a variable in a program containing the procedure call:

```
TaxCalc(MainVar);
```

The procedure TaxCalc is given a private copy of MainVar to manipulate.

The procedure can use this copy to make calculations, create displays, and make decisions. The procedure can even change the value of its copy of MainVar, while the actual parameters are not affected. Note, however, that nothing that goes on within the procedure affects the value of MainVar in the main program. To appreciate this point, consider the following program, called Value.

Listing 5.4. Value

```
program Value;
{Illustrates parameter passing}

  var
    MainVar : real;
```

```
procedure Test(    TestVar : real);
  begin {Test}
    TestVar := 3 * TestVar;
    writeln(TestVar:5:1)
  end; {Test}

begin {Value}
  MainVar := 5.0;
  writeln(MainVar:5:1);
  Test(MainVar);
  writeln(MainVar:5:1);
  readln
end. {Value}
```

Sample Run. Value

This program calls the simple procedure `Test`, which is passed the value parameter `TestVar`. The procedure multiplies `TestVar` by 3 and displays the result according to the format 5:1.

The main program uses a real variable `MainVar`. It begins by assigning the value 5.0 to `MainVar`. Next, it displays the value of `MainVar` to prove that the value was correctly assigned. Next, it makes the procedure call `Test(MainVar)`. That is, the value of `MainVar(5.0)` is passed to the procedure. The procedure multiplies this value by 3 and displays the result, 15.0. Finally, the program displays the value of `MainVar`. Note that the value of `MainVar` is still 5.0!

What happened is this. The procedure `Test` is given its own copy of `MainVar` to play with. Any changes that `Test` makes in `MainVar` are not reflected in the copy kept by the main program. Thus, after the procedure call, the value of `MainVar` is still 5.0.

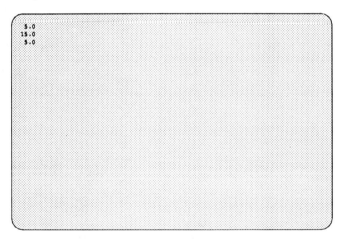

Applications of Procedures Using Value Parameters

In order to allow you to see a number of instances in which parameter passing is used, we present the following examples.

Example 1. Write a Pascal program to convert temperatures from Fahrenheit to Celsius.

Solution. Let the variable Fahr denote the temperature in degrees Fahrenheit. Let the variable Celsius denote the corresponding temperature in degrees Celsius. According to the well-known formula, we have:

```
Celsius := (5/9)*(Fahr - 32)
```

Our program will ask for a temperature in Fahrenheit and then use the formula to convert the given temperature to Celsius. Here is the pseudocode for the program:

```
program FToC.
  Display heading 'Conversion of Fahrenheit to
  Celsius'.
  Request Fahrenheit temperature.
  Input value of Fahrenheit temperature.
  Convert to Celsius.
  Output Celsius temperature.
```

It is clear that the program will need two variables, which we will name Fahr and Celsius. The actual conversion of the Fahr temperature to the Celsius temperature is an isolated task which is best to write as a procedure, which we will call Convert. The main program uses the real variable Fahr. However, the variable Celsius is not needed by the main program. So it is best to make it a local variable in the procedure Convert, that is, to declare it within the procedure. The value of Fahr is needed by Convert, so let's include a formal parameter in Convert to receive this value from the main program.

Here is the program:

Listing 5.5. FToC

```
program FToC;
{This program converts a user-supplied Fahrenheit temperature
into degrees Celsius.}

  var
    Fahr : real;

  procedure Convert(     Fahr : real);
  {Convert Fahr to Celsius}
```

```
    var
      Celsius : real;
    begin {Convert}
      Celsius := (5/9)*(Fahr - 32);
      write('This temperature equals ');
      write(Celsius:1:1);
      writeln(' degrees centigrade.')
    end; {Convert}

  begin {FToC}
    writeln('Conversion of Fahrenheit to centigrade');
    write('Temperature in degrees Fahrenheit? ');
    readln(Fahr);
    Convert(Fahr);
    readln
  end. {FToC}
```

Sample Run. Converting Fahrenheit to Centigrade

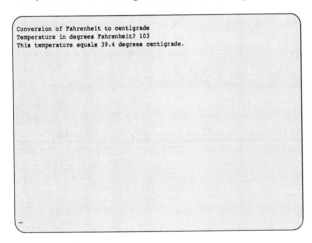

```
Conversion of Fahrenheit to centigrade
Temperature in degrees Fahrenheit? 103
This temperature equals 39.4 degrees centigrade.
```

Example 2. Write a Pascal program which computes the amount of change due if the user inputs the amount of a purchase and the amount of money paid.

Solution. We ask the user for two real (two decimal places) numbers: `Amount` and `Paid`. We compute the amount `Due` using the formula:

```
Due := Paid - Amount
```

Here is the pseudocode for the program.

```
program Purchase.
  Display 'What is the amount of the purchase?'.
  Input Purchase.
```

```
  Display 'What is the amount paid?'.
  Input Paid.
  Compute the change Due.
  Output result.
```

The pseudocode suggests that we include the details of computing the change in a procedure. Let's call this procedure `Change`. This procedure determines the amount of change and displays the amount. The new wrinkle here is that the procedure `Change` must be passed two data items: `Paid` and `Amount`. Since `Due` is used only within the procedure, we should make it local to the procedure. This variable is then undefined in the main program.

```
procedure Change(Purchase, Paid).
  Due := Paid - Purchase
  Display change due.
```

Here is the program.

Listing 5.6. Purchase

```
program Purchase;
{This program calculates the amount of change due
from a purchase of a user-specified amount with a
user-specified payment.}

  var
    Cost, Paid : real;

  procedure Change(     Cost, Paid : real);
    var
      Due : real;
begin {Change}
Due := Paid - Cost;
write('The change is: $');
writeln(Due:3:2)
end; {Change}

begin {Purchase}
write('What is the amount of the purchase? ');
readln(Cost);
write('What is the amount paid? ');
readln(Paid);
Change(Cost, Paid);
readln
end. {Purchase}
```

Sample Run. Purchase

```
What is the amount of the purchase? 14.38
What is the amount paid? 20.00
The change is: $5.62

_
```

One bit of cleverness in `Change` deserves special comment. Note the position of the $ in the output. It immediately precedes the first digit of the amount. This will be the case no matter how many digits are in the amount. This is because we specified a format string 3:2. That is, the field width is 3 and there are two places to the right of the decimal point. The specified field is completely taken up by the decimal point and the cents portion of the amount. Many versions of Pascal automatically expand the field to accommodate the number of digits actually present in the number. This puts the $ immediately preceding the first digit of the number.

Giving Names to Parameters

A procedure header identifies the parameters which are to be passed to the procedure. In the header and in the actual body of the procedure, the parameters used are formal parameters, which are replaced by actual parameters when the procedure is called. Since the formal parameters are eventually replaced, they are not program variables. In particular, you can assign to formal parameters the names of program variables which will eventually replace them. For example, if a formal parameter will eventually be replaced with the actual parameter Radius, then why not call the formal parameter Radius? Your procedure header will then give an indication of what will eventually become the actual parameter. There is no harm in this duplication of formal parameters and program variables, as long as you realize how Pascal is handling them both.

Variables Local to a Procedure

As mentioned above, a procedure can have a declaration section, just like a program. For example, let's go back to the procedure `NewStars` at the beginning of this section. The variable `J` is defined in a var declaration within the procedure itself. This variable is defined only for the duration of the procedure `NewStars`. In effect, the variable `J` is created when the procedure is called. When the procedure is completed, the variable `J` and its current value disappear. If you attempt to use `J` in the main program, you will get an error message (usually that the identifier `J` is undeclared). When a variable, such as `J`, is declared for use in a procedure, we say that the variable is *local to the procedure.*

Receiving Data from Procedures

In the preceding section, we learned to use procedures in order to modularize program design. You may isolate in a procedure a particular task required by the main program or another procedure. Whenever the task is needed, the procedure can be called. A procedure call can come from either within the main program or within a procedure. The section of the program originating a procedure call is referred to as the *calling program.*

In the preceding section, we learned how to use value parameters to send data to a procedure. However, we also learned that value parameters may only be used for one-way data passing: from the main program to the procedure. They cannot be used to pass data returned to the calling program. In many applications, however, two-way communications are required: It is necessary for the calling program to send data to a procedure and for the procedure to send information back to the calling program. In this section, we will discuss the most effective way of doing this, which is using *variable parameters.*

To illustrate the need for obtaining information back from procedures, let's consider the following problem.

Example 1. Design a procedure `TaxCalc` which calculates the 5% sales tax on a purchase.

Solution. Our procedure performs a rather simple task. It must be given the amount of the `Purchase` and it will calculate the amount of `Tax` (5% of the purchase amount). The procedure accomplishes the following calculation:

```
Tax := 0.05*Purchase;
```

The emphasis of our design, however, is not on the task itself, but on the communications which take place between the procedure and the calling program. It is clear that the procedure must have two parameters, `Purchase` and `Tax`. The first of these can be a value parameter, since it is used only for communicating from the calling program to the procedure `TaxCalc`.

We must communicate the value of `Tax`, calculated within the procedure `TaxCalc`, back to the main program. As we have seen, this can't be accomplished with a value parameter. To get a value back from a procedure, you must use a special sort of parameter, namely a *variable parameter.* A variable parameter is a procedure parameter which is replaced by a variable of the main program as part of the procedure call. Any alterations to the variable which occur within the procedure are reflected outside the procedure as well.

A variable parameter is declared by using the reserved word `var` preceding the variable parameter in the procedure heading. For example to declare a variable parameter `Tax` for the procedure `TaxCalc`, you would use a heading of the form:

```
procedure TaxCalc(Purchase : real;
                  var Tax : real);
```

Declaring `Tax` as a variable parameter tells Pascal that the procedure will be given a variable of the calling program to substitute for `Tax`. Any changes in the value of this variable made by the procedure are reflected in the main program. This is exactly what we have in mind.

Here is the coding for our procedure.

```
procedure TaxCalc(Purchase : real;
                  var Tax : real);
  begin {TaxCalc}
    Tax := 0.05*Purchase
  end; {TaxCalc}
```

Here are some typical statements which call the `TaxCalc` procedure.

Illustration A:

```
TaxCalc(100.0, Tax);
```

In this statement, `Purchase` is set equal to 100.0 and the value of `Tax` is calculated as 5.0. Note that `Tax` is a variable of the calling program, where it must be declared as a real variable. `TaxCalc` replaces the current value of `Tax` by 5.0. Any previous value of `Tax` is lost.

Illustration B:

```
TaxCalc(Amount,MdTax);
```

In this statement, Amount is a real variable of the calling program. Since Amount is an actual value parameter, a copy of its value is passed to the procedure and is assigned to the formal parameter Purchase. The variable MdTax is a real variable of the calling program. MdTax is a formal variable parameter, and the procedure call tells Pascal to use MdTax in place of the formal parameter Tax in executing the procedure. Suppose, for example, that Amount equals 200000.0. Then the procedure assigns to MdTax the value 0.05*200000.0 or 10000.0. It is the value of MdTax as the procedure ends. This value then becomes available to the calling program.

Illustration C:

```
TaxCalc(Total1+Total2,Tax);
```

In this illustration, Total1 and Total2 are calling program variables. Pascal calculates their sum and assigns it to the value parameter Purchase. For example, if Total1 has the value 1000.0 and Total2 has the value 3000.0, then Purchase is assigned the value 1000.0 + 3000.0 = 4000.0. Tax is a calling program variable which the procedure assigns the value 0.05*4000.0 = 200.0. This value then becomes available to the calling program.

Here is a program which uses the procedure TaxCalc to determine the amount of sales tax on a sale specified by the user. Note how the calling program is able to use the value of Tax after the procedure is done.

Listing 5.7. CashReg

```
program CashReg;
{This program calculates and displays the amount of
a 5% sales tax and the total amount due on a
purchase amount the user specifies.}

  var
    Purchase, Tax : real;

  procedure TaxCalc(    Purchase : real;
                    var Tax : real);
  {Calculate the tax and return the value to the
   main program}
    begin {TaxCalc}
      Tax := 0.05*Purchase
    end; {TaxCalc}
```

```
  begin {CashReg}
    write('Amount of purchase? ');
    readln(Purchase);
    TaxCalc(Purchase, Tax);
    write('The amount of tax is $');
    writeln(Tax:3:2);
    write('The total due is $');
    writeln(Purchase+Tax:3:2);
    readln
  end. {CashReg}
```

Sample Run. CashReg

```
Amount of purchase? 85.00
The amount of tax is $4.25
The total due is $89.25
```

Example 2. A program employs a menu of user choices. The user indicates a choice by typing one of the integers 1–5. Write a procedure `MenuChoice` which inputs the desired choice and checks that it is one of the appropriate integers. The procedure should return to the main program both the integer chosen and an indication that the integer is or is not one of the allowed integers.

Solution. We require that the procedure return two pieces of data to the calling program. The first is the integer itself. Let's store it in the variable `Choice`. The second is an indication whether the integer is allowed. Let's use the boolean variable `InputOk`. If the integer is one of the allowed choices, we will set `InputOk` equal to true; if not, we will set `InputOk` equal to false.

```
procedure MenuChoice(var Choice : integer;
                     var InputOk : boolean);
{This procedure accepts an integer Choice
from the user. It checks that Choice is between
```

```
1 and 5 inclusive. If so, InputOk is set equal to
TRUE; otherwise, InputOk is set equal to FALSE.}

  begin {MenuChoice}
    write('Input choice from menu: ');
    readln(Choice);
    InputOk := not((Choice 0) or (Choice 5));
  end; {MenuChoice}
```

Sample Run. MenuChoice

```
Procedure MenuChoice called.
Input choice from menu: 1
Return value of Choice and InputOk to calling program.
```

Example 3. Design a procedure which computes `Num` raised to the power `Exponent`, where `Num` is a real and `Exponent` is an integer which is positive or 0.

Solution. Recall that Pascal does not have a built-in mechanism for raising a number to a power. Let's remedy this omission by designing a procedure which can be used whenever we need to raise a number to a power. Let's confine ourselves to raising a real `Num` to a non-negative, integer power `Exponent`. In this case, the definition of raising to a power tells us that:

$Num^{Exponent}$ = Num*Num*...*Num (Exp times) if Exp > 0,
Num^{0} = 1.

Note that we are limiting the procedure to non-negative values of `Exponent`. To allow negative powers, it is necessary to introduce another formula. Moreover, we would have to worry about raising 0 to a negative power, in which case we would be dividing by 0. For the present, we will skirt these questions by limiting `Exponent` to non-negative integers.

Let's use a variable parameter `Pwr` to hold the power. This parameter will be used to communicate the value of the power to the calling program. To assign `Pwr` the desired value, requires several steps. First, we set:

```
Pwr := 1;
```

This assigns to `Pwr` the correct value for raising a number to the power 0. For positive powers we use a loop to multiply `Pwr` by `Num` a total of `Exponent` times.

Recall, however, that we are limiting `Exponent` to non-negative integers. We must design the procedure so that it rejects negative values of `Exponent` and tells the calling program that the value supplied was an error. The customary method for doing this is to introduce a boolean variable parameter `Error`, which returns true if the data supplied to the procedure was faulty (i.e., `Exponent` <0) and false otherwise.

The procedure `Power` will have four parameters: the numerical parameters `Num`, `Exponent`, and `Pwr` and the boolean parameter `Error`. The first two are provided by the calling program, but are not changed by the procedure, so we can make them value parameters. However, the parameters `Pwr` and `Error` must be communicated back to the calling program. So we must make them variable parameters.

Here is the code for the procedure:

```
procedure Power(     Num : real;
                     Exponent : integer;
                 var Pwr : real;
                 var Error : boolean);

{This procedure sets Pwr equal to Num raised
to the power Exponent, where Num is real and Exponent
is a non-negative integer.}

  var
    Lcv : integer;     {Lcv = counter variable for loop}

  begin {Power}
    Pwr := 1;
    Error := (Exponent < 0);
    if not Error
      then
        for Lcv := 1 to Exponent do
          Pwr := Pwr*Num
  end; {Power}
```

In case `Exponent` is 0, the loop is not executed so that `Pwr` retains its initial value 1, which is the correct value in this case.

Sample Run. Power

```
Procedure call: Power(12.0,2,Pwr,Error);

Returned to calling program:
Pwr:144.0
Error:FALSE

Procedure call: Power(12.0,-2,Pwr,Error);
Pwr: value is garbage.
Error:TRUE
-------------------------------------------------------
```

Later in this chapter, we will build a better procedure, which can be used for all values of `Exponent`. For now, however, this procedure is more than sufficient to be applied in a number of problems.

To test Power, we must incorporate it into a sample program, such as:

Listing 5.8. PowerTst

```
program PowerTst;
{This program tests the operation of the procedure
Power.}

  var
    Pwr, X : real;
    N : integer;
    Error : boolean;

  procedure Power(    Num : real;
                      Exponent : integer;
                  var Pwr : real;
                  var Error : boolean);
{This procedure sets Pwr equal to Num raised to
the power Exponent, where Num is real and Exp is a
non-negative integer}
  var
    Lcv : integer;  {Lcv = counter variable for loop}
  begin {Power}
    Pwr := 1;
    Error := (Exponent < 0);
    if not Error
      then
        for Lcv := 1 to Exponent do
          Pwr := Pwr*Num
  end; {Power}

  begin {PowerTst}
    writeln('Computing X to the power N.');
    writeln('Input a real value X.');
    readln(X);
    writeln('Input a non-negative integer N.');
    readln(N);
    Power(X, N, Pwr, Error);
    if (Error = false)
      then
        begin
          writeln ('X raised to the power N is:');
          writeln(Pwr:10:2)
        end
      else
        writeln('Negative exponent in Power.');
    readln
  end. {PowerTst}
```

Sample Run. PowerTst

```
Computing X to the power N.
Input a real value X.
5.0
Input a non-negative integer N.
3
X raised to the power N is:
    125.00
```

The Syntax of Variable Parameters

Variable parameters are declared within a procedure heading using the word `var` preceding a list of variables of a specific type:

```
var var1, var2, ..., varn : type;
```

For example, the procedure heading

```
procedure Diode(var X,Y,Z : integer);
```

defines the variables `X`, `Y`, and `Z` as variable parameters.

The word `var` must be repeated for separate variable lists, as in the procedure heading:

```
procedure Delete(var X : integer; var C : char);
```

Moreover, a procedure heading may include lists of both variable and value parameters, as in the procedure `TaxCalc` above.

Procedure headers which declare many parameters will generally require more than one line. This is nothing to worry about. A Pascal compiler reads source code lines based on their punctuation and use of keywords, and pays no attention to the arrangement of the source code in lines. Therefore you should attempt to arrange your procedure headings (and all other source code, for that matter) so that the procedure is easy to read. For example, the arrangement of the procedure heading:

```
procedure Graph(     X, Y, Z, Row, Column: integer;
                 var Min, Max : real;
                     Grid, Title : boolean);
```

is preferable to the arrangement:

```
procedure Graph(X, Y, Z, Row, Column: integer; var
Min, Max : real; Grid, Title : boolean);
```

In calling a procedure, you may substitute an expression for a value parameter. However, when using a variable parameter, you may only substitute a variable of the same type as specified in the procedure heading. You may not substitute a constant or an expression. For example, consider the procedure defined by the heading:

```
procedure Circle(var T : real);
```

You may call this procedure using statements of the form:

```
Circle(R);
Circle(S);
```

where R and S are real variables defined outside Circle. However, the following procedure calls are illegal:

```
Circle(2*R+1);
Circle(489.37);
```

In the first illegal call, we attempt to replace the formal variable parameter T by the expression 2*R+1. In the second, we attempt to replace T by the constant 489.37. Remember: A variable parameter may be replaced only by an actual variable of the same type.

The Mechanics of Passing Value and Variable Parameters

You have already seen how value parameters and variable parameters differ in their respective uses within a program. At times, beginners find the distinction between the two types of parameters confusing. To distinguish between the two, many beginners find it helpful to know how Pascal handles each of them "under the hood."

When a procedure is called, the calling program passes a value corresponding to each value parameter. Pascal determines these values from the procedure call, which specifies either a constant or an expression corresponding to each value parameter. The program evaluates any expressions it finds, using the current values of the variables in effect at the time. For each value parameter, after Pascal determines its value, a private copy is provided to the procedure for its use.

A value parameter results in passing a value to the procedure. For this reason, passing the value of a value parameter is referred to as a *call by value.*

In passing a variable parameter to a procedure, Pascal does not pass the actual value. Instead, it passes the address of the memory location holding the value of the variable being passed. For example, consider the procedure definition and procedure call:

```
Procedure       procedure Rect(Width, Length : real;
Definition          var Area : real);
                (formal parameters)

Procedure       Rect(W,L,A);
Call            (actual parameters)
```

where `Rect` is a procedure with value parameters `Width` and `Length` and a variable parameter `Area`. When the procedure `Rect` is called from the calling program, the main program passes the value stored in the memory locations of the actual parameters `W` and `L` to the procedure, and the formal parameters `Width` and `Length` are initialized to these values, respectively. `Area` is a variable parameter, and so, instead of passing the value stored in the memory location of the actual parameter to the procedure, the main program passes only the address of `A`.

In passing an address of a variable, Pascal passes only a reference to the variable rather than an actual value. For this reason, passing a variable parameter is often referred to as a *call by reference.*

From our above description of passing variable parameters, it should be clear why you can't pass the value of an expression via a variable parameter. What address would be passed?

In the case of procedures employing more than one variable parameter, several addresses are passed to the procedure. If a procedure employs both value parameters and variable parameters, Pascal passes both values and addresses.

More About Procedures

In Chapter 4 and this chapter, we have so far concentrated on the mechanics of designing, coding, and calling procedures. In this section, let's use what we have learned to concentrate on the application of procedures within a program.

When to Use a Procedure

Many beginners turn each statement in the first level of pseudocode into a procedure. If you followed this principle without exception, it would lead to an overzealous use of procedures. If an isolated task can be coded in a single statement and it is clear what that statement accomplishes, then you shouldn't try to bury the statement in a procedure.

On the other hand, if there are nasty details (say a complicated formula or a long sequence of steps to accomplish a single task) then you should bury the details in a procedure. At all times, your goal should be to design programs whose logic is transparent. You should use procedures to help you carry this aspect of design over into your implementation.

Not only does use of procedures help to clarify the logic of a program, it can also help to shorten the code. Indeed, code within a procedure needs to be included in a program only once, no matter how many times the procedure is called.

Procedures Called from Within Procedures

So far, all our procedures have been called from the main program. However, it is perfectly legal for a procedure to be called from within a procedure, as the following example shows.

Example 1. Suppose that `Amount` dollars are deposited in a bank account paying `Rate` percent interest compounded `Periods` times per year. Write a procedure `Interest` which calculates the amount in the bank account after a given `Time`.

Solution. From a course in business mathematics, let's pull the following formula:

$$\texttt{Balance := Amount*(1+Rate/Periods)}^{\texttt{Periods*Time}}$$

Don't worry about where this formula came from. A mathematician derived it and it is there to be used! Our problem is how to calculate with this formula in Pascal. We observe that the formula includes a power. To compute this part of the formula, we may use the procedure `Power` which we designed earlier in the chapter. Recall the code for this procedure:

```
procedure Power(     Num : real;
                     Exponent : integer;
                 var Pwr : real
                 var Error : boolean);
```

```
{This procedure sets Pwr equal to Num raised
to the power Exponent, where Num is real and Exponent
is a non-negative integer.}

  var
    Lcv : integer;    {Lcv = counter variable for loop}

  begin {Power}
    Pwr := 1;
    Error := (Exponent < 0)
    if not Error
      then
        for Lcv := 1 to Exponent do
          Pwr := Pwr*Num
  end; {Power}
```

In our current application, the only tricky part is to get the parameters correct. We wish to use Power to calculate:

```
(1+Rate/Periods)^(Periods*Time)
```

Thus, we need to apply the procedure Power (Num,Exponent,Pwr, Error), with Num replaced by 1+Rate/Periods and Exponent replaced by Periods*Time. The desired power is returned in the variable parameter Pwr. Therefore, the desired procedure call is:

```
Power(1+Rate/Periods, Periods*Time, Pwr, Error);
```

Once we obtain the value of the power in Pwr, we just multiply it by Amount.

The variable parameter Pwr required by Power will never be required outside the procedure Interest. So let's make it a variable of the procedure Interest. The procedure has two real value parameters, Rate and Amount, and two integer value parameters, Periods and Time. Balance must be a variable parameter since it returns a value to the calling program. The implementation of our procedure follows.

As in the procedure Power, we have included a variable parameter Error, which protects the caller from using garbage produced if the procedure is passed negative values for Amount, Periods, or Time. Error is returned true if any of these values is negative. Otherwise, it is returned false.

```
procedure Interest (     Rate, Amount : real;
                         Periods, Time : integer;
                     var Balance : real;
                     var Error : boolean);
{This procedure determines the value of an initial
 Amount placed in an account earning compound interest.
 The final amount is returned in the variable Balance.
  Amount = initial deposit
  Rate = the annual rate of interest
```

```
  Periods = the number of times annually that the
          money is compounded
  Time = the number of years the money is in the
       account.}

  var
    Pwr : real;
    Err : boolean;
  begin {Interest}
    Err := (Amount < 0) or (Periods < 0) or (Time < 0);
    if not Err
      then
        begin
          Power(1+Rate/Periods, Time*Periods, Pwr, Error);
          Balance := Amount*Pwr
        end
  end; {Interest}
```

Sample Run. Interest

```
Procedure call: Interest(.05, 100, 1, 1, Pwr, Error);

Returned to calling program: Balance:105.00
                             Error:false
```

To test the procedure Interest, we must include it within a program, which we will call IntTest. Of course, IntTest must also include the source code for the procedure Power, which is called by Interest. The called procedure must precede the calling procedure in the source code. Here is the coding of IntTest.

Listing 5.10. IntTest

```
program IntTest;
{Test out the procedure Interest by calling the
procedure and printing out the returned results.}

  var
    Balance : real;
    Error : boolean;

procedure Power(     Num : real;
                     Exponent : integer;
                 var Pwr : real;
                 var Error : boolean);
{This procedure sets Pwr equal to Num raised to
 the power Exponent, where Num is real and Exp is a
 non-negative integer}
  var
    Lcv : integer;  {Lcv = counter variable for loop}
  begin {Power}
    Pwr := 1;
```

```
    Error := (Exponent < 0);
    if not Error
      then
        for Lcv := 1 to Exponent do
          Pwr := Pwr*Num
  end; {Power}

procedure Interest (    Rate, Amount : real;
                        Periods, Time : integer;
                    var Balance : real;
                    var Error : boolean);
{This procedure determines the value of an initial
 Amount placed in an account earning compound interest.
 The final amount is returned in the variable Balance.
 Amount = initial deposit
 Rate = the annual rate of interest
 Periods = the number of times annually that the
money is compounded
 Time = the number of years the money is in the
account.}
  var
    Pwr : real;
    Err : boolean;

  begin {Interest}
    Err := ((Amount < 0) or (Periods < 0) or (Time < 0));
    if not Err
      then
        begin
          Power(1+Rate/Periods, Time*Periods, Pwr, Error);
          Balance := Amount*Pwr
        end
  end; {Interest}
```

Sample Run. IntTest

```
If $1000 is deposited at 12 percent
interest, compounded monthly, for
10 years, the balance will be
$   3300.39

_
```

The procedure Power, as simple as it is, is the key to solving many applied problems. In the next example, we solve a problem which is faced by many families: determining the required payments on a loan, such as a mortgage, an education loan, or a car loan.

Example 3. Design and implement a Pascal procedure for calculating the monthly payment on a loan at an annual interest of Rate, initial amount equal to Principal, and lasting for length Years.

Solution. As in the preceding example, the key is a formula which we pluck out of thin air. Let Payment denote the monthly payment. Then

$$\text{Payment} := \text{Rate*Principal*} (1+\text{Rate}/12)^{12*\text{Years}}/(12*((1+\text{Rate}/12)^{12*\text{Years}}-1))$$

To implement the desired calculation, we need the procedure Power once again. This allows us to compute the quantity:

$$(1+\text{Rate}/12)^{12*\text{Years}}$$

Here is the implementation of the procedure Loan. For brevity, we will leave out the source code for Power. However, in using the procedure, don't forget to include it.

```
procedure Loan(     Rate, Principal : real;
                    Years : integer;
               var Payment : real);
{This procedure calculates the monthly Payment on a mortgage
given the following data:
  Rate = the annual interest rate on the mortgage,
         expressed as a decimal.
  Principal = the initial balance on the mortgage
  Years = the length of the mortgage (an integer number
          of years). }

  var Pwr : real; {A temporary variable used to calculate
                   the power in the formula}
      Error : boolean; {Variable used to record error
                        condition in the procedure Power}

  begin {Loan}
    Power (1+Rate/12, 12*Years, Pwr, Error);
    if not Error
      then
        Payment := Rate*Pwr*Principal/(12*(Pwr-1))
  end; {Loan}
```

Sample Run. Loan

```
Procedure call: Loan(0.09, 100000.0, 30, Payment);
Returned to calling program: Payment:804.62261
```

Local and Global Identifiers

Now that we have become experienced in using procedures to organize a program, let's take a further look at the structure of a Pascal program and the way data are exchanged between different parts of a program.

The Organization of a Pascal Program

We have seen that a Pascal program may consist of the following components:

```
program heading
declarations
  constant declarations
  type declarations
  variable declarations
  procedure declarations
  function declarations
body
period
```

Note that various declaration categories may appear in any order. The components without the program heading and period is known as a *block*. That is, a block consists of

```
declarations
  constant declarations
  type declarations
  variable declarations
  procedure declarations
  function declarations
body
```

A program may be defined as consisting of a program heading, a block, and a period.

We have mentioned that a procedure is very similar to a program. And indeed it is. A procedure consists of a procedure heading followed by a block and a semicolon.

A procedure contains a block. And according to our definition of a block, it may contain procedure declarations. Thus a procedure may contain other procedures. Actually, these second-level procedures may also contain procedures, and so on to any level of nesting.

Scope Rules

Each block can have its own set of constants, variables, and procedures. Since each block can define its own set of identifiers, it is important to have a set of rules for determining where in a program a particular identifier may be used. The section of a program in which an identifier is valid is called the scope of the identifier. The rules defining the scope of an identifier are called *scope rules.*

Scope Rule 1

An identifier may be used anywhere within the block in which it is declared (and in any block contained within that block).

For example, consider the program `IntTest` of the preceding section. The outermost block defines the identifiers `Balance`, `Power`, and `Interest`. These identifiers may be used anywhere within the outermost block (subject to the other rules of Pascal, of course).

The real variable `Balance` can be used within the body of either of the procedures or within the main program body. Likewise, the procedure `Power` can be used within the procedure body for `Interest` or within the main program body.

Finally, the procedure `Interest` can be used within the main program body. Note, however, that `Interest` cannot be used within the body for `Power`, because of the following:

According to Scope Rule 1, a procedure may be used anywhere in the block in which it is defined. However, due to the manner in which Pascal compilers work, when a procedure is referenced, it must have already been declared earlier in the source code. This can create a problem. For example, suppose that procedure `Power` needed to reference Interest. The procedure declaration for `Interest` doesn't occur in the source code until after the declaration of `Power`. To get around this requires the notion of a forward declaration, which we will cover later in the book. For now, however, be aware of the problem and structure your programs so that all procedures are declared before they are called.

The block corresponding to the procedure `Interest` defines identifier `Pwr`. This identifier may be used anywhere within its block, that is, within the body of the procedure `Interest`.

The block corresponding to the procedure `Power` defines the identifier `Lcv`. This identifier may be used anywhere within its block, namely within the body of the procedure `Power`.

Reused Identifiers

The same Pascal identifier may be reused within different blocks of a single program. For example, two blocks of the same program could declare a variable `X`. This creates a potential for confusion as there could be two definitions of the same variable being used in the same procedure. This potential confusion is resolved by the following scope rule.

Scope Rule 2

In case an identifier is declared more than once within the same program, an identifier reference always refers to the definition in the innermost block defining the identifier.

This rule sounds confusing, but is really easy to understand in an example. Consider the following program structure:

Listing 5.11. Example

```
program Example;

  var
    X, Y : real; {Variables for main program}

  procedure Process1;
    var
      X, Z : real;  {Variables for procedure}

    begin {Process1}
    .
    .
    .
    end; {Process1}

  begin {Example}
  .
  .
  .
  end; {Example}
```

The variable `X` is defined in both the main program and in the procedure `Process1`. According to Scope Rule 2, any use of `X` refers to the definition made in the innermost block encompassing the reference. So if `X` is used in the main program body, then the first definition of `X` is used. If `X` is used within the body of `Process1`, then the second definition is used.

It may seem silly to allow an identifier to be used several times within a single program. Why doesn't Pascal just prohibit multiple definitions of an identifier? Not adopting such a restrictive rule has its advantages: Pascal is designed to encourage modular programming. When you are building a procedure, it is very convenient not to have to worry about which identifiers are already in use. Scope Rule 2 allows you to define identifiers for the private use of your procedure without worrying whether these identifiers conflict with those already in use.

As another example of the scope rules, consider the following procedure which was included in the program `AgeInDays` in Chapter 2.

```
procedure DetermineAge (var Age         : word;
                            BirthDay    : TypeDate;
                            CurrentDate : TypeDate;
                            MonthLen    : TypeMonthArray);

    var
      YearCounter : word;
    function NumDaysPastInYr (     DateToDo : TypeDate;
                                   MonthLen : TypeMonthArray) : word;

      var
        TempValue,
        MonthCounter : word;

      begin
        TempValue := 0;
        for MonthCounter := 1 to (DateToDo.Month - 1) do
          TempValue := TempValue + MonthLen [MonthCounter];
        TempValue := TempValue + DateToDo.Day;
        if LeapYear (DateToDo.Year) and (DateToDo.Month > 2)
          then
            TempValue := TempValue + 1;
        NumDaysPastInYr := TempValue
      end;
    function NumDaysInYr (YearToDetermine : word) : word;
      begin
        if LeapYear (YearToDetermine)
          then
            NumDaysInYr := 366
          else
            NumDaysInYr := 365
      end;
    begin
      Age := NumDaysInYr (BirthDay.Year) -
             NumDaysPastInYr (BirthDay, MonthLen);
      for YearCounter := (BirthDay.Year + 1) to (CurrentDate.Year - 1) do
        Age := Age + NumDaysInYr (YearCounter);
      if (BirthDay.Year = CurrentDate.Year)
        then
          Age := Age + NumDaysPastInYr (CurrentDate, MonthLen) -
                 NumDaysInYr (CurrentDate.Year)
        else
          Age := Age + NumDaysPastInYr (CurrentDate, MonthLen)
    end;
```

There are a number of identifiers belonging to this procedure block, namely: the variable `YearCounter` and the functions `NumDaysPastInYear`, `NumDaysInYear`. These identifiers are valid inside the block of the procedure. Each of the functions define blocks within the procedure block. Within their respective blocks, they declare identifiers whose scope is limited to the function block in which they are defined (but not in the larger procedure block).

Global Variables

If an inner block references an identifier defined in an outer block but does not redefine it, then the definition in the outer block is valid. In particular, an identifier defined in the outermost block can be used in any block in which it is not redefined. Of particular interest are the variables which are defined in the outermost block. These variables are called *global variables*. Such variables may be used throughout a program, hence the name. In particular, a global variable may be used within any procedure. However, as we will see below, doing so can create nasty problems.

Local Variables

In contrast to global variables, there are *local variables*. A variable defined within a block is said to be *local* to that block. In particular, if a variable is defined within a procedure, then it is said to be a local variable of the block defined by the procedure. For example, `J` is a local variable of the procedure Power.

A local variable comes into being when its procedure is called. When the procedure call is over, the variable is no longer available. In particular, a local variable may not be used outside the confines of its defining block. Moreover, there is no way to retain values of local variables for a procedure between consecutive procedure calls. A local variable is available only during the operation of its defining procedure.

The next example further illustrates the use of local variables.

Functions in Pascal

In modern mathematics, the notion of a function is fundamental. The concept of a function is, essentially, a modern reformulation of the classic notion of a `formula`. Here are some examples of functions of the variable `X`:

$f(X) = X$

$g(X) = X^2 + X + 1$

$h(X) = -X$

$k(X) = 1/X.$

Each of these functions provides a formula for determining, for each particular value of X, a function value. For example, the function f associates to a value of X, the function value X^2. If X is equal to 1, the function value, denoted f(1), is $1^2 = 1$; if X is assigned the value −2, then the function value, denoted f(−2), is $(-2)^2 = 4$; and so forth.

Functions are a convenient way of summarizing complex mathematical operations, and are extensively used throughout applied mathematics and the allied disciplines which utilize mathematics, such as computer science, physics, engineering, chemistry, biology, economics, statistics, and business.

Pascal allows you to use functions, both mathematical functions like the ones above and functions whose values are non-numerical data types like boolean and char. Standard Pascal includes a wide variety of predefined functions, which encompass most of those used in scientific and mathematical computations. Or you may declare your own functions in a manner that parallels the declaration of procedures.

Using Functions

To illustrate how functions work in Pascal, let's consider a concrete example, namely the function `Square(X)`, a user-defined function which calculates the square of the real number X. This function may be called by specifying an actual parameter for the formal parameter X. Here are some examples of function calls:

```
Square(0.0)

Square(1.5)

Square(-3.0)
```

In each case, the function calculates the square of the actual parameter and assigns this function value to the calling expression.

In the first case, the function value is $(0.0)^2 = 0.0$; the value 0.0 is then the value of the expression `Square(0.0)`. We say that the value 0.0 is returned to the expression `Square(0.0)`. In the third case, the function value is $(-3.0)^2 = 9.0$; the value 9.0 is returned to the expression `Square(-3.0)`.

A function resembles a procedure which returns a single value, the function value, to the calling program. A function value may be used in expressions, such as:

```
3*Square(1.5) - 2
```

This expression has the value:

```
3*(1.5)2 - 2 = 3*2.25 - 2
             = 4.75
```

A function differs from a procedure in an important respect: A procedure is an order to take an action. A function call produces a value which may be used as part of an action. For instance, here are some statements which make use of function calls involving `Square`:

```
writeln(Square(3.0));
X := Square(3.78);
if Square(X) > 4.5 then writeln(X);
```

Note how the function calls involving `Square` are used within statements.

Note, however, that a statement cannot consist of a function call all by itself. That is, a statement of the following sort makes no sense:

```
Square(5.8); {Error}
```

Indeed, this statement makes no more sense than the statement:

```
18; {Error}
```

Just like a procedure, a function may involve more than one parameter. For example, the function `Dist(X,Y)` is passed the two real parameters `X` and `Y` and assigns the value

```
Dist(X,Y) : X^2 + Y^2
```

Thus, for example, the function call `Dist(-1.0,2.0)` assigns the function value:

```
Dist(-1.0,2.0) = (-1.0)2 + (2.0)2 = 5.0
```

The parameters of a function may be of any data type and the same goes for the function value. For example, we can define a function `Caps(Ch)` which is passed the char parameter `Ch`. If `Ch` is a letter, then `Caps(Ch)` is assigned the corresponding capital letter; if `Ch` is not a letter, then `Caps(Ch)` is assigned just the value of `Ch`. Thus, for example:

```
Caps('a') is equal to 'A'.
Caps('N') is equal to 'N'.
Caps('>') is equal to '>'.
```

Declaring Functions

A function definition is made in a function declaration, which is very similar to a procedure declaration. For the sake of concreteness, let's discuss the definition for the function `Square(X)`, which assigns to `Square(X)` the function value `X*X`. Here is the coding for this function:

```
function Square(X : real) : real;
{This function returns the square of X.}

  begin {Square}
    Square := X*X
  end; {Square}
```

Let's analyze this function declaration in detail. Let's begin with the first line, which is the function heading. Just as does a procedure heading, a function heading ends in a semicolon.

The function heading begins with the reserved word `function`, which tells Pascal that what follows is a function declaration. Next, comes the identifier `Square`, which is the name of the function. Next, follows a formal parameter list which specifies the parameters which must be specified in a function call. The format of the formal parameter list is the same as that for a procedure. In this example, the function `Square` has a single real value parameter `X`.

A function returns a value, which in Turbo Pascal may be of any scalar data type. It is necessary to inform Pascal of the data type in advance. This is done at the end of the function heading. In this example, the function value is of type real. This is indicated by the notation:

```
: real
```

at the end of the function heading.

Following the function heading is the body, which consists of a declaration section and a statement section. In this example, the declaration section is empty. The statement section consists of the single statement:

```
Square := X*X;
```

This statement assigns the value of `X*X` to the identifier `Square`, which is used to define the function. This statement assigns the function value to `Square(X)`.

It may seem odd to use the function name within the body of the function. However, this is Pascal's mechanism for returning the function value. The function body should first calculate the function value using variables other than the function name. The last statement of a function body should always assign the desired value to the name of the function. It is hard to see this point in the above example, since there is only a single statement in the body. However, the point is more clearly illustrated in the following example.

Example 1. Design a function `Sum` which evaluates the sum:

```
1 + 2 + ... + Limit
```

Solution. The function value is

```
1 + 2 + ... + Limit
```

where `Limit` is a variable passed to the function via a formal parameter, which we'll also call `Limit`. Both the formal parameter and the function value are integers. So the function heading is:

```
function Sum(Limit : integer) : integer;
```

To calculate the sum, we use a loop. Here is the coding for the function:

```
function Sum (Limit : integer) : integer;
{This function calculates the sum
 1 + 2 + 3 + ... + Limit.}

  var
    Total, Lcv : integer;

  begin {Sum}
    Total := 0;              {Total holds the value of Sum}
    for Lcv := 1 to Limit do
      Total := Total + Lcv;     {Accumulate value of Total}
    Sum := Total                    {Assign Total to Sum}
  end; {Sum}
```

The function block's declaration section can be used to define variables, procedures, or functions which are local to the function. By the First Scope Rule, these identifiers can be used only within the block itself.

Functions, Parameter Passing, and Side Effects

A function may be passed parameters in much the same fashion as a procedure. The rules of the Pascal language allow for both value parameters and variable parameters to be used in connection with a function. A function's parameters are specified using formal parameters in the function heading. When the function is called, the formal parameters are replaced by actual parameters, which specify the actual values passed to the function.

We have seen examples of functions having one or several parameters. In addition, Pascal allows functions which have no parameters. Later in this chapter, we will discuss the random number generating function `Random` which is included in many versions of Pascal. The `Random` function has no parameters. Each time it is called, it returns a random real number between 0.0 and 0.999999999. A function, such as `Random`, which has no parameters, is called *parameterless.*

In connection with procedures, variable parameters are an extremely important tool. And although they may be used with a function, it is generally considered bad form to do so. Here's why.

The model for functions is provided by the functions of mathematics. A function is supposed to calculate a single value which can be used in calculations. If you allowed the function to modify values of variables it is given as parameters, then chaos could result. For example, suppose that the function `Square(X)` somehow modified the value of `X`. Now consider this expression:

```
Square(X)*Square(X)
```

The value of `X` used in the second function call might not be the same as the value used in the first. This would go counter to our usual mathematical expectations, which would say that X^2 times X^2 is X^4. This sort of craziness inevitably leads to confusion.

The moral is: Use only value parameters in defining a function.

As with procedures, it is possible to create nasty side effects by changing non-local variables within a function. Avoid these by only using variables which have been passed as value parameters. If you skirt the parameter-passing discipline of Pascal, you will often be condemned to tracking down bugs created by side effects.

Turbo Pascal's Predefined Functions

In solving problems using Pascal, it is often convenient to use the standard mathematical functions, such as those found on scientific calculators. Pascal includes the standard functions which allow you to calculate trigonometric functions, exponential functions, logarithms, and square roots as well as functions for truncation and rounding of real numbers.

Truncation and Rounding

Pascal includes two functions for converting real numbers to integers. The first function `Trunc(X)` truncates, or cuts off, the decimal portion of the real number `X`, leaving the whole portion. Here are some examples of this function evaluated at various parameter values.

X	value of Trunc(X)
5.878	5
–117.85	–117
12	12
–1	–1

Note that `Trunc` accepts either a real or integer parameter. However, its value is of the type integer.

The second function, `Round(X)`, rounds off the real number `X` to the nearest integer. For example, here are some illustrations of the operation of `Round(X)`:

X	value of Round(X)
5.878	6
1.5	2
9.8	10
–3.2	–3
–5.6	–6

As with the function `Trunc`, the parameter value for `Round` can be either real or integer. However, the function value is always of the type integer.

Mathematical Functions

Here is a list of the mathematical functions included in standard Pascal. In all cases, X denotes a variable of real or integer type.

Abs(X) = the absolute value of X
Example call: Abs(3) returns |3| = 3
Abs(–3) returns |–3| = 3

Exp(X) = the exponential function e^X
Example call: Exp(1) returns e1 = e = 2.718281

Ln(X) = the natural logarithm of X, defined for X > 0
Example call: Ln(1) returns 0

Sin(X) = the sine of angle X (in radians)
Example call: Sin(Pi/2) returns 9.999999E–01

Cos(X) = the cosine of angle X (in radians)
Example call: Cos(0) returns 9.999999E–01

Arctan(X) = the arctangent of X

Example call: Arctan(1) returns Pi/4

Sqr(X) = the square of X
Example call: Sqr(5) returns 25
Sqr(1.1) returns 1.21

Sqrt(X) = the square root of X, defined for X >= 0
Example call: Sqrt(4) returns 2.000000

The functions `Abs(X)` and `Sqr(X)` produce a value of the same type as `X`. That is, if `X` is of type real, then the output of the function is real; if `X` is of type integer, then the output of the function is integer. Here are some examples of values produced by the functions `Abs(X)` and `Sqr(X)`.

Abs(3) returns 3

Abs(0) returns 0

Abs(–1.5) returns 1.5

Sqr(3) returns 9

Sqr(–0.1) returns 0.01

All of the above functions other than `Abs(X)` and `Sqr(X)` produce real output, regardless of the type of `X`.

Applications of Pascal's Mathematical Functions

Example 1. Write a program which computes sin(X) for a value of X which the user supplies. The values of X and sin(X) should be rounded to five decimal places.

Solution. The problem is a reasonably straightforward one. The program will ask for a value of X and will compute the value of sin(X). The only problem is to reasonably present the output. Let's display it in the form:

```
Value of X    sin(X)
0.30000       0.29552
```

We will display both the headings and the numerical output in fields 15 characters wide. This size allows us room for the headings with some space between the two columns. The numerical output will be rounded to five decimal places, as required.

Here is the program.

Listing 5.11. Evaluate

```
program Evaluate;
{This function evaluates the sine of a user-specified number and rounds
the answer to 5 decimal places}

  var
    Angle : real;       {Value of angle in radians}

  begin {Evaluate}
    write('Type a value of Angle and press ENTER.');
    readln(Angle);
    writeln;
    writeln;
    writeln('Value of Angle':15, '     sin(Angle)     ':15);
    writeln(Angle:15:5, Sin(Angle):15:5);
    readln
  end. {Evaluate}
```

Sample Run. Evaluate

```
Type a value of Angle and press ENTER..3

Value of Angle    sin(Angle)
       0.30000       0.29552
```

The above example is rather pedestrian. However, the following example provides an interesting application of Pascal to biology and archaeology.

Example 2. Carbon 14 is a radioactive form of carbon found in all living things. When alive, the volume of carbon 14 in an organism remains approximately constant, with the portion lost to radioactive decay replaced by other carbon 14 from the environment. When an organism dies, the carbon 14 is no longer replaced. By measuring the fraction of carbon 14 remaining, it is possible to measure how long ago an organism died. If C14Frac denotes the fraction of carbon 14 remaining, then the organism died Ln(1/C14Frac)/0.00012 years ago. The use of carbon 14 for determining the ages of dead organisms was developed by Willard F. Libby of Columbia University in the late 1940s and is called radiocarbon dating or carbon dating. Libby was awarded the Nobel Prize in chemistry for this work.

Write a Pascal program to estimate the age of a dead organism given the fraction of carbon 14 remaining.

Solution. The program breaks down neatly into three steps as listed in the following pseudocode.

```
program CarbonDate.
   Obtain fraction of C14 from user
   Calculate estimated age
   Output estimated age to user.
```

The second step, that of calculating the estimated age makes use of the formula cited in the statement of the example. This calculation can be neatly done incorporating the formula in a function `EstimateAge` whose value is the estimated age. The remaining modules are fairly simple and can be included in the main program.

Here is the coding of the program.

Listing 5.12. CarbonDate

```
program CarbonDate;
{Calculate the age of an artifact based on the fraction of C14
remaining.
      Age = Estimated age of artifact
      C14Frac = fraction C14 remaining. Obtained from
                user.
      InputOk = boolean variable used to signify that
                valid input has been obtained.}

   var
      Age, C14Frac : real;
      InputOk : boolean;
```

```
function EstimateAge(     C14Frac : real) : real;
  begin {EstimateAge}
    EstimateAge := ln(1/C14Frac)/0.00012
  end; {EstimateAge}

begin {CarbonDate}
  writeln('What is the fraction of carbon-14');
  writeln('present in the artifact?');
  InputOk := false;
  {Obtain the fraction of C14. Must be > 0 and <= 1}
  while not InputOk do
    begin
      readln(C14Frac);
        if (C14Frac <= 0) or (C14Frac > 1)
          then
            begin
              writeln('Input error.');
              writeln('The fraction of C14 must be');
              writeln('a positive number less than 1');
              writeln('and greater than 0.');
              writeln('Input the fraction again.')
            end
          else
            InputOk := true
    end;
  {Calculate estimated age.}
  Age := EstimateAge(C14Frac);
  {Output to user.}
  writeln('The specimen is ', Age:6:0, ' years old.');
  readln
end. {CarbonDate}
```

Sample Run. CarbonDate

```
What is the fraction of carbon-14
present in the artifact?
0.5
The specimen is   5776 years old.
```

Random Numbers and Their Applications

The Random Function

Turbo Pascal contains the function Random, which can be used to generate events whose outcomes are "random." You may simulate the action of throwing a pair of dice by using Random to choose at random two integers between 1 and 6. Similarly, you may simulate the action of picking a card at random from a deck of cards by using Random to choose at random two integers, one an integer between 1 and 13 (1 = Ace, ..., 13 = King) and one an integer between 1 and 4 (1 = Spade, 2 = Diamonds, 3 = Hearts, 4 = Clubs).

Each time the function Random is called, it returns a real number between 0 (included) and 1 (excluded). The function values of Random are called *random numbers* and the function Random is called a *random number generator.*

The procedure used within Random for producing random numbers results in an unbiased, but unpredictable, value. The procedure for producing random numbers is unbiased in the sense that all numbers between 0 and 1 are equally likely. This means, for example, that numbers between 0 and 0.1 will occur about 10 percent of the time, numbers between 0.75 and 0.77 will occur about 2 percent of the time, and so forth.

The function Random can be used to make random choices within a program. For example, suppose you are writing a program to simulate traffic through an intersection. Suppose that 60 percent of all cars approaching the intersection go straight, 30 percent turn right and 10 percent turn left. The program can simulate the passage of each car through the intersection. The program can make a random choice of direction for each car using Random. Here's how: If you divide the real number line between 0.0 and 1.0 into tenths, then the distance from 0 to 0.6 is 60 percent of the distance, from 0.6 to 0.9 30 percent of the distance, and from 0.9 to 1.0 10 percent of the distance. This suggests that we let Straight correspond to a value of Random between 0 and 0.6, Right a value between 0.6 and 0.9, and Left a value between 0.9 and 1.0. Thus, our desired statement is:

```
X := Random;
if X < 0.6 then
  Straight
else if (X >= 0.6) and (X < 0.9) then
    Right
  else
    Left;
```

In repeated executions of this code, the procedure Straight will be executed approximately 60 percent of the time, the procedure Right approximately 30 percent of the time, and the procedure `Left` approximately 10 percent of the time. However, the actual sequence of turns made by the simulated car cannot be specified in advance (at least, not without knowing the internal operation of the random generator).

Different Sequences of Random Numbers

In some applications, you will need sequences of random numbers other than real numbers between 0 and 1. However, using the function `Random`, it is straightforward to manufacture almost any sequence of random numbers required.

By performing arithmetic operations on the value `Random`, it is possible to create sequences of real numbers lying between other bounds. For example, `6*Random` produces a real random number between 0 and 6. Thus, this expression produces a value between 5 and 6, say, approximately one-sixth of the time. Such an expression might be used in a quality control simulation in which a machine makes random errors in cutting boards, where the errors range from 0 to 6 centimeters.

The expression `10*Random + 5` produces real random numbers between 5 and 15. (`10*Random` produces random numbers between 0 and 10. Adding 5 increases each 5 units.)

In many applications, it is necessary to use random integers lying within a given range. For example, in simulating flipping a coin, we would use the random integers 0 and 1. In simulating throwing a die, we would use the random integers 1, 2, 3, 4, 5, 6.

To create sequences of integer random numbers, we combine the `Random` function with the `Trunc` function. For example, the expression `Trunc(2*Random)` creates random integers 0 or 1. Indeed, `2*Random` is a random real number between 0 (included) and 2 (excluded). By truncating the decimal part of such a number we obtain either of the integers 0 or 1.

Similarly, the expression `Trunc(6*Random)` creates random integers chosen from the list 0, 1, 2, 3, 4, 5. Furthermore, the expression, `Trunc (6*Random+1)` creates random integers chosen from the list 1, 2, 3, 4, 5, 6. It is this last expression which can be used to simulate throwing a die.

Applications of Random Numbers

Example 1. Write a function which simulates throwing two dice. The function should return to the calling program the total shown on the two dice.

Solution. The value of the function DiceTot returns the total of the two dice thrown. Further, let's use variables Die1 and Die2, local to the procedure DiceTot, to store the values obtained by throwing the two dice. From our discussion above, the values of Die1 and Die2 may be obtained using the statements:

```
Die1  := Trunc(6*Random + 1);
Die2  := Trunc(6*Random + 1);
```

Note that we are not necessarily assigning the same values to each of the dice. Successive calls to Random generally produce different random numbers. Here is our function:

```
function DiceTot : integer;
{This function simulates rolling two die and returns the sum
 of the values on the dice.}

  var Die1, Die2 : integer; {Values rolled on two dice}

  begin {DiceTot}
    Die1  := Trunc(6*Random + 1);
    Die2  := Trunc(6*Random + 1);
    DiceTot := Die1 + Die2;
  end; {DiceTot}
```

Sample Run. DiceTot

```
Function call: DiceTot
Returned value: 11

Function call: DiceTot
Returned value: 2
```

The Starting Point for Random Number Generation

Internal to Turbo Pascal, there is a routine for generating the numbers returned by the Random function. It is not really necessary for you to understand how this routine works. However, it is important to recognize that this routine starts from a particular number called the *seed.* From this seed, the routine generates a sequence of random numbers which are returned by successive calls to Random. If you start with the same seed, then the sequence of random numbers will be the same. This would make for very uninteresting random numbers! However, you may start with a randomly chosen seed (determined by the current reading of the system clock) using the procedure Randomize. The statement Randomize; instructs Turbo Pascal to set the seed of the random number generator.

In debugging programs involving random numbers, you may wish to omit the `Randomize` statement so that the output will be reproducible. Once the program is operating properly, you may insert the `Randomize` statement to introduce the desired unpredictability.

The Game of Craps

As an application of random numbers, let's design a program to play the popular dice game of craps.

To begin with, let's review the rules of the game. Craps can be played with any number of players. However, for simplicity, let's consider a single player playing against the house. The player places a bet. As a result of a single play, the player either loses the bet or wins an amount equal to the bet. A single play consists of a sequence of throws of a pair of dice. If the first roll is a 7 or 11, the player wins. If the first roll is a 2, 3, or 12, the player loses. If the first throw is 4, 5, 6, 8, 9, or 10, that number becomes the player's "point." The player continues to throw the dice until throwing the "point," in which case the player wins, or until throwing a 7, in which case the player loses.

To make the game realistic, let's keep track of the player's bankroll. For each play, we ask the player for a bet and then simulate rolling the dice. If the player wins, an amount equal to the bet is added to the bankroll. If the player loses, an amount equal to the bet is subtracted from the bankroll. The player is then asked if another play is desired.

Here is a program design in pseudocode:

```
program Craps.
  Set Continue equal to true.
  Obtain initial Bankroll.
  repeat
    Obtain Bet.
    Roll Dice.
    If player wins then
    Add Bet to Bankroll.
    If player loses then
    Subtract Bet from Bankroll.
    Continue ?(Y or N).
    If No, set Continue equal to false.
  until Continue = false.
```

In order to complete the program design, we must construct a second-level design corresponding to `Roll Dice`. Let's store the result of throwing the dice in the variable `Total`. We may distinguish between the various outcomes using a case statement.

```
Roll Dice.
Get dice Total.
```

```
case Total of
  7, 11 : Player wins;
  2, 3, 12 : Player loses;
  4,5,6,8,9,10 :
    Point := Total;
    repeat
      Get dice Total.
    until Total=7 or Total=Point;
    if Total=7 then
      Player Loses
    else
      Player Wins
    end; {case}
```

This second-level design shows that we need yet a further level of refinement to describe obtaining the value of `Total`. Here is the module corresponding to the third level of design.

```
Dice Total.
  Die1 := Trunc(6*Random+1);
  Die2 := Trunc(6*Random+1);
  Total := Die1 + Die2;
```

Let's implement `Roll Dice` as a procedure `RollDice` declared in the main program block. Further, let's declare a function, `DiceTot`, corresponding to `Dice Total`.

Let's now define the program variables and plan the parameter passing which must take place. The main program requires the boolean variable `Continue`, a char variable `Ch` to store the user response "Y" or "N," and integer variables `Bankroll` to store the amount of money the player currently has, and `Bet` to store the amount of the current bet. (We're assuming that bankroll is an integer since no sensible casino bothers with change at the craps table.)

Let's now code the program.

Listing 5.13. Craps

```
program Craps;
{This program plays the traditional game of CRAPS.
The player plays against the house. The player is
initially asked for the amount of his bankroll. This
is the total amount of money available for betting.
The game proceeds one play at a time. At the end of
each play, the player is asked whether to continue
or not.
  Continue = boolean variable indicating continue
             game
  Win = boolean variable indicating result of a
        throw
  Bankroll = total amount player has for betting
```

```
Bet = Amount of current bet
 Ch = character for inputting Y/N response.}

  var
  Continue, Win : boolean;
  Bankroll, Bet : integer;
  Ch : char;

 function DiceTot : integer;
{This function simulates rolling two dice and
 returns the sum of the values on the dice.}
  var
    Die1, Die2 : integer; {Values rolled on two dice}
  begin {DiceTot}
    Die1 := trunc(6*random + 1);
    Die2 := trunc(6*random + 1);
    DiceTot := Die1 + Die2
  end; {DiceTot}

 procedure RollDice(var Win : boolean);
{This procedure simulates one play of the game.
 The variable Win passes the win or lose status
 of the game back to the main program.}
  var
    Point, Total: integer;
  begin {RollDice}
    Total := DiceTot;
    writeln('The roll is ', Total);
    case Total of
      7,11       : Win := true;
      2,3,12     : Win := false;
      4,5,6,8,9,10 :
        begin
          Point := Total;
          writeln('The point is ',Point);
          repeat
            Total := DiceTot;
            writeln('The roll is ', Total)
          until (Total = 7) or (Total = Point);
          Win := (Total = Point)
        end
    end
  end; {RollDice}

begin {Craps}
  randomize;
  Continue := true;
  write('What is your initial bankroll ');
  write('(an integer number in dollars)? ');
  readln(Bankroll);
  repeat
    write('What is your bet (in integer number in dollars)? ');
    readln(Bet);
```

```
      RollDice(Win);
      if Win
        then
          begin
            writeln('You win $', Bet:1);
            Bankroll := Bankroll + Bet
          end
        else
          begin
            writeln('You lose $',Bet:1);
            Bankroll := Bankroll - Bet
          end;
      writeln('Current bankroll: $', Bankroll:1);
      write('Another roll? (Y/N)');
      readln(Ch);
      if (Ch = 'N') or (Ch = 'n')
        then
          Continue := false
    until (Continue = false)
  end.
```

Sample Run. Craps

```
What is your initial bankroll (an integer number in dollars)? 100
What is your bet (in integer number in dollars)? 10
The roll is 5
The point is 5
The roll is 6
The roll is 3
The roll is 7
You lose $10
Current bankroll: $90
Another roll? (Y/N)n
_
```

Note that your output may be different because of the randomness.

Generating Random Integers

In our discussion above, we used the function `Random`, together with `Trunc`, to generate random sequences of integers, such as those used in `Dice` and `Craps`. Turbo Pascal offers a short cut to generating such sequences, the function `Random(Num)`, which generates random integers between 0 and

Num. For example, you may generate the rolls of a die as values of the function Random(5)+1. (This generates random integers in the range 1–6).

You should note that Random(Num) is a function with a single parameter, whereas Random is a parameterless function.

Recursion

Let's begin by recalling a discussion from our introduction of functions. In the body of a function declaration, you were instructed to calculate the function value without using the name of the function. You were told to use the last statement in the body to assign the function value to the function name. We mumbled that the reason for this strange set of instructions had to do with something called recursion. In this section, we will explain this cryptic remark.

Within a body of a function or a procedure, it is possible to make function or procedure calls. We have seen a number of examples of this in functions and procedures which we have designed. Actually, Pascal allows a procedure or a function to call itself. That is, the body of a procedure or a function may contain references to the procedure or function itself. Such procedure or function calls are said to be *recursive.*

At first, the idea of recursive calls may seem like nonsense. After all, how can you define a function or procedure in terms of itself? It seems that you would be going around in circles, chasing your tail in search of a proper definition. However, as we shall see, recursive calls are a powerful tool in the hands of a programmer and often allow you to define complex procedures and functions with a minimum of coding.

Introduction to Recursion

To get an idea of what recursion is all about, let's reconsider the function Power(Num,Exponent), which we defined earlier in the chapter. Previously, we used a loop to multiply Num times itself Exponent times. However, an alternate way to calculate $Num^{Exponent}$ is:

multiply Num times $Num^{Exponent-1}$

This appears to beg the question, since we haven't computed $Num^{Exponent-1}$. The simplest way to do this is to invoke the procedure call Power(Num, Exponent-1). Using the same logic as before, we calculate Power(Num, Exponent-1) as follows:

```
multiply Num times Num^(Exponent-2)
```

And so forth. We compute each power in terms of the next lowest power. Eventually, we reduce the computation down to computing `Power(Num,0)`, which is assigned the value 1 (since $\text{Num}^0 = 1$). This computation scheme may be summarized in the following function coding:

```
function Power(Num : real;
               Exponent : integer) : real;

{Return Num raised to the power Exponent. Here Num is a
real and Exponent is an integer. In case Exponent is
negative, the value 1 is returned.}

 begin {Power}
    if Exponent <= 0 then {Exponent is non-positive}
        Power := 1
    else {Exponent is positive}
      Power := Num*Power(Num,Exponent-1)
  end; {Power}
```

This function declaration defines `Power(Num,Exponent)` using a recursive function call. Let's go over this code in detail. If `Exponent` is less than or equal to 0, then `Power(Num,Exponent)` is assigned the value 1. Otherwise, `Exponent` is positive and `Power(Num,Exponent)` is assigned the value

```
Num*Power(Num,Exponent-1)
```

To calculate `Power(Num,Exponent-1)`, the function is called again. If `Exponent-1` is positive, `Power(Num,Exponent-1)` is assigned the value

```
Num*Power(Num,Exponent-2)
```

so that `Power(Num,Exponent)` is now calculated as:

```
Num*Num*Power(Num,Exponent-2)
```

The function `Power` is called yet again. And so on, until, after `Exponent` steps, we compute `Power(Num,Exponent)` as:

```
Num*Num*...*Num*Power(Num,0) (Exponent factors of Num)
```

In a final function call, `Power(Num,0)` is assigned the value 1, and `Power(Num,Exponent)` is computed correctly as:

```
Num*Num*...*Num*1 (Exponent factors of Num)
```

To summarize: The statement

```
Power := Num*Power(Num,Exponent-1);
```

defines Power (on the left side of: =) in terms of itself. Pascal unravels the definition computing Power in a number of steps, each one reducing the computation of Power to another computation (namely that of Power (Num,Exponent-1). This process of reducing the computation comes to a stop in a finite number of steps, since it eventually comes down to computing Power(Num,0), which is set equal to 1.

Yet Another Example of Recursion

The process of factoring numbers gives us another instance where recursion is useful. For many applications, such as cryptography (the science of making and breaking codes), it is necessary to factor integers into their prime factors. Examples of such factorizations are:

15 = 5*3

12 = 2*2*3

56 = 2*2*2*7

Suppose that N is a positive integer. A factor of N must lie between 2 and N/2. One way of factoring N is to begin testing N for factors, starting with 2. If we find a factor, divide it out and repeat the process for the integer which is left.

For example, to factor 56, here is how we proceed:

```
N                  First factor found
56                        2
56 div 2 = 28             2
28 div 2 = 14             2
14 div 2 =  7            none

Factorization : 56 = 2*2*2*7
```

At each step, we attempt to find a factor between N and N/2. If we find one, we continue to factor the number N div (the factor found). If no factor is found, then the factorization process is complete and can be read off from the factors listed and the final value of N. The crucial step is where the factoring is reduced to factoring a smaller number. This is recursion.

1. It begins by asking for an integer N to factorize.
2. If N is 1, 0 or negative, the program halts. (We never try to factor numbers less than 2.)

3. If N is positive, the program calls the procedure Factor(N). We consider numbers K between 2 and N/2 to determine whether K is a factor of N. We use the boolean expression N mod K = 0. If this expression is true, then K is a factor of N. Otherwise, it is not. If a factor K is found (N mod K equals 0), N is replaced by N div K and Factor(N) is called again. If a factor K is not found, then N is declared a prime and the factorization process is complete.

Let's now design the program. Here is the pseudocode.

```
program Factor.
  Get number N from user.
  Factor the number.
  Display results.
```

The factorization process described above is essentially the contents of the second routine, which we implement as a procedure Factor(N). This procedure calls itself recessively. In this procedure, we use a loop to look for a factor K of N. If a factor is found, we print out the factor K, replace N by N mod K and make the recursive call Factor(N).

We use the boolean variables Continue and Prime as local variables in the procedure Factor(N). Prime indicates that a factor of N has not yet been found. If Prime is false]after all values of K have been tested (namely those between 2 and N/2), Prime is set equal to true, the current value of N is printed out as a factor, and the procedure terminates. This description suggests a while loop which continues as long as Prime is false.

Listing 5.14. Factors

```
program Factors;
{Determine the factors of a user-supplied integer N.}

    var
     InputOk : boolean;
     N : integer;

    procedure Factor( N : integer);
   {Obtain the factors of N and display them.
     K = a potential factor of N
     Prime = true if N is a prime, otherwise false
     Continue = true if a factor of N has not been found.}
     var
       K : integer;
       Success : boolean;
     begin {Factor}
       K := 1;
       Success := false;
```

```
      while (not Success) and (K < N div 2) do
        begin
          K := K+1;
          Success := ((N mod K) = 0)
        end;
      if Success
        then
          begin
            write(K:0, ' ');
            Factor(N div K)
          end
        else
          write(N:0, ' ')
    end; {Factor}

   begin {Factors}
    InputOk := false;
    while (InputOk = false) do
      begin
        write('Input number to factor: ');
        readln(N);
        if (N >=2) then
          InputOk := true
      end;
    write('The factors are: ');
    Factor(N);
    writeln;
    readln
  end.
```

Sample Run. Factors

```
Input number to factor: 12
The factors are: 2 2 3

Input number to factor: 210
The factors are: 2 3 5 7
```

In theory, there is no limit to the complexity of a recursive function or procedure call. Such a call can generate a very long sequence of procedure or function calls, each one calling the next. In practice, there is a system-dependent limit on the length of such sequences. Pascal keeps track of recursive calls using a section of memory called the stack. The allowable length of a recursive sequence depends on the amount of memory allocated for the stack. A recursive call which is too complex will overflow the space allotted. Therefore, if your system suddenly gives you an error which says something about the stack overflowing, a possible source is a recursive call.

It is very possible to accidentally set up an infinite recursive call. This is a recursive call that never ends. Eventually, such a recursive call will overflow the stack space and generate an error. Thus, if you use a recursive call, make sure that it ends after a finite number of steps.

Recursion versus Iteration

In this section, we have introduced the concept of recursion. In effect, a recursive procedure or function call is a kind of loop in which a sequence of repetitive function calls are made. This looping is somewhat different from the standard looping techniques we have previously introduced, which are referred to as iteration. Most (if not all) applications using recursion can be also programmed using iteration. Therefore, it seems in order to compare the two methods of performing repetitive actions.

Recursive calls are easy to describe and generally result in shorter code. On the other hand, recursive calls can be tricky to debug due to possible infinite recursions and branches that only are taken in some of the calls. Recursive procedures are also harder to understand than iterative procedures.

Recursive definitions save on the amount of code required as compared to iteration, but tend to need more RAM as stack space. It is very difficult to say with certainty which method results in lower overall RAM requirements. However, when programmed efficiently, recursive procedures typically execute faster.

On balance, both iteration and recursion have their places in your programming toolbox. In each application, you will need to decide the relative merits in deciding which one to use.

String Handling Functions and Procedures

Turbo Pascal includes a collection of procedures and functions for manipulation of strings. These predeclared functions and procedures are not part of standard Pascal. However, they are extremely useful and save you from writing your own collection of string handling routines. In this section, we survey Turbo Pascal's string handling procedures and functions. In the next section, we present some applications of these to various text processing problems.

Turbo Pascal String Handling Functions

Length(St)

This function returns the length of the string `St`. The returned value is an integer in the range 0..255. For example:

```
Length('ABCDEFG') returns 7
Length('     Alpha') returns 9
Length(' ') returns 0
```

Pos(Obj, Target)

This function returns the character position of the first occurrence of the string `Obj` in the string `Target`. This character position is expressed as an integer in the range 0..255. If `Obj` does not occur within the string `Target`, then the function `Pos` returns 0. For example:

```
Pos('CDE','ABCDEFGH') returns 3
Pos('grand', 'baby grand') returns 6
Pos('z', 'abcde') returns 0
```

Copy(St, Posit, Num)

This function extracts a string of `Num` characters from `St`, beginning with character position `Posit`. Both `Posit` and `Num` are integers in the range 1..255. For example:

```
Copy('ABCDEFG',3,2) returns 'CD'
Copy('ABCDEFG',3,5) returns 'EFG'
Copy('ABCDEFG',8,5) returns ''
```

Turbo Pascal String Handling Procedures

Turbo Pascal includes four predeclared procedures for dealing with strings, namely `Delete`, `Insert`, `Val`, and `Str`.

Delete(St, Posit, Num)

This procedure deletes `Num` characters from the string `St`, beginning with characters position `Posit`. Here `Posit` is an integer in the range 1..255 and `St` is a variable of string type. For example, suppose that `St` initially equals the string 'ABCDEFG'. Then

```
Delete(St,2,3) passes the value 'AEFG' back to St
Delete(St,2,8) passes the value 'A' back to St
Delete(St,3,2) passes the value 'ABEFG' back to St
```

Insert(Obj, Target, Posit)

This procedure inserts the string `Obj` within the string `Target` beginning at character position `Posit`, where `Posit` is an integer in the range 1..255, and `Target` is a variable of string type and `Obj` is either a constant or variable of string type. For example, suppose that `Target` has the value 'ABCDEFG'. Then:

```
Insert('XYZ',Target,3) passes Target with the value 'ABXYZCDEFG'
Insert('XYZ',Target,10) passes Target with the value 'ABCDEFGXYZ'
```

Str(Number, St)

A string which provides the character representation of a number is not the same thing as the number itself. That is, '1234' is a string constant and is not the same as the number 1234. Turbo Pascal provides procedures for converting back and forth from strings representing real and integer numbers and the corresponding numbers. The procedure `Str` converts a number to a string; the procedure `Val` converts a string to a number.

```
Str(501, St) passes St with the value '501'
Str(5000, St) passes St with the value '500'
  (St cannot accommodate the entire string representation, so
  truncation occurs.)
```

Val(St, Number, Code)

Converts the string `St` to a numerical representation, if possible. The numerical representation is passed in `Number`. If conversion is not possible, `Code` passes the character position of the first error which disallows conversion. Here `St` is a string constant or variable, `Number` is a variable of type either integer or real, and `Code` is a variable of type integer. If conversion is successful, then Code passes the value 0. If the type of `Number` is incorrect (that is, integer where real is required), then the position where the error occurs in the string will be returned. For example:

```
Val('-1234',Number,Code) passes Number with the value -1234
  and Code with the value 0.

Val(-1E5,Number,Code) passes the real variable with the value -1E5
  and Code with the value 0.

Val(123A,Number,Code) passes a garbage value in Number and Code
  with the value 4.
```

Text Processing Applications

Using the concept of a string and the string manipulation procedures and functions of the preceding section, we can present a number of very interesting applications and develop our programming technique at the same time.

Removing Trailing Blanks

Example 1. In many text applications, you may wish to remove blanks from the end of a string. For instance, in interpreting a command typed from the keyboard, a command processor should ignore any extra spaces which you inadvertently type. Blanks at the end of a string are called *railing blanks*. Design a procedure for removing such blanks.

Solution. The procedure strips away any trailing blanks in the string `Source` and stores the resulting string in `Target`. For instance, if `Source` is 'Love   ', then `Target` is 'Love'. Here is the code for the procedure.

```
procedure RemTrBlanks(var Source, Target : string);
{Strips away any trailing blanks in Source and
stores the resulting string in Target.}

  const
  Blank = ' ';

  var
    Posit : integer;
  begin {RemTrBlanks}
    Posit := Length(Source);
    While Source[Posit] = Blank DO
      Posit := Posit-1;
    Delete(Source, Posit+1, Length(Source)-Posit);
```

```
    Target := Source
  end; {RemTrBlanks}
```

Sample Run. RemTrBlanks

```
Suppose that Name stores the string:
'Hathaway, Sam      '

Procedure call: RemTrBlanks(Source, Target);
Result: Target stores the string:
'Hathaway, Sam'
```

Counting the Number of Words in a String

Example 2. Computer programs are used to prepare and analyze all kinds of text. Design a procedure to count the number of words in a string. For our purposes, a word will mean any string of characters not containing a space.

Solution. Our procedure counts the number of words in the string `Source` and returns the value of `Number`, the number of words in `Source`. For instance, if `Source` stores

```
'Now is the time for all good people to come to the aid of their party.'
```

then the statement:

```
Count(Source,Number);
```

will set `Number` equal to 16. Note that the result should be the same no matter how many spaces separate each of the words or if there are leading or trailing spaces.

To keep track of where words start and end, we will use the boolean variable `InWord`, which will be true when the last character was within a word (that is, a non-space) and false if the last character was a space. Whenever `InWord` changes its value from false to true, we increase a counter `Number` which counts the word which has just begun.

Here is the coding of the procedure.

```
procedure Count(var Source : String;
                var Number : integer);
{Count the number of words in the string
 Source and return the count in Number.}

  const
    Blank = ' ';
```

```
var
  I : integer;
  InWord : boolean;

 begin {Count}
  Number := 0;
  InWord := false;
  for I := 1 to Length(Source) do
    if InWord then
      InWord := (Source(I) <> Blank)
    else
      if (Source(I) <> Blank) then
        begin
          InWord := true;
          Number := Number + 1
        end
end; {Count}
```

Sample Run. Count

Suppose that Message stores the string:

```
'Daylight savings time begins today.     '

Procedure call: Count(Message,Number);
Result: Number is returned with the value 5.
```

6 More Data Types

All problem solving, whether or not it involves computer programming, involves data. Data can be of many different forms: letters, words, numbers, sentences, paragraphs, or pictures. And data are used for different purposes: Summarizing the given facts about a problem, providing the solution to a problem, or providing some intermediate information derived from the given facts and required for a solution.

The first step in solving a problem is to determine the given problem data (the *inputs*) and the data to be derived from it (the *outputs*). The second step is to determine how to derive the outputs from the inputs. This generally involves data manipulation. There are many forms of data manipulation, including arithmetic operations, sorting, text operations, graphics operations, display operations, print operations, storage operations, and reference operations. The particular data manipulations which are required will vary from problem to problem, depending on what is necessary to derive the outputs from the inputs.

In all problems, it is necessary to find a way to represent the data of the problem. The data representation you choose can go a long way toward organizing the data and aiding in any data manipulations you must perform. Turbo Pascal provides you with a number of very helpful data representations you can use. These data representations are called data structures.

We have already encountered the simplest of the data structures, the simple Turbo Pascal data types. These data types are useful in handling simple problems. However, for handling more complex problems, Turbo Pascal provides a number of other data types which provide various useful data organizations. Using these data types, allows you to clearly and efficiently represent data in Turbo Pascal and perform required manipulations.

For example, you may use an array to represent a list of numbers, such as:

14.1

11.2

11.3

 4.7

You may refer to single entries in the list, use them in calculations, modify them, and display them.

You may use a file to represent an open-ended list of data—say, a list of customers stored on disk—to which you may refer or add data.

Or you may introduce a user-defined data type whose values consist of the following list of colors: (Red, Green, Yellow, Blue).

Our goal in this chapter is to introduce some of Turbo Pascal's more advanced data types and show how they may be used in problem solving. The data types we are concerned with in this chapter are the so-called *static* data types. We will discuss dynamic data types later in the book.

Scalar, Ordinal, and Subrange Types

Scalar and Ordinal Data Types

The four basic data types integer, char, boolean, and real are called *scalar data types.* The scalar data types are those which serve as the building blocks for the more complex data types.

An *ordinal type* is a data type whose values can be arranged in order so that:

1. There is a first and last data value.
2. Each data value other than the last has a next larger value, called its *successor.*
3. Each data value other than the first has a next smaller value, called its *predecessor.*

Among the scalar data types, integer, char, and boolean are ordinal types. Let's see why. The integers are arranged according to their usual numerical order:

$... < -2 < -1 < 0 < 1 < 2 ...$

The first integer is `-maxint` and the last integer is `maxint`. (Recall that `maxint` is the largest integer allowed in Turbo Pascal. This number is predeclared as a constant.) The successor of each integer other than the last is obtained by adding 1. The predecessor of each integer other than the first is obtained by subtracting 1. For example, the predecessor of 3 is $3 - 1 = 2$ and the successor of 5 is $5 + 1 = 6$.

There are many ways to arrange the characters in order. In any reasonable ordering scheme, however, the letters should be in alphabetical order. That is, we should always have the following ordering:

'A' < 'B' < 'C' < ...

'a' < 'b' < 'c' < ...

Moreover, the letters should come one after the other according to the alphabet. (No character should be allowed to come between 'M' and 'N,' for example.) All schemes for arranging the characters in order satisfy these criteria just mentioned. Where they differ is in their placement of the digits, punctuation marks, and other symbols. In Turbo Pascal, characters are arranged according to the ASCII system. That is, each character is assigned an integer from 0 to 255. The characters are arranged in order according to their ASCII values. We will discuss ASCII values in more detail later. There is a first character (ASCII value 0) and a last character (ASCII value 255); each character other than the first has a predecessor; each character other than the last has a successor. In other words, char is an ordinal data type.

There are only two values of the type boolean, namely true and false. These values are ordered so that: false < true.

With respect to this ordering, boolean becomes an ordinal data type.

Other Ordinal Data Types

We will meet other ordinal data types as we proceed. In particular, in the next section, we will discuss the user-defined enumerated data types, which are ordinal.

Note that real is not an ordinal data type. It fails on three counts:

1. There is no first data value.
2. There is no last data value.
3. A data value does not have an unambiguously defined successor or predecessor. (What is the successor of 5.723571 ?)

The Functions succ and pred

Once a data type has been arranged in order, it is natural to ask what data value follows or precedes a given value. To answer such questions, you may use the predeclared standard Turbo Pascal functions `succ` and `pred`. The function `succ` may be used to determine the successor of a data value belonging to an ordinal data type. The function `pred` may be used to determine the predecessor of a data value belonging to an ordinal data type. So, for example,

`succ(3)` returns the value 4

`succ('A')` returns the value 'B'

`pred(7)` returns the value 6

`pred('m')` returns the value 'l'

`pred(false)` returns the value true

`succ(false)` returns the value true

Note that `succ(X)` is undefined if X is the last data value and `pred(X)` is undefined if X is the first data value. In these two cases, Turbo Pascal will report a run-time error.

The Functions chr and ord

The functions `chr` and `ord` are Turbo Pascal functions that are useful in doing manipulation of characters. As we shall see, you can use these functions in text-processing programs.

The function `chr(X)` returns the character whose ASCII code is given by the value of the integer X.

`chr(32)` returns the value ' ' (space)

`chr(65)` returns the value 'A'

`chr(97)` returns the value 'a'

The function `ord(C)` returns the ASCII code corresponding to the character C. For example:

`ord('A')` returns the value 65

`ord('a')` returns the value 97

`ord(' ')` returns the value 32

Subrange Data Types

Turbo Pascal allows you to create new data types in several ways. One method is to start with an ordinal data type and restrict data to lie within a particular subrange. For example, here is a subrange of the integers:

```
1..10
```

This subrange consists of the integers from 1 to 10, inclusive (that is, the integers, 1, 2, 3, 4, 5, 6, 7, 8, 9, 10). Similarly, here is a subrange of char:

```
'D..''H'
```

This subrange consists of the characters from 'D' to 'H' inclusive (that is, the characters 'D,' 'E,' 'F,' 'G,' 'H').

You can create variables whose values are restricted to a given subrange. Just write the subrange as a data type within the variable declaration. For example, consider the following declaration:

```
var
  Num : 1..10;
  Ch  : 'D..''H';
```

Suppose that a variable is of a subrange type. Giving it a value outside of its defined range results in a run-time error. For example, if you attempt to assign the above variable Num the value 15 or –1, then a run-time error results.

In using subranges, you may assign values of variables belonging to the larger type so long as the value belongs to the subrange. For example, suppose that Num is an integer variable and Small belongs to the subrange 0..10. The assignment:

```
Small := Num;
```

is legal so long as the value of Num lies in the range 0..10. Otherwise, a run-time error results.

You may always assign a variable of the larger type the value of a subrange variable. For example, the assignment:

```
Num := Small;
```

is always legal.

The above examples of subrange types were created from the standard data types integer and char, respectively. However, you may define subrange types of any ordinal type. In the next section, we will learn to create other ordinal types—namely, enumerated data types. There, we will illustrate how to define subrange types from these types.

Enumerated Data Types

Turbo Pascal allows the user to define ordinal data types which consist of a list of user-declared identifiers. For example, you may use a data type of colors:

```
(Red, Green, Blue)
```

This is a data type consisting of three identifiers: Red, Green, and Blue.

A user-defined data type such as this is called an *enumerated data type,* since it is defined by enumerating the data values in a list. By using enumerated data types, you can greatly improve program readability. You should choose the identifiers for your constants with this in mind. Your goal should be to write programs whose function is clear even to a person who did not write them!

In general, an enumerated data type is defined by listing the data values within parentheses:

```
(constant1, constant2, ... , constantn)
```

An enumerated data type is an ordinal type with the order given by the arrangement of the values within the defining parentheses. For example, in the above enumerated data type, the order of the values is:

```
Red < Green < Blue
```

To define the variable Color which can be assigned values belonging to the above data type, we may use a declaration of the form:

```
var Color : (Red, Green, Blue)
```

The following are then valid statements using the variable Color:

```
Color := Red;
if Color = Red
  then
    FillRegion;
for Color := Red to Blue do
  TestSize(Color);
```

Note that readln and writeln don't work with user-defined data types. You cannot use writeln or readln in connection with a value belonging to a user-defined type. For example, each of the following statements will result in a run-time error:

```
writeln(Color);
Readln(Color);
```

More About the Function ord

The function `ord(X)` is defined for `X` belonging to an ordinal data type. Its value is defined as follows:

- If `X` is of integer or an integer subrange type, then `ord(X)` is equal to `X`.
- If `X` is of char or a char subrange type, then `ord(X)` is equal to the ASCII code assigned to `X`.
- If `X` is a boolean variable, then `ord(X)` is 0 if `X` is false and 1 if `X` is true.
- If `X` is an enumerated type, then `ord(X)` is the numerical position of `X` within the listing of data values, where the numbering of data values begins with 0.

For example:

`ord(100)` is equal to 100;

`ord(-5)` is equal to –5;

If `X` belongs to the subrange type 3..10 and `X` has the value 5, then `ord(X)` is equal to 5.

If `X` has the value 'a,' then `ord(X)` is equal to 97, the ASCII code of 'a.'

In the enumerated type `(Green, Yellow, Red, Blue)`, `ord(Green)` is equal to 0, whereas `ord(Blue)` is equal to 3.

Type Declarations

In the above examples of subrange and enumerated data types, we introduced variables of the desired types by describing the data type directly within the variable declaration. However, in many applications, it is convenient to be able to assign a name to a data type. For example, this allows us to pass parameters of the type to functions and procedures. We assign a name to a data type using a type declaration.

A type declaration has the syntax:

```
type typename = datatype;
```

For example, consider the above data type which lists the colors (Red, Green, Blue). We can assign the name Colors to this data type using the declaration:

```
type Colors = (Red, Green, Blue);
```

Once such a type declaration is included, we can declare the variable Color to be of type Colors using a declaration of the form:

```
var Color : Colors;
```

Type declarations are placed preceding the variable declaration section in a block.

Each block within a program can have its own type declaration section. The same scope rules that apply to variables and procedures also apply to types: The scope of a data type consists of the block in which it is declared. Outside of the block, the data type is undefined.

Note that when passing enumerated or subrange type parameters to or from a procedure or function, it is necessary to declare an appropriate type rather than explicitly describe the data type in the procedure or function header. For instance, the following procedure header is incorrect:

```
procedure Test(var Color : (Red, Green, Blue));
```

Rather, you should use a type declaration to define a type Colors, as above, and declare the procedure as:

```
procedure Test(var Color : Colors);
```

Records

An array allows you to collect under a common name a number of data items with a common type. In many applications, however, it is necessary to consider collections of data items with different types. In many such applications, it is useful to describe your data using the record data type.

Consider a calendar date, such as: Mar 15, 1987. It consists of three data items: The month Mar, the day 15, and the year 1987. Each of these data items can be described in Pascal, but using different data types. The month can be described using an identifier Month having values from an enumerated data type listing the 12 months:

```
Month : (Jan, Feb, Mar, Apr, May, Jun, Jul, Aug, Sep,
         Oct, Nov, Dec)
```

The day can be described using the identifier `Day` having values in the integer subrange type 1..31:

```
Day : 1..31
```

The year can be described using the identifier `Year` having values in the integer subrange type 0..2000 (at least, for years 0 through 2000):

```
Year : 0..2000
```

A date can be described using a data structure consisting of a sequence of three data items: a month, a day, and a year. Schematically, such a data structure can be described as follows:

```
Date = (Month, Day, Year)
```

This data structure resembles an array in that it consists of a sequence of data items. However, it differs from an array in that the data items are of different types. This data structure is an example of a record. More precisely, we can make the following definition.

A *record* is a data type with a number of components (or *fields*). A record is defined in a declaration which lists the fields and their data types. In the declaration, each field is assigned a name, or field identifier, which can be used to access the data item contained in the field.

The Syntax of a Record Declaration

A *record* type declaration consists of the type name followed by an equal sign, the reserved word record, a field list, and the reserved word end. The *field list* consists of entries of the form:

```
field_identifier : data_type;
```

In other words, the general syntax of a record type declaration is as follows:

```
type typename = record
                  identifier1 : type1;
                  identifier2 : type2;
                  .
                  .
                  .
                  identifiern : typen
                end;
```

For example, here is a declaration of a record type corresponding to calendar dates, as described above:

```
type Date = record
              Month : (Jan, Feb, Mar, Apr, May, Jun,
                       Jul, Aug, Sep, Oct, Nov, Dec;
              Day  : 1..31;
              Year  : 0..2000;
            end;
```

This declaration creates a data type called `Date` which has three fields, `Month`, `Day`, and `Year`, with the data types as specified in the declaration.

You can create variables of type `Date` using a `var` declaration of the usual sort. For example, the declaration:

```
var BegDate, EndDate : Date;
```

declares variables `BegDate` and `EndDate` whose values are data structures of type `Date`.

You can refer to the individual components of the data structure using the field names appended to the variable name with a period. For instance, the first component of `BegDate` is stored in the variable `BegDate.Month`; the second component is stored in the variable `BegDate.Day`, and the third component is stored in the variable `BegDate.Year`. For example, we may set `BegDate` to the date Mar 15, 1987 using the statements:

```
BegDate.Month := Mar;
BegDate.Day := 15;
BegDate.Year := 1987;
```

The variables which identify the components of a record can be manipulated just like any other variables, as shown in the following statements:

```
BegDate.Month := Succ(Jan);
{assigns the Month component of BegDate the value succ(Jan) or Feb}

if EndDate.Day > 15
  then
    writeln('You are late!');
  {If the Day component of EndDate is larger than 15,
   print out the message 'You are late!'}
```

In the above discussion, we have introduced a user-defined type (`Date`) defined in terms of the record data type. We then defined variables of type `Date` using a `var` declaration. However, you may define the variables directly, using a `var` declaration of the form:

```
var
  BegDate,
  EndDate  :  record
                Month  :  (Jan, Feb, Mar, Apr, May, Jun,
                           Jul, Aug, Sep, Oct, Nov, Dec);
                Day  :  1..31;
```

```
      Year  :  0..2000
    end;
```

By defining the variables in this way, there is no necessity to define the data type Date and so the code is shorter. However, the advantage of introducing the type Date is that the declaration of the variables BegDate and EndDate automatically describes what role the variables are meant to play. This self-documenting feature makes the original method of declaration the preferable one. Furthermore, as we shall shortly see, we can pass records to a procedure or a function only in case the record description consists of a single identifier. This is a further impetus for defining record data types.

Passing Records as Parameters

You may pass records as parameters in procedure and function calls. Moreover, they may be used in connection with either value parameters or variable parameters.

Note, however, that in specifying a record type as a parameter, you must use only a single identifier. This is the same sort of restriction that applied in the case of passing arrays as parameters. In the case of records, the following construction is not allowed:

```
procedure Example( Alpha : record
                             x : integer;
                             y : integer
                           end;);
{Error}
```

Instead, you must assign the record structure a type name and refer to the type name in the procedure call, as follows.

```
type
  Beta = record
           x : integer;
           y : integer
         end;
procedure Example( Alpha  :  Beta);
```

Example 1. Design a procedure InputDate which inputs a date from the user and stores it in a record of type Date which is passed back to the calling program.

Solution. The procedure must ask for values to insert into the three fields of the record to be passed back: the month, day, and year. We could input the month as a string. However, it is simpler to input it as an integer 1 to 12 and convert the integer into one of elements of the data type Month. This can be done by assigning:

```
FirstMonth := Jan;
```

Then Month can be assigned the value of the Nth month using the loop:

```
Month := FirstMonth;
for J := 2 to N do
  Month := Succ(Month);
```

Here is the implementation of InputDate.

```
procedure InputDate(var UserDate : Date);

var
  J, Mnth, Yr : integer;
  {J is a loop counter
   Mnth is the numerical representation of the month
   Yr consists of the last two digits of the year}

begin {UserDate}
  FirstMonth := Jan;
  write('Month(1-12): ');
  readln(Mnth);
  UserDate.Month := FirstMonth;
  for J := 2 to Mnth do
    UserDate.Month := Succ(UserDate.Month);
  write('Day (1-31): ');
  readln(UserDate.Day);
  write('Year (19??): ');
  readln(Yr);
  UserDate.Year := 1900 + Yr
end; {UserDate}
```

Sample Run. InputDate

```
Procedure call: InputDate(BegDate);
Result:
Month (1-12): 12
Day (1-31): 15
Year (19??): 88
```

(This corresponds to the date: Dec 15 1988)

Further Examples of Records

Records can be used to describe the data in a wide variety of applications, as the following examples show.

Records with Array Components

A record can incorporate fields having any data type, even arrays. For instance, you can use a record field to store a character string. Here is the declaration of a record for storing the results of a survey on employment:

```
type
  SurveyForm = record
                 Name : string[30];
                 Address : string[30];
                 City : string[30];
                 State : string[10];
                 Zipcode : string[15];
                 Employed : boolean;
               end;
```

The first five fields are used to store strings. For instance, the first field is used to store the name of an individual surveyed. The name can contain as many as 30 characters.

Suppose that a teacher uses a computerized system of testing, using multiple choice tests having 25 questions of 5 choices each, with the choices labeled A to E. A set of answers can be stored in a data structure of the type `Test`, declared as follows:

```
type
  Test = record
           Name : string[30];
           Course : 1..1000;
           Exam : 1..10;
           Answers : array [1..25] of A..E
         end;
```

Records with Record Components

Records can have components which are other records. For instance, consider a data type used to store appointments recording the person, date, and purpose of the meeting. Such a data type can be described by the following declaration:

```
type
  Appointment = record
                  Person : string[30];
                  When : Date;
                  Purpose : string[30]
                end;
```

Note that the second field gives the time for the appointment and is given in terms of a variable of type `Date`, which we defined at the start of the section.

The type `Date` was defined as a record. So the data type `Appointment` is a record, one of whose fields is a record.

Suppose that `Scheduled` is a variable of type `Appointment`. The value of `Scheduled.When` is a date, which has three fields. You may refer to these fields using the variables:

```
Scheduled.When.Day
Scheduled.When.Month
Scheduled.When.Year
```

Records which have fields defined as records are said to be *hierarchical.*

Arrays of Records

Example 2 (Inventory). A small computer software company maintains an inventory consisting of five products: command cards, documentation, diskettes, binders, and labels. Write a program to keep track of the inventory. The program should allow the user to display the inventory, add to the inventory, and remove items from the inventory.

Solution. Organize the program around a loop in which the user is asked to make a choice from a menu. There are three choices: Add inventory, remove inventory, and quit. Here is pseudocode to describe the tasks:

```
program Inventory.
Initialize inventory.
Continue := true
while Continue do
  Display menu and make choice.
  case Choice of
    1 : Add inventory;
    2 : Remove inventory;
    3 : Quit;
```

The tasks of adding and removing inventory will be relegated to procedures.

The only remaining part of the design process is to decide the data structures needed to store the data of the program. The main data item manipulated by the program is the inventory. For each of five data items, the inventory data structure must store the item name and the quantity of the item in inventory. This suggests that we use an array of records. We declare data types corresponding to the array and the records as follows:

```
type Item = record
              Product : string[13];
              Quantity : integer;
            end;
     Parts = array[1..5] of Item;
```

To store the inventory, we declare a variable Invntry of type Parts. The procedures for initializing, adding and removing inventory all manipulate the components of the data structure Invntry, as shown in the listing below.

Here is the implementation of the program Inventory.

Listing 6.1. Inventory

```
program Inventory;
{Maintain the inventory of parts for a small software company.
There are five items kept in inventory: command cards, documen-
tation, diskettes. binders, and labels. The program sets up an
initial inventory setting of 50 units each and allows the user
to add or subtract items from the inventory.}

type
  Item = record
           Product : string[13];
           Quantity : integer
         end;
  Parts = array [1..5] of Item;

var
  Invntry : Parts;   { array of records to store inventory data }
  Choice : integer;    { stores the response to the menu choice }
  Continue : boolean;        { indicates program should continue }

procedure Initialize(var Invntry : Parts);
{Set up the initial inventory.}

  var
    I : integer; {Loop variable}

    begin {Initialize}
      Invntry [1].Product := 'Command Cards';
      Invntry [2].Product := 'Documentation';
      Invntry [3].Product := 'Diskettes';
      Invntry [4].Product := 'Binders';
      Invntry [5].Product := 'Labels';
      for I := 1 to 5 do
        Invntry [I].Quantity := 50
    end; {Initialize}

procedure DisplayInvntry(var Invntry : Parts);
{Display the current status of the inventory and
 display the menu for selection of inventory operations.}

  var
    X : integer; {Loop variable}
  begin {DisplayInvntry}
    writeln;
    writeln('Identification Number':21, 'Product':11,'Quantity':20);
    for X := 1 to 5 do
```

```
      writeln(X:11, ' ':11, Invntry [X].Product:13,
              Invntry [X].Quantity:14);
    writeln;
    writeln;
    writeln('1. Add Inventory');
    writeln('2. Take Away Inventory');
    writeln('3. Quit')
  end; {DisplayInvntry}

procedure AddInvntry(var Invntry : Parts);
{Make an addition to the inventory.}

  var
    ProdNum, Change : integer;

  begin {AddInvntry}
    writeln;
    writeln('Enter the identification number of');
    write('the product to be added: ');
    readln(ProdNum);
    write('Number of units to add? ');
    readln(Change);
    Invntry [ProdNum].Quantity := Invntry [ProdNum].Quantity + Change
  end; {AddInvntry}

procedure RemoveInvntry(var Invntry : Parts);
{Make a removal from the inventory.}

  var
    ProdNum, Change : integer;

  begin {RemoveInvntry}
    writeln;
    writeln('Enter the identification number of');
    write('the product to be removed: ');
    readln (input, ProdNum);
    write('Number of units to remove: ');
    readln (input, Change);
    Invntry [ProdNum].Quantity := Invntry[ProdNum].Quantity - Change
  end; {RemoveInvntry}

  begin {Inventory}
    Initialize(Invntry);
    Continue := true;
    while Continue do
      begin
        DisplayInvntry(Invntry);
        writeln;
        write('Choose an operation to perform (1-3): ');
        readln(Choice);
        case Choice of
          1 : AddInvntry(Invntry);
          2 : RemoveInvntry(Invntry);
          3 : Continue := false
        end
```

```
    end
  end. {Inventory}
```

Sample Run. Inventory

```
Identification Number       Product             Quantity
        1                   Command Cards          50
        2                   Documentation          50
        3                   Diskettes              50
        4                   Binders                50
        5                   Labels                 50

1. Add Inventory
2. Take Away Inventory
3. Quit
Choose an operation to perform (1-3): 2
Enter the identification number of
the product to be removed: 4
Number of units to remove: 2
Identification Number       Product             Quantity
        1                   Command Cards          50
        2                   Documentation          50
        3                   Diskettes              50
        4                   Binders                48
        5                   Labels                 50

1. Add Inventory
2. Take Away Inventory
3. Quit
Choose an operation to perform (1-3): 3
```

The with Statement

Referring to the field identifiers can result in a lot of typing and code that is cumbersome to read. Pascal allows a shortcut to assist with this problem, namely, the `with` statement. To illustrate the use of the with statement, consider the variable `UserDate` of type `Date` introduced above. The individual fields of the record `UserDate` can be referred to using the field identifiers

```
UserDate.Day
UserDate.Month
UserDate.Year
```

You can set up a section of code in which you can refer to these variables simply as `Day`, `Month`, and `Year`, respectively. Simply use the statement:

```
with UserDate do
  begin
    <statements>
  end;
```

In the section of the code between the begin and end, you may refer to the field identifiers simply as Day, Month, and Year, respectively. For example, here is a rewritten version of the procedure InputDate of the preceding section which utilizes the with statement. Notice how much more compact this makes the statements.

```
procedure InputDate(var UserDate : Date);

  var J, Mnth, Yr : integer;
  {J is a loop counter
    Mnth is the numerical representation of the month
    Yr consists of the last two digits of the year}

  begin {InputDate}
    with UserDate do
      begin
        FirstMonth := Jan;
        write('Month(1-12): ');
        readln(Mnth);
        Month := FirstMonth;
        for J := 2 TO Mnth do
          Month := Succ(Month);
        write('Day (1-31): ');
        readln(Day);
        write('Year (19??): ');
        readln(Yr);
        Year := 1900 + Yr
      end {with}
    end; {InputDate}
```

A field identifier may be the same as another identifier in the same block. Ordinarily, this doesn't cause any problems because the field identifier is used preceded by the record variable identifier and a period, and these serve to distinguish the two uses of the field identifier. However, in using a with statement, this means of distinguishing the two uses of the field identifier vanishes and confusion can result.

As we have already observed, a record may have components which are records. You may use the with statement to omit more than one nested layer of field identifiers. For example, consider the variable Scheduled of type Appointment, where

```
type Appointment = record
                     Person : string[30];
                     When : Date;
                     Purpose : string[30]
                   end;
```

You may use a `with` statement of the form:

```
with Scheduled.When do
  begin
    .
    .
    .
  end;
```

Within the program segment defined by the `begin` and `end`, you may use the identifier `Day` instead of the more cumbersome `Schedules.When.Day`. However, the above caution about reused identifiers applies here as well. For example, using the identifier `Day` in the above program segment, where `Day` has a meaning other than `Scheduled.When.Day` will create confusion. You should take care never to let this happen.

You may also use the `with` statement in connection with several record variables simultaneously, as in the statement:

```
with BegDate, Purpose do
  begin
    .
    .
    .
  end;
```

This allows you to use the field identifiers of both `BegDate` and `Purpose` without including the record identifiers. Be very careful in using this construction, however, with record variables having the same declaration. This is a ticket to programming chaos, as illustrated by the statement:

```
with BegDate, EndDate do
  begin
    .
    .
    .
  end;
```

In this example, both `BegDate` and `EndDate` use the same field identifiers, since they are record variables of the same type. Thus, there is an ambiguity in this program segment as to the meaning, for example, of `Day`.

Moral: The `with` statement is very convenient, but requires some care in its use so that you don't create identifiers which have two different definitions in the same segment of code.

Variant Records

The structure of a record is determined by the record declaration. In some circumstances, it is helpful to allow the record structure to vary among several possible ones. Pascal allows this possibility using what are called variant records. For example, consider the following record structure:

```
type
  EmpStatus  = (Active, Retired, Quit, Fired);
  EmpSummary = record
                 Name : string[20];
                 Address : string[20];
                 case Status : EmpStatus of
                   Active : (Dept : string[20]);
                   Retired : (DateRet : Date);
                   Quit,
                   Fired : (DateTerm : Date;
                            Reason : string[20])
                 end
               end;
```

This record consists of a fixed part and a variant part. The fixed part remains constant for all employees and stores for all employees their name, address, just as in an ordinary record. Note, however, the case portion of the definition. It defines separate record structures depending on the value of the variable `Status`. For example if the value of `Status` is `Active`, then the record structure contains the field:

```
Dept : string[20];
```

which records the employee's department. If, however, the value of `Status` is `Retired`, then the record structure contains the field:

```
DateRet : Date;
```

which records the date of retirement. Finally, if `Status` has either of the values `Quit` or `Fired`, then the record structure has the fields:

```
DateTerm : Date;
Reason : string[20];
```

Note that the number of fields and their definition can vary with the value of `Status`. Moreover, note that `Status`—in addition to being used to determine the record structure—determines a field in the record. That is, you can refer to:

```
EmpSummary.Status
```

to obtain the value of `Status`.

A record such as EmpSummary is called a *variant record.* The field which determines the various record structures (Status in the above example) is called the *tag field* of the record.

Variant records are a very powerful tool in designing data structures to match the requirements of applications. However, you should be careful in using them. Indeed, you may refer to any of these fields, whether or not they make sense. For instance, you may refer to

```
EmpSummary.DateTerm
```

even for a record in which Status is Active. If you do, the value of the field will be garbage.

Example 1. Write a procedure which stores employee data into an record having the structure defined above.

Solution. The procedure must ask for the data in the record a field at a time. However, in the case of the tag field, you must employ a case statement to take into account the various possibilities.

To input the strings, we use the previously defined procedure InputStr. To input dates, we use the previously defined procedure InputDate.

Here is the implementation of the procedure.

```
procedure EnterData(var Employee : EmpSummary);

  var
    Status : 1..4;
  begin {EnterData}
    write('Enter name of employee: ');
    InputStr(Employee.Name);
    write('Address: ');
    InputStr(Employee.Address);
    writeln('Employee Status: ');
    writeln('1 = Active, 2 = Retired, 3 = Quit, 4 = Fired');
    readln(Status);
    case Status of
      1 : begin
            writeln('Department:');
            InputStr(Employee.Dept)
          end;
      2 : begin
            writeln('Date retired:');
            InputDate(Employee.DateRet)
          end;
      3,4 : begin
              writeln('Date terminated');
              InputDate(Employee.DateTerm);
              writeln('Reason terminated: ');
              InputStr(Employee.Reason);
            end
```

```
    end {case}
  end; {EnterData}
```

Sample Run. EnterData

```
Enter name of employee: John Becker
Address: 12 Oakview Court, Chicago, IL
Employee Status:
1 = Active, 2 = Retired, 3 = Quit, 4 = Fired
2
Date retired:
Month (1-12): 12
Day (1-31) : 14
Year (19??) : 86
```

Sets

A *set* is a data type made up of a collection of data objects of the same type. The objects are called the *elements* of the set and their common data type is called the *base type* of the set. A set is defined by listing its elements within brackets. Here are some examples of sets:

1. The set of integers between 1 and 10 inclusive:
   [1, 2, 3, ..., 10]
2. The set consisting of the letters 'a,' 'b,' 'c.'
   ['a,' 'b,' 'c']
3. The set consisting of the colors Red, Green, and Blue.
   [Red, Green, Blue]

A set is completely determined by its elements, without regard to order. That is, the sets [1, 2, 3] and [2, 1, 3] are regarded as the same.

An element of a set is said to be *in the set.* Thus, for instance, 1 is in [1, 2, 3], and 'a' is in ['a,' 'b,' 'c']. However, 5 is not in [1, 2, 3].

Sets are extremely useful in programming. For instance, in analyzing input data, suppose that you wish to determine whether or not the character `Ch` is one of the digits '0,' '1,' '2,' '3,' ..., '9.' You could do this using a compound condition of the form:

```
if (Ch >= '0') and (Ch <= '9') then ...
```

It is much simpler to use the set ['0'..'9'] which consists of the desired digits and to write the test in the form:

```
if Ch in ['0'..'9'] then ...
```

Or, you may introduce the variable Digit which has as its value the set ['0'..'9'] of digits and write the test in the more suggestive form:

```
if Ch in Digit then ...
```

Set Data Types, Constants, and Variables

Pascal allows sets consisting of elements from an ordinal type. The ordinal type may be one of the predefined ones: integer, char, or boolean. Or it may be a subrange type (such as 1..10) or a user-defined ordinal type (such as (Red, Green, Blue)). However, in Pascal, you may not have a set of elements from a non-ordinal type, such as real. Thus, for example, you may not have a set of the form (1.5, 3.8, 1E12).

In Pascal, a set can be explicitly defined by listing its elements within brackets, either individually or as part of a range. For instance, the set consisting of the integers 1, 2, 3, 4, 5, 10, 11, 20 can be written in the form:

```
[1..5, 10..11, 20]
```

The set [] which contains no elements is called the *null set.*

You can test whether a particular element belongs to a set using the reserved word in. For example, the expression:

```
1 in [1..5, 10..11, 20]
```

is true, whereas the expression:

```
18 in [1..5, 10..11, 20]
```

is false. Such expressions may be used in conditional statements just like expressions involving numerical conditions.

You specify a set data type by using the reserved words set of. Here are some examples of set data types:

```
type
  Numbers = set of 1..100;
  Digits = set of ['0..''9'];
  LowerCase = set of ['a..''z'];
  Color = set of [Red, Green, Blue];
  Committee = set of [John, Joe, Sally, Bill];
```

Corresponding to a set data type, we can define constants and variables. For instance, to hold the readings in an experiment, we can define the variable Readings to be of type Numbers.

```
var Readings : Numbers;
```

The values of `Readings` are then sets of integers and the following are valid assignments:

```
Readings := [1..10];
Readings := [15, 38, 42, 21];
```

In Turbo Pascal, a set can contain as many as 255 elements.

Union, Intersection, and Difference of Sets

In preceding chapters, we learned about numerical expressions, such as

1*2 + 3/5

X*Y*(Z+W)/3

A *numerical expression* involves a combination of various numbers (or variables with numerical values) via numerical operations. Pascal evaluates such an expression to obtain a number. Correspondingly, there are set expressions in which sets (or variables whose values are sets) are combined using various set operations. Pascal evaluates such expressions to form a set. Let us begin the subject of set expressions by introducing the various set operations which Pascal allows.

The *union* of the two sets A and B, denoted A+B, is the set consisting of the elements which are either in A or in B. For example,

```
[1,2,3] + [3,4,5]
```

is the union of the two sets [1, 2, 3] and [3, 4, 5] and is equal to:

```
[1,2,3,4,5]
```

Note that the element 3, which is common to the two sets is listed only once in the union. Here is another example:

```
[1..10]+[20..30]
```

is equal to the set:

```
[1..10, 20..30]
```

The *intersection* of the two sets A and B, denoted A*B, is the set consisting of the elements which are in common to A and B. For example,

```
[1,2,3]*[3,4,5]
```

is the set

```
[3]
```

As another example,

```
[1..10]*[20..30]
```

is equal to the null set [].

The difference of the sets A and B, denoted A–B, is the set of elements which are in A but not in B. For example,

```
[1,2,3] - [3,4,5]
```

is equal to the set:

```
[1,2]
```

Using the operations of union intersection and difference, you can form set expressions which can be evaluated as sets. Here are some examples of set expressions:

```
([1,2,3]*[1..10]) - [2,3,5]
A*B - C
```

Such expressions are evaluated according to similar rules of precedence as used for evaluation numerical expressions. That is, first all intersections (*) are performed in left-to-right order. Then unions (+) and differences (–) are performed in left-to-right order. Parentheses are evaluated first, with nested parentheses evaluated from the inside out. The exercises will provide some practice in evaluating various set expressions.

Relational Set Operators

In preceding chapters, we learned about relational numerical expressions, such as:

```
X = Y
X <= Y
X > Y
```

We used such expressions in conditional statements, such as:

```
if X = Y then ...
if X <= Y then ...
if X > Y then ...
```

There are corresponding simple relational set expressions. They are constructed by relating a pair of sets using one of the seven set relational operators: =, <>, <, >, <=, >=, in.

Two sets A and B are *equal* if they contain precisely the same elements. In this case, we write A = B. If A is not equal to B, then we write A <> B.

We say that the set A is *contained in* the set B provided that each element of A is contained in B. If A is contained in B, we write: A <= B. We write A >= B to mean that B is contained in A. We say that A is a subset of B provided that A is contained in B.

Here are some examples of simple set expressions formed from the relational operators =, <=, and >=.

```
[1,2] = [2,1] is true. (The order of the elements of a set is immaterial.)
[] <= [1] is true. (The null set is a subset of every set.)
['a'..'k'] <> ['a'..'z'] is true.
[1,2,3,4] <= [1..100] is true.
[true] >= [true,false] is false.
[Red, Green] >= [Red] is TRUE.
```

More general relational set expressions may be formed by joining simple relational set expressions using the logical operators `and`, `or`, and `not` as in the following examples:

```
(A <= B) or (A <> D)
(A <> B) and (A >= C)
NOT (A <= C)
```

Example 1 (Employment Agency). An employment agency stores data about its applicants for jobs. The file of applicants for secretarial positions records the following skills: typing, filing, word processing (wp), shorthand, research, telephone. Write a procedure which inputs data corresponding to an applicant for a secretarial position.

Solution. Each applicant's data has two parts: personal data and a set of skills. For the sake of simplicity, let's keep the personal data to a minimum and record only the application number in this category. The skills consist of a set drawn from the above list. This suggests that we define data types as follows:

```
type
  Tasks = (typing, filing, wp, shorthand, research, telephone)
  Profile = set of Tasks;
  Applicant = record
                AppNumber : 1..MaxInt;
                Skills : Profile
              end;
```

To input data corresponding to an applicant, we must ask which skills the applicant possesses. This can be done by asking a series of questions, one for each task and recording the answer. The `Skills` set for a given applicant can be built up by successively including in it the tasks for which the answers are 'Y.'

For displaying the various tasks listed, it is convenient to create an array `SkillWords` which contains names of the various tasks as strings. To do this, we can define a type

```
type SkillsList = array[1..6] of string[9];
```

Then `SkillWords` can be of type `SkillsList`. It is most convenient to store the words in `SkillsList` within the main program with the idea that the same list of skills will be needed to input data for many applicants. Here is the code needed to store the data in `SkillsList`:

```
SkillsList[1] := 'typing   ';
SkillsList[2] := 'filing   ';
SkillsList[3] := 'wp       ';
SkillsList[4] := 'shorthand';
SkillsList[5] := 'research ';
SkillsList[6] := 'telephone';
```

Here is the procedure.

```
procedure GetClientData(var Client : Applicant;
                        var SkillWords : SkillsList);

  var
    SkillNum : integer;
    Response : char;
    NewSkill : Tasks;

  begin
    with Client do
      begin
        NewSkill := typing; {Initial skill to add}
          Skills := [ ]; {Set Skills to empty set}
        write('Applicant Number: ');
        readln(AppNumber);
        for SkillNum := 1 to 6 do
          begin
            write('Does applicant have skills in: ');
            write(SkillsList[SkillNum]:0, '? (Y/N)');
            readln(Response);
            if Response in ['Y,' 'y'] then
            Skills := Skills + [NewSkill]; {Add skill}
            NewSkill = succ(NewSkill) {Go to next skill}
          end
      end
    end {with}
  end; {GetClientData}
```

```
Sample Run. GetClientData

Procedure call: GetClientData(Client, SkillsList);
Result:
Applicant Number: 4832
Does applicant have skills in: typing   ? (Y/N)
Y
Does applicant have skills in: filing   ? (Y/N)
N
Does applicant have skills in: wp       ? (Y/N)
Y
Does applicant have skills in: shorthand? (Y/N)
Y
Does applicant have skills in: research ? (Y/N)
N
Does applicant have skills in: telephone? (Y/N)
N
```

More About Arrays

Scope Rules and Arrays

An array may be defined within any block. If defined within an interior block, the array is a local identifier for the block and the usual scope rules apply. If an array is defined in the outermost block, then its components are global variables.

Passing Arrays to Functions and Procedures

You may pass arrays to functions and procedures. However, the syntax of parameter passing requires that you assign a type name to the array you are passing. Thus, for example, it is incorrect to write:

```
procedure Avg(var Grades : array[1..5] of integer);
{Error}
```

Rather, you must assign a type name to array[1..5] of integer and use this type name in the procedure header. For example, you might call the type `Test`. Then the type declaration for `Test` would be:

```
type Test = array[1..5] of integer;
```

A valid procedure header would then be:

```
procedure Avg(var Grades : Test);
```

With this minor syntactic caution, arrays may be passed via either variable or value parameters to procedures and functions.

Pascal allows you to pass arrays using either value or variable parameters. However, you should get into the habit of using only variable parameters. Here's why. Arrays are memory hogs. Consider, for example, an array declared as `array[1..1000 of integer]`. This array has 1,000 components and each integer requires 2 bytes of memory. As a result, the array requires 2,000 memory locations. If you pass this array via a value parameter, the procedure or function is given its own copy of the array. This uses another 2,000 memory locations. If you pass the array via a variable parameter, the procedure or function is passed only the address of the first component of the array.

There may be times when you will want to use value parameters, however. For example, if the array will be manipulated in the procedure but you wish the original to remain unchanged. In this case, you will need to make a copy of the original array anyway, so you may as well let Pascal do it for you by using a value parameter.

Earlier in this book, we advised you never to use variable parameters with a function. Limitations on memory usually force us to allow an exception for array passing. However, if you pass an array to a function, you should exercise extreme care not to create side effects.

Multidimensional Arrays

Our discussion of arrays has so far centered on arrays with a single column of entries, the so-called one-dimensional arrays. In many applications, however, it is necessary to deal with arrays having several columns. For instance, here is a table of temperatures at various times in various cities.

Time	Los Angeles	San Diego	San Francisco
9:00 AM	58	61	49
12:00 PM	62	66	52
3:00 PM	65	72	60
6:00 PM	62	68	57
9:00 PM	54	58	53

The data in this data structure consists of 15 integers, arranged in three columns with five entries per column. Suppose that you wish to store the data in a single array, namely an array with two subscripts, one corresponding to row names, and one to column names. An array with two subscripts is called a two-dimensional array. In this example, let's number the rows with the integers 1 to 5 and the columns with cities from the data type:

```
type City = (LosAngeles, SanDiego, SanFrancisco)
```

Let's name the array to store the data Temperatures. Then the array may be declared using a statement of the form:

```
var Temperature : array[1..5,LosAngeles..SanFrancisco]
                  of integer;
```

or equivalently

```
var Temperature : array[1..5, City] of integer;
```

The data may be stored in the array using a sequence of assignment statements of the form:

```
Temperature[1,LosAngeles] := 58;
Temperature[3,SanDiego] := 72;
Temperature[5,SanFrancisco] := 53;
```

Pascal allows arrays with any number of subscripts. A subscript may be any ordinal type and the various subscripts can be of differing types. For instance, the array Temperature has two subscripts, the first running over the range 1..5, and the second over the range LosAngeles..SanFrancisco. Each subscript is called a *dimension* of the array. Arrays with a single index are called *one-dimensional,* arrays with two indexes *two-dimensional,* and so forth.

Here is a declaration for a three-dimensional array:

```
var SalesReport : array[1..10, 1..4, 1..3] of real;
```

This array has 10*4*3 = 120 components, each of which stores a real number. Here is an assignment statement which assigns one of these components a value:

```
SalesReport[2,3,1] := 42.5;
```

As with one-dimensional arrays, the indexes may come from any ordinal type and a single array may use indexes of several different types. Note, however, that the component values of an array must belong to the same ordinal data type.

In dealing with multidimensional arrays, you should exercise great care in assigning values to components, especially if there are two indexes which share common values. It is very easy to confuse the components of SalesReport[5,2,3] and SalesReport[5,3,2], especially if you are computing indexes as values of expressions. If a program is producing strange results, trace through the array values you have assigned and see whether you have mixed up your indexes.

A Detailed Example

Let's now return to the program AgeInDays which we introduced in Chapter 2. We are now at the point where we can understand the program. We begin by declaring two user-defined types:

```
type
  TypeMonthArray = array[1..12] of integer;
  TypeDate       = record
                     Year : word;
                     Month : word;
                     Day : word
                   end;
```

We then declare a variable MonthLen of type TypeMonthArray. The array MonthLen stores the lengths of the months. That is, MonthLen[1] stores 31, the number of days in January, MonthLen[2] stores 28, the normal number of days in February, and so forth. The variables BirthDay and CurrentDate are of type TypeDate. The program begins by initializing the variables. First it assigns the lengths of months, then it determines the value of CurrentDate from the system clock.

The program then asks the user for his or her birthday. This is handled in the procedure GetInput. The date is read in as a string. Then it is broken down into its component parts (month, day, year). Then the component parts are converted into numerical values using the procedure val. Finally, the procedure tests the date for validity. (All numbers must be positive, the month number must be less than 13, and the day of the month must correspond to a real day.) The program keeps requesting a birthdate until a valid date is entered.

The program then determines the age of the person in days. This is a complex computation since it involves the number of days in the birth year, the number of elapsed days in the current year, and a tally of leap years during the person's life. The count of days proceeds one year at a time, from the birth year to the current year. The age in days is accumulated in the variable Age.

Finally, the result is displayed.

You should study the code of this program very carefully. It incorporates everything we have learned up to this point about arrays, records, procedures, and functions, as well as numerical calculation and string manipulation.

Sorting and Searching Using Arrays

In many applications, it is necessary to arrange the components of a list in some sort of order. The simplest and most familiar types of order are those associated with numbers and letters. Numbers can be arranged according to their numerical size, in either ascending or descending order. Letters can be arranged in either alphabetical or reverse alphabetical order. The process of arranging a list in order is called *sorting*. In this section, we will discuss some of the basics of sorting. For simplicity, we will confine ourselves to lists of numbers, sorted according to numerical size. In the next chapter, we will return to sorting and consider the sorting of text data in alphabetical order.

Again for simplicity, let's assume throughout this section that we are to sort lists in increasing numerical order. To sort lists in decreasing numerical order, you can make slight alterations in the procedures we develop.

Let's begin by stating a problem in precise terms in a Pascal setting. Suppose that we have an array Arr of real numbers, such as:

```
J       Arr[J]
1       90
2       38
3       15
4       48
5       80
6        1
```

We wish to rearrange the components of the array so that they are in numerically increasing order. That is, we wish to change the value of Arr[] to:

```
J       Arr[J]
1        1
2       15
3       38
4       48
5       80
6       90
```

Of course, in this simple case, we can do the rearrangement by inspection and don't need a computer program to solve the problem. However, in many applications, the lists involved have hundreds or even thousands of components. To handle such large lists, it is necessary to have an algorithm for obtaining the new, sorted, value of `Arr[]`. There are many such algorithms known, of varying degrees of complexity. Generally speaking, the more complex algorithms balance their complexity with speed of operation.

The Bubble Sort Algorithm

In this section, we present two simple algorithms for sorting which are variations on a very simple idea, called the *bubble sort algorithm.* You pay for the algorithm's great simplicity with its slow execution speed.

The bubble sort algorithm (and just about all sorting algorithms) sorts a list in a succession of elementary steps (called *passes*) in which only two components are interchanged. Each pass consists of the following steps:

The Nth Pass of the Bubble Sort Algorithm

Compare consecutive components, starting from the bottom of the list and proceeding up. In any comparison, interchange components so that the smallest one is on the top. Stop with the first comparison involving the `N`th component from the top of the list.

For instance, let's carry out the first pass using the above array as an example. In this case, `N=1` so that we compare all the components. Start at the bottom of the list and compare 1 and 80. Since 1 is smaller, interchange the two to get:

```
90
38
15
48
 1
80
```

Now perform the comparison between 1 and 48. Since 1 is smaller, the two are interchanged.

```
90
38
15
 1
48
80
```

The next comparison is 1 and 15. Again, an interchange takes place.

```
90
38
 1
15
48
80
```

The next comparison is 1 and 38. Again, 1 comes out on top.

```
90
 1
38
15
48
80
```

Finally, the last comparison is 1 and 90. Again, the 1 comes out on top.

```
 1
90
38
15
48
80
```

This completes the first pass of the algorithm. Note that after this pass, the 1 is in its proper position, as the least component in the list.

For the second pass, we start at the bottom of the list again and compare consecutive entries again. We stop with the second component from the top. (There is no point in comparing with the top component, since it is already in its proper position and will therefore not require any interchange.) The result of the second pass is:

```
 1
15
90
38
48
80
```

Now the first two components, 1 and 15, are in their proper places.

For the third pass, we start at the bottom of the list again and compare consecutive entries stopping with the third entry from the top:

```
 1
15
38
90
48
80
```

Here are the results of the fourth pass:

```
 1
15
38
48
90
80
```

Here are the results of the fifth pass:

```
 1
15
38
48
80
90
```

The list is now in order. For a list of 6 components, it took 5 passes through the bubble sort algorithm. In general, for a list of N components, it generally takes N–1 passes. If you are lucky, the list may be in order in fewer passes. However, as the above example shows, some lists require the full N–1 passes.

The bubble sort is so named because, if you think of the value of each component as measuring its physical weight and think of each component as a bubble, then the bubble sort allows each "bubble" to rise in accordance with its weight. The lightest bubbles rise to the top and rise earliest.

Let's now write a Pascal procedure BubbleSort which implements the above algorithm to sort a list of real numbers stored in an array. We will want to pass the array to be sorted to the procedure, so let's define a data type corresponding to the procedure. To make things match up with the above discussion, let's consider 6-component arrays. Accordingly, we define the type:

```
type NumArray = array[1..6] of real ;
```

Since we will be working with arrays of size 6, it seems reasonable to define the variable ArraySize and assign it the value 6.

```
ArraySize := 6;
```

We will assume that both NumArray and ArraySize are declared outside the bubble sort procedure.

The heart of the algorithm is the swapping of values between consecutive components of the list. This suggests that we start off with a procedure Swap for accomplishing this. The following procedure swaps the values of the variables First and Second. The value of First is assigned to Second and the value of Second is assigned to First. To make these assignments, the value of `First` needs to be temporarily stashed in some other variable, in this case the local variable `Temp`.

```
procedure Swap(var First, Second : real);
{Swap the values of the variables First and Second}

  var
    Temp : real;

  begin {Swap}
    Temp := First;
    First := Second;
    Second := Temp
  end; {Swap}
```

We could make this procedure local to the sorting procedure. However, since it is useful in its own right, let's leave it as an independent procedure.

Now we are ready for the procedure `BubbleSort` itself. There are two loops, one to make repeated passes (a loop controlled with variable `PassNum` which runs from 1 to `ArraySize-1`), and one to make comparisons between consecutive pairs of components (which we control with the variable `Pos` which measures the position of the topmost component). With each comparison, the position goes down so the value of `Pos` decreases. The first comparison occurs with `Pos` equal to `ArraySize-1` and the last with `Pos` equal to `PassNum`. Here is the coding for the algorithm.

```
procedure BubbleSort(var Arr : NumArray;
                     var ArraySize : integer);

  var
    PassNum, Pos : integer; {Loop counters}

  begin {BubbleSort}
    for PassNum := 1 TO ArraySize-1 do
      for Pos := ArraySize-1 downto PassNum do
        if Arr[Pos] Arr[Pos+1] then
          Swap(Arr[Pos],Arr[Pos+1])
  end; {BubbleSort}
```

In order to use the procedure for a different sized list, you must redefine the type `NumArray`. For example, to sort a list of 100 numbers, you must replace the definition of the type `NumArray` with:

```
type NumArray = array[1..100] OF real;
```

Moreover, you must set:

```
ArraySize := 100;
```

As sorting algorithms go, the bubble sort is extremely inefficient. Even on a fast computer, sorting a list of 1,000 entries using the bubble sort method will usually take many minutes. One source of this inefficiency is the fact that the bubble sort doesn't know whether the list is already sorted. If the list ends up sorted on an early pass, the bubble sort just keeps on going with repeated passes, even though no interchanges take place.

One way to improve the bubble sort is to introduce a flag, called `SortFlag`, which is usually false, but is set equal to true after an interchange takes place. Then at the end of each pass, the procedure can inspect `SortFlag` to determine if any interchanges took place. If so, then the sorting process should continue for another pass. Thus, the procedure resets `SortFlag` to false and goes to the next pass. If, however, at the end of a pass, `SortFlag` is false, then no interchanges took place during the pass. This means that the list is already sorted. In this case, the procedure ends.

Here is the code for the improved version of the bubble sort procedure.

```
procedure BubbleSort2(var Arr : NumArray ;
                      var ArraySize : integer);
{A faster version of the bubble sort algorithm.}

  var
    PassNum, Pos : integer;
    SortFlag : boolean;

  begin {BubbleSort2}
    Sortflag := False;
    PassNum := 0;
    while not SortFlag do
      begin {while}
        SortFlag := true;
        PassNum := PassNum + 1;
        for Pos := ArraySize-1 downto PassNum do
          if arr[Pos] arr[Pos+1] then
            begin
              Swap(Arr[Pos],Arr[Pos+1]);
              SortFlag := false
            end
      end {while}
  end; {BubbleSort2}
```

The Selection Sort Algorithm

There are many different algorithms used for sorting. To give you some idea of the variety, let's discuss a second method of sorting an array of numbers, the so-called `selection sort`. As in the bubble sort algorithm, the selection sort operates as a sequence of passes. Each pass involves a number of interchanges. The selection sort will generally involve fewer interchanges but more passes than the bubble sort.

The Nth Pass of the Selection Sort Algorithm

Determine the smallest entry among the last N entries. Interchange the largest entry with the Nth entry. To sort a list of N entries into increasing order requires N–1 passes.

Here is a concrete example of the selection sort applied to the list:

```
90 38 15 48 1 80
```

Pass 1. Consider the entries beginning with the first. The smallest is 1. Therefore, we interchange the 1 with the first entry to obtain the modified list:

```
1 90 38 48 15 80
```

Pass 2. Consider the entries beginning with the second. The smallest is 15. Therefore, we interchange 15 with the second entry 90 to obtain:

```
1 15 38 48 90 80
```

Pass 3. Consider the entries beginning with the third. The smallest is 38. It is already in the third position, so no interchange need take place. The list remains the same:

```
1 15 38 48 90 80
```

Pass 4. Consider the entries beginning with the fourth. The smallest is 48. Again no interchange takes place.

```
1 15 38 48 90 80
```

Pass 5. Consider the entries beginning with the fifth. The smallest is 80. Interchange 80 with the fifth entry to obtain.

```
1 15 38 48 80 90
```

The original list had 6 elements and after 6 – 1 = 5 passes, the list is now sorted into ascending order.

As with the bubble sort, we can describe the selection sort for sorting the elements of an integer array `Arr` of size `ArraySize`. Here is a procedure for carrying out the selection sort on such an array.

```
procedure SelectionSort(var Arr : NumArray;
                            ArraySize : integer);

  var
    Temp, PassNum, Pos : integer;
    {PassNum is the pass number,
    Pos is the position of the entry being compared,
    Temp temporarily holds an array value during an
    interchange}

  begin {SelectionSort}
    for PassNum := 1 to ArraySize -1 do
      for Pos := PassNum+1 to ArraySize do
        if Arr[PassNum] Arr[Pos] then
          Swap(Arr[PassNum], Arr[Pos])
  end; {SelectionSort}
```

Sorting is an immense field within computer science, a field within which research is still going on. Indeed, sorting is an extremely important operation for applications. However, it is one which can take up large amounts of computer time, even on the fastest machines. Accordingly, the search goes on for ever more efficient sorting algorithms.

7 Turbo Pascal Units and Error Handling

Thus far, we have designed programs of only modest length. However, programs of even moderate length typically consist of hundreds of lincs of source code. A complex program can consist of hundreds of thousands of lines of source code! Clearly, in dealing with programs of such magnitude, you must take great care in planning and organizing. In this chapter, we discuss the notion of a *unit*, which is one method for modularizing large programs.

As we shall see, Turbo Pascal comes with several precompiled units consisting of procedures for performing the most command tasks. In this chapter, we will discuss the contents of one of these units, `Crt`, which contains procedures and functions for *screen handling.*

In addition, we will discuss two topics which are closely related to screen handling, namely *keyboard handling* and *input/output error handling.*

Introduction to Units

What Is a Unit?

A *unit* is a file of precompiled code which can be selectively used within a program. A unit may contain declarations of constants, variables, and data types. Furthermore, a unit may contain procedures and functions. A unit may consist of self-contained code or it may refer to other units. You can arrange your code into units which mirror the structure of your program, thereby modularizing your code. A skillful use of units can guarantee that no single source code file is too large and that details are relegated to their proper level.

Once a unit is created, you may use its declared elements in any program. Thus units give you a simple mechanism for creating reusable program elements.

Predefined versus User-Defined Units

Turbo Pascal comes with a number of predefined units which provide many useful procedures and functions. Among these predefined units are:

Crt	provides screen and keyboard handling
Printer	provides a convenient printer interface
DOS	provides file handling and other DOS functions
Graph	provides graphics routines
System	provides access to system functions
Overlay	provides access to routines to manage overlays

In addition, you may create your own units.

Declaring Units Within a Program

A unit is contained in a file whose name has the extension TPU. To make use of the program elements within a unit, declare the unit with a *Uses* clause placed just after the program header. For instance, to make use of the Graph unit, place the declaration

```
Uses Graph;
```

just after the program header. Note that the file extension TPU should be omitted.

You may declare a number of units with a single `Uses` statement by separating the unit names by commas.

Once a unit has been declared, you may use the program elements anywhere within the program, just as if they had been declared explicitly in the outermost block.

Where to Store Compiled Units

When you compile your program, the compiler requires the code for any program elements declared in units. It will look for such program code in the appropriate TPU files. The compiler will first look for a TPU file in the *current directory* (the directory where you are creating your source code). It will then look for a TPU file in the Units directory, which is set by the command **Options-Directories-Units**. If a declared unit cannot be found, the compiler will report an error and quit.

The Crt Unit

As a way of getting acquainted with the application of units, let's explore one of the predefined units, namely `Crt`. This unit provides program elements for manipulating the screen and keyboard. Let's discuss the various program elements which this unit contains.

Setting Screen Mode

The unit `Crt` contains the procedure `TextMode` which allows you to set the text mode of the display. The syntax of this procedure is:

```
TextMode(Mode)
```

where `Mode` is one of the following constants (declared within the unit)

```
BW40 (black and white 40 column mode)
BW80 (black and white 80 column mode)
Mono (monochrome mode)
CO40 (color 40 column mode)
CO80 (color 80 column mode)
Font8x8 (use 8 bit × 8 bit characters-for 43 or 50 line EGA or VGA)
```

In order to speed screen display, you may declare the display to be a file of text using a declaration of the form:

```
var Screen : text;
```

and then associating the screen with the variable `Screen` using the `Crt` procedure `AssignCrt`:

```
AssignCrt(Screen);
```

Cursor Motion

Crt includes the GotoXY procedure for moving the cursor. The statement:

```
GotoXY(20,15);
```

moves the cursor to column 20 and row 15.

The Crt variables WhereX and WhereY allow you to read the current position of the cursor. For instance, the statements:

```
X := WhereX;
Y := WhereY;
```

assign to X and Y, respectively, the current column and row of the cursor.

Character Attributes

Within Crt are assigned constants which represent the various colors. The actual numbers assigned to the colors are not important. The point of declaring the constants is to allow you to call the colors by name rather than by their codes. The colors declared within Crt are:

```
Black
Blue
Green
Cyan
Red
Magenta
Brown
LightGray
DarkGray
LightBlue
LightGreen
LightCyan
LightRed
LightMagenta
Yellow
White
Blink
```

A color is a constant of type word.

Crt declares a byte variable TextAttr which holds the current text attribute. This byte records the color, intensity, and blinking attributes for subsequent text to be displayed. To set the intensity portion of TextAttr, use one of these statements:

```
HighVideo; {High intensity}
LowVideo; {Low intensity}
NormVideo; {Original intensity at startup}
```

To set the color portion of TextAttr use the procedure

```
TextColor(Color:word);
```

To set the blinking attribute of TextAttr use the statement:

```
TextColor(Blink);
```

To set the background color, use the procedure

```
TextBackground(Color:word);
```

Displaying Characters and Editing

Crt includes a number of procedures for performing editing, as follows:

```
ClrEol; {Erase the screen from the cursor position to the end of the line}
ClrScr; {Erase the screen}
Delay(Time : word); {Halt the program for Time milliseconds}
DelLine; {Delete the line containing the cursor and scroll the screen}
InsLine; {Insert a blank line at the cursor position.
         Move the cursor to the first character of this line.}
```

Using Windows

Crt includes the ability to restrict work to a window of the screen. To create a window, say from column 5, row 5, to column 60, row 15, use the statement:

```
Window(5,5,60,15);
```

The cursor is initially moved to the upper left corner of the window. All subsequent write statements will be limited to the window.

The top and bottom X positions on the window are given by the values Lo(WindMin) and Lo(WindMax), respectively. The right and left Y positions on the window are given by the values Hi(WindMin) and Hi(WindMax), respectively.

Sound

The Crt unit includes two procedures to create sound. To create a sound of 3000 hz, use the statement:

```
Sound(3000);
```

The sound continues until it is turned off by the statement:

```
NoSound;
```

Miscellaneous Contents of Crt

There are several other variables and functions of a more technical variety which are also included within `Crt`. Here is a list of them:

```
CheckBreak
CheckEof
CheckSnow
DirectVideo
LastMode
```

Consult your manual for details of these.

Keyboard Handling

In addition to the program elements described above, the unit `Crt` provides the functions `KeyPressed` and `ReadKey`. The function `KeyPressed` is a function with boolean value which returns true when there is a keystroke waiting to be read and false otherwise. This function allows you to read input if it is there, but otherwise to proceed with the program. Here is the code which accomplishes exactly that:

```
if KeyPressed then
    read(Ch);
```

The function `ReadKey` reads a keystroke from the keyboard. If there is no keystroke, this function waits until there is one. The syntax of this function is:

```
function ReadKey : char
```

This function returns one of the characters of the IBM character set, whose ASCII codes range from 0 to 255. If a null (ASCII code 0) is returned, then this indicates that the character is an *extended* character (i.e., it corresponds to one of the function keys, arrow keys, etc.) The extended character can be then obtained by using `ReadKey` a second time. The interpretation of the character so obtained is according to the following table:

Key	Second Character Returned
F1–F10	Chr(59)–Chr(68)
Rt Arrow	Chr(77)
Left Arrow	Chr(75)
Down Arrow	Chr(80)
Up Arrow	Chr(72)
Home	Chr(71)
End	Chr(79)
PgUp	Chr(73)
PgDn	Chr(81)
Ins	Chr(82)
Del	Chr(83)

Error Handling

Detecting Input/Output Errors

Input/output errors are run-time errors that occur because of incorrect user interaction with the program. Examples are:

1. Entering data of an incorrect type from the keyboard. (e.g., char instead of integer or real instead of integer).
2. Specifying an incorrect file name, with the result that the program cannot find the file specified.
3. Not inserting a diskette into the diskette drive, with the result that the computer reports a read error in attempting to access the drive.

There are two possible responses to such errors. The active response is to stop the program and report the error to the user. The passive response is to allow the user to react to the error and continue the program after correcting the error. The default response is active. And this is the approach we have been observing until now.

You can control the response to errors using the {$I} compiler directive. {$I+} turns on the active response and {$I–} turns it off. These compiler directives may be used for an entire program or only for a particular section of a program (possibly only for single statements).

If {$I–} is used, then the variable IOResult is used to record the result of input/output operations. This function returns an integer which is 0 if no error has occurred and a non-zero value if an error has occurred. After returning a value, IOResult is reset to 0 until a subsequent error occurs. For example, here is a code fragment which asks the user to input an integer. To guard against the possibility that the user types in an invalid input, the {$I–} directive is used. If the user types in an incorrect value, the code segment requests reentry of the value.

```
OK := false;
while not OK do
  begin
    write('Input integer value: ');
    {$I-} readln(Value); {$I+}
    OK := (IOResult = 0)
    If not OK
      then
        writeln('Error. Non-integer value')
  end;
```

Here is a list of the standard Turbo Pascal procedures which can generate input/output errors:

Append

Assign

BlockRead

BlockWrite

ChDir

Close

Erase

Exec

Flush

GetDir

MkDir

Read

Readln

Rename

Reset

Rewrite

RmDir

Seek

Write

Writeln

IOResult Codes

Actually, the value returned by `IOResult` gives an explicit description of the nature of the error which most recently caused `IOResult` to be assigned a value. All of the error conditions correspond to non-zero integers. The number of possible different values is rather large. Rather than list them, we merely refer you to the table contained in Appendix A of the *Turbo Pascal Programmer's Guide.*

Error Handling Procedures

In dealing with errors, it is customary to build a single procedure, called an *error handler,* which responds to all input/output errors. Any time within the program a non-zero value of `IOResult` is detected, a call is made to the error handling routine. This routine examines the value of `IOResult` to determine the nature of the error. The error handler then displays a message to the user indicating the error and an action to take (e.g., repeat the input, insert the correct diskette, etc.) The error handler then passes control back to the calling routine, which should allow the user to continue as suggested by the error handler. If the user makes another input/output error, then the program is sent to the error handler again and the error analysis is repeated.

Building Your Own Units

Now that we have seen how useful units can be, let's show how to build your own units. To do this, let's return to the program `AgeInDays`, which was introduced in Chapter 2. If you will recall, that program computes the user's age in days. It used a number of procedures and introduced data types `TypeMonthArray` and `TypeDate`. Let's create a unit which declares these two data types as well as the procedures use in the main program. Also, let's include within the unit the function `LeapYear` (which might be useful elsewhere).

The Source Code of a Unit

The first step in creating a unit is to create the source code for the unit, just as if you were creating the source code for a program. Let's call the unit `Age`. The source code for the unit is shown in Listing 7.1.

There are a number of things to note. First observe that the first line is a header which begins with the keyword `Unit` followed by the unit name and a semicolon. Next, is the keyword `interface` without a semicolon. The interface section of a unit lists the data types and procedure headers, exactly as they appeared in the program. The interface section lists the program elements which will be usable by other programs.

Following the interface section is the keyword `implementation`, again without a semicolon. The implementation section of a unit lists the source code for the procedures and functions declared in the interface section. Note that the data types, constants, and variables of the interface need not be repeated in this section. However, any other units referred to within the code must be declared via a `Uses` declaration.

Note that any program elements which are local to the blocks within the implementation may not be used by programs using the unit. Rather, the local elements are strictly private to the internal code of the unit. Thus, for instance, the procedure `InitDate` may not be used outside of the unit. The same applies to the type `TypeDateStr`.

At the end of the source code in the implementation is the keyword `end` followed by a period.

Listing 7.1. Source code for the unit Age

```
unit Age;
{Contains the data types and procedures for AgeInDays}

interface

  type
    TypeMonthArray = array [1..12] of integer;
    TypeDate = record
                 Year,
                 Month,
                 Day : word
               end;

  procedure InitVariables(var MonthLen : TypeMonthArray;
                          var CurrentDate : TypeDate);

  function LeapYear(    YearToTest : word) : boolean;

  procedure GetInput(var BirthDay : TypeDate;
                         MonthLen : TypeMonthArray);

  procedure DetermineAge(var Age : word;
                             BirthDay : TypeDate;
                             CurrentDate : TypeDate;
                             MonthLen : TypeMonthArray);

  procedure PrintOutput( Age : word);

implementation

  uses
    crt,
    dos;

  procedure InitVariables(var MonthLen : TypeMonthArray;
                          var CurrentDate : TypeDate);

    procedure InitDate(var CurrentDate : TypeDate);

      var
        DummyVar : word;

      begin {InitDate}
        with CurrentDate do
          GetDate (Year, Month, Day, DummyVar)
      end; {InitDate}

    procedure InitMonthVar(var MonthLen : TypeMonthArray);

      begin {InitMonthVar}
        MonthLen[1] := 31;
        MonthLen[2] := 28;
```

```
      MonthLen[3]  := 31;
      MonthLen[4]  := 30;
      MonthLen[5]  := 31;
      MonthLen[6]  := 30;
      MonthLen[7]  := 31;
      MonthLen[8]  := 31;
      MonthLen[9]  := 30;
      MonthLen[10]  := 31;
      MonthLen[11]  := 30;
      MonthLen[12]  := 31
    end; {InitMonthVar}

  begin {InitVariables}
    InitMonthVar(MonthLen);
    InitDate(CurrentDate);
  end; {InitVariables}

function LeapYear( YearToTest : word) : boolean;

  begin {LeapYear}
    LeapYear := (YearToTest mod 4 = 0) and
                ((YearToTest mod 100 <> 0) or
                 (YearToTest mod 400 = 0))
  end; {LeapYear}

procedure GetInput(var BirthDay  : TypeDate;
                       MonthLen  : TypeMonthArray);

  type
    TypeDateStr = string[10];

  var
    DateEntered : TypeDateStr;
    ValidDate : boolean;

  function NextPart(var DateEntered : TypeDateStr) : word;

    var
      NumString : TypeDateStr;
      ErrorCode, ActualNum : integer;

    begin {NextPart}
      NumString := '';
      repeat
        NumString := concat(NumString, copy(DateEntered, 1, 1));
        DateEntered := copy(DateEntered, 2, length(DateEntered) - 1)
      until (DateEntered [1] = '/') or (length(DateEntered) = 0);
      DateEntered := copy(DateEntered, 2, length(DateEntered) - 1);
      val (NumString, ActualNum, ErrorCode);
      NextPart := ActualNum;
      if (ErrorCode <> 0)
        then
          NextPart := 0
    end; {NextPart}
```

```
  begin {GetInput}
    repeat
      clrscr;
      write('Enter birth date in --/--/---- form: ');
      readln(DateEntered);
      BirthDay.Month := NextPart(DateEntered);
      BirthDay.Day := NextPart(DateEntered);
      BirthDay.Year := NextPart(DateEntered);
      ValidDate := ((BirthDay.Month < 13) and (BirthDay.Month > 0)) and
                   (((BirthDay.Day <= MonthLen[BirthDay.Month]) and
                     (BirthDay.Day > 0)) or
                     (LeapYear(BirthDay.Year) and
                     (BirthDay.Month = 2) and (BirthDay.Day = 29))) and
                   (BirthDay.Year <> 0);
    until ValidDate
  end; {GetInput}

procedure DetermineAge(var Age : word;
                           BirthDay : TypeDate;
                           CurrentDate : TypeDate;
                           MonthLen : TypeMonthArray);

  var
    YearCounter : word;

  function NumDaysPastInYr(    DateToDo : TypeDate;
                               MonthLen : TypeMonthArray) : word;

      var
        TempValue, MonthCounter : word;

    begin {NumDaysPastInYr}
      TempValue := 0;
      for MonthCounter := 1 to (DateToDo.Month - 1) do
        TempValue := TempValue + MonthLen[MonthCounter];
      TempValue := TempValue + DateToDo.Day;
      if LeapYear(DateToDo.Year) and (DateToDo.Month > 2)
        then
          TempValue := TempValue + 1;
      NumDaysPastInYr := TempValue
    end; {NumDaysPastInYr}

  function NumDaysInYr( YearToDetermine : word) : word;

    begin {NumDaysInYr}
      if LeapYear(YearToDetermine)
        then
          NumDaysInYr := 366
        else
          NumDaysInYr := 365
    end; {NumDaysInYr}
```

```
  begin {DetermineAge}
    Age := NumDaysInYr(BirthDay.Year) -
              NumDaysPastInYr(BirthDay, MonthLen);
    for YearCounter := (BirthDay.Year + 1) to (CurrentDate.Year - 1) do
      Age := Age + NumDaysInYr(YearCounter);
    if (BirthDay.Year = CurrentDate.Year)
      then
        Age := Age + NumDaysPastInYr(CurrentDate, MonthLen) -
                 NumDaysInYr(CurrentDate.Year)
      else
        Age := Age + NumDaysPastInYr(CurrentDate, MonthLen)
  end; {DetermineAge}

procedure PrintOutput( Age : word);

  begin {PrintOutput}
    writeln('You are ', Age, ' days old.');
    readln
  end; {PrintOutput}

end. {Age}
```

Compiling a Unit

Once you have entered the source code for a unit, compile it exactly as if it were a program. You will get the same sort of error messages as you would for any syntax errors in a program. Moreover, you will get additional messages indicating any deviation from the syntax of a unit which we have described. The compiler knows that you are compiling a unit rather than a program, since the source code begins with the keyword `Unit`.

To create a TPU file corresponding to the unit, compile the unit to disk rather than memory. The compiler in this case creates a unit file named AGE.TPU.

Using a Unit

To use the unit within a program, just list the unit name in a `Uses` declaration. For example, Listing 7.2 shows the revised version of the program `AgeInDays` which makes use of the unit. Note how simple the program is in comparison with the original program. All of the details are buried in the procedures of the unit. Note that we must still declare the variables used in the program since we did not include these within the unit. (We could have, but chose not to.)

Listing 7.2. Using the unit Age

```
program AgeInDays2;
{Revised version of AgeInDays, using Age unit.}

  uses
    crt,
    dos,
    Age;

  var
    MonthLen : TypeMonthArray;
    BirthDay, CurrentDate : TypeDate;
    Days : word;

  begin {AgeInDays2}
    InitVariables(MonthLen, CurrentDate);
    GetInput(BirthDay, MonthLen);
    DetermineAge(Days, BirthDay, CurrentDate, MonthLen);
    PrintOutput(Days)
  end. {AgeInDays2}
```

After seeing the simplicity of the above program, we can devise the following strategy for using units to structure a program. Design the program at the first level and create source code which calls procedures that are not yet written. Create a unit containing headers for the desired procedures, but create an implementation section which has empty blocks for the procedures. Both the unit and the program will compile at this stage. Moreover, you are now through with the first level of design and can now concentrate on the procedures in the unit, which constitute the second level of design. These procedures in turn, may reference more detailed procedures in a unit representing the third level of design. And so forth. Units allow you to implement top-down design and simultaneously keep the size of the source code files as small as possible.

8 Objects and Methods

As you may have already noticed, the subtitle of this book mentions *object-oriented programming*, but we have not as yet said a word about this topic. We haven't forgotten! In order to discuss object-oriented programming, it is necessary first to have a command of the basic notions of Turbo Pascal, especially user-defined data types, records, and units, all of which have counterparts in the study of objects.

In this chapter, we introduce object-oriented programming and its fundamental elements, objects, and methods.

What Is Object-Oriented Programming?

We have already mentioned on several occasions that even medium-length programs can be quite long and involve complex interrelationships among the various parts of the program. Procedures and functions call other procedures and functions, which in turn call other procedures and functions, and so on. It is often very difficult to cut through this maze of calls to determine the origin of a bug. Other complications arise from the fact that source code is maintained in a number of different files, each of which may be worked on by more than one programmer. The principal problem of programming today is how to plan and reliably develop programs not subject to the problems we have just mentioned.

We have already presented a few ideas which can provide a partial solution to the problem. Our discussions of top-down design showed how to plan programs by considering levels of detail from the most general down to the most specific. Careful planning is, in itself, an aid in avoiding errors in complex programs or in tracking down errors when they occur.

A second ingredient in a solution to our problem is the use of parameter passing to and from procedures and functions. By carefully passing parameters from one section of the program to another, we can go a long way in insulating one part of the program from another. Another technique in this regard is the use of units to create separately compiled files of procedures, functions, data types, constants, and variables.

However, all of the techniques described have their particular problems. For instance, consider the use of units to design a large program. Programmer A might be given the assignment of designing a series of procedures and functions, to be contained in a unit. Suppose that in this design, he (or she) declares a set of variables to be exported. Because of the complexity of the program, the list of variables is rather long. Programmer B uses the unit of Programmer A, but uses one of the variables exported by the unit for his own purposes. Suddenly the program begins to exhibit strange problems. Tracking them down to the overuse of a variable can be quite a chore. And this is just one problem which can occur when more than one programmer works on a program!

Object-oriented programming was invented as a style of programming suited to creating reliable programs. Its fundamental idea is to create packets of code, called *objects,* which contain both data structures *and* procedures and functions for manipulating them. By limiting manipulations of a particular data structure to those specified within the object, you can provide a reliable method for dealing with the object while hiding all details of the methods for doing so.

But enough of this abstract discussion. Let's get down to concrete terms and introduce Turbo Pascal's objects.

Objects

Declaring an Object

A *Turbo Pascal object* consists of a data structure plus a set of procedures and functions for manipulating the object. As a concrete example of an object, let's consider Turbo Pascal in text mode. The screen is divided into a certain number of rows, each containing a certain number of character positions. Let's consider abstractly the notion of a character position. How can we describe it? Well, a character position is described by two integers, X and Y, with X giving the column number and Y giving the row number. Therefore, the data structure describing a character position consists of a pair of integers.

What about the allowable data manipulations to this data structure? Let's be very simplistic and allow only one, moving the cursor to a given character position.

Let's call by the name `Position` our abstraction of a character position and create a corresponding object using the following declaration:

```
type
  Position = object
               X, Y : integer;
               procedure MoveTo( XPos, YPos : integer);
             end;

procedure Position.MoveTo( XPos, YPos : integer);

  begin
    {Make sure (XPos,YPos) is on the screen}
    if (XPos >= 1) and (XPos <= 80) and
       (YPos >= 1) and (YPos <= 25)
      then
        begin
          X := XPos;
          Y := YPos
      end
  end;
```

Let's analyze the structure of this object declaration. First of all, the declaration contains a description of the object as a type. The description begins as would any type declaration with the keyword `type`. Then comes the name of the type followed by =, and then the keyword `object`. Then follows the data portion of the object. In this case, the data portion consists of two variables of integer type. However, the object could contain any number of data items of any types. The types of the data items may be user-defined as long as the appropriate types are declared (possibly in the same type declaration used for the object).

After the data portion of the object declaration comes a list of the headers for the functions and procedures included in the object.

The type declaration for the object concludes with the keyword `end;`.

Following the type declaration, but in the same block, the object's procedures and functions must be declared. In this case, the code for `MoveTo` is placed directly after the object declaration. Note that in this code, `MoveTo` is denoted `Position.MoveTo` to indicate that the procedure is bound to (that is, belongs to) the object `Position`.

The procedures and functions of an object are called *methods* of the object. An object's methods provide the manipulations of the object's data.

Instances of an Object

Note that the object `Position` is a data type. This means that we can create variables of type `Position`. Such a variable is called an *instance* of the object. An instance is declared in a `var` declaration just like any other variable. For example, here is a declaration of a `Position` variable `PositionA`:

```
var
  PositionA : Position;
```

The data portion of the variable is treated as if it were a record. The X component of `PositionA` is accessed as `PositionA.X` and the Y component as `PositionA.Y`. For example, we may set X and Y to 50 and 10, respectively with the statements:

```
PositionA.X := 50;
PositionA.Y := 10;
```

The same thing can be accomplished using the procedure `MoveTo`.

```
PositionA.MoveTo(50,10);
```

(Of course, this last statement includes a check that (50,100) is within the current window. If it isn't, then no assignment of X and Y is made.)

It is possible to create many instances of a single object. For instance, we may create instances `PositionA`, `PositionB`, `CursorPosition`, and so forth. It is also possible to create constants whose type corresponds to an object. For instance, we can create the constant `HomePosition` corresponding to the coordinates (X,Y) = (0,0) using the declaration:

```
const
  HomePosition : Position = (X:0; Y:0);
```

In this case, `HomePosition.X` and `HomePosition.Y` are constants with value 0.

An Object's Fields

The various components of an instance, are called *fields*. These components may be either data, function, or procedure components and are indicated by the name of the instance followed by a period, followed by the name of the component (e.g., `PositionA.MoveTo`).

At first, it may seem strange to have a procedure or a function as the component of a structure. However, that's one of the great benefits of using objects. It is perfectly permissible to have different objects with component names in common. For example, you may have an object other than Position which incorporates a component named MoveTo. When the component is used in an instance of the object, the different instance names allow the compiler to distinguish between the two uses of the same name. This helps solve the problem of the two programmers using the same identifiers!

Inheritance

Inherited Objects

One of the most significant features of objects is that of inheritance. To explain what this means, let's consider an example. Go back to the object `Position`, which is an abstraction of the concept of a character position on the screen. Let's now create an object which abstracts the concept of a data field on the screen. The data components of the object are as follows:

```
Position = X,Y : integer; {location of the field}
Length : integer {length of the data field}
Protect : boolean {allow writing to field or not}
Color : word {background color of the field}
Contents : string {contents of the field}
```

The procedures which we will define for a data field are: `InitField`, which initializes a field with specific values, `DisplayField`, which displays the field, and `EnterField`, which allows data entry into the field.

The first thing to realize is that in specifying `Position`, we really need to specify a position on the screen. For this purpose, we want to use the definition of `Position` that we have already created. This is what inheritance is all about. In defining an object, we can specify that `Position` is an *ancestor* type of `Field`—that is, `Field` incorporates all of the data elements and methods of `Position`. Listing 8.1 shows the code for both of our objects `Position` and `FieldInput` set up as a unit.

Listing 8.1. The unit FieldInput

```
unit FieldInp;

interface

  type
    Position = object
                 X, Y : integer;
                 procedure MoveTo( XPos, YPos : integer);
               end;

    Field = object
              (Position)
              Width : word;
              Color : byte;
              Contents : string;
              Protect : boolean;
              procedure InitField(    XPos, YPos : integer;
```

```
                                   FWidth : word;
                                   FColor : byte;
                                   FContents : string;
                                   FProtect : boolean);
              Procedure EnterField;
              procedure Display;
            end;

implementation

  uses
    crt;

  {-----------------------------------------------------------
  Method implementations for Position
  -----------------------------------------------------------}
  procedure Position.MoveTo( XPos, YPos : integer);

    begin
      {Make sure (XPos,YPos) is on the screen}
      if (XPos >= 1) and (XPos <= 80) and
         (YPos >= 1) and (YPos <= 25)
        then
          begin
            X := XPos;
            Y := XPos
          end
    end;

  {-----------------------------------------------------------
  Method implementations for Field
  -----------------------------------------------------------}
  procedure Field.InitField(    XPos, YPos : integer;
                                FWidth : word;
                                FColor : byte;
                                FContents : string;
                                FProtect : boolean);

    begin
      MoveTo(XPos, YPos);
      Width := FWidth;
      Color := FColor;
      Contents := FContents;
      Protect := FProtect
    end;

  procedure Field.EnterField;

    begin
      if not Protect
        then
          begin
            Display;
            readln(Contents)
          end
    end;
```

```
procedure Field.Display;

  var
    OldText : byte;

  begin
    OldText := textattr;{Crt unit's current color byte}
    textbackground (Color);
    window(X, Y, X+Width-1, Y);
    clrscr;
    write(Contents);
    gotoxy (1, 1);
    textattr := OldText
  end;

end.
```

Note the type declaration of the object `Field`. It begins with the line (`Position`). The identifier `Position` refers to the previously defined object `Position`. The parentheses indicate that we wish the object `Field` to inherit the elements of `Position`. What this means is that `Field` will have fields `X`, `Y`, and `MoveTo`, just as if they were explicitly declared in the Field declaration.

Here is an important point to note about coding methods. Note that the variables `X`, `Y`, `Width`, `Contents`, and so forth are not passed via parameters to the methods. They are used just as if they were global variables. This certainly makes writing methods easier. But what about all the warnings to always pass data via parameters? In the case of objects, the methods are tightly bound to the variables in the object declaration. Thus, there never can be any confusion as to what variables are meant. The method declarations can be coded with simpler headers and still have the same tight control over variables as if they were passed via parameters. This is one of the principal advantages of using objects.

Let's now illustrate the advantage of using objects by using the object field to define two fields on the screen. The first will contain the word `NAME` and will be located at position (0,0). The second field will be for entry of a name and will be located beginning at (6,0) and will be of length 30. Let's illuminate each of these fields in blue. The first field will be protected, since it is not meant for data entry. To create these fields, we merely create two variables of type `Field`, initialize them, and display them. The program then allows the user to enter a name into the second field. Here is the code:

```
program Illustration;

  uses
    crt,
    FieldInp;
```

```
var
  NameField, NameEntryField : Field;

begin {Illustration}
  NameField.InitField(1, 1, 5, Blue, 'NAME', true);
  NameEntryField.InitField(6, 1, 30, Cyan, '', false);
  NameField.Display;
  NameEntryField.Display;
  NameEntryField.EnterField
end. {Illustration}
```

Note how simple the code is. Once we have conceptualized the notion of a `Field`, we can create any number of fields that will simply use instances of the object `Field`. The methods associated to the object allow us to simply manipulate the data associated to each of the instances.

Note that the above example assumes that unit `FieldInput` has been compiled as a TPU file as previously discussed.

The with Clause with Objects

The use of dotting allows us to distinguish data elements and methods belonging to different instances of an object. However, use of dotting leads to rather verbose source code. Using the `with` clause, you can suppress use of the instance name, just as you can use `with` in connection with records to work only with record field names. For instance, using `with`, we may rewrite the program developed above as follows:

```
program Illustration2;

 uses
   crt,
   FieldInp;

 var
   NameField, NameEntryField : Field;

 begin {Illustration2}
   with NameField do
     begin
       InitField(1, 1, 5, Blue, 'NAME', true);
       Display
     end;
   with NameEntryField do
     begin
       InitField(6, 1, 30, Cyan, '', false);
       Display;
       EnterField
     end
 end. {Illustration2}
```

Object Hierarchies

You may construct hierarchies of objects using previously defined objects as ancestors. Just remember: An object can have only a single ancestor. However, a single object can have many descendants. This is an important point, so let's elaborate on it a bit. For instance, consider the `Field` object. We can construct a number of different descendant objects using `Field` as ancestor. For example, we might create a series of specialized objects which allow only a particular type of data, say a `BooleanField` which only allows `Contents` to be equal to one of the characters "Y," "N," "y," or "n." For such an object, we would add another data element, `Meaning`, which is boolean, equal to true if `Contents` is "Y" or "y," and equal to false if `Contents` is equal to "N" or "n." In addition, this object would have a revised `EnterField` method which would test the input and reject all strings except for one of the four single character strings: "Y," "N," "y," or "n." The object `BooleanField` is then a descendant of `Field`. Another possible descendant of `Field` is the object `NumericField`, which allows you to enter only real numbers in the field. That is, the string in `Contents` must be a valid string representing a real number. `EnterField` would include code to test input strings and reject those which are not of the proper type. Both `BooleanField` and `NumericField` are descendants of the single object `Field`. That is, an object can have many descendants.

However, an object cannot have more than a single ancestor. You might think that you could allow an object to inherit fields and methods from more than one object. However, this is not the case.

A Philosophical Note

Note that you may refer to the data fields of an instance of an object using the dot convention of identifying the fields. However, one of the philosophical tenets of object oriented programming is that it is bad form to do so. You should try, insofar as possible, to perform all manipulations which involve the data fields using the methods of the object. If you find that there is a manipulation which you can't perform using the predefined methods, you should inherit off the object and add the method you need.

Assignment Rules for Inherited Objects

A descendant object has all the data fields of its ancestors which lie above it in the object hierarchy. Therefore, it makes sense to be able to assign to an object instance an instance of any descendant object. That's a bit to swallow.

So let's take an example. Suppose that `PositionA` and `PositionB` are instances of type `Position`. Then the following assignment is legal:

```
PositionA := PositionB;
```

This assignment is equivalent to making the assignments:

```
PositionA.X := PositionB.X;
PositionA.Y := PositionB.Y;
```

However, suppose that `Name` is an instance of type `Field`, a descendant of `Position`. Then the following assignment is legal:

```
PositionA := Name;
```

It is equivalent to the assignments:

```
PositionA.X := Name.X;
PositionA.Y := Name.Y;
```

However, note that the following assignment is illegal:

```
Name := PositionA; {ERROR}
```

Indeed, `Name` has data fields which are not present in `Position`. What would such an assignment statement assign to these data fields?

When passing object instances to a procedure or function, similar assignment rules apply. For instance, consider a procedure with header:

```
procedure Test(var Posn : Position);
```

The formal parameter `Posn` may be replaced by an actual parameter of type `Position` or of any descendant type (say, of type `Field`).

Although this doesn't seem very exciting, it is a very important feature of objects. Consider the following implications. Suppose that you are given a library of objects compiled as a unit. This unit was written some time ago by a person who is no longer with your company. Moreover, suppose that the source code is unavailable. All you are given is the compiled code in the form of a TPU file and a listing of the data fields and method headers. Suppose that you wish to modify the operation of one of the methods. In standard Pascal, this would be an impossible task. However, in object-oriented Pascal, it's easy. Just create a descendant type with all data elements and methods inherited. However, include code for the method you wish to change. Call the modified method by the same name. Now use the descendant object in your program. All of the methods of the ancestor object are inherited by the new object, except for the new method which replaces the one of the same name in the ancestor. Simple? You bet! (There are some traps in this simplistic description.) Before you try this, be sure to read the discussion of virtual and static methods.

Polymorphism

As we have seen, a descendant object inherits all the data fields and all the methods of its ancestor object. In addition, of course, the descendant object can have methods and/or data fields which are not inherited. One possibility which is legal is for a descendant object to redefine methods it inherits, using the same name, but different source code. Thus, for example, the object `Field` could refine the method `MoveTo` which it inherits from `Position`. The ability to use a single identifier to represent different methods is called *polymorphism.*

Given that a single identifier may stand for several different procedures, Turbo Pascal needs a rule for determining which of the possible procedures it is to use. The rule is this: Use the method closest to the object which does the calling. For instance, suppose that you are using an instance of the object `Field` and call the method `MoveTo`. Turbo Pascal first looks among the methods implemented specifically for `Field` to determine if there is a method `MoveTo`. There is no such method. Therefore, it then goes one step up the object hierarchy and looks at the ancestor `Position` for the method `MoveTo`. And so forth, up the object hierarchy. The first method with the correct name is the one which is used.

Thus, if you redefined `MoveTo` and gave it a separate implementation in `Field`, the redefined method would be used with instances of `Field`, whereas the original implementation would be used with instances of `Position`.

Static versus Virtual Methods

All of the methods we have considered so far have been examples of *static methods.* These are methods in which all calls to other methods are specified during compilation. In addition, Turbo Pascal supports *virtual methods* in which calls to other methods are determined during program execution.

Static and virtual methods work out nested method calls very differently. Any nested calls within a static method are interpreted as if the calls were made in the earliest ancestor from which the method was inherited. In a virtual method, nested calls to a method use the most recent method of that name.

A method is made virtual by using the keyword `virtual` in its object declaration, as in the following:

```
Procedure EnterField; virtual;
```

Depending on what calling convention you wish to have for nested calls, some methods can be made virtual and some static. Note, however, that once a method is made virtual, all of its descendants must be virtual, even if they are redefined.

If a method does not have any nested calls, then it makes no difference whether the method is static or virtual.

Let's now discuss how to use virtual methods. Each object with virtual procedures must have an initialization procedure, called a *constructor.* This procedure is typically called `Init`, and must be called to initialize *each instance* of the object. The constructor can have code which initializes variables and performs other housekeeping chores. However, a constructor automatically (no code needed on your part) creates a *virtual method table* for the instance. This table lists the methods which will be used in response to each possible nested method call. Without this table, a call of a virtual method will cause a system crash! Here is the format for a typical constructor:

```
Constructor Field.InitField(XPos, YPos : integer;
                            FWidth : word;
                            FColor : word;
                            FContents : string;
                            FProtect : boolean);
```

Note that a constructor begins with the keyword `constructor` instead of `procedure` or `function`. Other than that, the constructor header looks exactly like any other method header. This example is the constructor for the object `Field`, in which the methods are all declared as virtual. (See Listing 8.2.) Note that the implementation of the constructor hasn't changed at all. The code for creating the virtual method table is added automatically by the compiler.

In the case of `InitField`, there already was an initialization procedure to use as the constructor for the object. As another example, consult Listing 8.2, where the object `Position` includes a virtual method. We have added a constructor which has no body. This constructor does nothing else but construct the virtual method table.

Note that a constructor must not be declared as virtual. If you attempt to do so, the compiler will report an error.

Listing 8.2. The unit FieldInput using virtual methods

```
unit FieldInp;

interface

  type
    Position = object
                 X, Y : integer;
                 procedure MoveTo(XPos, YPos : integer);
               end;

    Field = object
              (Position)
              Width : word;
              Color : byte;
              Contents : string;
              Protect : boolean;
              constructor InitField(    XPos, YPos : integer;
                                        FWidth : word;
                                        FColor : byte;
                                        FContents : string;
                                        FProtect : boolean);
              procedure EnterField; virtual;
              procedure Display; virtual;
            end;

implementation

  uses
    crt;

  {--------------------------------------------------------
  Method implementations for Position
  --------------------------------------------------------}
  procedure Position.MoveTo(XPos, YPos : integer);

    begin
      {Make sure (XPos,YPos) is on the screen}
      if (XPos >= 1) and (XPos <= 80) and
         (YPos >= 1) and (YPos <= 25)
        then
          begin
            X := XPos;
            Y := XPos
          end
    end;
```

```
{------------------------------------------------------------
Method implementations for Field
------------------------------------------------------------}
constructor Field.InitField(   XPos, YPos : integer;
                               FWidth : word;
                               FColor : byte;
                               FContents : string;
                               FProtect : boolean);

  begin
    MoveTo(XPos, YPos);
    Width := FWidth;
    Color := FColor;
    Contents := FContents;
    Protect := FProtect
  end;

procedure Field.EnterField;

  begin
    if not Protect
      then
        begin
          Display;
          readln(Contents)
        end
  end;

procedure Field.Display;

  var
    OldText : byte;

  begin
    OldText := textattr;   {Crt unit's current color byte}
    textbackground (Color);
    window(X, Y, X+Width-1, Y);
    clrscr;
    write(Contents);
    gotoxy (1, 1);
    textattr := OldText
  end;

end.
```

In order to make programs using virtual methods easier to debug, Turbo Pascal includes the {$R} compiler flag. If you put the flag {$R+} at the beginning of the program, any calls to uninitialized instances will result in an error message rather than a system crash. After you have debugged your program, you can remove this flag. (The flag results in slower program operation and increased code size).

9 Files

In the preceding chapters, we learned about a number of Pascal's data structures. All of these data structures were fixed in size throughout the execution of the program, with the size of the data structure determined by a declaration. In addition to these data structures, Pascal allows for data structures that vary in size during program execution. In this chapter, we introduce the most elementary of these, the file data type. We will learn to declare files, associate them to physical files on floppy or hard disk, read and write contents of files, and apply our knowledge to write several programs which maintain a telephone directory file.

The File Data Type

What Is a File?

In Pascal, a *file* is a data structure consisting of a sequence of components all of the same data type. Unlike an array, a file does not have a fixed size. It may consist of any number of components. After the last component is a marker `<eof>` which indicates the end of the file.

Here are some examples of files.

1. A file of integers consists of a sequence of integers:

   ```
   3  17  23  48  51  321  480  ...58<eof>
   ```

   Each component of this file is an integer. The first component is 3, the second 17, the last component 58.

2. A file of characters consists of a sequence of characters:

   ```
   'a'  'b'  'e'  '{'  ...  '$'<eof>
   ```

   The first component is 'a', the second 'b', and the last component '$'.

3. An entry in a telephone directory may be defined as a record of type `PhoneDir`, where:

```
type PhoneDir = record
                   Name  : string[20];
                   Phone : string[12];
                end;
```

   You may use a file of components of type `PhoneDir` to store a sequence of phone directory entries.

4. An inventory control system uses a list of products currently stored in a warehouse. Each product may be described by a text string. The list of products in the warehouse may be stored in a file of components of type `string[255]`. (The maximum length of a product name is chosen as 255 to allow for detailed product descriptions.)

Pascal includes mechanisms for creating files, writing components to a file and reading the components of a file. For the remainder of this section, we will concentrate on the first of these: how to declare a file. In the next two sections, we will discuss writing and reading files.

Declaring Files

Declaring a file consists of three steps:

1. Declare a suitable file type.
2. Declare a file variable of a declared file type.
3. Associate the file variable with a physical file recognized by your computer's operating system.

You declare a file type just as you do any other custom data type in the type declaration section of a block. The syntax of a file type declaration is:

```
type filetype = file of datatype;
```

Here `filetype` is a Pascal identifier which is assigned as the name of the file type and `datatype` is the data type of the components in the file.

For instance, the type of the file of integers in Step 1 above can be declared with a declaration of the form:

```
type IntFile = file of integer;
```

The type of the file of characters in Step 2 above can be declared with:

```
type CharFile = file of char;
```

The type of the phone directory file of Step 3 above can be declared with:

```
type PhoneFile = file of PhoneDir;
```

(Of course, for Pascal to make any sense of this declaration, the type declaration for `PhoneDir` needs to come first.)

The type of the parts file of Step 4 above can be declared with:

```
type PartsFile = file of Parts;
```

You may declare a file type using any data type, with two notable exceptions. First, Pascal does not allow a file of files, or a file of a data type defined in terms of files. Second, datatype in a file type declaration must be described using a single Pascal identifier. Thus, for instance, the following declaration is invalid:

```
type Alpha = file of array[1..10] of char;
```

Rather this last file type should be defined using declarations of the form:

```
type CharArray = array[1..10] of char;
     Alpha = file of CharArray;
```

To define a file in Pascal, you merely declare a file variable. For example, to create a file of integers named `Survey`, we declare a file variable `Survey` using a declaration of the form:

```
var Survey : IntFile;
```

You may define several different files of the same type. Suppose, for instance, you wish to maintain separate inventories for two warehouses. You can define corresponding inventory files `CarParts1` and `CarParts2` using the declaration:

```
var CarParts1, CarParts2 : PartsFile;
```

You can take a shortcut and combine the type declaration and variable declaration for a file with a single declaration of the form:

```
var Survey : file of integer;
```

Each file variable must be associated with a corresponding physical file recognized by the operating system. This association is defined using the procedure `Assign`. For example, to associate the file variable `Survey` declared above with the disk file named A:SURVEY.DAT, you would use the statement:

```
Assign(Survey, 'A:SURVEY.DAT');
```

Note that the name of the physical file is enclosed in single quotation marks: Syntactically, it is a literal string constant.

The `Assign` statement must be used prior to executing any other statements which refer to the file variable. A reference to a file variable which has not been assigned to a physical file will result in an I/O (Input/Output) error when the program is run.

Once a file variable is assigned to a physical file, no further reference is made in the program to the physical file. All subsequent references (for example, to read or write to or from the file) involve only the file variable.

Writing Components to a File

Generalities About Writing Files

Let's consider a file identified by its file variable `F`. To prepare a file for writing (also referred to as *opening the file*), you must first issue the statement:

```
rewrite(F);
```

The rewrite procedure erases the current contents of the file and positions the file pointer to component 0 (that is, the beginning of the file).

The statement:

```
write(F,x);
```

writes x as the next component in the file.

Once a file is open for writing, you may write any number of consecutive data items into the file. When you are done writing, you must close the file using a statement of the form:

```
close(F);
```

Some Examples

Example 1. Create a file containing the following integers:

1 1 2 4 3 9 4 16 5 25 ... 100 10000

(Each number is followed by its square.)

Solution. The program is a simple application of the procedures introduced above. We first assign the file to a physical file. We choose the file name NUMBERS for the physical file. Then we rewrite the file and use a loop to write the desired data items to the file. Then we close the file. Here is the program.

Listing 9.1. Squares

```
program Squares;
{This program makes a file of all the integers
from 1 to 100 and their squares.}

  const
    SquaresFileName = 'NUMBERS';
    Max = 100;

  var
    SquaresFile : file of integer;
    Number, Square : integer;

  begin {Squares}
    assign(SquaresFile, SquaresFileName);
    rewrite(SquaresFile);
    for Number := 1 to Max do
      begin
        Square := Number*Number;
        write(SquaresFile, Number, Square)
      end;
    close(SquaresFile)
  end. {Squares}
```

Example 2. Write a program which creates a telephone directory consisting of entries supplied by the user.

Solution. Each telephone directory entry will consist of a name, street address, city, state, zipcode, and telephone number. We define variables to each of these pieces of data. Our program will keep asking the user if there is another entry to create. The program loops until the user answers "No." For each telephone entry, the program prompts for each of the pieces of data in order. When all of the data items have been entered, the record is written to the file.

For simplicity, let's store each of the data items in a variable of type string. That is, a variable of type `string[255]`. This is wasteful since it allocates 255 characters for each data item. A more reasonable limit would be to allocate for each variable a maximum length. Say, 30 for `name`, 5 for `zipcode`, etc.

Here is the program.

Listing 9.2. Make Directory

```
program MakeDirectory;
{This program creates a file holding entries from
a telephone directory which are entered by the user.}

  const
    DirectoryFileName = 'TELEPHON';

  type
    Directory = file of string;

  var
    DirectoryFile : Directory;
    Name, Street, City,
    State, ZipCode, Phone : string;

  procedure GetEntry(var Name, Street, City,
                         State, ZipCode, Phone : string);
  {Reads data from the keyboard into the strings.}
    begin {GetEntry}
      write('Name? ');
      readln(Name);
      write('Street Address? ');
      readln(Street);
      write('City? ');
      readln(City);
      write('State? ');
      readln(State);
      write('Zip Code? ');
      readln(ZipCode);
      write('Telephone? ');
      readln(Phone)
    end; {GetEntry}

  procedure WriteEntry(var DirectoryFile : Directory;
                           Name, Street, City,
                           State, ZipCode, Phone : string);
  {Writes the strings to DirectoryFile.}
    begin {WriteEntry}
      write(DirectoryFile, Name);
      write(DirectoryFile, Street);
      write(DirectoryFile, City);
      write(DirectoryFile, State);
      write(DirectoryFile, ZipCode);
      write(DirectoryFile, Phone)
    end; {WriteEntry}

  function Finished : boolean;
  {Returns true if the user wants to quit, or
   false if the user wants to add another entry.}
    var
      Answer : char;
    begin {Finished}
```

```
      write('Another entry(Y/N)? ');
      readln(Answer);
      Finished := (Answer <> 'Y') and (Answer <> 'y')
    end; {Finished}

  begin {MakeDirectory}
    assign(DirectoryFile, DirectoryFileName);
    rewrite(DirectoryFile);
    repeat
      GetEntry(Name, Street, City, State, ZipCode, Phone);
      WriteEntry(DirectoryFile, Name, Street, City, State, ZipCode, Phone)
    until Finished;
    close(DirectoryFile)
  end. {MakeDirectory}
```

Let's introduce the variables `Directory` of type `PhoneDir` as our file variable and `Entry` of type `PhoneNum` to store the current phone number input by the user. Our program will consist of a loop which inputs a single directory `Entry` with each repetition. The loop inputs the record components `Entry.Name` and `Entry.Number` using `readln` to accept user responses to prompts the program displays. The program then uses `write` to record `Entry` into the file. Here is a listing of the program.

Listing 9.3. Input Phone Directory

```
program InputPhoneDir;
type PhoneNum = record
                   Name : String[20];
                   Number : String[20];
                end;
     PhoneDir = file of PhoneNum;
var Directory : PhoneDir;
    Entry : PhoneNum;
    Continue : boolean;
    Response : char;
begin {InputPhoneDir}
  assign(Directory,'TELEPHON')
  rewrite(Directory);
  Continue := true;
  while Continue do
    begin
      writeln('Input phone directory entry.');
      writeln('Name (at most 20 characters): ');
      readln(Entry.Name);
      writeln('Phone Number: ');
      readln(Entry.Number);
      write(Directory,Entry);
      writeln('Another Entry (Y/N)?');
      readln(Response);
      if (Response = 'N') or (Response = 'n') then
        Continue := false
    end {while}
end. {InputPhoneDir}
```

Sample Run. InputPhoneDir

```
Name (at most 20 characters):
John Jones
Phone Number:
(301)-777-3201
Another Entry (Y/N)?
Y
Input phone directory entry.
Name (at most 20 characters):
Sally Smith
Phone Number:
(212)-593-2200
Another Entry (Y/N)?
N
```

The write statement also allows you to write more than one component at a time to the file. Indeed, suppose that `var1`, `var2`, `...`, `varn` are variables whose type is the same as the component type of `F`. Then the statement:

```
write(F,var1,var2,...varn)
```

writes the value of `var1` as the next component of `F`, `var2` as the component after that, and so forth for all the variables listed.

Reading Files

Once you create a file and write data into it, you may read the file and recover the data for further use. In this section, we discuss how this is done.

Reading Components from a File

The statement

```
reset(F);
```

causes the file pointer to be reset to component 0 of the file.

The statement

```
read(F,X);
```

reads the next component of the file F and assigns it to the variable `X` (which, of course, must be of the same type as the component type of F).

The component to be read is determined by the current position of the file pointer. This position must be set prior to reading. You may position the file pointer either using the Seek procedure (to position the pointer at a specified component) or the Reset procedure (to position the pointer at the beginning of the file). For example, the statement:

```
Reset(Numbers);
```

positions the file pointer to the beginning of the file. The procedure

```
Seek(Numbers,5);
```

positions the file pointer on the fifth component of the file.

After a read statement, the file pointer is moved to point to the next component of the file, if there is one, or to the <eof> marker, if not.

If the file pointer is pointing at the <eof> marker, then attempting to read a component results in an I/O error. When such an error occurs, the program is halted and an error message is printed.

The most general form of the read statement is:

```
read(F, var1,...varn)
```

This statement reads the next n components of F and assigns the first to var1, the second to var2, the nth to varn.

Example 1. Write a program to count the number of entries in a file of integers.

Solution. Listing 9.4. Count entries

```
program CountEntries;
{This program counts the number
of entries in a file of integers.}

  const
    NumbersFileName = 'NUMBERS';

  var
    NumbersFile : file of integer;
    Count, Number : integer;

  begin {CountEntries}
    assign(NumbersFile, NumbersFileName);
    reset(NumbersFile);
    Count := 0;
    while not eof(NumbersFile) do { repeat until end of file }
      begin
        read(NumbersFile, Number);
        Count := Count + 1
      end;
```

```
    writeln('The number of numbers in the file is ', Count);
    close(NumbersFile)
  end. {CountEntries}
```

Example 2. Consider the file `Directory` created earlier in this chapter. Write a program which accepts the name of a person and searches the file for the corresponding phone number.

Solution. The program consists of the following steps: Open the file, obtain from the user the name to search for, read file entries and compare with the given name, display any match which is found.

Listing 9.5. Search

```
program Search;
{This program searches a file of telephone listings
for the entry of a name given by the user.}

  uses
    crt;

  type
    Directory = file of string;

  const
    DirectoryFileName = 'TELEPHON';

  var
    DirectoryFile : Directory;
    NameToSearchFor,
    Name, Street, City,
    State, ZipCode, Phone : string;

  procedure GetNameToSearchFor(var NameToSearchFor : string);
    begin {GetNameToSearchFor}
      write('Name to search for? ');
      readln(NameToSearchFor)
    end; {GetNameToSearchFor}

  procedure ReadEntry(var DirectoryFile : Directory;
                      var Name, Street, City,
                          State, ZipCode, Phone : string);
 {Reads an entry from DirectoryFile into the strings.}
  begin {ReadEntry}
    read(DirectoryFile, Name);
    read(DirectoryFile, Street);
    read(DirectoryFile, City);
    read(DirectoryFile, State);
    read(DirectoryFile, ZipCode);
    read(DirectoryFile, Phone)
  end; {ReadEntry}
```

```
procedure SearchForName(var DirectoryFile : Directory;
                            NameToSearchFor : string;
                        var Name, Street, City,
                            State, ZipCode, Phone : string);
{Reads entries from DirectoryFile until the name matches the
 name we're searching for or until we hit end of file.}
  begin {SearchForName}
    Name := '';
    while (not eof(DirectoryFile)) and not (Name = NameToSearchFor) do
      ReadEntry(DirectoryFile, Name, Street, City, State, ZipCode, Phone)
  end; {SearchForName}

procedure DisplayResult(    NameToSearchFor,
                            Name, Street, City,
                            State, ZipCode, Phone : string);
  begin {DisplayResult}
    clrscr; { clear the screen }
    if (Name = NameToSearchFor)
      then
        begin
          writeln(Name);
          writeln(Street);
          writeln(City, ', ', State, ' ', ZipCode);
          writeln(Phone)
        end
      else
        writeln('The name is not on file.')
  end; {DisplayResult}

begin {Search}
  assign(DirectoryFile, DirectoryFileName);
  reset(DirectoryFile);
  GetNameToSearchFor(NameToSearchFor);
  SearchForName(DirectoryFile, NameToSearchFor,
                Name, Street, City,
                State, ZipCode, Phone);
  DisplayResult(NameToSearchFor, Name, Street,
                City, State,
                ZipCode, Phone);
  close(DirectoryFile)
end. {Search}
```

Example 3. Write a program which prints out a mailing list corresponding to each entry of the telephone directory file previously created.

Solution. For this program, we read the entries in the file sequentially. For each entry we print the address portion on the printer, taking care to format the output in the conventional form of an address. We use the `Printer` unit to allow us to print to the device `Lst`.

Listing 9.6. Print directory

```
program PrintDirectory;
{This program prints a mailing label for each
entry in a directory of telephone book
listings.}

  uses
    printer; { This unit lets us write to "Lst", the printer }

  const
    DirectoryFileName = 'TELEPHON';

  type
    Directory = file of string;

  var
    DirectoryFile : Directory;
    Name, Street, City,
    State, ZipCode, Phone : string;

  procedure ReadEntry(var DirectoryFile : Directory;
                      var Name, Street, City,
                          State, ZipCode, Phone : string);
{Reads an entry from DirectoryFile into the strings.}
  begin {ReadEntry}
    read(DirectoryFile, Name);
    read(DirectoryFile, Street);
    read(DirectoryFile, City);
    read(DirectoryFile, State);
    read(DirectoryFile, ZipCode);
    read(DirectoryFile, Phone)
  end; {ReadEntry}

begin {PrintDirectory}
  assign(DirectoryFile, DirectoryFileName);
  reset(DirectoryFile);
  while not eof(DirectoryFile) do
    begin
      ReadEntry(DirectoryFile, Name, Street,
                City, State, ZipCode, Phone);
      writeln(Lst, Name); { Print the name }
      writeln(Lst, Street); { Print the street }
      writeln(Lst, City, ', ',
              State, ' ', ZipCode) { Print the rest }
    end;
  close(DirectoryFile)
end. {PrintDirectory}
```

Example 4. Write a program which adds entries to the file `Telephon` previously created. New entries should be added at the end of the file.

Solution. Note that we don't use `rewrite` to open the file since this would erase all of its current contents. Here is the program.

Listing 9.7. Add Entries

```
program AddEntries;
{This program adds entries to a
file of telephone listings.}

  uses
    crt;

  const
    DirectoryFileName = 'TELEPHON';

  type
    Directory = file of string;

  var
    DirectoryFile : Directory;
    Name,
    Street,
    City,
    State,
    ZipCode,
    Phone         : string;

  procedure GetEntry(var Name, Street, City,
                         State, ZipCode, Phone : string);
  {Reads data from the keyboard into the strings.}
    begin {GetEntry}
      write('Name? ');
      readln(Name);
      write('Street Address? ');
      readln(Street);
      write('City? ');
      readln(City);
      write('State? ');
      readln(State);
      write('Zip Code? ');
      readln(ZipCode);
      write('Telephone? ');
      readln(Phone)
    end; {GetEntry}
```

```
procedure WriteEntry(var DirectoryFile : Directory;
                     Name, Street, City,
                     State, ZipCode, Phone : string);
{Writes the strings to DirectoryFile.}
  begin
    write(DirectoryFile, Name);
    write(DirectoryFile, Street);
    write(DirectoryFile, City);
    write(DirectoryFile, State);
    write(DirectoryFile, ZipCode);
    write(DirectoryFile, Phone)
  end;

function Finished : boolean;
{Returns true if the user wants to quit, or
 false if the user wants to add another entry.}
  var
    Answer : char;
  begin {Finished}
    write('Another entry (Y/N)? ');
    readln(Answer);
    Finished := (Answer <> 'Y') and (Answer <> 'y')
  end; {Finished}

begin {AddEntries}
  assign(DirectoryFile, DirectoryFileName);
  reset(DirectoryFile); {reset can be used for read/write}
  repeat
    clrscr;
    GetEntry(Name, Street, City, State, ZipCode, Phone);
    WriteEntry(DirectoryFile, Name, Street, City, State, ZipCode, Phone)
  until Finished;
  close(DirectoryFile)
end. {AddEntries}
```

Example 5. Create a single program for creating, maintaining, and searching a telephone directory.

Solution. This program combines all of the elements of the programs in the preceding examples. The new element is the menu selection required to choose different operations. This program looks complex. However, the piece-by-piece approach to building its components allows us to structure it so that it is easy to plan and code.

Here is the program.

Listing 9.8. Directory Manager

```
program DirectoryManager;
{This program incorporates all of the
routines needed to create and manage
a telephone directory file using
random access file techniques.}

  uses
    crt;

  const
    MaxStringLength = 20;
    MaxZipCodeLength = 5;

  type
    TypeString = string [MaxStringLength];
    TypeZipCode = string [MaxZipCodeLength];
    TypeEntry = record
                  Name, Street,
                  City, State : TypeString;
                  ZipCode : TypeZipCode;
                  Phone : TypeString;
                end;
    TypeDirectoryFile = file of TypeEntry;

  var
    DirectoryFile : TypeDirectoryFile;
    Option : integer;

  function FileExists( FileName : string) : boolean;
  {Tries to open the file named in FileName for reading.
   If the file can be opened for reading, it must exist, so
   FileExists returns true. Otherwise, FileExists returns
   false.}
    var
      TempFile : TypeDirectoryFile;
    begin {FileExists}
      assign(TempFile, FileName);
      {$i-} { Disable i/o error checking
              so the program won't crash
            { if it tries to open a file
              that doesn't exist }
      reset(TempFile);
      {$i+} { Re-enable i/o error checking }
      if(ioresult = 0) { ioresult = 0 if the file was opened }
        then
          begin
            FileExists := true;
            close(TempFile) { TempFile is open, so we must close it }
          end
        else
          FileExists := false
    end; {FileExists}
```

```
procedure OpenDirectoryFile(var DirectoryFile :
                                TypeDirectoryFile);
{Opens the directory file, retaining the
 old contents if the file already exists.}
  const
    DirectoryFileName = 'DIRECTRY.DAT';
  begin {OpenDirectoryFile}
    assign(DirectoryFile, DirectoryFileName);
    if FileExists(DirectoryFileName)
      then
        reset(DirectoryFile) { Open old file without
                               destroying contents }
      else
        rewrite(DirectoryFile) { Create a new file }
  end; {OpenDirectoryFile}

procedure GetOption(var Option : integer);
{Displays a menu and reads the menu choice
  (option) from the keyboard.}
   begin {GetOption}
    clrscr;
    writeln('Options:');
    writeln('1. Make entry in directory');
    writeln('2. Search directory');
    writeln('3. Exit program');
    write('Choose option (1/2/3)? ');
    readln(Option)
   end; {GetOption}

procedure AddEntry(var DirectoryFile : TypeDirectoryFile);
{Reads an entry from the keyboard and
 writes it to the end of the file.}
  var
    Entry : TypeEntry;
  begin {AddEntry}
    clrscr;
    with Entry do
      begin
        write('Name? ');
        readln(Name);
        write('Street Address? ');
        readln(Street);
        write('City? ');
        readln(City);
        write('State? ');
        readln(State);
        write('Zip Code? ');
        readln(ZipCode);
        write('Telephone? ');
        readln(Phone)
      end;
    seek(DirectoryFile, filesize(DirectoryFile));
        {Go to end of file}
    write(DirectoryFile, Entry)
  end; {AddEntry}
```

```
procedure DisplayEntry( Entry : TypeEntry);
{Displays the contents of Entry.}
  begin {DisplayEntry}
    with Entry do
      begin
        writeln(Name);
        writeln(Street);
        writeln(City, ',', State, ' ', ZipCode);
        writeln(Phone)
      end
  end; {DisplayEntry}

procedure Search(var DirectoryFile : TypeDirectoryFile);
{Asks for the name and searches for a matching entry.}
  var
    NameToSearchFor : TypeString;
    Entry : TypeEntry;
  begin {Search}
    clrscr;
    write('Name to search for? ');
    readln(NameToSearchFor);
    seek(DirectoryFile, 0); {Go to beginning of file}
    Entry.Name := '';
    while(not eof(DirectoryFile)) and
          (Entry.Name <> NameToSearchFor) do
      read(DirectoryFile, Entry);
    if (Entry.Name = NameToSearchFor)
      then
        DisplayEntry(Entry)
      else
        writeln('Name not on file.');
    write('Press ENTER.');
    readln
  end; {Search}

begin {DirectoryManager}
  OpenDirectoryFile(DirectoryFile);
  repeat
    GetOption(Option);
    case Option of
      1 : AddEntry(DirectoryFile);
      2 : Search(DirectoryFile)
    end
  until (Option = 3);
  close(DirectoryFile)
end. {DirectoryManager}
```

Passing Files as Parameters

Files may be passed to a procedure via the usual parameter passing rules valid for any other data structures. However, a file may have many components and passing it by value to a procedure could therefore result in time-consuming copying of the components for the procedure's use. For this reason, the Pascal standard allows you to pass files via variable parameters. An attempt to pass a file via a value parameter is a syntax error.

Also, in passing files, it is necessary to assign type names for your file types. A procedure declaration such as the following is illegal:

```
procedure(var Format : file of char);
{Error}
```

Rather, you should declare a file type as follows:

```
type Characters : file of char;
```

The procedure heading can then be given as:

```
procedure(var Format : Characters);
```

More About Files

The File Pointer and Current Component

Turbo Pascal views a file as a sequence of components lined up in order. At any particular moment, one of the components is designated as the *current component.* This is the component which will be affected by the next read or write operation.

Turbo Pascal numbers the file components beginning with 0. The current size of a file may be determined from the integer value returned by the function `FileSize`. For example, if the file associated with the file variable `Test` currently has 10 components, then the function call

```
FileSize(Test)
```

returns the value 10.

The boolean function `EOF` indicates whether the file pointer is currently pointing at the last component of the file. That is, `EOF(Test)` is true if the file pointer for `Test` is pointing at the last component of the file. `EOF(Test)` is false otherwise.

The function `FilePos` returns the number of the component at which the file pointer is currently pointing. For example, if the file pointer is currently pointing at component number 5 of the file associated to the file variable `Test`, then the function call `FilePos(Test)` returns 5.

The procedure `Seek` is used to position the file pointer at a particular component of a file. For example, to position the file pointer on the 7th component of the file associated with the file variable `Test`, use the statement:

```
Seek(Test, 7);
```

To position the file pointer at the end of the last component of the file, use the statement:

```
Seek(Test, FileSize(Test))
```

This is because `FileSize(Test)` returns an integer which is one more than the last component number used. A statement of the latter sort can be used to position the file pointer for writing an additional component at the end of a file.

File Buffers and Closing Files

Rather than write to disk with every piece of data, no matter how small, most operating systems write to files using file buffers. A file buffer is an area of RAM which the operating system sets aside to aid in writing to a particular disk file. Data to be written to disk is accumulated in the appropriate file buffer rather than being written directly to disk. When the file buffer is full, its contents are written to disk. This arrangement greatly improves the efficiency of output to disk. However, it carries with it certain potential problems. At any given moment, some data which your program has ordered to be written to disk may, in fact, not yet have been transferred to disk from the file buffer. You may do this by closing the file. This causes the data in the buffer to be written to disk, the disk's directory to be updated, and the file buffer to be removed from RAM. To close the file associated with the file variable `Test`, you use the statement:

```
Close(Test);
```

In order to make sure that disk directories are properly updated and buffer contents are cleared, you should be sure to close each file after it is written to. Note, however, that it is not necessary to close files which were used solely for reading.

Text Files

A *text file* is a file of characters which is divided into lines of text separated by end of line markers. Text files are particularly useful for storing text documents, such as letters, reports, or memos. In addition, they may be used to store real, integer, string, and boolean data (see below).

A text file is declared using the predeclared type identifier text. For example, the declaration:

```
var Report : text;
```

declares the file Report as a text file.

Note that each line of a text file consists of a sequence of characters and terminates with the marker `<eoln>`, which indicates the end of the line. In Turbo Pascal, the marker `<eoln>` consists of a carriage return followed by a line feed (ASCII codes 10 and 13).

You may read or write a text file a line at a time or a character at a time. Alternatively, you may regard the characters as groups and read or write real, integer, or string data one value at a time. In what follows, we'll describe how to accomplish each of these tasks.

Writing Text Files

You may use `rewrite` with text files. Its effect is the same as with any other files—it erases the file, prepares it for writing, and positions the file pointer to the beginning of the file.

To write data to a text file, you may use the predeclared standard procedures `write` and `writeln`. These procedures have the syntax:

```
write(F, var1, ... , varn);
writeln(F, Var1, ... , Varn);
```

Here F is a text file identifier and `var1, ..., varn` are variables of real, integer, char, or string type. Moreover, in the case of real or integer data, expressions may be used in place of the corresponding variables.

If F is the standard file output, you may omit the file identifier F and write simply:

```
write(var1, ... , varn);
writeln(var1, ... , varn);
```

Actually, in the case of the standard file output, the procedures `write` and `writeln` are just the procedures we introduced at the beginning of the book!

The effect of the statement:

```
write(F, var1, ... , varn);
```

is to write the sequence of values var1, ..., varn to the file F. The form in which the variable values are written is as a sequence of characters. For example, the integer 1234 is written as the sequence of characters '1234'. Consecutive data items are separated by spaces only if the program is written to add spaces.

Note that in using write with a text file, you may mix variables of type real, integer, char, or string literals. This is in sharp distinction to write with non-text files, where all the variables must be of the declared file component type.

Note that no spaces are placed after numeric variables.

The effect of the statement:

```
writeln(F, var1, ... , varn);
```

is to write the sequence of values var1, ..., varn to the file F followed by <eoln>.

Suppose that Production is declared as array[1..100] of real. Here is a code fragment which writes the contents of Production to the text file Report:

```
rewrite(Production);
for J := 1 to 100 do
  write(Report,Production[J]);
```

Formatted Writing to Text Files

You may use format strings :n and :m:n in writing data to a text file. These formatting strings are used just as we discussed in the special case of writing to the standard output stream. For example, suppose that X is an integer variable whose value is 5. Then the statement:

```
writeln(F,X:8);
```

writes the following to the file F (asterisks denote blanks):

```
*******5<eoln>
```

Similarly, suppose that Y is a real variable with the value 4.88 and X is as above. Then the statement:

```
writeln(F,X:3,Y:8:5);
```

writes the following to the file F:

```
**5*4.88000<eoln>
```

Reading Text Files

To read data from a text file, you may use the predeclared standard procedures `read` and `readln`. These procedures have the syntax:

```
read(F, var1, ... , varn);
readln(F, var1, ... , varn);
```

Here `F` is a text file identifier and `var1, ..., varn` are variables of real, integer, or char type. If `F` is the standard file input, you may omit the file identifier `F` and write simply:

```
read(var1, ... , varn);
readln(var1, ... , varn);
```

Actually, in the case of the standard file input, the procedures `read` and `readln` are just the procedures we introduced at the beginning of the book!

The effect of the statement:

```
read(F, var1, ... , varn);
```

is to read a sequence of `n` values from `F` and assign them to the variables `var1, ..., varn`. The values are read from `F` using the same rules we described in connection with reading the standard input stream (see Chapter 3). Using these rules, Pascal attempts to read data from the file and assign to each of the variables `var1, ... , varn` a value of the appropriate type (integer, real, or char). If this is not possible, a run-time error occurs.

The effect of the statement:

```
readln(F, var1, ... , varn);
```

is the same as that of `read(F,var1,...,varn);`, except that after the variables are assigned values, the file pointer is advanced to the beginning of the next line of the file.

The File Browser Program

Many times you need to view the contents of a file without editing it. This need is fulfilled by the File Browser program. Explicitly, this program allows you to display the contents of a file and move around within the file to see various parts of it. The most interesting parts of the program involve the screen and keyboard management. The program allows 21 lines of the screen for displaying file contents. It allows for documents whose line length is greater than the width of the screen. For such documents, you can screen right or left and see the portion of the document "off the screen."

A second feature is the handling of the keyboard. At the beginning of the program is defined a set of "acceptable characters," i.e., those which are recognized by the program. Note that there are defined by ASCII codes. The codes listed within the program correspond to the arrow keys and the PgUp and PgDn keys. These keys allow you to position the cursor within the document and to scroll the document up or down on the screen. For simplicity, we have limited the document length to 500 lines.

The program first asks you for the file to browse. It then reads the document into an array of lines.

The program then waits for keystrokes. It accepts certain keystrokes and ignores others. Function key F10 is used to exit the program.

Study this program carefully. It contains many useful techniques. Moreover, it is the basis for building a full-fledged word processor.

Listing 9.9. FileBrowser

```
program FileBrowser;

  uses
    crt;

  const
    MaxDocumentLength = 500;
    PageLength = 21;
    AcceptedChars = [];
    AcceptedExt = [chr(68), chr(71)..chr(73), chr(75), chr(77),
                   chr(79)..chr(81)];
    BlankLine = '
';

  type
    TypeLine = string[81]; { 79 chars + 2 for CR/LF }
    TypeDocument = array[1..MaxDocumentLength] of TypeLine;
    TypeFileName = string[12];
    TypeModeString = string[9];
    TypeCharacterSet = set of char;

  var
    Document : TypeDocument;
    ExtKeyHit, FileChanged, Done : boolean;
    TopLine, CurrentLine, CurrentCol : integer;
    FileName : TypeFileName;
    KeyHit : char;

  procedure GetKey(var Key : char;
                   var Extended : boolean;
                       Acceptable,
                       ExtendedAcceptable : TypeCharacterSet;
                       CAPSOn : boolean);
```

```
  const
    ExtendedKey = chr(0); { 1st ASCII code returned by extended key }
    Beep = chr(7);

  function CharOk(    Key : char;
                      Extended : boolean;
                      Acceptable,
                      ExtendedAcceptable : TypeCharacterSet) : boolean;
    begin {CharOk}
      CharOk := (Extended and (Key in ExtendedAcceptable)) or
                ((not Extended) and (Key in Acceptable))
    end; {CharOk}

  begin {GetKey}
    repeat
      Key := readkey;
      Extended := (Key = ExtendedKey);
      if Extended
        then
          Key := readkey
        else
          if CAPSOn
            then
              Key := upcase(Key);
      if not CharOk(Key, Extended, Acceptable, ExtendedAcceptable)
        then
        write(Beep)
    until CharOk(Key, Extended, Acceptable, ExtendedAcceptable)
  end; {GetKey}

procedure InitVar(var Document : TypeDocument;
                  var Done : boolean;
                  var TopLine, CurrentLine, CurrentCol : integer);

  var
    LineInDocument : integer;

  begin {InitVar}
    for LineInDocument := 1 to MaxDocumentLength do
      Document[LineInDocument] := '';
    FileChanged := false;
    Done := false;
    TopLine := 1;
    CurrentLine := 1;
    CurrentCol := 1;
    FileName := ''
  end; {InitVar}

procedure UpdateScreen( CurrentLine, CurrentCol : integer);

  begin {UpdateScreen}
    gotoXY(36,1);
    write(CurrentLine, ' ');
    gotoXY(52, 1);
    write(CurrentCol, ' ');
    gotoxy(CurrentCol, CurrentLine - TopLine + 3)
  end; {UpdateScreen}
```

```
function LastCharPos(var Document : TypeDocument;
                         LineNum : integer) : integer;

    begin {LastCharPos}
      LastCharPos := length(Document[LineNum])
    end; {LastCharPos}

  procedure RedisplayPage(var Document : TypeDocument;
                              TopLine : integer);

    var
      LineToWrite : integer;

    begin {RedisplayPage}
      for LineToWrite := TopLine to TopLine + PageLength do
        begin
          gotoxy(1, LineToWrite - TopLine + 3);
          write(BlankLine);
          gotoxy(1, LineToWrite - TopLine + 3);
          write (copy(Document[LineToWrite], 1,
                      LastCharPos(Document, LineToWrite)))
        end
    end; {RedisplayPage}

  procedure SetupScreen(var Document : TypeDocument;
                            CurrentLine, CurrentCol : integer);

    begin {SetupScreen}
      clrscr;
      writeln('Document Name: ', FileName : 12, ' ', 'Line: ', ' ':8,
              'Column: ', ' ':17);
      write('----!----!----!----!----!----!----!----!');
      writeln('----!----!----!----!----!----!----!----!');
      gotoxy(1,25);
      write('Hit F10 to exit program');
      window(1, 1, 80, 24);
      RedisplayPage(Document, 1)
    end; {SetupScreen}

  procedure DoKey(     KeyHit : char;
                   var Document : TypeDocument;
                       ExtKeyHit : boolean;
                   var Done : boolean;
                   var TopLine, CurrentLine, CurrentCol : integer);

    procedure DoHome(var CurrentCol : integer);
      begin {DoHome}
        CurrentCol := 1
      end; {DoHome}

    procedure DoEnd(var Document : TypeDocument;
                        CurrentLine : integer;
                    var CurrentCol : integer);
      begin {DoEnd}
        CurrentCol := LastCharPos(Document, CurrentLine) + 1
      end; {DoEnd}
```

```
procedure DoUp(var Document : TypeDocument;
               var TopLine, CurrentLine, CurrentCol : integer);
  begin {DoUp}
    if (CurrentLine = TopLine) and (TopLine > 1)
      then
        begin
          TopLine := TopLine - 1;
          gotoxy(1, 3);
          insline;
          gotoxy(1, 3);
          write(copy(Document[TopLine], 1,
                     LastCharPos(Document, TopLine)))
        end;
    if (CurrentLine > 1)
      then
        CurrentLine := CurrentLine - 1;
    if LastCharPos(Document, CurrentLine) < CurrentCol
      then
        DoEnd(Document, CurrentLine, CurrentCol)
  end; {DoUp}

procedure DoDown(var Document : TypeDocument;
                 var TopLine, CurrentLine, CurrentCol : integer);
  begin {DoDown}
    if CurrentLine < MaxDocumentLength
      then
        begin
          if (CurrentLine = TopLine + PageLength)
            then
              begin
                TopLine := TopLine + 1;
                gotoxy(1, 3);
                delline;
                gotoxy(1, 24);
                write(copy(Document[TopLine + PageLength], 1,
                           LastCharPos(Document, TopLine + PageLength)))
              end;
          CurrentLine := CurrentLine + 1;
          if LastCharPos(Document, CurrentLine) < CurrentCol
            then
              DoEnd(Document, CurrentLine, CurrentCol)
        end
  end; {DoDown}

procedure DoPgUp(var Document : TypeDocument;
                 var TopLine, CurrentLine, CurrentCol : integer);
  begin {DoPgUp}
    if TopLine >= PageLength
      then
        begin
          TopLine := TopLine - PageLength + 1;
          CurrentLine := CurrentLine - PageLength + 1
        end
      else
        begin
```

```
          CurrentLine := CurrentLine - TopLine + 1;
          TopLine := 1
        end;
    if LastCharPos(Document, CurrentLine) < CurrentCol
      then
        DoEnd(Document, CurrentLine, CurrentCol);
    RedisplayPage(Document, TopLine)
  end; {DoPgUp}

procedure DoPgDn(var Document : TypeDocument;
                 var TopLine, CurrentLine, CurrentCol : integer);
  begin {DoPgDn}
    if TopLine <= (MaxDocumentLength - 2 * PageLength)
      then
        begin
          TopLine := TopLine + PageLength - 1;
          CurrentLine := CurrentLine + PageLength - 1;
        end
      else
        begin
          CurrentLine := CurrentLine - TopLine + MaxDocumentLength -
                         PageLength;
          TopLine := MaxDocumentLength - PageLength
        end;
    if LastCharPos(Document, CurrentLine) < CurrentCol
      then
        DoEnd(Document, CurrentLine, CurrentCol);
    RedisplayPage(Document, TopLine)
  end; {DoPgDn}

procedure DoLeft(var Document : TypeDocument;
                 var TopLine, CurrentLine, CurrentCol : integer);
  begin {DoLeft}
    if CurrentCol > 1
      then
        CurrentCol := CurrentCol - 1
      else
        if (CurrentLine <> 1)
          then
            begin
              DoUp(Document, TopLine, CurrentLine, CurrentCol);
              DoEnd(Document, CurrentLine, CurrentCol)
            end
  end; {DoLeft}

procedure DoRight(var Document : TypeDocument;
                  var TopLine, CurrentLine, CurrentCol : integer);
  begin {DoRight}
    if CurrentCol < LastCharPos(Document, CurrentLine) + 1
      then
        CurrentCol := CurrentCol + 1
      else
        begin
          DoDown(Document, TopLine, CurrentLine, CurrentCol);
          DoHome(CurrentCol)
```

```
        end
    end; {DoRight}

  begin {DoKey}
    if ExtKeyHit
      then
        case ord(KeyHit) of
          68 : Done := true;
          71 : DoHome(CurrentCol);
          72 : DoUp(Document, TopLine, CurrentLine, CurrentCol);
          73 : DoPgUp(Document, TopLine, CurrentLine, CurrentCol);
          75 : DoLeft(Document, TopLine, CurrentLine, CurrentCol);
          77 : DoRight(Document, TopLine, CurrentLine, CurrentCol);
          79 : DoEnd(Document, CurrentLine, CurrentCol);
          80 : DoDown(Document, TopLine, CurrentLine, CurrentCol);
          81 : DoPgDn(Document, TopLine, CurrentLine, CurrentCol);
        end
  end; {DoKey}

procedure OpenFileToRead(var FileToReadFrom : text);

  var
    FileName : string;

  begin {OpenFileToRead}
    {$I-}
    repeat
      clrscr;
      write('Enter file name: ');
      readln(FileName);
      assign(FileToReadFrom, FileName);
      reset(FileToReadFrom)
    until (ioresult = 0)
    {$I+}
  end; {OpenFileToRead}

procedure LoadDocument(var Document : TypeDocument);

  var
    LineInDocument : integer;
    FileToReadFrom : text;

  begin {LoadDocument}
    OpenFileToRead(FileToReadFrom);
    LineInDocument := 1;
    while not eof(FileToReadFrom) and
          (LineInDocument <= MaxDocumentLength) do
      begin
        readln(FileToReadFrom, Document[LineInDocument]);
        LineInDocument := LineInDocument + 1
      end;
    close(FileToReadFrom)
  end; {LoadDocument}
```

```
begin {FileBrowser}
  InitVar(Document, Done, TopLine, CurrentLine, CurrentCol);
  LoadDocument(Document);
  SetupScreen(Document, CurrentLine, CurrentCol);
  repeat
    UpdateScreen(CurrentLine, CurrentCol);
    GetKey(KeyHit, ExtKeyHit, AcceptedChars, AcceptedExt, false);
    DoKey(KeyHit, Document, ExtKeyHit, Done, TopLine,
          CurrentLine, CurrentCol)
  until Done
end. {FileBrowser}
```

File Manipulation Procedures

The computer operating system provides for many "housekeeping" functions, such as listing directories, changing the current directory, and creating or removing subdirectories. In many application programs, you will want to perform such functions. For this reason, Turbo Pascal provides you with access to the most important of these functions in the form of a number of predeclared procedures, namely `ChDir`, `Erase`, `GetDir`, `MkDir`, `Rename`, `RmDir`. In this section, we describe the operation of these procedures.

Chdir is used to change the current directory. This is the directory to which the files used in `case`, `Rename`, `GetDir`, and `Assign` refer. The syntax of the procedure is:

```
ChDir(PathName);
```

Here, `PathName` is a valid DOS path name. The procedure changes the current directory to the one specified in PathName. If this directory is not a valid path name, an I/O error occurs. For example, the following statement changes the current directory to C:\WORDPROC\LETTERS:

```
ChDir('C:\WORDPROC\LETTERS');
```

The `erase` procedure is used to erase a file stored on diskette. The file is assumed to be in the current directory. Here is the syntax of this procedure:

```
Erase(FileName);
```

Here, `FileName` is a valid name of a file in the current directory. If there is no such file, then an I/O error occurs. For example, the following statement erases the file LETTER1.DOC:

```
Erase('LETTER1.DOC');
```

The `GetDir` procedure displays the contents of a specified directory. The syntax of the procedure is:

```
GetDir(PathName);
```

Here, `PathName` specifies a valid path to a directory. If this path is invalid, then an I/O error occurs. If `PathName` is omitted, then the current directory is assumed. For example, the following statement displays the contents of the directory C:\WORDPROC\LETTERS:

```
GetDir('C:\WORDPROC\LETTERS');
```

The `MkDir` procedure is used to create a directory. The syntax of the procedure is:

```
MkDir(PathName);
```

Here, `PathName` is a path to the directory being specified. For example, the following statement creates the subdirectory LETTERS of C:\WORDPROC:

```
MkDir('C:\WORDPROC\LETTERS');
```

The `Rename` procedure is used to name files in the current directory. Its syntax is:

```
Rename(OldName, NewName);
```

Here, `OldName` is the current name of the file and `NewName` is the new name. If either there does not exist a file with the name `OldName` or if a file with name `NewName` already exists, then an I/O error occurs. For example, the following statement changes the name of the file LETTER1 to LETTER2:

```
Rename(Letter1,Letter2);
```

The `RmDir` procedure is used to delete a directory. Its syntax is:

```
RmDir(PathName);
```

Here, `PathName` is a path to the directory being deleted. If either the path is invalid or if the specified directory contains user files, then an I/O error occurs. For example, the statement deletes the subdirectory LETTERS of the directory C:\WORDPROC, assuming that the current directory is C:\WORDPROC:

```
RmDir('LETTERS');
```

In all cases, of I/O errors mentioned above, you may use the function `IOResult` together with the compiler directive `{$I-}` to treat the errors in a passive fashion, as described in Chapter 8.

10 Graphics and Sound

Turbo Pascal is capable of using the graphics and sound capabilities of the IBM PC and its compatibles. This chapter is an introduction to these capabilities and includes:

- Line graphics in text mode
- Setting colors and graphics modes
- Relative and absolute coordinates in graphics mode
- Drawing lines, rectangles, and circles
- Drawing bar charts and pie charts
- Filling regions of the screen
- Saving and recalling graphics images
- Setting user-defined viewports
- Using sound within a program

Graphics in Text Mode

IBM PCs and compatibles are capable of various screen display modes. Just which display modes you can use will depend on the particular video adapter you have equipped your computer with. In text mode, the video display can display only characters from the standard IBM character set (more about that below). All video display adapters can display text mode.

In text mode, the display contains 25 rows of either 40 or 80 characters each. In addition, EGA and VGA display adapters have 43 and 50 line display modes. The various character positions divide the screen into small rectangles. Figure 10.1 shows the subdivision of the screen corresponding to an 80-character line width for a 25-line display mode.

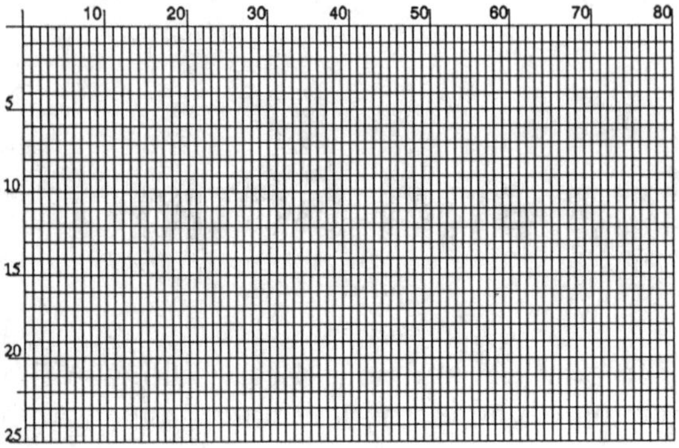

Figure 10.1.
Screen layout for text mode (80-character, 25-line width).

For simplicity, throughout this chapter, let's deal exclusively with the 25-line, 80-column text mode. The rectangles into which we have divided the screen are arranged in rows and columns. The rows are numbered from 1 to 25, with row 1 at the top of the screen and row 25 at the bottom. The columns are numbered from 1 to 80, with column 1 at the extreme left and column 80 at the extreme right. Each rectangle on the screen is identified by a pair of numbers, indicating the row and column. For example, the rectangle in the 12th row and 16th column is shown in Figure 10.2.

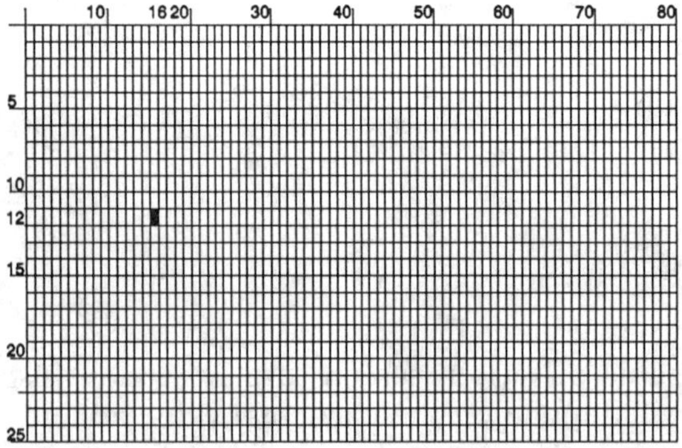

Figure 10.2.
Rectangle in the 12th row and 16th column.

To locate the cursor at column *x* and row *y*, we use the instruction:

```
gotoxy(x,y);
```

Remember that printing always occurs at the current cursor location.

Example 1. Write statements to print the words "IBM Personal Computer" beginning at column 20, row 10.

Solution.

```
gotoxy(20,10);
write('IBM Personal Computer');
```

Until now, we have printed only characters such as those found on a typewriter keyboard (letters, numbers, and punctuation marks). Actually, the IBM PC has a very extensive set of characters, including a collection of graphics characters, as shown in Figure 10.3. Note that each character (including graphics characters) is identified by an ASCII code. In Figure 10.3, we list the characters corresponding to ASCII codes 128–255. For example,

ASCII value	Character	ASCII value	Character	ASCII value	Character	ASCII value	Character
128	Ç	166	ª	204	╠	242	≥
129	ü	167	º	205	═	243	≤
130	é	168	¿	206	╬	244	⌠
131	â	169	⌐	207	╧	245	⌡
132	ä	170	¬	208	╨	246	÷
133	à	171	½	209	╤	247	≈
134	å	172	¼	210	╥	248	°
135	ç	173	¡	211	╙	249	∙
136	ê	174	«	212	╘	250	·
137	ë	175	»	213	╒	251	√
138	è	176	░	214	╓	252	ⁿ
139	ï	177	▒	215	╫	253	²
140	î	178	▓	216	╪	254	■
141	ì	179	│	217	┘	255	(blank 'FF')
142	Ä	180	┤	218	┌		
143	Å	181	╡	219	█		
144	É	182	╢	220	▄		
145	æ	183	╖	221	▌		
146	Æ	184	╕	222	▐		
147	ô	185	╣	223	▀		
148	ö	186	║	224	α		
149	ò	187	╗	225	β		
150	û	188	╝	226	Γ		
151	ù	189	╜	227	π		
152	ÿ	190	╛	228	Σ		
153	Ö	191	┐	229	σ		
154	Ü	192	└	230	μ		
155	¢	193	┴	231	τ		
156	£	194	┬	232	Φ		
157	¥	195	├	233	Θ		
158	Pts	196	─	234	Ω		
159	ƒ	197	┼	235	δ		
160	á	198	╞	236	∞		
161	í	199	╟	237	Ø		
162	ó	200	╚	238	ε		
163	ú	201	╔	239	∩		
164	ñ	202	╩	240	≡		
165	Ñ	203	╦	241	±		

Figure 10.3.
IBM graphics and special characters.

the character with ASCII code 179 is a vertical line (|). To place this character at the current cursor position, we use the instruction:

```
write(chr(179));
```

Note the use of `write` rather than `writeln` prevents the cursor from moving to the beginning of the next line. In most printing involving graphics, you will want to use write for this reason.

We may use the graphics characters to build up various images on the screen, as the next example shows. Note the use of the procedure `Clrscr`, which clears the screen. This procedure is contained in the unit `Crt`.

Example 2. Write a program that draws a horizontal line across row 10 of the screen. (Assume that you have a 80-column screen.)

Solution. Just in case the screen contains some unrelated characters, begin by clearing the screen using the `ClrScr` procedure. Then print character 196 (a horizontal line) across row 10 of the screen.

Here is the program:

Listing 10.1. Print Horizontal Line

```
program PrintHorizontalLine;
{This program prints a horizontal
line across row 10 of the screen.}

  uses
    crt;

  var
    X : integer;

  begin {PrintHorizontalLine}
    clrscr;
    gotoxy(1, 10);  { Move the cursor to column 1, row 10 }
    for X := 1 to 80 do
      write(chr(196));  { Write 80 horizontal line characters }
    readln
  end. {PrintHorizontalLine}
```

Example 3. Write a program that draws a vertical line in column 25 from row 5 to row 15. The program should blink the line 50 times.

Solution. The blinking effect may be achieved by repeatedly clearing the screen.

Here is our program:

Listing 10.2. Blinking Line

```
program BlinkingLine;
{This program draws a vertical line in column 25 from
row 5 to row 15, blinking 50 times before stopping.}

  uses
    crt;

  var
    Iteration, Y : integer;

  begin {BlinkingLine}
    clrscr;
    for Iteration := 1 to 50 do  { Blink 50 times }
      begin
        for Y := 5 to 15 do
          begin
            gotoxy(25, Y);  { Move the cursor to column 25, row Y }
            write(chr(179)) { Write vertical line character }
          end;
        clrscr  { Clear the screen }
      end;
      readln
  end. {BlinkingLine}
```

Example 4. Draw a pair of x- and y-axes as shown in Figure 10.4. Label the vertical axes with the word Profit and the horizontal axis with the word Month.

Figure 10.4.
X-axis = Month and Y-axis = Profit.

Solution. The program must draw two lines and print two words. The only real problem is to determine the positioning. The word Profit has six letters. Let's start the vertical line in the position corresponding to the seventh character column. We'll run the vertical line from the top of the screen (row 1)

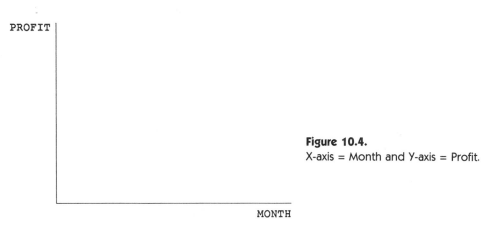

to within two character rows from the bottom. On the next-to-last row, we will place the word month. The layout of the screen is shown in Figure 10.5.

Here is our program to generate the display:

Listing 10.3. Axes

```
program Axes;
{This program draws a pair of axes labeled"PROFIT"
and"MONTH".}

  uses
    crt;

  procedure WriteLabels;
  {Writes "PROFIT" at upper left, "MONTH" at lower right.}
    begin {WriteLabels}
      gotoxy(1, 1);
      write('PROFIT');
      gotoxy(75, 23);
      write('MONTH')
    end; {WriteLabels}

  procedure DrawAxes;
  { Draws the vertical and horizontal axes and a corner character.}
    var
      X, Y : integer;
    begin {DrawAxes}
      { Draw the vertical axis }
      for Y := 1 to 22 do
        begin
          gotoxy(7, Y);
          write(chr(179))
        end;
      { Draw the corner }
      gotoxy(7, 22);
      write(chr(192));
      { Draw the horizontal axis }
      for X := 8 to 80 do
        begin
          gotoxy(X, 22);
          write(chr(196))
        end
    end; {DrawAxes}

begin {Axes}
    clrscr;
    WriteLabels;
    DrawAxes;
    readln
  end. {Axes}
```

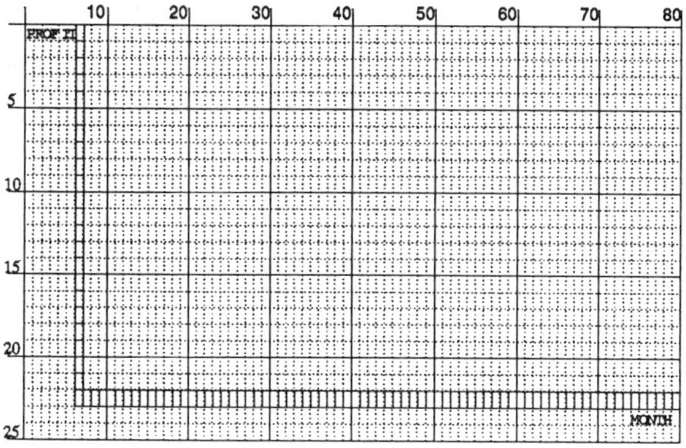

Figure 10.5.
Display layout for chart of Figure 10.4.

Colors and Graphics Modes

Now that we have explored some of the elements of producing pictures using the IBM character set, let's get into graphics proper. Depending on the video adapter of your computer, you may have available graphics modes which allow you to control the screen display at the individual dot level. Graphics modes differ both in the dimension of the screen in dots and in the number of permissible colors. In this section, we discuss the various graphics modes available and how to initialize them.

> **NOTE:** Much of the material in this chapter is not valid for versions of Turbo Pascal prior to 5.5.

The Graph Unit

The various graphics procedures and functions to be introduced in this chapter are contained in the unit `Graph`. To make use of these statements, your program must declare this unit using a statement of the form:

```
uses Graph;
```

Graphics versus Text Modes

Turbo Pascal 5.5 supports video adapter cards, as specified by the following predeclared constants:

CGA

MCGA

EGA

EGA64 (old EGA with 64K on card)

EGAMono (EGA in monochrome mode)

IBM8514 (IBM 8514 adapter)

HercMono (Hercules monochrome adapter)

ATT400 (AT&T video adapter)

VGA

PC3270 (IBM 3270 video adapter)

For each of these adapters, one or more video modes is supported, as defined by the following predefined constants.

CGAC0 (320 × 200, Colors: LightGreen, LightRed, Yellow)

CGAC1 (320 × 200, Colors: LightCyan, LightMagenta, White)

CGAC2 (320 × 200, Colors: Green, Red, Brown)

CGAC3 (320 × 200, Colors: Cyan, Magenta, LightGray)

CGAHi (640 × 200, Monochrome)

MCGAC0 (320 × 200, Colors: LightGreen, LightRed, Yellow)

MCGAC1 (320 × 200, Colors: LightCyan, LightMagenta, White)

MCGAC2 (320 × 200, Colors: Green, Red, Brown)

MCGAC3 (320 × 200, Colors: Cyan, Magenta, LightGray)

MCGAMed (640 × 200, Monochrome)

MCGAHi (640 × 480, Monochrome)

EGALo (640 × 200, 16 color)

EGAHi (640 × 350, 16 color)

EGA64Lo (640 × 200, 16 color)

EGA64Hi (640 × 350, 4 color)

EGAMonoMi (640 × 350, 2 pages if 256K present)

HercMonoHi (720 × 348, Monochrome)

ATT400C0 (320 × 200, Colors: LightGreen, LightRed, Yellow)

ATT400C1 (320 × 200, Colors: LightCyan, LightMagenta, White)

ATT400C2 (320 × 200, Colors: Green, Red, Brown)

ATT400C3 (320 × 200, Colors: Cyan, Magenta, LightGray)

ATT400Med (640 × 200, Monochrome)

ATT400Hi (640 × 400, Monochrome)

VGALo (640 × 200, 16 color)

VGAMed (640 × 350, 16 color)

VGAHi (640 × 480, 16 color)

PC3270Hi (720 × 350, Monochrome)

IBM8514Lo (640 × 480, 256 colors)

IBM8514Hi (1024 × 768, 256 colors)

Initializing and Terminating Graphics

Before using any graphics statements, you must initialize the graphics system using a statement of the form:

```
initgraph(GraphDriver, GraphMode, PathToDriver);
```

Here `GraphDriver` is the constant indicating the graphics adapter you wish to use and `GraphMode` is the constant indicating the graphics mode you wish to use. `PathToDriver` is a path which locates the graphics driver (.BGI file) appropriate for your video adapter.

The default value of `GraphDriver` indicates that the routine should automatically detect which graphics adapter you have and set `GraphMode` for the highest resolution mode which the hardware will support. In the case of the IBM8514 or ATT400 cards, autodetection is not available.

You may bypass autodetection and set the graphics mode and driver manually. For example, to choose the CGA driver and CGAHi mode, you would use the statements:

```
GraphDriver := CGA;
GraphMode := CGAHi;
initgraph(GraphDriver, GraphMode, '');
```

Note that `GraphDriver` and `GraphMode` are predeclared integer variables. In this example, even if you don't have a CGA card, if your card can emulate CGA (e.g., an EGA or VGA card), then that emulation will be used.

Usually, the first task you wish to undertake in graphics mode is to erase the screen. This can be done using the statement:

```
ClearDevice;
```

When you are done using the graphics system (possibly not until the end of your program), you should close the graphics system using the statement:

```
CloseGraph;
```

This statement returns the computer to the display mode in effect when the graphics system was initialized. If you fail to close the graphics system, you risk returning the machine to DOS in a different video mode than DOS expects, with some odd effects possible.

Determining the Current Coordinate System

You may have the program determine the maximum X and Y coordinates using the functions `GetMaxX` and `GetMaxY`, respectively. These functions have no parameters and return the maximum X and Y coordinates as integers. For example, if `MaxX` and `MaxY` are integer variables and we are in CGAHi mode, then

```
MaxX  := GetMaxX;
MaxY  := GetMaxY;
```

assigns `MaxX` the value 319 and `MaxY` the value 199.

Error Management in Graphics

After any graphics procedure, the variable `GraphResult` records any error which occurred during execution. A zero value indicates successful execution. Here are the meanings of the various nonzero values of `GraphResult`:

–1: No initgraph

–2: Specified adapter not detected

–3: File not found

–4: Invalid driver

–5: No Load Memory

–6: No Scan Memory

–7: No Flood Memory

−8: Font not found

−9: No Font memory

−10: Invalid graphics mode

−11: Generic error

−12: I/O Error

−13: Invalid Font

−14: Invalid Font Number

To build bulletproof graphics programs, you should test your graphics procedures for errors during execution.

Available Colors

Colors in Turbo Pascal may be specified using the following predeclared constants:

Black (0)

Blue (1)

Green (2)

Cyan (3)

Red (4)

Magenta (5)

Brown (6)

LightGray (7)

DarkGray (8)

LightBlue (9)

LightGreen (10)

LightCyan (11)

LightRed (12)

LightMagenta (13)

Yellow (14)

White (15)

You may set the color used by other graphics procedures using the `SetColor` procedure. This procedure sets the current color, which remains in effect until explicitly changed. For instance to make the current color LightBlue, use the statement:

```
SetColor(LightBlue);
```

You may set the background color using the `SetBkColor` statement. For instance, to set the background color to White, use the statement:

```
SetBkColor(White);
```

Pixels

Each of the small screen rectangles (more properly, dots) is called a pixel (i.e., a picture element). You may color each pixel on an individual basis. Of course, the number of dots on your screen depends on your choice of graphics mode. For instance, in CGAC1 mode, there are 320 dots across the screen and 200 dots down, for a total of 64,000 pixels.

Graphics Coordinates

Each pixel is specified by a pair of coordinates (x,y), where x is the column number and y is the row number (see Figure 10.6). Note the following important facts:

1. Rows and columns are numbered beginning with 0 (not 1 as in text mode). In the medium-resolution CGA graphics mode, the rows are numbered from 0 to 199 and the columns from 0 to 319. In high-resolution CGA graphics mode, the rows are numbered from 0 to 199 and the columns from 0 to 639.
2. Coordinates in graphics mode are specified with the column (x-coordinate) first.

You may illuminate the pixel with coordinates (x,y) in the color using the statement:

```
PutPixel(x,y,color);
```

For instance, to illuminate the pixel at (50,100) with the color Cyan, use the statement:

```
PutPixel(50,100,Cyan);
```

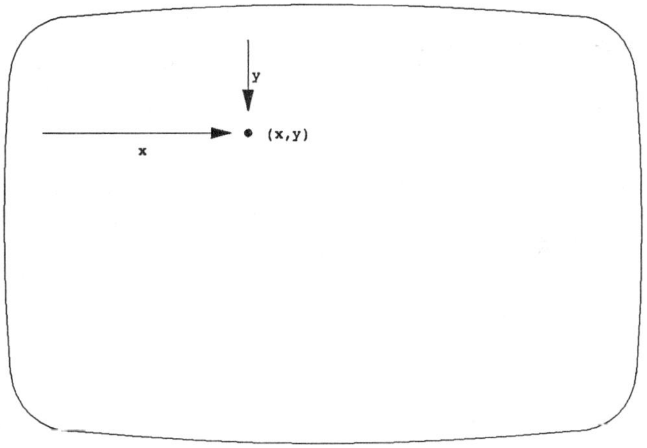

Figure 10.6.
Coordinates in graphics mode.

To "erase" a pixel, illuminate it using the background color.

In graphics mode, the cursor is not visible. Instead, the computer keeps a pointer to the last point referenced. This pointer is called the *current pointer.* You may determine the position of the current pointer using the two functions `GetX` and `GetY`, which return the X and Y coordinates of the current pointer, respectively. For instance, if X and Y are integer variables, then the following statements assign them the coordinates of the current pointer:

```
X := GetX;
Y := GetY;
```

When you first initialize the graphics system, the current pointer is in the upper-left corner of the screen, namely the point (0,0). The current pointer is changed by some graphics statements and not others. (More about that later.) You may move the current pointer using the `MoveTo` procedure. For instance, to move to the point (50,75), use the statement:

```
MoveTo(50,75);
```

Relative Coordinates in Graphics Mode

You may specify the position of new points by giving coordinates relative to the last point referenced. Such coordinates are called *relative coordinates.* For example, suppose that the last point referenced is (100,75), and that a point is specified by relative coordinates:

```
(20,30)
```

This is the point that is 20 units to the right and 30 units down from the last referenced point (see Figure 10.7). This is the point with coordinates (100,75).

Similarly, consider the point specified by the relative coordinates:

```
(-10,-40)
```

This is the point that is 10 units to the left and 40 units up from the point (120,105); that is, the point (90,35) (see Figure 10.7).

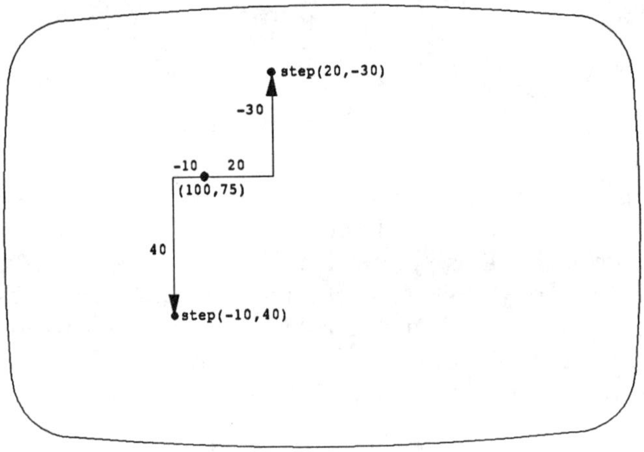

Figure 10.7.
Relative graphics coordinates.

You may move the current pointer relative to its current location using the statement `MoveRel`. For instance, to make the move specified by the relative coordinates (–10,–40), use the statement:

```
MoveRel(-10,-40);
```

Lines, Rectangles, and Circles

Let's now discuss the graphics statements available for drawing lines, rectangles, ellipses, circles, arcs, and sectors.

Lines

The `Line` statement draws a line between two specified points. The value of the current pointer remains unchanged by this command. For instance, to draw a line between the points (20,50) and (80,199), use the statement:

```
Line(20,50,80,199);
```

The LineTo statement draws a line from the current pointer to a designated point. The current pointer is changed to the designated point. For instance, the following statement draws a line from the current pointer to the point (50,75):

```
LineTo(50,75);
```

The LineRel statement draws a line from the current pointer to a point specified by a designated relative move. The current pointer is changed to the designated point. For instance, the following statement draws a line from the current pointer to the point specified by the relative move (10,–40):

```
LineRel(10,-40);
```

All three line statements draw the line using the current color (set by SetColor) and the current line style (see below).

Note that there are lines the computer cannot draw perfectly. Lines on a diagonal are displayed as a series of visible "steps." This is as close as the computer can get to a straight line within the limited resolution provided by the graphics modes. The higher the resolution (that is, the more pixels on the screen), the better your straight lines will look.

Example 1. Draw a triangle in CGAHi mode with corners at the three points (150,20), (50,100), and (250,130) (see Figure 10.8).

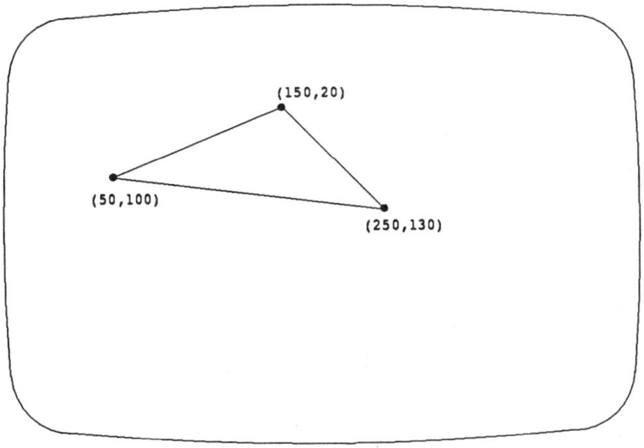

Figure 10.8.
A triangle.

Solution. We must draw three lines: from (150,20) to (50,100); from (50,100) to (250,130); and from (250,130) to (150,20). Here is the program.

Note that this coding assumes that the appropriate graphics driver (BGI file) is in the same directory as your program. If it is elsewhere, you *must* place a path to the driver within the single quotes. Be sure to include a backslash at the end of the path call. This applies to all programs in this and following chapters.

Listing 10.4. Triangle

```
program Triangle;
  uses
    graph;

  var
    GraphDriver, GraphMode  :  integer;

  begin {Triangle}
    GraphDriver  := CGA;
    GraphMode  := CGAHi;
    initgraph(GraphDriver, GraphMode, '');
    moveto(150, 20);
    lineto(50, 100);
    lineto(250, 130);
    lineto(150, 20);
    readln;
    closegraph
  end. {Triangle}
```

Example 2. Let's reconsider the triangle of Example 1. The point (150,80) is inside the triangle. Draw lines connecting this point to each of the corners of the triangle (see Figure 10.9).

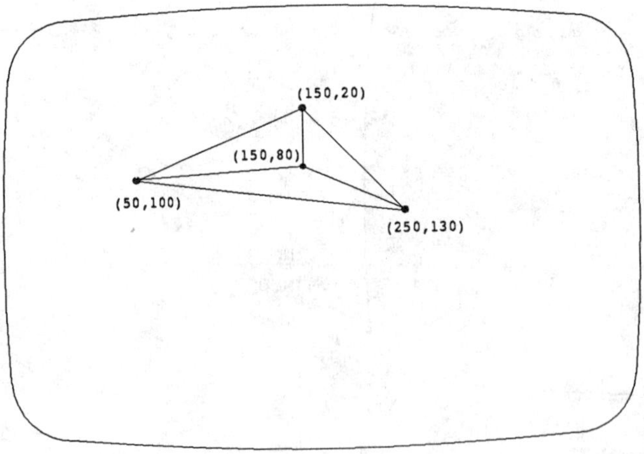

Figure 10.9.
More triangles.

Solution. Draw the triangle as before. Then `Moveto` the point (150,80) and draw the three new lines using `Line` so that the current pointer is not changed between statements.

Listing 10.5. Triangle 2

```
program Triangle2;
  uses
    graph;

  var
    GraphDriver, GraphMode : integer;

  begin {Triangle2}
    GraphDriver := CGA;
    GraphMode := CGAHi;
    initgraph(GraphDriver, GraphMode, '');
    moveto(150, 20);
    lineto(50, 100);
    lineto(250, 130);
    lineto(150, 20);
    moveto(150, 80);
    line(150, 80, 150, 20);
    line(150, 80, 50, 100);
    line(150, 80, 250, 130);
    readln;
    closegraph
  end. {Triangle2}
```

Using Colors with Line

To set the color of a line, execute the procedure `SetColor` prior to drawing the line. For instance, to draw a line between (50,80) and (130,40) in Cyan, use the statements:

```
SetColor(Cyan);
Line(50,80,130,40);
```

Line Styles

Turbo Pascal allows drawing of line figures (lines, rectangles, circles, arcs), using lines of various styles and thickness. There are four predeclared line styles:

SolidLn

DottedLn

CenterLn

DashedLn

There are two predeclared thicknesses:

NormWidth

ThickWidth

In addition, you can specify your own line style. We'll discuss how to do this in a later chapter.

Line styles and thickness are set using the procedure `SetLineStyle`, with the syntax:

```
SetLineStyle(LineStyle:word; Pattern:word;Thickness:word);
```

Here `LineStyle` is one of the line styles specified above, `Pattern` has the value 0 unless `LineStyle` equals `UserBitLn`, in which case `Pattern` equals the bit pattern describing the style, and `Thickness` is one of the two values described above.

For instance, to draw a thick dotted line between (50,50) and (100,100), use the statements:

```
SetLineStyle(DottedLn,0,ThickWidth);
Line(50,50,100,100);
```

A current line style and thickness is maintained and used by all subsequent line drawing commands. The default style is `SolidLn` and the default thickness is `NormWidth`.

Rectangles

You may draw rectangles using the procedure `Rectangle`. You specify a rectangle using the coordinates of a pair of opposite vertices. For instance, to draw a rectangle with opposite vertices (50,50) and (100,100), use the statement:

```
Rectangle(50,50,100,100);
```

The Rectangle statement draws using the current color and the current line style and thickness.

Circles and Ellipses

To draw a circle, you use the `Circle` statement. For example, to draw a circle at center (100,100) and radius 50, you would use a statement of the form:

```
Circle(100,100,50);
```

The `Circle` statement uses the current color to draw the circular boundary.

Note that the circles on the screen are not smooth, but have a "ragged" appearance. This is due to the limited resolution of the screen. If you use high-resolution mode, you will notice that the appearance of your circles improves greatly.

You may draw ellipses using the `Ellipse` command. This is a very versatile command using 5 parameters. Its syntax is:

```
Ellipse(X,Y:Integer; StAngle, EndAngle:Word;Xradius, YRadius:Word);
```

Here `(X,Y)` is the center of the ellipse, `Xradius` is the horizontal radius, `Yradius` is the vertical radius, and `StAngle` and `EndAngle` are, respectively, the starting and ending angle. Angles are expressed in degrees, with a 0 angle pointing toward 3 o'clock.

For example, in CGAHi mode, consider the statement:

```
Ellipse(300,100,0,360,100,50);
```

This statement draws a complete ellipse with center (100,300) with x-radius 100 and y-radius 50 (see Figure 10.10).

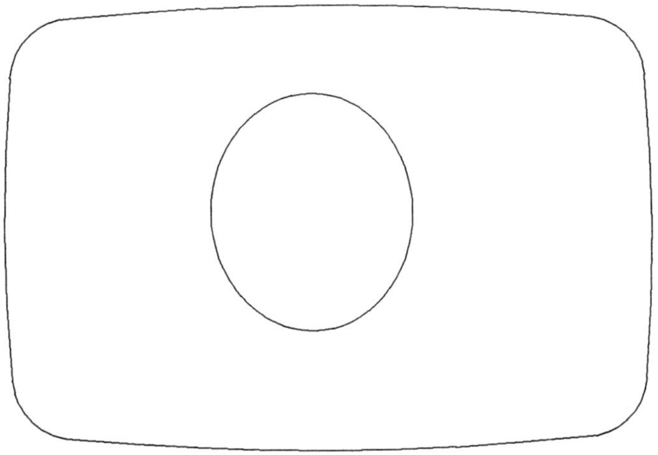

Figure 10.10.
The result of
Ellipse(300,100,0,360,100,50);

You can get even finer-grained control over circles and ellipses if you apply some mathematics. Suppose that an ellipse (or circle) has its center at the point with coordinates (x0,y0). Suppose that the horizontal half-axis has length A and the vertical half-axis has length B. Then a typical point (x,y) on the ellipse takes the form

```
x = x0 + A*cos(t)
y = y0 + B*sin(t)
```

where t is an angle between 0 and 2*pi radians. The geometric meaning of the angle t is shown in Figure 10.11. The above equations are called the *parametric equations for the ellipse.* They are very useful in drawing graphics.

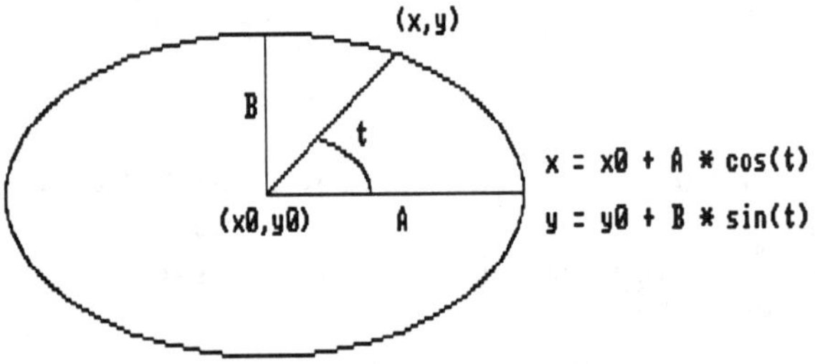

Figure 10.11.
An ellipse in parametric form.

For example, here is a program that draws an ellipse with center (320,100) (the center of the screen in high-resolution mode) by plotting dots in a "sweep" fashion. This graph may be used to simulate the motion of a planet around the sun.

Listing 10.6. Orbit

```
program Orbit;
{This program depicts the orbit of a planet as
it travels about the sun in an elliptical path.}

  uses
    crt,
    graph;

  var
    GraphDriver, GraphMode : integer;
    T : real;           {Angle, in radians}
    X, Y : integer;  {Coordinates of the planet at angle T}
```

```
begin {Orbit}
  GraphDriver := CGA;
  GraphMode := CGAHi;
  initgraph(GraphDriver, GraphMode, '');
  T := 0;  {Angle T will go from 0 to 6.28 radians}
  repeat
    X := 320 + round(200 * cos(T));  {Compute column at angle T}
    Y := 100 + round(30 * sin(T));   {Compute row at angle T}
    putpixel(X, Y, 1);               {Draw the planet}
    delay(100);                      {Pause 1/10 sec}
    T := T + 0.05
  until (T > 6.28);
  closegraph
end. {Orbit}
```

Arcs, Sectors, and Pie Slices

The three procedures `Arc`, `Sector`, and `PieSlice` are similar. The first draws an elliptical arc, the second an elliptical sector (the sides are included), and the third draws a filled pie slice. (In the latter case, you can choose the fill pattern. But for the moment, let's deal only with the default fill pattern, a solid fill).

For instance, to draw a circular arc of radius 20, centered at (40,100), from angle 90 to 120, use the statement:

```
Arc(40,100,90,120,20);
```

Just like the `Ellipse` procedure, the `Arc` procedure allows drawing arcs of ellipses.

To draw a circular sector (arc plus sides) of radius 20, centered at (40,100), from angle 90 to 120, use the statement:

```
Sector(40,100,20,20,90,120);
```

To draw a circular pie slice (filled sector) of radius 20, centered at (40,100), from angle 90 to 120, use the statement:

```
PieSlice(40,100,90,120,20);
```

Aspect Ratio

Drawing circles and ellipses has an added complication we haven't yet mentioned—the aspect ratio. Usually, when you plot circles on graph paper you use the same scale on the x-axis as on the y-axis. For example, if a unit on the x-axis is larger than a unit on the y-axis, your circle will appear as an ellipse stretched out in the x-direction. Similarly, if the unit on the y-axis is larger than the unit on the x-axis, the circle will appear as an ellipse stretched out in the y-direction. Like it or not, the geometry of circles is intimately bound up with that of ellipses.

What is the aspect ratio for a circle? Well, that's a tricky question. On first glimpse, you probably guessed that the aspect ratio is 1. And indeed it is, if you are looking for a mathematical circle. However, if you draw a circle with an aspect ratio of 1, you will get an ellipse because the scales on the x- and y-axes are different. Let's consider CGAHi graphics mode: The screen is 640×200 pixels, the ratio of width to height is 200/640, or 5/16. To achieve a circle, you would expect to have to multiply the x-radius by 5/16 to get the proper y-radius; that is, an aspect ratio of 5/16. Well, not quite! Video monitors are not square because the ratio of width to height is 4/3. In order to achieve an ellipse that is visually a circle, we must multiply by 5/16 and by 4/3. In other words, the aspect ratio is

```
(5/16) * (4/3) = 5/12
```

Turbo Pascal computes the aspect ration from the current graphics driver setting. With these aspect ratios, circles look like circles. However, the y-radius is quite different from the x-radius! If you wish to set the aspect ratio for yourself, you may use the `SetApectRatio` statement. But beginners should probably not need to use it.

Computer Art

The graphics statements of Turbo Pascal may be used to draw interesting computer art on the screen. As a taste of what can be done, the program below draws random polygons on the screen. The program is written in CGAHi graphics mode, so that the screen has dimensions 640×200. The program first chooses the number of sides of the polygon. The polygon may have up to six sides. Next, the program picks out random points in numbers one more than the number of sides (it takes that number of points to draw a polygon with the given number of sides). The program then draws lines between consecutive points. The last point is made equal to the first point to make a closed polygon. Figure 10.12 shows a typical polygon.

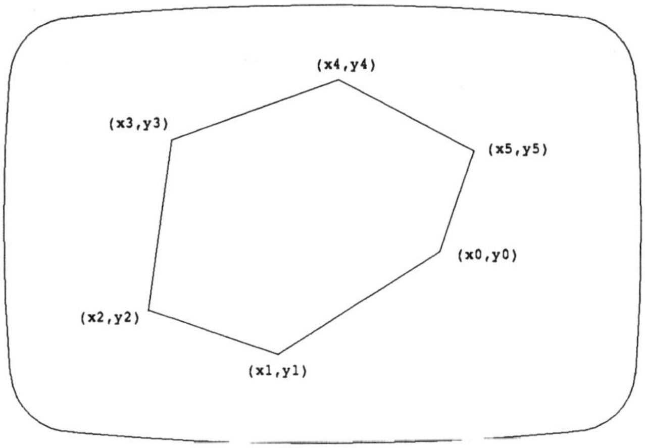

Figure 10.12.
A typical polygon.

The program then erases the polygon and repeats the entire procedure to draw a different polygon. The program draws 50 polygons.

Listing 10.7. Random Polygons

```
program RandomPolygons;
{This program draws a number of randomly
shaped polygons. After each polygon is
drawn, it is erased, giving a flickering
effect.}

  uses
    graph;

  const
    MaxSides  = 6;    {Max number of sides for any polygon}
    MaxPoints = 7;    {N sides means N+1 points}

  type
    TypeCoordinate = record
                       X, Y : integer
                     end;
    TypePoints = array[1..MaxPoints] of TypeCoordinate;
    TypePolygon = record
                    NumberOfSides  : integer;
                    Points         : TypePoints
                  end;
```

```
var
  GraphDriver, GraphMode : integer;
  Iteration : integer;    {Controls # of polygons to be drawn}
  Polygon : TypePolygon; {Holds poly points}

procedure DrawPolygon(    Polygon : TypePolygon;
                          Color : integer);
{Draws the polygon in the given color.}
  var
    CurrentPoint : integer;
  begin {DrawPolygon}
    setcolor(Color);    { set graphics drawing color }
    with Polygon do
      for CurrentPoint := 2 to (NumberOfSides + 1) do
        line (Points[CurrentPoint - 1].X, Points[CurrentPoint - 1].Y,
              Points[CurrentPoint].X, Points[CurrentPoint].Y)
  end; {DrawPolygon}

procedure MakePolygon(var Polygon : TypePolygon);
{Fills Polygon with random points and draws it.}
  var
    CurrentPoint : integer;
  begin {MakePolygon}
    with Polygon do
      begin
        {Choose 1 <= NumberOfSides <= MaxSides}
        NumberOfSides := 1 + random(MaxSides);
        for CurrentPoint := 1 to NumberOfSides do
          begin
            Points[CurrentPoint].X := random(640);
            Points[CurrentPoint].Y := random(200)
          end;
        Points[NumberOfSides + 1] := Points[1]   {Close polygon}
      end;
    DrawPolygon(Polygon, 1)
  end; {MakePolygon}

begin {RandomPolygons}
  GraphDriver := CGA;
  GraphMode := CGAHi;
  initgraph(GraphDriver, GraphMode, '');
  randomize;
  for Iteration := 1 to 50 do
    begin
      Delay(500);
      MakePolygon(Polygon); {Make and draw polygon}
      DrawPolygon(Polygon, getbkcolor)
        {Erase polygon by drawing}
    end;                                    {in background color}
  closegraph;
  readln
end. {RandomPolygons}
```

Here is a second program that draws a regular polygon (one with equal sides and angles) and then draws inscribed replicas of the original polygon, each of smaller size, until the interior of the original polygon is filled with the inscribed replicas (see Figure 10.13).

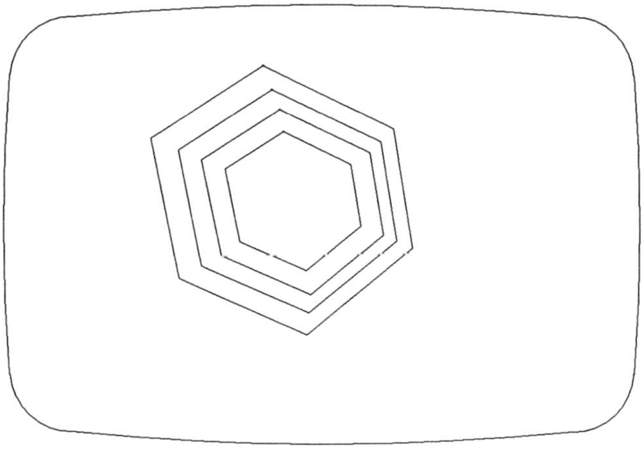

Figure 10.13.
Inscribed polygons.

Here are the mathematics necessary to draw a regular polygon. Suppose that you wish to draw a regular polygon having N sides and inscribed in a circle of radius R and centered at the point (X0,Y0) (see Figure 10.14). The vertices are then the points (X[J],Y[J]) (J := 0,1,2,...,N), where

```
X[J] = X0 + R*COS(2*PI*J/N)
Y[J] = Y0 + R*(5/12)*SIN(2*PI*J/N)
```

The user chooses the value of N (up to 20) for our program. The center of the polygon is the center of the screen (320,100) in CGAHi mode. Use an initial value of 100 for the radius R, then draw polygons corresponding to the same value of N, but with successively smaller values of R. Shrinking the radius circle in which the polygon is inscribed gives the illusion that the polygon is growing inward. Here is the program:

Listing 10.8. Inscribed Polygons

```
program InscribedPolygons;
{This program draws a sequence of inscribed
polygons which grow inward.}

  uses
    graph;
```

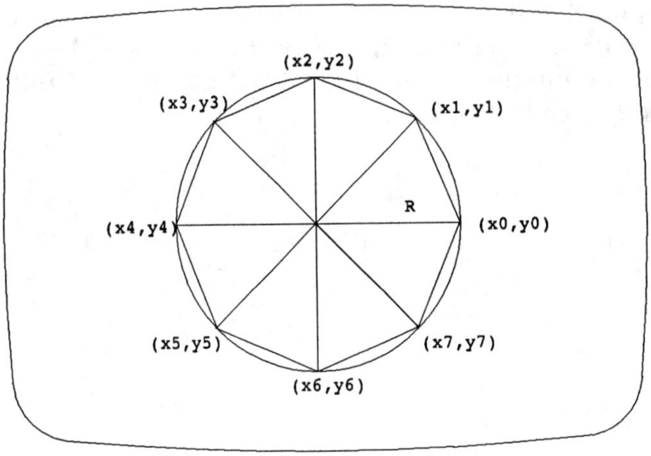

Figure 10.14.
An inscribed polygon.

```
const
  MaxSides = 20;  {Max number of sides for any polygon}
  MaxPoints = 21; {N sides means N+1 points}

type
  TypeCoordinate = record
                     X, Y : integer
                   end;
  TypePoints = array[1..MaxPoints] of TypeCoordinate;
  TypePolygon = record
                  NumberOfSides : integer;
                  Points : TypePoints
                end;

var
  Polygon : TypePolygon;
  Size : integer;

procedure GetNumberOfSides(var NumberOfSides : integer);
{Reads values for NumberOfSides from the keyboard until
 NumberOfSides is equal to or less than MaxSides.}
  begin {GetNumberOfSides}
    repeat
      write('Number of sides? ');
      readln(NumberOfSides)
    until (NumberOfSides <= MaxSides)
  end; {GetNumberOfSides}

procedure OpenGraph;
{Initializes the graphics system into C/GA hi-res mode.}
  var
    GraphDriver, GraphMode : integer;
  begin {OpenGraph}
    GraphDriver := CGA;
    GraphMode := CGAHi;
```

```
    initgraph(GraphDriver, GraphMode, '')
  end; {OpenGraph}

procedure CalculateVertices (     Size : integer;
                            var Polygon : TypePolygon);
{Calculates the vertices for the polygon at the size
 contained in Size.}
  var
    Current : integer;
  begin {CalculateVertices}
    with Polygon do
      begin
        for Current := 1 to NumberOfSides do
          with Points[Current] do
            begin
              X := 320 + round
                    (Size * cos (2 * pi * Current / NumberOfSides));
              Y := 100 + round
                    (Size * (5/12) * sin(2 * pi * Current / NumberOfSides))
            end;
          Points[NumberOfSides + 1] := Points[1]
      end
  end; {CalculateVertices}

procedure DrawPolygon (     Polygon : TypePolygon);
{Draws the polygon}
  var
    CurrentPoint : integer;
  begin {DrawPolygon}
    with Polygon do
      for CurrentPoint := 2 to (NumberOfSides + 1) do
        line (Points[CurrentPoint - 1].X, Points[CurrentPoint - 1].Y,
              Points[CurrentPoint].X, Points[CurrentPoint].Y)
  end; {DrawPolygon}

begin {InscribedPolygons}
  GetNumberOfSides(Polygon.NumberOfSides);
  OpenGraph;
  for Size := 25 downto 0 do
    begin
      CalculateVertices(Size * 8, Polygon);  {Sizes 200,192,184,etc}
      DrawPolygon(Polygon)
    end;
  closegraph;
  readln
end. {InscribedPolygons}
```

Text on a Graphics Screen

In order to dress up your graphics displays, it is useful to include explanatory text. In fact, in order to enhance the graphic message, various type sizes and styles are used. In this section, we discuss how to employ text along with your graphics.

Text Fonts

Turbo Pascal 5.5 allows you to make use of a number of different text fonts within graphics mode. The most rudimentary font is a bit-mapped font in which the characters are formed in a rectangle 8 pixels wide and 8 pixels high. Using procedures within the `Graph` unit, you may alter the size of these characters by a specified magnification factor.

The character font and the size of the characters are both specified using the procedure `SetTextStyle`, which has the syntax:

```
SetTextStyle(Font:Word; Direction:Word; CharSize:Word);
```

The various parameters may be specified using the following predeclared constants. The Font parameter may be one of the following:

DefaultFont

TriplexFont

SmallFont

SansSerifFont

GothicFont

The first choice corresponds to the bit-mapped font. The remaining four correspond to stroke fonts. Note that the stroke fonts must be installed prior to their being called in the `SetTextStyle` procedure.

The parameter `Direction` may take on one of the values:

```
HorizDir (horizontal text)
VertDir (vertical text)
```

The parameter `CharSize` has default value 1 for the bit-mapped font and 4 for the stroked fonts. Other values can be chosen for larger font sizes.

Text Justification

In text mode, characters are placed in a predetermined position in one of the character positions on the screen. However, in graphics work, it is necessary to place text much more precisely. Text is placed at a particular pixel location. The `SetTextJustify` procedure sets how the text will be placed relative to the pixel. Horizontally, the pixel may be at the left, center, or right edge of the character. Vertically, the pixel may be at the top, center, or bottom edge of the character. The syntax of the `SetTextJustify` procedure is:

```
SetTextJustify(Horiz, Vert: Word);
```

The choices for Horiz are:

LeftText

CenterText

RightText

The choices for Vert are:

BottomText

CenterText

TopText

Text Placement

The actual output of text in graphics modes can be accomplished using either the `OutText` or `OutTextXY` procedure. The procedure `OutText` displays specified text at the position of the current pointer. For instance, suppose that the current pointer is (50,100). Then the statement:

```
OutText('Hello');
```

displays the string `'Hello'` beginning at pixel (50,100). The type font, style, and direction are specified either by the last setting of `SetTextStyle` (if used) or the default values (otherwise). The justification is set either by the last setting of `SetTextJustify` (if used) or the defaults (otherwise).

The procedure `OutTextXY` is used to display text at a specified pixel location. For instance, the statement:

```
OutTextXY(50,100,'Hello');
```

displays the string 'Hello' beginning at the pixel (50,100), regardless of the value of the current pointer.

Neither of the statements OutText or OutTextXY changes the value of the current pointer.

Drawing Bar Charts

In this section, we'll apply what we have just learned about drawing lines and rectangles to draw the bar chart shown in Figure 10.15.

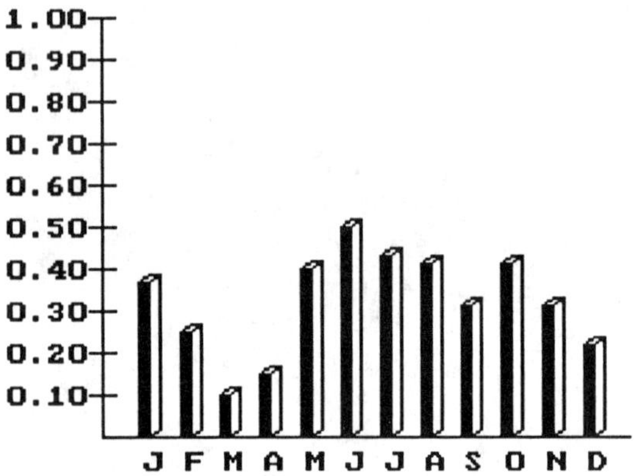

Figure 10.15.
A bar chart.

Before we begin discussing the design of the bar chart itself, let's discuss the Turbo Pascal procedures available for drawing the bars. The Bar procedure allows you to draw 2-dimensional bars and has the syntax:

```
Bar(x1,y1,x2,y2:integer);
```

This procedure draws a filled-in bar with a pair of opposite corners at (x1,y1) and (x2,y2). The fill pattern and color are taken from the settings of the current fill pattern and current color, respectively. You may set these using the procedure SetFillStyle.

The second procedure for drawing bars is Bar3D, which is used to draw 3-dimensional bars. It has the syntax:

```
Bar3D(x1,y1,x2,y2:integer; Depth:word; Top:boolean);
```

This procedure draws a 3-dimensional bar with opposite corners at (x1,y1) and (x2,y2). It handles fill style and color just like the procedure Bar. The parameter `Depth` specifies the number of pixel deep the bar is drawn. The parameter `Top` specifies whether or not to draw the bar with a top.

Let's now draw the bar chart shown above. Since the bars are 3-dimensional, we will be using the `Bar3D` procedure.

In setting up any graphics display, some planning is necessary to make the display look "pretty." The main goal in this section is to illustrate the planning procedure.

This display is not too complicated, so let's stick to CGAC0 (320 × 200) graphics.

Note that there are 10 bars to be displayed. Also, we must put a tick mark under each bar and line up and center a letter under the tick mark. Each letter is eight pixels wide, so we can approximate the centering of the letters on the tick marks by placing the tick marks in one of the columns 4, 12, 20, 28,.... (The corresponding letters occupy columns 0–7, 8–15, 16–23, 24–31,....)

Similarly, to center the labels on the vertical axis on the tick marks there, choose the rows for the tick marks from among 4, 12, 20,....

Let's place the vertical axis beginning in row four. This allows us to place the top tick mark in the proper row. There are at most 195 screen rows in which to place the rest of the vertical axis. We must divide the vertical axis into 10 equal parts. This suggests that each vertical part is 16 rows high. This causes the vertical axis to be 160 rows high and ends in row 164. We need to leave room for four characters (32 columns) to the right of the vertical axis as well as the tick marks, and let's not push the labels too far to the left. Finally, the vertical axis must be in one of the columns 4, 12, 20, 28,.... One possibility is to put the vertical axis in column 52. It turns out that this gives a reasonable-looking display.

The horizontal axis begins at the point (52,164). The horizontal axis is divided into 13 equal parts. Let's make each part two characters (32 columns) wide. This means that the right endpoint of the horizontal axis is (52+13*16,164).

First the program draws the axes. Then it draws the tick marks along the axes and the labels beside the tick marks.

Now we have drawn everything but the bars. We store the height of the Jth bar in the variable bar[ ]. The scale on the vertical axis is from 0 to 1 and the axis is 160 rows high. The height of the Jth bar is bar[J]*160. The Jth bar runs from row 164 to row 164-bar[J]*160. Let's make the bar extend for four columns, two on either side of the tick mark. This means that the Jth bar starts in column

```
52+16*J - 2 = 50+16*J
```

Similarly, the Jth bar ends in column

```
52+16*J + 2 = 54+16*J
```

Finally, we assemble the various pieces into a single program.

Listing 10.9. Bar Chart

```
program BarChart;
{This program draws a bar chart corresponding
to data read from the file BARDEMO.DAT.}

  uses
    graph;

  const
    Max = 12; {Number of columns in bar chart}

  type
    TypeNameArray = array[1..Max] of char;
    TypeBarArray = array[1..Max] of real;

  var
    Name : TypeNameArray;
    Bar : TypeBarArray;

  procedure OpenGraph;
  {Opens the graphics system in CGA med-res mode.}
    var
      GraphDriver, GraphMode : integer;
    begin {OpenGraph}
      GraphDriver := CGA;
      GraphMode := CGAC0; {Medium res, 4 colors}
      initgraph(GraphDriver, GraphMode, '');
      cleardevice
    end; {OpenGraph}

  procedure AssignData(var Name : TypeNameArray;
                       var Bar : TypeBarArray);
  {Fills Name and Bar with the data in BarFileName.}
    const
      BarFileName = 'BARDEMO.DAT';
    var
      BarFile : text;
      Column : integer;
    begin {AssignData}
      assign(BarFile, BarFileName);
      reset(BarFile);
      for Column := 1 to Max do
        readln(BarFile, Name[Column], Bar[Column]);
      close(BarFile)
    end; {AssignData}

  procedure DrawFrame(    Name : TypeNameArray);
  {Draws and labels the axes.}
    var
      Step : integer;
      StepString : string;
```

```
  begin {DrawFrame}
    line(52, 164, (52 + 16 * 13), 164); {Horizontal axis}
    line(52, 164, 52, 4);               {Vertical axis}
    for Step := 1 to 10 do
      begin
        line(47, (164 - 16 * Step), 57, (164 - 16 * Step));
        str((Step / 10):4:2, StepString);   {Convert number to string}
        outtextxy(15, (164 - 3 - 16 * Step), StepString) {Write string}
      end;                                                {at (X,Y)}
    for Step := 1 to Max do
      outtextxy((52 + 16 * Step), 170, Name[Step])
  end; {DrawFrame}

procedure DrawBars(     Bar : TypeBarArray);
{Uses the Graph unit "bar3d" procedure to draw
 pictorial representations of the values in Bar.}
  var
    Step, X : integer;
  begin {DrawBars}
    for Step := 1 to Max do
      begin
        X := (50 + 16 * Step);
        bar3d(X, 164, (X + 4), round(164 - Bar[Step] * 160), 4, topon)
      end
  end; {DrawBars}

begin {BarChart}
  OpenGraph;
  AssignData(Name, Bar);
  DrawFrame(Name);
  DrawBars(Bar);
  readln;
  closegraph
end. {BarChart}
```

Drawing Pie Charts

As an application of the `Circle` command, let's draw the pie chart shown in Figure 10.16.

To draw this pie chart, let's begin by creating an array to contain the various data, and to list the data as shown on the left. We put the category names (Food, Clothing, and so forth) in an array `Name[]`. The numerical quantities are put in an array `Amount[]`. The first part of the program is to initialize the graphics system. The next part of our program consists of initializing the arrays.

Our next step is to create the left portion of the display. This requires some care and planning. Let's skip the top four text lines (32 pixels) and begin the display on the fifth text line. To display percentages we multiply

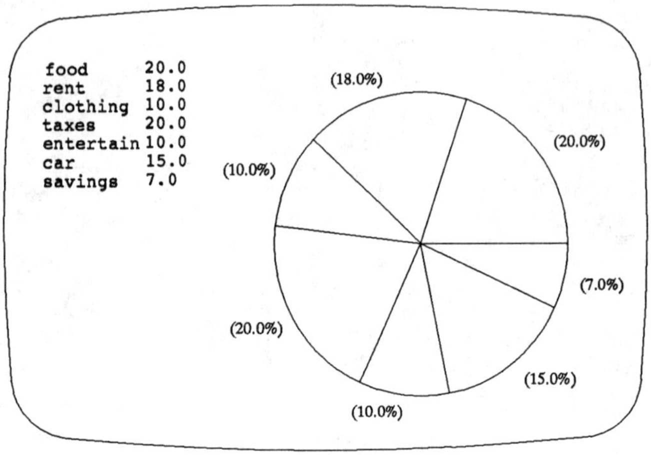

Figure 10.16. A pie chart.

each number Amount[J] by 100. We then convert the numbers to strings for output to the display. For this purpose, we use the Str function.

Finally, we come to the section of the program in which we draw the pie. The Jth data item corresponds to the proportion Amount(J) of the total pie. In angular measure, this corresponds to Amount(J)*(360). The first slice of the pie begins at angle 0; it ends at Angle[1] = Amount(1)*(360). The second slice begins where the first slice ends. It ends at Angle[1]+A(2)*(360), and so forth. We use the PieSlice procedure to draw the pie slices.

Here is the program.

Listing 10.10. Pie Chart

```
program PieChart;
{This program draws a simple pie graph
for the data given in the program.}

  uses
    graph;

  const
    NumberOfItems = 7;

  type
    TypeNameArray = array[1..NumberOfItems] of string;
    TypeAmountArray = array[1..NumberOfItems] of real;
    TypeAngleArray = array[0..NumberOfItems] of integer;

  var
    Name : TypeNameArray;
    Amount : TypeAmountArray;
```

```
procedure OpenGraph;
{Opens the graphics system in CGAHi mode.}
  var
    GraphDriver, GraphMode : integer;
  begin {OpenGraph}
    GraphDriver := CGA;
    GraphMode := CGAHi;
    initgraph(GraphDriver, GraphMode, '');
    cleardevice
  end; {OpenGraph}

procedure AssignData(var Name : TypeNameArray;
                     var Amount : TypeAmountArray);
{Assigns names and amounts to be graphed.}
  begin {AssignData}
    Name[1] := 'Food           ';    Amount[1] := 0.20;
    Name[2] := 'Rent           ';    Amount[2] := 0.18;
    Name[3] := 'Clothing       ';    Amount[3] := 0.10;
    Name[4] := 'Taxes          ';    Amount[4] := 0.20;
    Name[5] := 'Entertainment ';    Amount[5] := 0.10;
    Name[6] := 'Car            ';    Amount[6] := 0.15;
    Name[7] := 'Savings        ';    Amount[7] := 0.07
  end; {AssignData}

procedure DisplayListedData(    Name : TypeNameArray;
                                Amount : TypeAmountArray);
{Writes the names and amounts in the upper-left corner.}
  var
    Step : integer;
    AmountString : string;
  begin {DisplayListedData}
    for Step := 1 to NumberOfItems do
      begin {Convert number to string for outtextxy}
        str((100 * Amount[Step]):5:2, AmountString);
        outtextxy(0, (Step * 10), Name[Step] + AmountString)
      end
  end; {DisplayListedData}

procedure DrawPie(    Amount : TypeAmountArray);
{Draws a pie chart representing the contents of Amount.}
  var
    Angle : TypeAngleArray;
    Step, CurrentAngle : integer;
  begin {DrawPie}
    Angle[0] := 0;
    for Step := 1 to NumberOfItems do
      begin
        setfillstyle(Step, 1);
        CurrentAngle := round((180 / pi) * (Amount[Step] * (2 * pi)));
        Angle[Step] := Angle[Step - 1] + CurrentAngle;
        PieSlice(450, 100, 360 - Angle[Step], 360 - Angle[Step - 1], 100)
      end   {PieSlice (X, Y, StAngle, EndAngle, Radius) -- Draws and}
  end;      {fills a pie slice, using (X,Y) as the center point, and}
            {drawing from StAngle to EndAngle using given Radius.}
```

```
begin {PieChart}
  OpenGraph;
  AssignData(Name, Amount);
  DisplayListedData(Name, Amount);
  DrawPie(Amount);
  readln;
  closegraph
end. {PieChart}
```

Painting Regions of the Screen

Using the graphics commands of Turbo Pascal, it is possible to draw a tremendous variety of shapes. For example, Figure 10.17 shows a triangle you may draw using several `Line` statements. Figure 10.18 shows a circle drawn using the `Circle` statement. The boundary lines of each shape are specified in the graphics statements used to draw it.

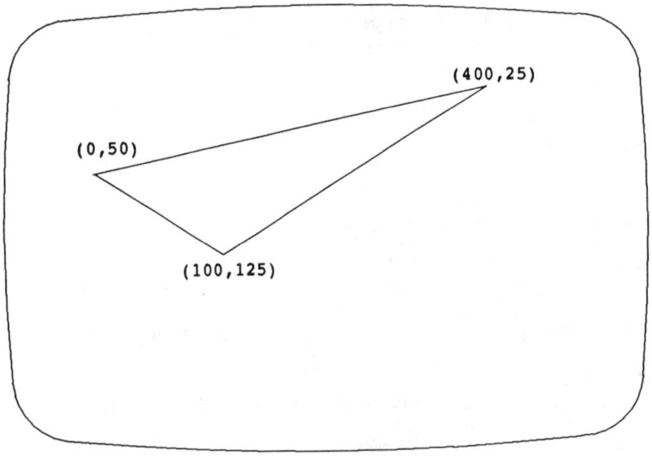

Figure 10.17.
A triangle.

Turbo Pascal allows you to fill a region with a pattern. For example, we may fill the interiors of the triangle of Figure 10.17 and the circle of Figure 10.18. The patterns allowed are defined by the following predeclared constants:

EmptyFill (solid fill in background color)

SolidFill (solid fill in specified color)

LineFill (fill with dashed lines)

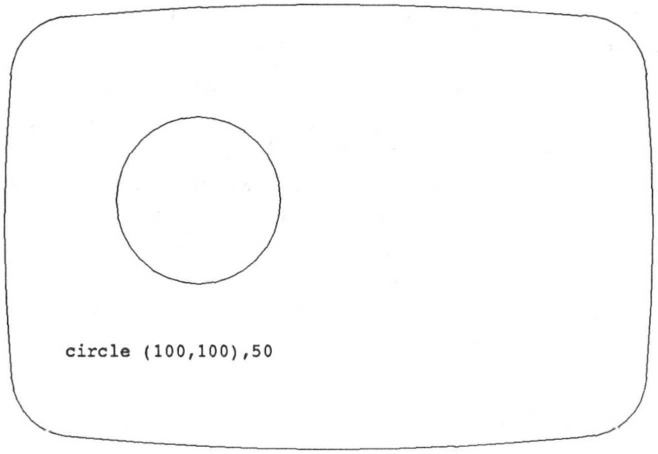

Figure 10.18.
A circle

LtSlashFill (/// fill)

SlashFill (/// fill with thick lines)

LtBkSlashFill (/// fill)

BkSlashFill (\\\ fill with thick lines)

HatchFill (light hatch fill)

XHatchFill (heavy hatch fill)

InterleaveFill (interleaving line fill)

WideDotFill (sparse dot fill)

CloseDotFill (dense dot fill)

UserFill (user-defined fill pattern)

We will discuss the creation of user-defined fill patterns later in the book. For now, however, let's confine ourselves to the predefined fill patterns. For purposes of filling regions, Turbo Pascal maintains a current fill style and a current fill color. These are set using the `SetFillStyle` procedure. For example, to set a `SlashFill` in Magenta, use the statement:

```
SetFillStyle(SlashFill, Magenta);
```

The default fill style is `SolidFill` and the default color is the background color.

There are two procedures which can be used for filling regions. The `FloodFill` procedure fills a region specified by a point in the region and the color of the boundary. For example, to fill the region containing the point (50,100) and bounded by the color Red, use the statement:

```
FloodFill(50,100,Red);
```

For example, consider the triangle in Figure 10.19. The point (75,75) lies inside the triangle, and suppose the triangle itself is drawn in Red. Suppose that we wish to fill the interior of the triangle with a `SlashFill` in color Blue. The appropriate statements to do this are:

```
SetFillStyle(SlashFill,Blue);
FloodFill(75,75,Red);
```

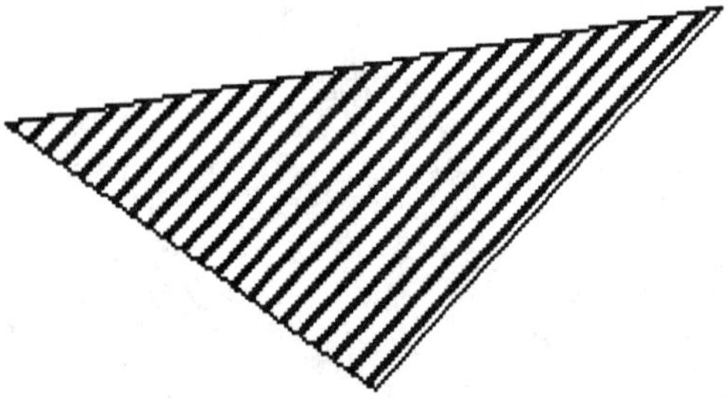

Figure 10.19. PAINTing the interior of the triangle.

`FloodFill` is a very straightforward statement to understand. The main difficulty, however, is in specifying a point within the region. Or, to put it more precisely, if we are given a region how do we specify a point within it? Well, that's a mathematical question. I just happen to be a mathematician so I can't resist explaining a little mathematics at this point!

Let's begin by considering the case of the rectangle (x1,y1,x2,y2). The center of the rectangle is at the point ((x1+x2)/2, (y1+y2)/2); that is, to obtain the coordinates of the center of the rectangle we average the values of the coordinates of the opposite corners (see Figure 10.20).

Another way of getting the same answer is to average the values of the coordinates of all four corners: (x1,y1), (x1,y2), (x2,y2), (x2,y1). Now there are four x-coordinates to add up, but we must divide by four. We obtain (2*x1+2*x2)/4 = (x1+x2)/2 and do the same for the y-coordinate.

Let's now consider a triangle with vertices (x1,y1), (x2,y2), and (x3,y3). Suppose that you average the coordinates to obtain

```
( (x1+x2+x3)/3, (y1+y2+y3)/3 )
```

This point is called the *centroid* of the triangle and is always inside the triangle.

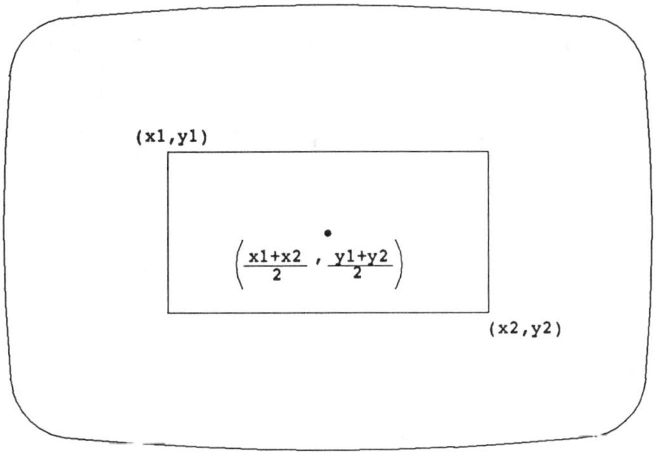

Figure 10.20. The center of a rectangle.

Well, what works for 3- and 4-sided figures works in a more general setting. For many figures bounded by straight lines, you may compute a point within the figure simply by averaging the coordinates of the vertices. For which figures does this apply? The simplest such figures are the so-called *convex bodies.* We say that a figure is convex if, whenever you connect two points within the figure by a line, all points of the line are inside the figure (see Figure 10.21).

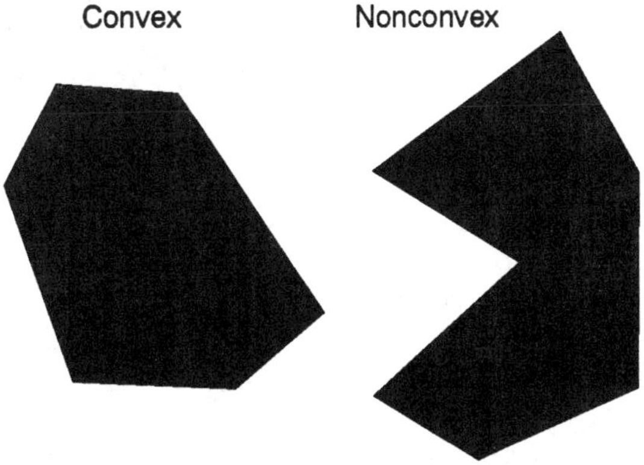

Figure 10.21. Convex and nonconvex figures.

A convex figure bounded by line segments is a type of polygon. Suppose that the vertices of such a polygon are (x1,y1), (x2,y2),...., (xn,yn). Then the point

```
( (x1+...+xn)/n, (y1+...+yn)/n )
```

obtained by averaging the x- and y-coordinates is called the *centroid of the polygon.* And the centroid is always inside the polygon. If you wish to fill a convex polygon, just compute the centroid. This will give you the point to use in the `FloodFill` statement!

The second fill procedure is `FillPoly`, which is used to fill a polygonal region. The syntax of this procedure is:

```
FillPoly(Numpoints:word; Polypoints)
```

Here, `NumPoints` is the number of vertices of the polygon and `Polypoints` is a list of the vertices.

Saving and Recalling Graphics Images

Turbo Pascal contains commands that allow you to save and recall the contents of any rectangle on the screen. This is extremely convenient in many graphics applications, particularly animation.

Let's begin this discussion with a description of the image to be saved. The image must consist of a rectangular portion of the screen. The rectangle in question may start and end anywhere, and may contain text characters, portions of text characters, or a graphics image. You specify the rectangle by giving the coordinates of two opposite vertices: either the upper left and lower right, or the lower left and upper right. Thus, a rectangle is specified in the same way as in drawing a rectangle. Here are some specifications of rectangles:

```
(0,0)-(100,100)
(3,8)-(30,80)
```

As an example, consider a text character in CGAHi mode. In this mode, text characters occupy 8 × 8 rectangles. For example, the character in the upper-left corner of the screen occupies the rectangle (0,0)–(7,7). (Lines of text are always eight pixels high.)

The `GetImage` statement allows you to store the contents of a rectangle in an array. You may use any array of byte, as long as it is big enough. The first six byte entries are reserved. The remainder are used to record the image. In CGAHi mode, each pixel can be stored in a single bit. (There are only two possible colors.) Thus, the 64 pixels require 64 bits, or 64/8 = 8 bytes. Therefore, an array of 14 bytes is required to store a character. More generally, to calculate the number of bytes required to store a rectangle, you may use the `ImageSize` function, whose syntax is:

```
ImageSize(x1,y1,x2,y2:integer);
```

This function returns the number of bytes required to store the image in the rectangle (x1,y1,x2,y2) in the current graphics mode.

To store an image in a specified array, we use the `GetImage` procedure. For example, to store the rectangle (0,0,9,49) (this rectangle is 10 by 50) in the array `A[ ]`, use the statement

```
GetImage(0,0,9,49,A);
```

To summarize, to store the contents of a rectangle in an array you must:

1. Define an array of sufficient size in var declaration.
2. Execute a `GetImage` statement.

You may redisplay the rectangle at any point on the screen by using the `PutImage` statement.

For example, to redisplay the rectangle stored in `A`, with the upper left corner at (100,125), use the statement

```
PutImage(100,125,A,CopyPut);
```

The last parameter, `CopyPut`, specifies how the image is to be copied relative to any existing pixels in the target rectangle. In this case, we have specified that the image is to be copied over any existing pixels.

To see `GetImage` and `PutImage` in action, examine the following program:

Listing 10.11. Get and Put

```
program GetAndPut;
{This program prints a letter A in the
0, 0 position. It copies the letter to
an array and redisplays it at graphics
location 100, 100.}

  uses
    crt, graph;

  const
    MaxImageSize = 14;  {8x8 letter, 6 + 8 = 14}

  type
    TypeImage = array[1..MaxImageSize] of byte;  {An array of MaxImageSize}
                                                  {bytes is needed to store}
                                                  {the letter}

  var
    Letter : TypeImage;
```

```
procedure OpenGraph;
{Opens the graphics system in CGAHi mode.}
  var
    GraphDriver, GraphMode : integer;
  begin {OpenGraph}
    GraphDriver := CGA;
    GraphMode := CGAHi;
    initgraph(GraphDriver, GraphMode, '');
    cleardevice
  end; {OpenGraph}

begin {GetAndPut}
  OpenGraph;
  outtextxy(0, 0, 'A');                 {Write "A" at (0,0)}
  getimage(0, 0, 7, 7, Letter);         {Store "A" in Letter}
  Delay(500);
  cleardevice;                          {Clear the graphics screen}
  putimage(100, 100, Letter, copyput);  {Display it at (100,100)}
  readln;
  closegraph
end. {GetAndPut}
```

We are out to store an 8 × 8 image, so we use the above formulas to calculate the required array size. The `OutTextXY` procedure draws the letter A, and `GetImage` stores the image in the array `Letter`. We then clear the screen. A call to `PutImage` recovers the image from the array and places it with its upper-left corner at (100,100).

If we were to replace `CopyPut` in `PutImage` with `XorPut` and recover the image twice on the same area of the screen, it would disappear. With a third call to `PutImage`, the image would reappear. Use this feature to create the illusion of motion across the screen. Suppose that you wish to create the illusion that the letter A is moving across the screen—merely display it and erase it from consecutive screen positions. The screen creates the displays faster than the eye can view them. What you see is a continuous motion of the letter across the screen. Here is a program to create this animation:

Listing 10.12. Animation

```
program Animation;
{This program prints a letter A in the
1, 1 position. It copies the letter to
an array and redisplays it at graphics
location 100, 100.}

  uses
    graph;

  const
    MaxImageSize = 14;
```

```
type
  TypeImage = array[1..MaxImageSize] of byte;  {An array of MaxImageSize}
                                               {bytes is needed to store}
                                               {the letter            }

var
  Letter : TypeImage;
  X : integer;

procedure OpenGraph;
{Opens the graphics system in CGA med-res mode.}
  var
    GraphDriver, GraphMode : integer;
  begin {OpenGraph}
    GraphDriver := CGA;
    GraphMode := CGAC0;
    initgraph(GraphDriver, GraphMode, '');
    cleardevice
  end; {OpenGraph}

begin {Animation}
  OpenGraph;
  outtextxy(0, 0, 'A');                     {Write "A" at (0,0)}
  getimage(0, 0, 7, 7, Letter);             {Store "A" in Letter}
  cleardevice;                              {Clear the graphics screen}
  for X := 0 to 311 do
    begin
      putimage(X, 100, Letter, XorPut);      {Display in opposite color}
                                             {of what it's on top of}
      delay(200);
      putimage(X, 100, Letter, XorPut)       {and erase it}
    end;
  closegraph;
  readln
end. {Animation}
```

Note that the X runs from 0 to 311. Although the screen is 319 pixels wide, the variable X specifies the upper-left corner of the rectangle, which is 8 × 8. Therefore, 311 is the largest possible value of the variable.

Animation is the backbone of all the arcade games that have become so popular in recent years. We will apply the above principles of animation in designing several computer games later in the book.

The Viewport and Clipping

In many applications, you will wish to display graphics only within a rectangular portion of the screen. Such a region of the screen is called a *viewport.* To define a viewport, use the `SetViewPort` procedure, whose syntax is:

```
SetViewPort(x1,y1,x2,y2 : Integer; Clip : boolean);
```

Here, (x1,y1,x2,y2) are the coordinates of the rectangular region which defines the viewport. The variable `Clip` determines whether drawing operations are clipped (that is, limited) by the boundaries of the viewport. For example, to define a clipping viewport for the region (50,50,100,100), use the statement:

```
SetViewPort(50,50,100,100,ClipOn);
```

To define the same viewport without clipping, replace `ClipOn` with `ClipOff`.

When a viewport is in effect, all coordinates are relative to the viewport. For instance, suppose that the viewport is set using the statement above. Then the statement:

```
PutPixel(5,5,white);
```

will illuminate the pixel whose coordinates is (5,5) relative to the viewport. That is, the pixel (55,55). By defining appropriate viewports, you can often make drawing calculations simpler, since they may be made relative to the viewport.

The default viewport is the one with coordinates `(0,0,GetMaxX,GetMaxY)` and no clipping.

To erase the current viewport and move the current pointer to (0,0) in the viewport, use the statement:

```
ClearViewPort;
```

Example 1. Use the `ViewPort` command to draw a family of 15 concentric rectangles centered at the center of the screen.

Solution.

Listing 10.13. Viewport example

```
program ViewPortExample;
{This program draws a sequence of
rectangles with one nested inside
the next.}

  uses
    graph;

  var
    GraphDriver, GraphMode : integer;
    Step, X1, Y1, X2, Y2 : integer;
```

```
begin {ViewPortExample}
  GraphDriver := CGA;
  GraphMode := CGAHi;
  initgraph(GraphDriver, GraphMode, '');
  cleardevice;
  for Step := 0 to 15 do  {Draw 15 rectangles}
    begin
      X1 := Step * 16;
      Y1 := Step * 5;
      X2 := getmaxx - X1;
      Y2 := getmaxy - Y1;
      setviewport(X1, Y1, X2, Y2, clipon);
      bar(0, 0, getmaxx, getmaxy);  { Fill the window with white }
      setviewport(X1 + 1, Y1 + 1, X2 - 1, Y2 - 1, clipoff); {1 smaller}
      clearviewport    {Clear the window, which is 1 pixel smaller on each}
    end;               {side than the white-filled window, leaving a thin}
  readln;              {white border on each side.}
  closegraph
end. {ViewPortExample}
```

The output of the program is shown in Figure 10.22.

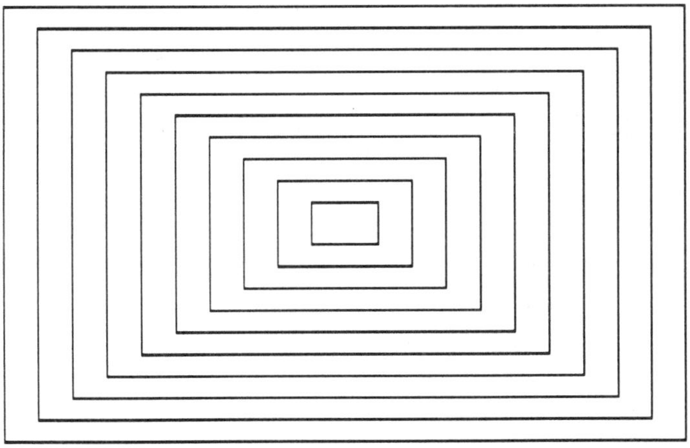

Figure 10.22. Expanding rectangles.

Sound

IBM PCs and compatibles have a small speaker located within the system unit that you may use to introduce sound and music into your programs.

ASCII code 7 provides a character (called Beep) for beeping the speaker. Thus, by outputting the character Chr(7) to the standard output stream, you cause the speaker to beep.

Professional programs employ sophisticated input routines that subject user input to a number of tests to determine if the input is acceptable. (Is the length correct? Does the input employ any illegal characters?) Here is a simple subroutine of this type: The main program assigns a value to the variable LENGTH, which gives the maximum length of an input string. The subroutine illuminates a box, beginning at text location (1,1) (top left corner of the screen) to indicate the maximum field size for the input. The routine then allows you to input characters and to display them in the appropriate position in the illumination field. For each character displayed part of the illumination disappears. Moreover, using the backspace key restores one character space illumination. If you attempt to input characters beyond the illuminated field, the routine beeps the speaker.

Listing 10.14. Fancy Input

```
program FancyInput;
{This program has the user input a string
of fixed length into an illuminated box,
beeping when the user attempts to input
a value that is not legal.}

  uses
    crt;

  const
    MaxTestLength = 20;

  var
    Test : string;

  procedure ReadLnString(var AString : string;
                             MaxLength : integer);
  {Clears the screen, draws a box, and has the user
   input a string which cannot exceed MaxLength
   characters, beeping when the user attempts to input
   a value that is not legal.}
    const
      Beep = chr(7);
      Backspace = chr(8);
      Enter = chr(13);
      Box = chr(219);
    var
      X : integer;
      Key : char;
    begin {ReadLnString}
      clrscr;
      gotoxy(1, 1);
      for X := 1 to MaxLength do
        write(Box);
```

```
    gotoxy(1, 1);
    AString := '';
    repeat
      Key := readkey;
      if (Key = Backspace)
        then
          if (AString = '')
            then
              write(Beep)
            else
              begin
                delete(AString, length(AString), 1);
                write(Backspace, Box, Backspace)
              end
        else
          if (Key <> Enter)
            then
              if (length(AString) = MaxLength)
                then
                  write(Beep)
                else
                  begin
                    AString := AString + Key;
                    write(Key)
                  end
    until (Key = Enter)
  end; {ReadLnString}

begin {FancyInput}
  ReadLnString(Test, MaxTestLength)
end. {FancyInput}
```

This handy little command enables you to access any frequency between 37 and 32767 Hertz (cycles per second, also abbreviated Hz). The sound continues until turned off. To produce a sound at 500 Hz, use this statement:

```
Sound(500);
```

To turn off the current sound, use the statement:

```
NoSound;
```

Here is an elementary graphics program that has been enhanced by the Sound procedure. It draws fixed triangles and random circles and blinks them in a manner suitable for illuminating a rock concert. Sound provides some audio accompaniment.

Listing 10.15. Sound and Light Show

```
program SoundAndLightShow;
{This program creates a sound and light show
with random sounds and randomly-placed shapes.}

  uses
    crt,
    graph;

  var
    Iteration : integer;

  procedure OpenGraph;
  {Opens the graphics system in C/GA med-res mode.}
    var
      GraphDriver, GraphMode : integer;
    begin {OpenGraph}
      GraphDriver := CGA;
      GraphMode := CGAC0;
      initgraph(GraphDriver, GraphMode, '');
      cleardevice
    end; {OpenGraph}

  procedure DrawRandomCircle;
  {Draws a circle with radius 30 at a random position on the screen.}
    begin {DrawRandomCircle}
      setcolor(random(getmaxcolor) + 1);
      circle(random(250), random(200), 30);  {random circle}
    end; {DrawRandomCircle}

  procedure DrawRandomTriangle;
  {Draws a polygon with three random points.}
    const
      MaxPoints = 4;
    type
      TypeCoordinate = record
                         X, Y : integer
                       end;
      TypePointsArray = array[1..MaxPoints] of TypeCoordinate;
    var
      CurrentPoint : integer;
      Points : TypePointsArray;
    begin {DrawRandomTriangle}
      for CurrentPoint := 1 to 3 do
        begin
          Points[CurrentPoint].X := random(getmaxx);
          Points[CurrentPoint].Y := random(getmaxy)
        end;
      Points[MaxPoints] := Points[1];
      setcolor(random(getmaxcolor) + 1);
      drawpoly(MaxPoints, Points)
    end; {DrawRandomTriangle}
```

```
begin {SoundAndLightShow}
  OpenGraph;
  randomize;
  for Iteration := 1 to 100 do
    begin
      DrawRandomCircle;
      sound(random(1000) + 37);  {From 37 to 1037 Hz}
      cleardevice;
      DrawRandomTriangle;
      sound(random(1000) + 37);
      cleardevice
    end;
  nosound;  {turn off sound}
  closegraph;
  readln
end. {SoundAndLightShow}
```

A Detailed Graphics Example

In this section, we present a detailed graphics program to draw bar charts. This program incorporates much of what we have covered in this chapter. Moreover, it presents a number of valuable techniques to have in your toolbox. This program presents a main menu of six choices, as shown in Figure 10.23.

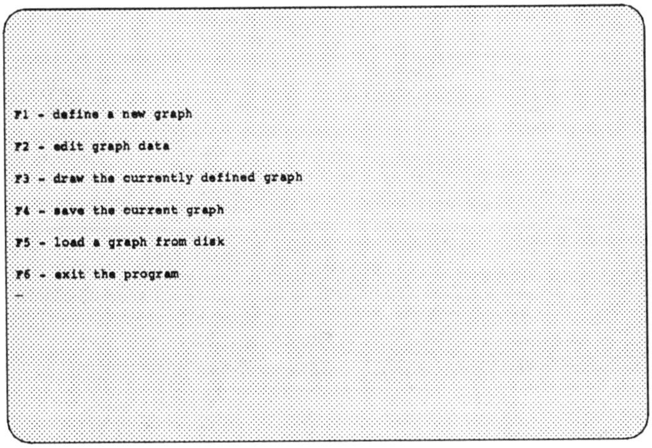

Figure 10.23.
Main menu.

Note that the various choices are made by pressing one of the function keys F1–F6. By pressing F1, you are presented with a fill-in menu (a so-called *dialogue box*) in which you specify various parameters of the bar chart (see Figure 10.24).

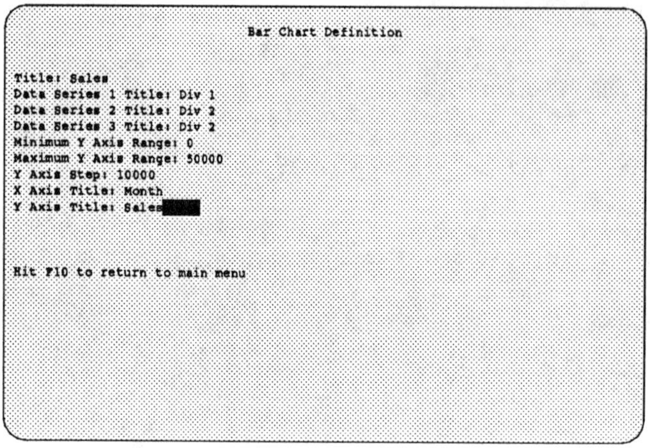

Figure 10.24.
Bar chart.

Press F10 to get back to the main menu. Now press F2 to define the data in X-axis labels (see Figure 10.25). Note that you may specify as many as three sets of data, labelled Series 1, Series 2, and Series 3. The sets of data are translated in heights of bars. Note that you may use the cursor motion keys to move from field to field of this screen. This is typical in many of today's programs. You should examine the code carefully to see how this is done. In addition, note that you may edit the entries in a field using the backspace key to erase characters.

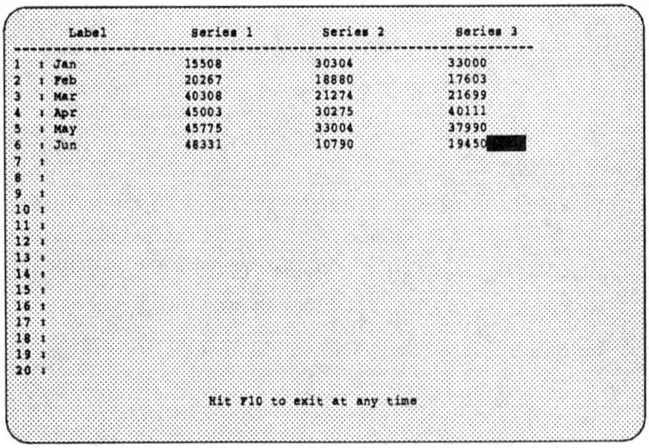

Figure 10.25.
Data in X-axis labels

When you are done entering the data, press F10 to return to the main menu. Now press F3 to view the graph you have defined (see Figure 10.26).

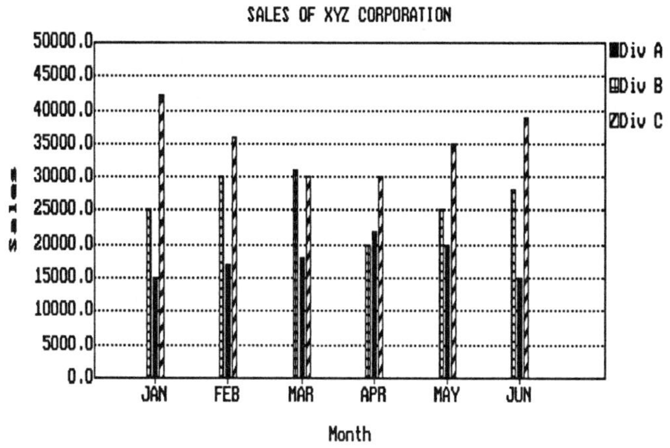

Figure 10.26. Graph of XYZ corporation

The main program is simplicity itself:

```
begin
  Initialize(Done, MainTitle, Ser1Title, Ser2Title, Ser3Title, XTitle,
             YTitle, YMin, YMax, YStep, DataArray);
  repeat
    DisplayMainMenu;
    GetKey(MainChoice, Extended, [], F1ToF6, false);
    DoMainChoice(MainChoice, MainTitle, Ser1Title, Ser2Title, Ser3Title,
                 XTitle, YTitle ,YMin, YMax, YStep, DataArray)
  until Done
end.
```

You should examine the procedure GetKey which is used as a general keyboard input routine. It allows you to specify a set of acceptable ordinary keystrokes and a set of acceptable extended keystrokes. The procedure DoMainChoice executes the choice passed by GetKey. There are routines for each of the main menu choices.

Listing 10.16. Bar Chart

```
program BarChart;

  uses
    crt,
    graph;

  const
    F10 = 68;
    F1ToF6 = [chr(59)..chr(64)];
    AllCharSet = [chr(32)..chr(126), chr(13), chr(27), chr(8)];
```

```
  ExtendedSet = [chr(72), chr(80), chr(71), chr(79), chr(83),
                 chr(68), chr(75), chr(77)];
  NumSet = ['0'..'9', '.', '+', '-', chr(13), chr(27), chr(8)];
  Return = -1;
  Up = 72;
  Down = 80;
  Right = 77;
  Left = 75;

type
  TypeCharacterSet = set of char;
  TypeDataArray    = array[1..20, 1..4] of string;

var
  MainChoice : char;
  Done, Extended : boolean;
  MainTitle : string;
  Ser1Title, Ser2Title, Ser3Title,
  XTitle, YTitle, YMin, YMax, YStep : string;
  DataArray : TypeDataArray;

procedure GetKey(var Key : char;
                 var Extended : boolean;
                     Acceptable,
                     ExtendedAcceptable : TypeCharacterSet;
                     CAPSOn : boolean);
  const
    ExtendedKey = chr(0);  { 1st ASCII code returned by extended key }
    Beep = chr(7);

  function CharOk(    Key : char;
                      Extended : boolean;
                      Acceptable,
                      ExtendedAcceptable : TypeCharacterSet) : boolean;
    begin {CharOk}
      CharOk := (Extended and (Key in ExtendedAcceptable)) or
                ((not Extended) and (Key in Acceptable))
    end; {CharOk}

  begin {GetKey}
    repeat
      Key := readkey;
      Extended := (Key = ExtendedKey);
      if Extended
        then
          Key := readkey
      else
          if CAPSOn
            then
              Key := upcase(Key);
      if not CharOk(Key, Extended, Acceptable, ExtendedAcceptable)
        then
          write(Beep)
    until CharOk(Key, Extended, Acceptable, ExtendedAcceptable)
  end; {GetKey}
```

```
procedure GetField(var Field : string;
                       MaxLength, X, Y : integer;
                       Acceptable,
                       ExtendedAcceptable : TypeCharacterSet;
                       CAPSOn : boolean;
                   var Result : integer);
  const
    Beep = chr(7);
    Backspace = chr(8);
    Return = chr(13);
    Escape = chr(27);
    Blank = chr(219);
    Del = chr(83);
  var
    Cursor : integer;
    Key : char;
    Extended : boolean;

  procedure DrawField(     Field : string;
                           MaxLength, X, Y : integer);
    var
      Space : integer;

    begin {DrawField}
      gotoxy(X, Y);
      write(Field);
      for Space := 1 to (MaxLength - length(Field)) do
        write(Blank)
    end; {DrawField}

  procedure InitField(var Field : string;
                      var Cursor : integer;
                          MaxLength, X, Y : integer);
    begin {InitField}
      Field := '';
      Cursor := 0;
      DrawField(Field, MaxLength, X, Y)
    end; {InitField}

  procedure AddKey(var Field : string;
                   var Cursor : integer;
                       MaxLength : integer;
                       Key : char);
    begin {AddKey}
      if (Cursor = MaxLength)
        then
          write(Beep)
        else
          begin
            write(Key);
            if (Cursor = length(Field)) or (length(Field) = 0)
              then
                Field := Field + Key
              else
                Field[Cursor + 1] := Key;
            Cursor := Cursor + 1
          end
    end; {AddKey}
```

```
procedure DeletePreviousChar(var Field : string;
                             var Cursor : integer;
                                 MaxLength : integer);
  begin {DeletePreviousChar}
    if (Cursor > 0)
      then
        begin
          write(Backspace, copy(Field, Cursor + 1, MaxLength), Blank);
          delete(Field, Cursor, 1);
          Cursor := Cursor - 1
        end
      else
        write(Beep)
  end; {DeletePreviousChar}

procedure DeleteCurrentChar(var Field : string;
                            var Cursor : integer;
                                MaxLength : integer);
  begin {DeleteCurrentChar}
    if (Cursor > length(Field))
      then
        begin
          write(copy(Field, Cursor + 2, MaxLength), Blank);
          delete(Field, Cursor + 1, 1)
        end
      else
        write(Beep)
  end; {DeleteCurrentChar}

procedure ClearBlanks(var Field : string;
                      MaxLength, X, Y : integer);
  var
    Space : integer;

  begin {ClearBlanks}
    while (copy(Field, length(Field), 1) = ' ') do
      delete(Field, length(Field), 1);
    gotoxy(X + length(Field), Y);
    for Space := 1 to (MaxLength - length(Field)) do
      write(' ')
  end; {ClearBlanks}

begin {GetField}
  Cursor := 0;
  DrawField(Field, MaxLength, X, Y);
  repeat
    gotoxy(X + Cursor, Y);
    GetKey(Key, Extended, Acceptable, ExtendedAcceptable, CAPSOn);
    if Extended
      then
        if (Key = Del)
          then
            DeleteCurrentChar(Field, Cursor, MaxLength)
          else
            Result := ord(Key)
      else
        case Key of
          Return    : Result := -1;
```

```
          Backspace : DeletePreviousChar(Field, Cursor, MaxLength);
          Escape    : InitField(Field, Cursor, MaxLength, X, Y)
          else
            AddKey(Field, Cursor, MaxLength, Key)
        end
    until ((not Extended) and (Key = Return)) or
          (Extended and (Key <> Del));
    ClearBlanks(Field, MaxLength, X, Y)
  end; {GetField}

procedure Initialize(var Done : boolean;
                     var MainTitle, Ser1Title, Ser2Title, Ser3Title,
                         XTitle, YTitle, YMin, YMax, YStep : string;
                     var DataArray : TypeDataArray);
  var
    Row,
    Column : integer;

  begin {Initialize}
    Done := false;
    MainTitle := '';
    Ser1Title := '';
    Ser2Title := '';
    Ser3Title := '';
    XTitle    := '';
    YTitle    := '';
    YMin      := '0';
    YMax      := '0';
    YStep     := '0';
    for Row := 1 to 20 do
      for Column := 1 to 4 do
        DataArray[Row, Column] := ''
  end; {Initialize}

procedure DisplayMainMenu;

  begin {DisplayMainMenu}
    clrscr;
    gotoxy(1, 6);
    writeln('F1 - define a new graph');
    writeln;
    writeln('F2 - edit graph data');
    writeln;
    writeln('F3 - draw the currently defined graph');
    writeln;
    writeln('F4 - save the current graph');
    writeln;
    writeln('F5 - load a graph from disk');
    writeln;
    writeln('F6 - exit the program')
  end; {DisplayMainMenu}

procedure ChangeReal(var RealString : string;
                         StartXPos, StartYPos : integer;
                     var LastHitKey : integer);
  var
    RealNum : real;
    ErrorCode : integer;
```

```
begin {ChangeReal}
      repeat
        GetField(RealString, 10, StartXPos , StartYPos, NumSet, ExtendedSet,
                 false, LastHitKey);
        val(RealString, RealNum, ErrorCode)
      until (ErrorCode = 0) or (RealString = '')
    end; {ChangeReal}

  procedure ChangeDefineField(     CurrentLine : integer;
                               var LastHitKey  : integer;
                               var MainTitle, Ser1Title, Ser2Title,
                                   Ser3Title, XTitle, YTitle,
                                   YMin, YMax, YStep : string);
    begin {ChangeDefineField}
      case CurrentLine of
        1 : GetField(MainTitle, 50, 8, 4, AllCharSet, ExtendedSet, false,
                     LastHitKey);
        2 : GetField(Ser1Title, 10, 22 , 5, AllCharSet, ExtendedSet, false,
                     LastHitKey);
        3 : GetField(Ser2Title, 10, 22, 6, AllCharSet, ExtendedSet, false,
                     LastHitKey);
        4 : GetField(Ser3Title, 10, 22, 7, AllCharSet, ExtendedSet, false,
                     LastHitKey);
        5 : ChangeReal(YMin, 23, 8, LastHitKey);
        6 : ChangeReal(YMax, 23, 9, LastHitKey);
        7 : ChangeReal(YStep, 14, 10, LastHitKey);
        8 : GetField(XTitle, 10, 15, 11, AllCharSet, ExtendedSet, false,
                     LastHitKey);
        9 : GetField(YTitle, 10, 15, 12, AllCharSet, ExtendedSet, false,
                     LastHitKey)
      end
    end; {ChangeDefineField}

  procedure DisplayDefineMenu(var MainTitle, Ser1Title, Ser2Title,
                                  Ser3Title, XTitle, YTitle,
                                  YMin, YMax, YStep : string);

    begin {DisplayDefineMenu}
      clrscr;
      writeln('                              Bar Chart Definition');
      writeln;
      writeln;
      writeln('Title: ', MainTitle);
      writeln('Data Series 1 Title: ', Ser1Title);
      writeln('Data Series 2 Title: ', Ser2Title);
      writeln('Data Series 3 Title: ', Ser3Title);
      writeln('Minimum Y Axis Range: ', YMin);
      writeln('Maximum Y Axis Range: ', YMax);
      writeln('Y Axis Step: ', YStep);
      writeln('X Axis Title: ', XTitle);
      writeln('Y Axis Title: ', YTitle);
      writeln;
      writeln;
      writeln;
      writeln('Hit F10 to return to main menu')
    end; {DisplayDefineMenu}
```

```
procedure AdjustLineNum(var CurrentLine : integer;
                        var Done : boolean;
                            LastHitKey : integer);
  begin {AdjustLineNum}
    case LastHitKey of
      F10          : Done := true;
      Return, Down : if CurrentLine < 9
                       then
                         CurrentLine := CurrentLine + 1;
      Up           : if CurrentLine > 1
                       then
                         CurrentLine := CurrentLine - 1
    end
  end; {AdjustLineNum}

procedure DefineChart(var MainTitle, Ser1Title, Ser2Title,
                          Ser3Title, XTitle, YTitle,
                          YMin, YMax, YStep : string);
  var
    LastHitKey, CurrentLine : integer;
    Done : boolean;

  begin {DefineChart}
    CurrentLine := 1;
    Done := false;
    DisplayDefineMenu(MainTitle, Ser1Title, Ser2Title, Ser3Title, XTitle,
                      YTitle, YMin, YMax, YStep);
    repeat
      ChangeDefineField(CurrentLine, LastHitKey, MainTitle, Ser1Title,
                        Ser2Title, Ser3Title, XTitle, YTitle, YMin, YMax,
                        YStep);
      AdjustLineNum(CurrentLine, Done, LastHitKey)
    until Done
  end; {DefineChart}

procedure DrawBorders;
  var
    X : integer;

  begin {DrawBorders}
    writeln('       Label       Series 1         Series 2         Series 3');
    writeln('---------------------------------------------------------------');
    for X := 1 to 20 do
      writeln(X:2, ' :');
    writeln;
    write ('                              Hit F10 to exit at any time')
  end; {DrawBorders}

procedure DrawData(var DataArray : TypeDataArray);
  var
    Row, Column : integer;

  begin {DrawData}
    for Row := 1 to 20 do
      for Column := 1 to 4 do
        begin
          gotoxy((Column - 1) * 17 + 6, Row + 2);
```

```
          write(DataArray[Row, Column])
        end
  end; {DrawData}

procedure DrawEditScreen(var DataArray : TypeDataArray);

  begin {DrawEditScreen}
    clrscr;
    DrawBorders;
    DrawData(DataArray)
  end; {DrawEditScreen}

procedure ChangeEditField(var FieldToChange : string;
                              CurrentLine,
                              CurrentField : integer;
                          var LastHitKey : integer);
  begin {ChangeEditField}
    if (CurrentField = 1)
      then
        GetField(FieldToChange, 10, (CurrentField - 1) * 17 + 6,
                 CurrentLine + 2, AllCharSet, ExtendedSet, false,
                 LastHitKey)
      else
        ChangeReal(FieldToChange, (CurrentField - 1) * 17 + 6,
                   CurrentLine + 2, LastHitKey)
  end; {ChangeEditField}

procedure AdjustLinColNum(var CurrentLine,
                              CurrentField : integer;
                          var Done : boolean;
                              LastHitKey : integer);
  begin {AdjustLinColNum}
    case LastHitKey of
      Return, Down : if CurrentLine < 20
                       then
                         CurrentLine := CurrentLine + 1;
      Up           : if CurrentLine > 1
                       then
                         CurrentLine := CurrentLine - 1;
      Left         : if CurrentField > 1
                       then
                         CurrentField := CurrentField - 1;
      Right        : if CurrentField < 4
                       then
                         CurrentField := CurrentField + 1;
      F10          : Done := true
    end
  end; {AdjustLinColNum}

procedure EditData(var DataArray : TypeDataArray);

  var
    Done : boolean;
    LastHitKey, CurrentLine, CurrentField : integer;
```

```
  begin {EditData}
    CurrentLine  := 1;
    CurrentField := 1;
    Done         := false;
    DrawEditScreen(DataArray);
    repeat
      ChangeEditField(DataArray[CurrentLine, CurrentField], CurrentLine,
                      CurrentField, LastHitKey);
      AdjustLinColNum(CurrentLine, CurrentField, Done, LastHitKey)
    until Done
  end; {EditData}

procedure DrawChart(var DataArray : TypeDataArray;
                        MainTitle, Ser1Title, Ser2Title,
                        Ser3Title, XTitle, YTitle,
                        YMinString, YMaxString,
                        YStepString : string);
  const
    WinXMin = 80;
    WinYMin = 16;
    WinXMax = 559;
    WinYMax = 169;
    CharWidth = 8;
    CharHeight = 8;

  var
    YMin, YMax, YStep : real;
    Key : char;
    Extended : boolean;

  procedure OpenGraph;

    var
      GraphDriver, GraphMode : integer;

    begin {OpenGraph}
      GraphDriver := CGA;
      GraphMode := CGAHi;
      initgraph(GraphDriver, GraphMode, '');
      cleardevice
    end; {OpenGraph}

  function WinY(    Y, YMin, YMax : real) : integer;

    begin {WinY}
      WinY := WinYMax - round
              ((WinYMax - WinYMin) * (Y - YMin) / (YMax - YMin))
    end; {WinY}

  function WinX(    X, XMin, XMax : real) : integer;

    begin {WinX}
      WinX := round ((WinXMax - WinXMin) * (X - XMin) / (XMax - XMin))
    end; {WinX}

  procedure WriteLabels(    MainTitle, XTitle, YTitle : string;
                             YMin, YMax, YStep : real);

    var
      Y : real;
      ScreenY : integer;
      YString : string;
```

```
  begin {WriteLabels}
    outtextxy(((getmaxx+1) div 2) -
              ((CharWidth*length(MainTitle)) div 2), 0, MainTitle);
    outtextxy(((getmaxx+1) div 2) -
              ((CharWidth*length(XTitle)) div 2), (getmaxy-CharHeight),
              XTitle);
    settextstyle(defaultfont, vertdir, 1);
    outtextxy(CharWidth, (WinYMax div 2) + (WinYMin div 2) -
              ((CharWidth*length (YTitle)) div 2), YTitle);
    settextstyle(defaultfont, horizdir, 1);
    setlinestyle(dottedln, 0, normwidth);
    Y := YMin;
    repeat
      ScreenY := WinY(Y, YMin, YMax);
      str(Y:0:1, YString);
      outtextxy((WinXMin - (CharWidth*length(YString))),
                (ScreenY-(CharWidth div 2)), YString);
    line(WinXMin, ScreenY, WinXMax, ScreenY);
    Y := Y + YStep
  until (Y > YMax);
  setlinestyle(solidln, 0, normwidth)
end; {WriteLabels}

procedure BoxedBar(    X1, Y1, X2, Y2, Series : integer);

  const
    Ser1Fill = solidfill;
    Ser2Fill = hatchfill;
    Ser3Fill = slashfill;

  begin {BoxedBar}
    case Series of
      1 : setfillstyle(Ser1Fill, 1);
      2 : setfillstyle(Ser2Fill, 2);
      3 : setfillstyle(Ser3Fill, 3)
    end;
    bar(X1, Y1, X2, Y2);
    rectangle(X1, Y1, X2, Y2)
  end; {BoxedBar}

procedure DrawKey(    Ser1Title, Ser2Title, Ser3Title : string);

  begin {DrawKey}
    BoxedBar(WinXMax + 4, WinYMin, WinXMax + 12, WinYMin + 6, 1);
    outtextxy(WinXMax + 14, WinYMin, Ser1Title);
    BoxedBar(WinXMax + 4, WinYMin + 16, WinXMax + 12, WinYMin + 22, 2);
    outtextxy(WinXMax + 14, WinYMin + 16, Ser2Title);
    BoxedBar(WinXMax + 4, WinYMin + 32, WinXMax + 12, WinYMin + 38, 3);
    outtextxy(WinXMax + 14, WinYMin + 32, Ser3Title)
  end; {DrawKey}

function ColumnMax(var DataArray : TypeDataArray) : integer;

  var
    Column : integer;
```

```
    begin {ColumnMax}
      ColumnMax := 0;
      for Column := 1 to 20 do
        if (DataArray[Column, 2] <> '') or
           (DataArray[Column, 3] <> '') or
           (DataArray[Column, 4] <> '')
          then
           ColumnMax := Column
    end; {ColumnMax}

  function ValueOf(    Str : string) : real;

    var
      Temp : real;
      ErrorCode : integer;

  begin {ValueOf}
    val(Str, Temp, ErrorCode);
    ValueOf := Temp
  end; {ValueOf}

procedure DrawBars(var DataArray : TypeDataArray;
                       Ser1Title, Ser2Title, Ser3Title : string;
                       YMin, YMax, YStep : real);
  const
    Name = 1;
    Ser1 = 2;
    Ser2 = 3;
    Ser3 = 4;

  var
    Column, ScreenX : integer;

  begin {DrawBars}
    DrawKey(Ser1Title, Ser2Title, Ser3Title);
    for Column := 1 to ColumnMax(DataArray) do
      begin
        ScreenX := WinX(Column + 1, 0, ColumnMax(DataArray) + 1);
        line(ScreenX, WinYMax - 2, ScreenX, WinYMax + 2);
        outtextxy(ScreenX -
                   ((CharWidth*length(DataArray[Column, Name])) div 2),
                   WinYMax + 4, DataArray[Column, Name]);
        BoxedBar(ScreenX - 2, WinY(ValueOf(DataArray[Column, Ser1]),
                 YMin, YMax), ScreenX + 2, WinYMax, 1);
        BoxedBar(ScreenX - 8, WinY(ValueOf(DataArray[Column, Ser2]),
                 YMin, YMax), ScreenX - 4, WinYMax, 2);
        BoxedBar(ScreenX + 4, WinY(ValueOf(DataArray[Column,Ser3]),
                 YMin, YMax), ScreenX + 8, WinYMax, 3)
      end
  end; {DrawBars}

  begin {DrawChart}
    YMin := ValueOf(YMinString);
    YMax := ValueOf(YMaxString);
    YStep := ValueOf(YStepString);
    OpenGraph;
```

```
    rectangle (WinXMin, WinYMin, WinXMax, WinYMax);
    WriteLabels (MainTitle, XTitle, YTitle, YMin, YMax, YStep);
    DrawBars (DataArray, Ser1Title, Ser2Title, Ser3Title, YMin, YMax, YStep);
    GetKey(Key, Extended, AllCharSet, AllCharSet, false);
    closegraph
  end; {DrawChart}

procedure OpenFileToWrite(var FileToSaveTo : text);

  var
    FileName : string;

  begin {OpenFileToWrite}
    {$I-}
    repeat
      clrscr;
      write('Enter file name: ');
      readln(FileName);
      assign(FileToSaveTo, FileName);
      rewrite(FileToSaveTo)
    until (ioresult = 0)
    {$I+}
  end; {OpenFileToWrite}

procedure SaveChart(     MainTitle, Ser1Title, Ser2Title,
                         Ser3Title, XTitle, YTitle,
                         YMin, YMax, YStep : string;
                     var DataArray : TypeDataArray);

  var
    FileToSaveTo : text;
    Row, Column : integer;

  begin {SaveChart}
    OpenFileToWrite(FileToSaveTo);
    writeln(FileToSaveTo, MainTitle);
    writeln(FileToSaveTo, Ser1Title);
    writeln(FileToSaveTo, Ser2Title);
    writeln(FileToSaveTo, Ser3Title);
    writeln(FileToSaveTo, XTitle);
    writeln(FileToSaveTo, YTitle);
    writeln(FileToSaveTo, YMin);
    writeln(FileToSaveTo, YMax);
    writeln(FileToSaveTo, YStep);
    for Row := 1 to 20 do
      for Column := 1 to 4 do
        writeln(FileToSaveTo, DataArray[Row, Column]);
    close(FileToSaveTo)
  end; {SaveChart}

procedure OpenFileToRead(var FileToReadFrom : text);

  var
    FileName : string;
```

```
  begin {OpenFileToRead}
    {$I-}
    repeat
      clrscr;
      write('Enter file name: ');
      readln(FileName);
      assign(FileToReadFrom, FileName);
      reset(FileToReadFrom)
    until (ioresult = 0)
    {$I+}
  end; {OpenFileToRead}

procedure LoadChart(var MainTitle, Ser1Title, Ser2Title,
                        Ser3Title, XTitle, YTitle,
                        YMin, YMax, YStep : string;
                    var DataArray : TypeDataArray);
  var
    Row, Column : integer;
    FileToReadFrom : text;

  begin {LoadChart}
    OpenFileToRead(FileToReadFrom);
    readln(FileToReadFrom, MainTitle);
    readln(FileToReadFrom, Ser1Title);
    readln(FileToReadFrom, Ser2Title);
    readln(FileToReadFrom, Ser3Title);
    readln(FileToReadFrom, XTitle);
    readln(FileToReadFrom, YTitle);
    readln(FileToReadFrom, YMin);
    readln(FileToReadFrom, YMax);
    readln(FileToReadFrom, YStep);
    for Row := 1 to 20 do
      for Column := 1 to 4 do
        readln(FileToReadFrom, DataArray[Row, Column]);
    close(FileToReadFrom)
  end; {LoadChart}

procedure DoMainChoice(    MainChoice : char;
                       var MainTitle, Ser1Title, Ser2Title,
                           Ser3Title, XTitle, YTitle,
                           YMin, YMax, YStep : string;
                       var DataArray : TypeDataArray);

  begin {DoMainChoice}
    case ord(MainChoice) of
      59 : DefineChart(MainTitle, Ser1Title, Ser2Title, Ser3Title, XTitle,
                       YTitle, YMin, YMax, YStep);
      60 : EditData(DataArray);
      61 : DrawChart(DataArray, MainTitle, Ser1Title, Ser2Title, Ser3Title,
                     XTitle, YTitle, YMin, YMax, YStep);
      62 : SaveChart(MainTitle, Ser1Title, Ser2Title, Ser3Title,
                     XTitle, YTitle, YMin, YMax, YStep, DataArray);
      63 : LoadChart(MainTitle, Ser1Title, Ser2Title, Ser3Title,
                     XTitle, YTitle, YMin, YMax, YStep, DataArray);
      64 : Done := true
    end
  end; {DoMainChoice}
```

```
begin {BarChart}
  Initialize(Done, MainTitle, Ser1Title, Ser2Title, Ser3Title, XTitle,
           YTitle, YMin, YMax, YStep, DataArray);
  repeat
    DisplayMainMenu;
    GetKey(MainChoice, Extended, [], F1ToF6, false);
    DoMainChoice(MainChoice, MainTitle, Ser1Title, Ser2Title, Ser3Title,
              XTitle, YTitle ,YMin, YMax, YStep, DataArray)
  until Done
end. {BarChart}
```

11 Building Computer Games

In the last decade, computer games have captured the imaginations of millions of people. In this chapter, we will build several computer games which utilize both the random number generator and the graphics capabilities of the IBM personal computer. Actually, as we shall shortly see, these games utilize most of what we have learned and provide a good test of our programming prowess. In order to get the most out of this chapter, you should carefully analyze the games, proceeding in top-down fashion from the main program through the procedures at various levels. Study how the games are designed, as well as how the details of keyboard, user interface, and graphics are handled.

Several of the games require that we keep track of time, so we begin this chapter with a discussion of Turbo Pascal's mechanisms for timing.

Measuring Time Within a Program

Introducing Delays

Often it is necessary to introduce delays within a program to create timing effects. You may do this using the procedure `delay`, with the syntax

```
delay(time)
```

where `time` is given in milliseconds. When this statement is encountered, program execution is halted for the specified number of milliseconds. For instance, to halt a program for 2 seconds (2000 milliseconds), you would use the statement:

```
delay(2000)
```

As an illustration of the use of the delay procedure, consider the following program which tests the user's mastery of addition of two-digit numbers. The program loops through 10 consecutive problems and gives the user 10 seconds to answer. The 10 second timing is created using the `delay` procedure.

Listing 11.1. TimedAdd

```
program TimedAdd;
{This program provides a timed test of
addition of 2-digit numbers.}

  uses
    crt;

  var
    Number, Score : integer;
    A, B, C : real;

  begin {TimedAdd}
    randomize;
    Score := 0;
    for Number := 1 to 10 do
      begin
        A := int(100*random);
        B := int(100*random); {A,B random 2-digit numbers}
        writeln('Problem ', Number, ': A=', A :5:0,  ' B=', B :5:0);
        writeln('Determine their sum.');
        delay (10000); {Delay 10000 ms, or 10 seconds}
        write('Time is up! What is your answer? ');
        readln(C);
        if (A + B = C)
          then
            begin
              writeln('Your answer is correct! Congratulations!');
              Score := Score + 1
            end
          else
            writeln('Sorry, the correct answer is ', A + B:5:0, '.')
      end;
    writeln ('Your score is ', Score, '.');
    writeln;
    readln
  end. {TimedAdd}
```

Calculating Elapsed Time

The delay procedure is used for creating delays within a program. However, often you wish to keep track of elapsed time within a program without halting the program. This may be accomplished by reading the system clock. Recall that a PC compatible running under MS-DOS has a clock which keeps track of the date and time. In some machines, the time and date are set manually each time you start DOS. In others, the time and date are stored in a memory preserved by a battery between sessions. In any case, during a session, the date and time are available from DOS. Within a Turbo Pascal program, the date and time may be read using the procedures `GetDate` and `GetTime`. The declaration of these procedures is:

```
GetTime(var Hour, Minute, Second, Sec100 : word);
GetDate(var Year, Month, Day, DayOfWeek : word);
```

Here `Sec100` provides hundredths of a second and `DayOfWeek` provides the day of the week, with 0 corresponding to Sunday. For instance, if the current time is 17:05:01.03, then the procedure call:

```
GetTime(Hour, Minute, Second, Sec100);
```

will assign `Hour` equal to 17, `Minute` to 5, `Second` to 1, and `Sec100` to 3. Of course, the variables must be declared within the calling program.

By recording the times at various points in the program, you may keep track of the time which elapses. This is a way of measuring time without causing the program to halt.

Blind Target Shoot (Text Mode)

The object of this game is to shoot down a target on the screen by moving your cursor to hit the target. The catch is that you only have a two-second look at your target! The program begins by asking if your are ready. If so, you press any key. The computer then randomly chooses a spot to place the target and it lights up the spot for two seconds. The cursor is then moved to the upper left position of the screen (the so-called "home" position). You must then move the cursor to the target based on your brief glimpse of it. You have five seconds to hit the target (see Figure 11.1).

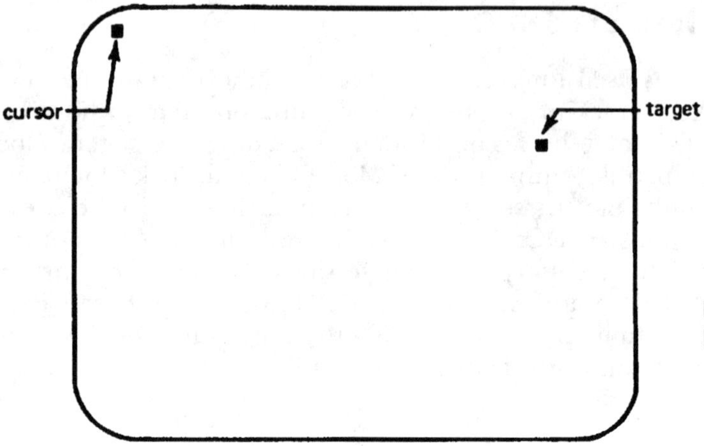

Figure 11.1.
Blind target shoot.

Your score is based on your distance from the target as measured in terms of the moves it takes to get to the target from your final position. Here is the list of possible scores:

Distance from Target	Score
0	100
1 or 2	90
3 to 5	70
6 to 10	50
11 to 15	30
16 to 20	10
over 20	0

You move the cursor using the cursor motion keys on the numeric keypad.

Here is a sample session with the game. When the game starts, the target is displayed (see Figure 11.2).

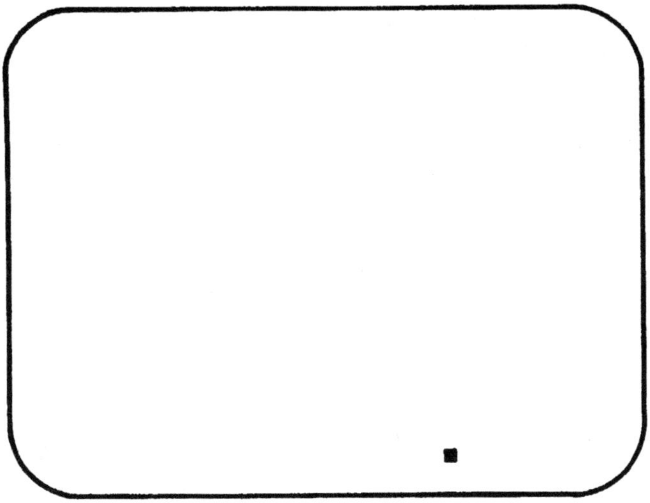

Figure 11.2.
Target displayed.

The screen is cleared and the cursor is moved to the home position (see Figure 11.3a). The cursor is then moved to the remembered position of the target (see Figure 11.3b). Time runs out (see Figure 11.3c).

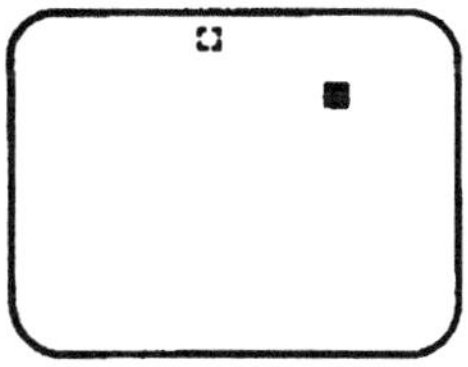

Figure 11.3a.
Cursor moved to home position.

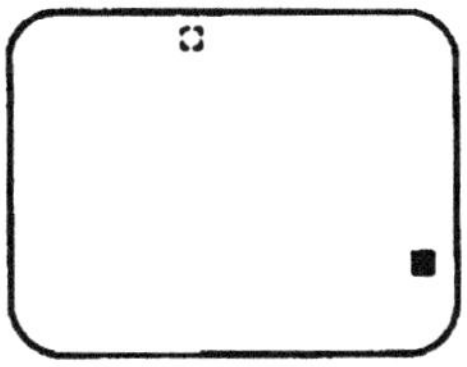

Figure 11.3b.
Cursor moves to position of target.

Figure 11.3c.
Time runs out.

The score is calculated (see Figure 11.4).

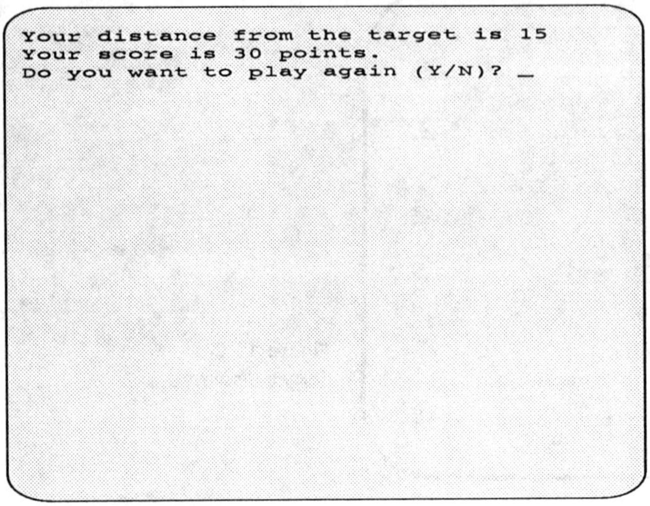

Your distance from the target is 15
Your score is 30 points.
Do you want to play again (Y/N)? _

Figure 11.4.
Score calculated.

Here is a listing of our program:

Listing 11.2. Blind target shoot

```
program BlindTargetShoot;
{This program plays the blind target shoot game.}

  uses
    crt,
    dos;

  var
    TargetX, TargetY,
    PlayerX, PlayerY : integer;

  procedure TitleScreen;
    var
      Dummy : char;

    begin {TitleScreen}
      textmode(bw40); {Enter 40-column black & white text mode}
      writeln(‘Blind Target Shoot’:29);
      gotoxy(1, 20);
      write(‘To begin game, press any key’:34);
      Dummy := readkey
    end; {TitleScreen}

  procedure SetUpTarget(var TargetX, TargetY : integer);
  {Clears the screen and shows the target at a random location
   (stored in TargetX,TargetY) for a certain number of seconds.}

    const
      SecondsToDisplay = 2;
```

```
  begin {SetUpTarget}
    clrscr;
    randomize;
    TargetX := random(40) + 1; {Choose random target column}
    TargetY := random(25) + 1; {Choose random target row}
    gotoxy(TargetX, TargetY); {Move to target location}
    write(chr(219)); {Draw target}
    gotoxy(81, 26); { Move cursor off the screen to hide it }
    delay(SecondsToDisplay * 1000);
    gotoxy(TargetX, TargetY);
    write(' ') { Erase target }
  end; {SetUpTarget}

procedure Aim(var PlayerX, PlayerY : integer);
{Allows the player to use the arrow keys to move the cursor (aim).}

  const
    SecondsToMove = 5;
    ExtendedKey = chr(0);   { 1st character returned when an extended }
                            { key (F-keys, arrows, etc.) is pressed  }
    UpArrow = chr(72);      { 2nd character returned when up is pressed }
    DownArrow = chr(80);    { 2nd character       ""     down      ""     }
    LeftArrow = chr(75);    { 2nd character       ""     left      ""     }
    RightArrow = chr(77);   { 2nd character       ""     right     ""     }

  type
    TypeTimer = record
                  Hour, Minute, Second, Sec100 : word
                end;

  var
    Timer : TypeTimer;
    Key : char;
    ArrowKeyPressed : boolean;

  procedure StartTimer(var Timer : TypeTimer);
  {Stores the current time in Timer.}

    begin {StartTimer}
      with Timer do
        gettime(Hour, Minute, Second, Sec100)
    end; {StartTimer}

  function ElapsedTime( Timer : TypeTimer) : real;
  {Returns the time difference (in seconds) between the time contained
  in Timer and the current time. Accurate to over 24 hours.}

    var
      Current : TypeTimer;

    begin {ElapsedTime}
      StartTimer(Current);
      if (Current.Hour < Timer.Hour)  {Hour has looped to next day}
        then                          {add 24 hours for previous day}
          Current.Hour := Current.Hour + 24;
      if (Current.Minute < Timer.Minute)  {Minute looped to next hour}
```

```
      then                                {add 60 min for prev hour}
        Current.Minute := Current.Minute + 60;
    if (Current.Second < Timer.Second)  {Second looped to next min.}
      then                                {add 60 sec for prev min}
        Current.Second := Current.Second + 60;
    if (Current.Sec100 < Timer.Sec100)  {1/100 sec looped to next}
      then                                {add 100 for prev second}
        Current.Sec100 := Current.Sec100 + 100;
    ElapsedTime := ((Current.Hour - Timer.Hour) * 60 * 60) +
                   ((Current.Minute - Timer.Minute) * 60) +
                   (Current.Second - Timer.Second) +
                   ((Current.Sec100 - Timer.Sec100) / 100)
  end; {ElapsedTime}

procedure ReadArrowKey(var Key : char;
                       var ArrowKeyPressed : boolean);
{Reads from the keyboard, accepting only the arrow
 keys; if no key is pressed, it doesn't do anything.}

  begin {ReadArrowKey}
    if not keypressed
      then
        ArrowKeyPressed := false
      else
        begin
          Key := readkey;
          if (Key <> ExtendedKey)
            then
              ArrowKeyPressed := false
            else
              begin
                Key := readkey;
                ArrowKeyPressed :=
                  (Key in [UpArrow, DownArrow, LeftArrow, RightArrow])
                end
        end
  end; {ReadArrowKey}

begin {Aim}
  PlayerX := 1;
  PlayerY := 1;
  StartTimer(Timer);
  repeat
    gotoxy(PlayerX, PlayerY);
    ReadArrowKey(Key, ArrowKeyPressed);
    if ArrowKeyPressed
      then
        case Key of
          UpArrow : if (PlayerY = 1)
                      then
                        PlayerY := 25 {Loop around}
                      else
                        PlayerY := PlayerY - 1;
          DownArrow : if (PlayerY = 25)
                      then
                        PlayerY := 1
```

```
                        else
                          PlayerY := PlayerY + 1;
             LeftArrow : if (PlayerX = 1)
                        then
                          PlayerX := 40
                        else
                          PlayerX := PlayerX - 1;
             RightArrow : if (PlayerX = 40)
                        then
                          PlayerX := 1
                        else
                          PlayerX := PlayerX + 1
           end
    until (ElapsedTime(Timer) >= SecondsToMove)
  end; {Aim}

procedure DisplayResults(    TargetX, TargetY,
                             PlayerX, PlayerY : integer);

  function Distance(    X1, Y1, X2, Y2 : integer) : integer;
  {Distance formula for (X1,Y1) to (X2,Y2).}

    begin {Distance}
      Distance := round(sqrt(sqr(X2 - X1) + sqr(Y2 - Y1)))
    end; {Distance}

  begin {DisplayResults}
    clrscr;
    write('Your distance from the target is ');
    writeln(Distance(TargetX, TargetY, PlayerX, PlayerY));
    write('Your score is ');
    case Distance(TargetX, TargetY, PlayerX, PlayerY) of
      0 : writeln('100 points!!!');
      1..2 : writeln('90 points!');
      3..5 : writeln('70 points.');
      6..10 : writeln('50 points.');
      11..15 : writeln('30 points.');
      16..20 : writeln('10 points.')
      else
        writeln('0 points.')
    end
  end; {DisplayResults}

function Finished : boolean;

  var
    Answer : char;
  begin {Finished}
    write('Do you want to play again (Y/N)? ');
    readln(Answer);
    Finished := (Answer <> 'Y') and (Answer <> 'y')
  end; {Finished}

begin {BlindTargetShoot}
  TitleScreen;
  repeat
```

```
      SetUpTarget(TargetX, TargetY); {Find location, display, and erase}
      Aim(PlayerX, PlayerY);
      DisplayResults(TargetX, TargetY, PlayerX, PlayerY)
    until Finished
  end. {BlindTargetShoot}
```

Shooting Gallery

In this section we develop a game called Shooting Gallery that simulates the shooting galleries of carnivals. The player has a gun that he or she may fire at a moving target (see Figure 11.5). The program keeps track of the hits. The game shows 20 moving targets during one play.

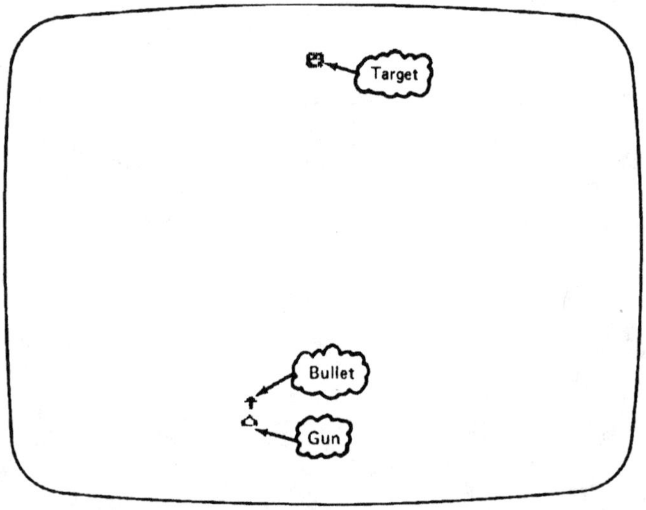

Figure 11.5.
The game of Shooting Gallery.

The design of this game incorporates most of what we know. The right and left motions will tell the program that we wish to move the gun to the right or left. The cursor-up key will fire the gun.

This program will be in the medium-resolution CGA graphics mode (320 × 200). The gun will initially be in the center of the last text row of the screen. The first position of the bullet after being fired will be in pixel row 185.

For the gun, we will use the small house-shaped figure (ASCII character 127). The bullet will be a vertical arrow (ASCII character 24) and the target will be a happy face (ASCII character 2). It is necessary to animate the motion of these figures. To do this, we declare a data type `TypePicture` which is an array of bytes which describe the pixels. A second data type `TypeSprite` consists of a picture plus a screen location corresponding to the upper left corner of the picture.

The program begins by placing the gun in its initial position. There is an outer loop for 20 targets and an inner loop each step of which moves the target two columns across the screen and the bullet (if any have been fired) eight rows up the screen. If you fire the gun (cursor-up key), the gun firing routine is called. This displays the bullet in its initial position. All subsequent motion of the bullet is controlled by the main loop. The bullet disappears when it reaches the row of the target. The target disappears when it hits the right edge of the screen. If the bullet and the target are at the same place at the same time, both disappear and you are credited with a hit.

Listing 11.3. Shooting Gallery

```
program ShootingGallery;
{This program plays the shooting gallery game.}

  uses
    crt,
    graph;

  const
    PictureSize = 20;
    NumTargets = 20;
    PictureHeight = 8;
    PictureWidth = 8;

  type
    TypePicture = array[1..PictureSize] of byte;
    TypeSprite = record
                   X, Y : integer;
                   Picture : TypePicture
                 end;

  var
    Gun, Bullet, Target : TypeSprite;
    Score, TargetNumber : integer;
    BulletInMotion, TargetHit : boolean;

  {----- Sprites routines ---}

  procedure DisplaySprite(var Sprite : TypeSprite;
                              XStart, YStart : integer);
  {Displays a sprite on the screen at (XStart,YStart).}
```

```
  begin {DisplaySprite}
    with Sprite do
      begin
        if (XStart >= 0) and (XStart = (getmaxx - PictureWidth))
          then
            X := XStart
          else
            X := 0;
        if (YStart >= 0) and (YStart = (getmaxy - PictureHeight))
          then
            Y := YStart
          else
            Y := 0;
        putimage(X, Y, Picture, xorput)
      end
  end; {DisplaySprite}

procedure RemoveSprite(var Sprite : TypeSprite);
{Removes a sprite from the screen.}

  begin {DisplaySprite}
    with Sprite do
      putimage(X, Y, Picture, xorput)
  end; {DisplaySprite}

procedure MoveSprite(var Sprite : TypeSprite;
                         XRel, YRel : integer);
{Moves a sprite from one location on the screen to another
 location, relative to the current (X,Y) location. MoveSprite
 assumes the sprite has been already drawn on the screen at
 the current location.}

  begin {MoveSprite}
    RemoveSprite(Sprite);
    with Sprite do
      begin
        if ((X + XRel) >= 0) and
           ((X + XRel) <= (getmaxx - PictureWidth))
          then
            X := X + XRel;
        if ((Y + YRel) >= 0) and
           ((Y + YRel) <= (getmaxy - PictureHeight))
          then
            Y := Y + YRel;
        putimage(X, Y, Picture, xorput) {Draw picture in new position}
      end
  end; {MoveSprite}

{----- End of sprites routines -----}

procedure DisplayScore( Score : integer);
  var
    ScoreString : string;

  begin {DisplayScore}
    str(Score, ScoreString);
    ScoreString := concat('Score: ', ScoreString);
```

```
    setfillstyle(emptyfill, 1);
    bar(0, 186, getmaxx, getmaxy);
    moveto(0, 186);
    outtext(ScoreString)
  end; {DisplayScore}

procedure InitGame(var Gun, Bullet, Target : TypeSprite;
                   var Score : integer;
                   var BulletInMotion : boolean);

  procedure OpenGraph;
  {Opens the graphics system in C/GA med-res mode.}

    var
      GraphDriver, GraphMode : integer;

    begin {OpenGraph}
      GraphDriver := CGA;
      GraphMode := CGAC0;
      initgraph(GraphDriver, GraphMode, '');
      cleardevice
    end; {OpenGraph}

  procedure CreatePictures(var Gun, Bullet, Target : TypeSprite);
  {Draws and stores each sprite's picture.}

    begin {CreatePictures}
      setcolor(1);
      outtext(chr(127));
      getimage(0, 0, (PictureWidth - 1), (PictureHeight - 1), Gun.Picture);
      cleardevice;
      setcolor(2);
      outtext(chr(24));
      getimage(0, 0, (PictureWidth - 1), (PictureHeight - 1),
               Bullet.Picture);
      cleardevice;
      setcolor(3);
      outtext(chr(2));
      getimage(0, 0, (PictureWidth - 1), (PictureHeight - 1),
               Target.Picture);
      cleardevice
    end; {CreatePictures}

  begin {InitGame}
    OpenGraph;
    CreatePictures(Gun, Bullet, Target);
    DisplaySprite(Gun, 160, 177);
    Score := 0;
    DisplayScore(Score);
    BulletInMotion := false
  end; {InitGame}

procedure PlayARound(var Gun, Bullet, Target : TypeSprite;
                     var BulletInMotion, TargetHit : boolean);
  var
    Column : integer;
```

```
procedure InitRound(var Target : TypeSprite;
                    var TargetHit : boolean);

  begin {InitRound}
    DisplaySprite(Target, 0, 8);
    TargetHit := false
  end; {InitRound}

function Even( Number : integer) : boolean;

  begin {Even}
    Even := not odd(Number)
  end; {Even}

procedure DoHit(var Target : TypeSprite;
                var TargetHit : boolean;
                var Score : integer);

  begin {DoHit}
    RemoveSprite(Target);
    TargetHit := true;
    Score := Score + 1
  end; {DoHit}

procedure CheckBullet(var Bullet, Target : TypeSprite;
                      var BulletInMotion, TargetHit : boolean;
                      var Score : integer);
{Performs movement and collision-checking for the bullet.}

  begin {CheckBullet}
    MoveSprite(Bullet, 0, -PictureHeight);
    if (Bullet.Y <= (PictureHeight + 8))
      then
        begin
          RemoveSprite(Bullet);
          BulletInMotion := false;
          if (abs(Bullet.X - Target.X) < 7)
            then
              DoHit(Target, TargetHit, Score)
        end
  end; {CheckBullet}

procedure CheckKeyboard(var Gun, Bullet : TypeSprite;
                        var BulletInMotion : boolean);
{Accepts the up, left, and right arrow keys from the keyboard
 and fires if the up arrow is pressed or moves if the left/right
 arrow keys are pressed.}

  const
    SpecialKey = chr(0);
    UpArrow = chr(72);
    LeftArrow = chr(75);
    RightArrow = chr(77);

  var
    Key : char;
```

```
    begin {CheckKeyboard}
      if keypressed
        then
          begin
            Key := readkey;
            if (Key = SpecialKey)
              then
                case readkey of
                  UpArrow : if not BulletInMotion
                              then
                                begin
                                  DisplaySprite(Bullet, Gun.X, 169);
                                  BulletInMotion := true
                                end;
                  LeftArrow : MoveSprite(Gun, -8, 0);
                  RightArrow : MoveSprite(Gun, +8, 0)
                end
          end
      end; {CheckKeyboard}

  begin {PlayARound}
    InitRound(Target, TargetHit);
    for Column := 2 to (getmaxx - PictureWidth) do
      if Even(Column) and not TargetHit
        then
          begin
            MoveSprite(Target, +2, 0);
            if BulletInMotion
              then
                CheckBullet(Bullet, Target, BulletInMotion, TargetHit,
                            Score);
            CheckKeyboard(Gun, Bullet, BulletInMotion);
            delay(20)
          end
  end; {PlayARound}

procedure DetermineResults(var Target : TypeSprite;
                               TargetHit : boolean;
                           var Score : integer);

  begin {DetermineResults}
    if not TargetHit
      then
        RemoveSprite(Target);
    DisplayScore(Score)
  end; {DetermineResults}

  begin {ShootingGallery}
    InitGame(Gun, Bullet, Target, Score, BulletInMotion);
    for TargetNumber := 1 to NumTargets do
      begin
        PlayARound(Gun, Bullet, Target, BulletInMotion, TargetHit);
        DetermineResults(Target, TargetHit, Score)
      end;
    closegraph
  end. {ShootingGallery}
```

Tic-Tac-Toe (Graphics Mode)

In this section, we present a program for the traditional game of tic-tac-toe. We won't attempt to let the computer execute a strategy. Rather, we will let it be fairly stupid and choose its moves randomly. Throughout the program, you will be O and the computer will be X. The start of the game is shown in Figure 11.6.

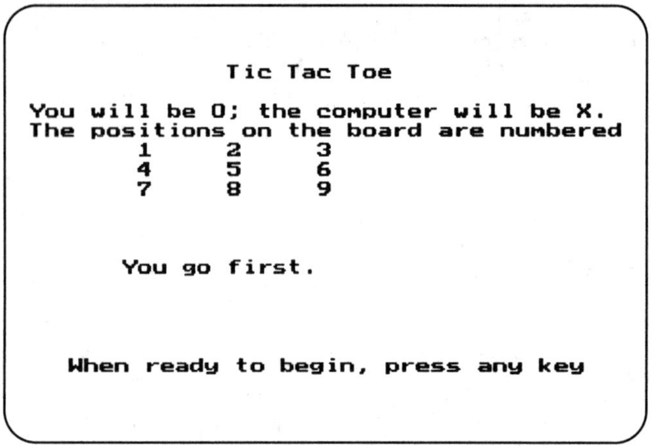

Tic Tac Toe
You will be O; the computer will be X.
The positions on the board are numbered
1 2 3
4 5 6
7 8 9
You go first.
When ready to begin, press any key

Figure 11.6.
Sample tic-tac-toe game.

The computer now draws a tic-tac-toe board (see Figure 11.7).

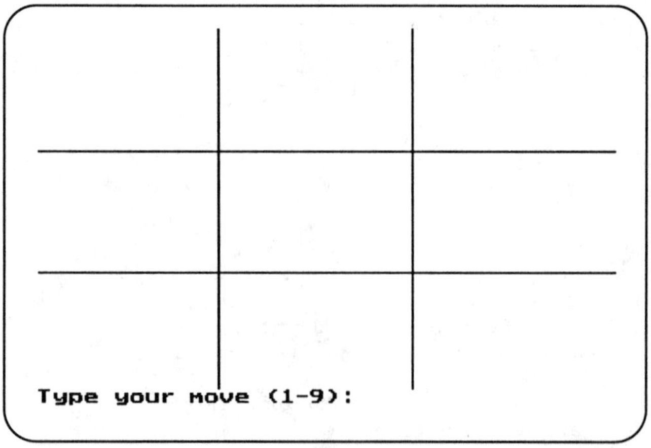

Figure 11.7.
The computer draws a tic-tac-toe board.

The computer now displays your move and makes a move of its own (see Figure 11.8).

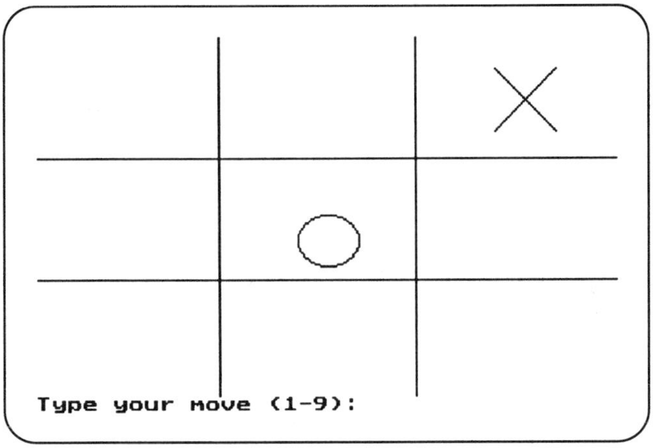

Figure 11.8. The computer displays your move and makes one of its own.

The computer now makes its move until someone wins or a tie game results.

To implement this game, we represent each square on the board by a data type which consists of one of the three values (`empty`, `O`, `X`). We declare a data type for the game board, namely an array of squares. We number the squares from 1 to 9, starting from the first row and numbering left to right. We declare a data type to correspond to whose turn it is. This data type has one of the two values (`Computer`, `Human`).

The main program is very simple to describe in terms of three procedures:

```
begin
  OpenGraph;
  repeat
    InitializeGame (Board, Turn);
    PlayGame (Board, Turn);
    DisplayOutcome (Board)
  until Finished;
  closegraph
end.
```

Each trip through the loop corresponds to a single move. At the end of each move, the variable `Turn` is set so that the next turn is taken by the other player. The loop continues until there is a winner, in which case the variable `Finished` is set equal to true by the procedure `DisplayOutcome`.

The details of the program are contained in the coding of the three procedures. Here is a listing of our program:

Listing 11.4. Tic Tac Toe

```
program TicTacToe;
{This program plays the traditional game
of tic tac toe against an opponent,
```

```
drawing a board on the screen, and
determining when there is a winner.}

  uses
    crt,
    graph;

  const
    MaxSquares = 9;

  type
    TypeSquare = (Empty, O, X);
    TypeBoard = array[1..MaxSquares] of TypeSquare;
    TypeTurn = (Computer, Human);

  var
    Board : TypeBoard;
    Turn : TypeTurn;

  procedure OpenGraph;
  {Opens the graphics system in CGA med-res mode.}

    var
      GraphDriver, GraphMode : integer;

    begin {OpenGraph}
      GraphDriver := CGA;
      GraphMode := CGAC0;
      initgraph(GraphDriver, GraphMode, '');
      cleardevice
    end; {OpenGraph}

  procedure InitializeGame(var Board : TypeBoard;
                           var Turn : TypeTurn);
  var
    Dummy : char;

  procedure InitializeBoard(var Board : TypeBoard);

    var
      CurrentSquare : integer;

    begin {InitializeBoard}
      for CurrentSquare := 1 to MaxSquares do
        Board[CurrentSquare] := Empty
    end; {InitializeBoard}

  procedure FlipForTurn(var Turn : TypeTurn);

    begin {FlipForTurn}
      randomize;
      if (random(2) = 1)
        then
          begin
            outtextxy(48, 100, 'You go first.');
            Turn := Human
          end
```

```
      else
        begin
          outtextxy(48, 100, 'I will go first.');
          Turn := Computer
        end
  end; {FlipForTurn}

procedure DrawBoard;

  begin {DrawBoard}
    cleardevice;
    line(103, 8, 103, 191);
    line(206, 8, 206, 191);
    line(8, 70, 311, 70);
    line(8, 132, 311, 132)
  end; {DrawBoard}

begin {InitializeBoard}
    cleardevice;
    outtextxy(104, 0, 'Tic Tac Toe');
    outtextxy(0, 20, 'You will be O; the computer will be X.');
    outtextxy(0, 30, 'The positions on the board are numbered');
    outtextxy(56, 40, '1 2 3');
    outtextxy(56, 50, '4 5 6');
    outtextxy(56, 60, '7 8 9');
    FlipForTurn(Turn);
    outtextxy(20, 150, 'When ready to begin, press any key');
    Dummy := readkey;
    InitializeBoard(Board);
    DrawBoard
  end; {InitializeBoard}

procedure BlankTextLine;
{Clears the bottom row, where text is written}

  begin {BlankTextLine}
    setfillstyle(emptyfill, 1);
    bar(0, 192, 319, 199)
  end; {BlankTextLine}

function Won(     Board : TypeBoard;
                  Side : TypeSquare) : boolean;
{Determines whether a side (O or X) has won the game.}

  begin {Won}
    Won :=
    ((Board[1]=Board[2]) and (Board[2]=Board[3]) and (Board[3]=Side)) or
    ((Board[4]=Board[5]) and (Board[5]=Board[6]) and (Board[6]=Side)) or
    ((Board[7]=Board[8]) and (Board[8]=Board[9]) and (Board[9]=Side)) or
    ((Board[1]=Board[4]) and (Board[4]=Board[7]) and (Board[7]=Side)) or
    ((Board[2]=Board[5]) and (Board[5]=Board[8]) and (Board[8]=Side)) or
    ((Board[3]=Board[6]) and (Board[6]=Board[9]) and (Board[9]=Side)) or
    ((Board[1]=Board[5]) and (Board[5]=Board[9]) and (Board[9]=Side)) or
    ((Board[3]=Board[5]) and (Board[5]=Board[7]) and (Board[7]=Side))
  end; {Won}
```

```
procedure PlayGame(var Board : TypeBoard;
                       Turn : TypeTurn);

  procedure FindCenter(     Square : integer;
                       var CenterX, CenterY : integer);
  {Returns in CenterX,CenterY the center coordinates of square 1-9.}

    begin {FindCenter}

      case Square of
        1, 2, 3 : CenterY := 5 * 8;
        4, 5, 6 : CenterY := 14 * 8;
        7, 8, 9 : CenterY := 21 * 8
      end;
      case Square of
        1, 4, 7 : CenterX := 7 * 8;
        2, 5, 8 : CenterX := 20 * 8;
        3, 6, 9 : CenterX := 33 * 8
      end
    end; {FindCenter}

procedure DrawX( Square : integer);
{Draws an "X" in the square.}

  var
    CenterX, CenterY : integer;

  begin {DrawX}
    FindCenter(Square, CenterX, CenterY);
    line(CenterX - 16, CenterY - 16, CenterX + 16, CenterY + 16);
    line(CenterX + 16, CenterY - 16, CenterX - 16, CenterY + 16)
  end; {DrawY}

procedure DrawO( Square : integer);
{Draws an "O" in the square.}

  var
    CenterX, CenterY : integer;

  begin {DrawO}
    FindCenter(Square, CenterX, CenterY);
    circle(CenterX, CenterY, 16)
  end; {DrawO}

procedure DoComputerMove(var Board : TypeBoard;
                         var Turn : TypeTurn);
{Places an "X" on the board.}

  var
    Move : integer;

  procedure FindMove(     Board : TypeBoard;
                     var Move : integer);

    function ComputerWillWin(     Board : TypeBoard;
                                  Move : integer) : boolean;
```

```
  {Determines whether the computer will win if it
   places an "X" in the tentative square, Move.}

    begin {FindMove}
      Board[Move] := X;
      ComputerWillWin := Won(Board, X)
    end; {FindMove}

  procedure FindWinningMove(     Board : TypeBoard;
                             var Move : integer);

      begin {FindWinningMove}
        repeat
          repeat
            Move := Move + 1
          until (Board[Move] = Empty) or (Move = MaxSquares)
        until (Move = MaxSquares) or ComputerWillWin(Board, Move)
      end; {FindWinningMove}

    procedure FindRandomMove(     Board : TypeBoard;
                             var Move : integer);

      begin {FindRandomMove}
        repeat
          Move := random(MaxSquares) + 1
        until (Board[Move] = Empty)
      end; {FindRandomMove}

    begin {FindMove}
      Move := 0;
      FindWinningMove(Board, Move);
      if not ComputerWillWin(Board, Move)
        then
          FindRandomMove(Board, Move)
    end; {FindMove}

  begin {DoComputerMove}
    FindMove(Board, Move);
    BlankTextLine;
    outtextxy(8, 192, 'Here's my move!');
    delay(500);
    Board[Move] := X;
    DrawX(Move);
    Turn := Human
  end; {DoComputerMove}

procedure LetPlayerMove(var Board : TypeBoard;
                        var Turn : TypeTurn);
{Lets the user place an "O" on the board.}

  var
    Move : integer;

  begin {LetPlayerMove}
    BlankTextLine;
    outtextxy(8, 192, 'Type your move (1-9): ');
```

```
      repeat
        repeat
          Move := ord(readkey) - ord ('0')
        until (Move in [1..9])
      until (Board[Move] = Empty);
      Board[Move] := O;
      DrawO(Move);
      Turn := Computer
    end; {LetPlayerMove}

  function Full( Board : TypeBoard) : boolean;
  {Determines whether the board is full (Cat's Game).}

    var
      CurrentSquare : integer;

    begin {Full}
      Full := true;
      for CurrentSquare := 1 to MaxSquares do
        if (Board[CurrentSquare] = Empty)
          then
            Full := false
    end; {Full}

  begin {PlayGame}
    repeat
      if (Turn = Computer)
        then
          DoComputerMove(Board, Turn)
        else
          LetPlayerMove(Board, Turn)
    until Won(Board, O) or Won(Board, X) or Full(Board)
  end; {PlayGame}

procedure DisplayOutcome( Board : TypeBoard);

  begin {DisplayOutcome}
    if Won(Board, O)
      then
        outtextxy(96, 0, '*** You win ***')
      else
        if Won(Board, X)
          then
            outtextxy(104, 0, '*** I win ***')
          else
            outtextxy(84, 0, '*** Cat''s game ***')
  end; {DisplayOutcome}

function Finished : boolean;

  var
    Answer : char;

  begin {Finished}
    BlankTextLine;
    outtextxy(8, 192, 'Another game (Y/N)? ');
```

```
    repeat
      Answer := readkey
    until (Answer in ['Y', 'y', 'N','n']);
    Finished := (Answer in ['N', 'n'])
  end; {Finished}

begin {TicTacToe}
  OpenGraph;
  repeat
    InitializeGame(Board, Turn);
    PlayGame(Board, Turn);
    DisplayOutcome(Board)
  until Finished;
  closegraph
end. {TicTacToe}
```

Blackjack

In this section, we present a version of the popular card game Blackjack. In this game, the player (we will allow only one at a time) vies with the dealer. The player makes a bet. The player and dealer are then dealt two cards each. The dealer's first card is face down and the others are face up. The object is to get a hand that totals as closely as possible to 21 without going over. Numbered cards have their usual values; jacks, queens, and kings all have value 10; and aces have a value of either 1 or 11 at the player's (or dealer's) discretion. The player goes first, deciding, one card at a time, whether to be hit (given another card) or to stand (decline further cards). If the player's total goes over 21, the player busts and loses the amount bet. If the player hits 21 exactly, he or she automatically wins the amount bet. And if a player hits BlackJack, that player should get/win 1 1/2 times his bet.

If the player stops before busting or achieving 21, the dealer plays. First the dealer turns over his first card. As long as the dealer's total is less than 16, he must draw a card. The dealer continues until he either busts, gets 21, or gets at least 16. If the dealer busts, the player wins. Otherwise, the player with the highest total wins. In case of ties, the dealer wins.

Our program to implement this game employs most of what we have learned about string manipulation. The deck of cards is represented as a string:

"AHADACAS2H2D2C2S......"

Here AH stands for the ace of hearts, 2D for the two of diamonds, and so forth. Picking a card involves choosing a random odd position in the string. The card chosen is then determined by extracting the two-character substring that stands for the character.

The program uses the various graphics characters in the IBM PC's character set to draw the cards on the screen. These are characters with ASCII codes from 0 to 31 and from 128 to 255. In this program, we use characters to form rectangles (ASCII codes 187, 188, 200, 201, 205) and the characters for the various card suits (ASCII codes 3, 4, 5, and 6). (IBM wisely chose to include these in its character set.)

Listing 11.5. Blackjack

```
program Blackjack;

  uses
    crt;

  type
    TypeDeck = string[104];

  var
    DealerFirstCard, Deck  : TypeDeck;
    GameIsOver : boolean;
    PlayerTotal, DealerTotal,
    PlayerNumAce, DealerNumAce,
    BetAmount,
    PlayerNumCard, DealerNumCard,
    NumChips : integer;

  procedure GetNumChips(var NumChips : integer);

    begin {GetNumChips}
      repeat
        clrscr;
        write('Enter the number of chips to start with : ');
        readln(NumChips)
      until (NumChips > 0)
    end; {GetNumChips}

  procedure PlaceBet(var BetAmount : integer;
                         NumChips  : integer;
                         GameIsOver : boolean);

    var
      ErrorCode : integer;
      ChoiceString : string[10];

    begin {PlaceBet}
      repeat
        ErrorCode := 0;
        clrscr;
        writeln('You have ', NumChips, ' chips to bet.');
        write('(Q)uit or enter bet: ');
        readln(ChoiceString);
        if (ChoiceString[1] = 'Q') or
           (ChoiceString[1] = 'q')
          then
            begin
              GameIsOver := true;
```

```
          BetAmount := 1
        end
      else
        val (ChoiceString, BetAmount, ErrorCode);
  until (BetAmount > 0) and (BetAmount < = NumChips) and (ErrorCode = 0)
end; {PlaceBet}

procedure DrawCard(     Card : TypeDeck;
                        NumCard : integer;
                        DealerCard : boolean;
                        DealFirstOver : boolean);
  const
    TopOfCard = chr(201) + chr(205) + chr(205) + chr(205) + chr(205) +
                chr(205) + chr(205) + chr(205) + chr(205) + chr(187);
    SideOfCard = chr(186) + '  ' + chr(186);
    BottomOfCard = chr(200) + chr(205) + chr(205) + chr(205) +
                   chr(205) + chr(205) + chr(205) + chr(205) +
                   chr(205) + chr(188);
  var
    SideNum, XPos, YPos : integer;

  function CardSymbol(CharSymbol : char) : char;

    begin {CardSymbol}
      case CharSymbol of
        'H' : CardSymbol := chr(3);
        'D' : CardSymbol := chr(4);
        'C' : CardSymbol := chr(5);
        'S' : CardSymbol := chr(6)
      end
    end; {CardSymbol}

  begin {DrawCard}
    XPos := 11 * (NumCard - 1) + 1;
    if DealerCard
      then
        YPos := 1
      else
        YPos := 14;
    gotoxy(XPos, YPos);
    write(TopOfCard);
    for SideNum := 1 to 5 do
      begin
        gotoxy(XPos, YPos + SideNum);
        write(SideOfCard)
      end;
    gotoxy(XPos, YPos + 6);
    write(BottomOfCard);
    gotoxy(XPos + 4, YPos + 3);
    if not (DealerCard and (NumCard = 1)) or DealFirstOver
      then
        begin
        if (Card[1] = '0')
          then
            write('1');
        write(Card[1]);
```

```
          write(CardSymbol(Card[2]))
        end
    end; {DrawCard}

  procedure DealACard(var DealerFirstCard, Deck : TypeDeck;
                      var TotalValue, NumCard, NumAce : integer;
                          DealerCard : boolean);
    var
      Card : TypeDeck;

    function PointValue(Card : char) : integer;

      begin {PointValue}
        case Card of
          'A' : PointValue := 11;
          'J', 'Q', 'K', '0' : PointValue := 10;
          else
            PointValue := ord(Card) - 48
        end
      end; {PointValue}

    begin {DealACard}
      Card := copy(Deck, 1, 2);
      Deck := copy(Deck, 3, length(Deck) - 2);
      TotalValue := TotalValue + PointValue(Card[1]);
      if Card[1] = 'A'
        then
          NumAce := NumAce + 1;
      if (TotalValue > 21) and (NumAce > 0)
        then
          begin
            TotalValue := TotalValue - 10;
            NumAce := NumAce - 1
          end;
      NumCard := NumCard + 1;
      if DealerCard and (NumCard = 1)
        then
          DealerFirstCard := Card;
      DrawCard(Card, NumCard, DealerCard, false)
    end; {DealACard}

  procedure SetupHand(var DealerFirstCard, Deck : TypeDeck;
                      var PlayerTotal, DealerTotal,
                          PlayerNumAce, DealerNumAce,
                          PlayerNumCard, DealerNumCard : integer);

    procedure SetupDeck (var Deck : TypeDeck);

      const
        FullDeck =
'AH2H3H4H5H6H7H8H9H0HJHQHKHAD2D3D4D5D6D7D8D9D0DJDQDKDAC2C3C4C5C6C7C8C9C0CJCQCKCAS2S3S4S5S6S7S8S9S0SJSQSKS';

      var
        CardNum, CardToAdd : integer;
        TempDeck : TypeDeck;
```

```
    begin {SetupDeck}
      Deck := '';
      TempDeck := FullDeck;
      randomize;
      for CardNum := 1 to 52 do
        begin
          CardToAdd := random(length(TempDeck) div 2) * 2 + 1;
          Deck := concat(Deck, copy(TempDeck, CardToAdd, 2));
          TempDeck := concat(copy(TempDeck, 1, CardToAdd - 1),
                             copy(TempDeck, CardToAdd + 2,
                                  length(TempDeck) - (CardToAdd + 2)))
        end
      end; {SetupDeck}

  procedure DealCards(var DealerFirstCard, Deck : TypeDeck;
                      var PlayerTotal, DealerTotal,
                          PlayerNumAce, DealerNumAce,
                          PlayerNumCard, DealerNumCard : integer);

    begin {DealCards}
      DealACard(DealerFirstCard, Deck, PlayerTotal, PlayerNumCard,
                PlayerNumAce, false);
      DealACard(DealerFirstCard, Deck, PlayerTotal, PlayerNumCard,
                PlayerNumAce, false);
      DealACard(DealerFirstCard, Deck, DealerTotal, DealerNumCard,
                DealerNumAce, true);
      DealACard(DealerFirstCard, Deck, DealerTotal, DealerNumCard,
                DealerNumAce, true)
    end; {DealCards}

  procedure SetupScreen;
    begin {SetupScreen}
      clrscr;
      gotoxy(32, 9);
      write('Dealer''s Hand');
      gotoxy(32, 22);
      write('Player''s Hand')
    end; {SetupScreen}

  begin {SetupHand}
    PlayerTotal := 0;
    DealerTotal := 0;
    PlayerNumAce := 0;
    DealerNumAce := 0;
    PlayerNumCard := 0;
    DealerNumCard := 0;
    SetupScreen;
    SetupDeck(Deck);
    DealCards(DealerFirstCard, Deck, PlayerTotal, DealerTotal,
              PlayerNumAce, DealerNumAce, PlayerNumCard, DealerNumCard)
  end; {SetupHand}

procedure DoPlayersHand(    DealerFirstCard : TypeDeck;
                        var Deck : TypeDeck;
                        var PlayerTotal,
                            PlayerNumAce,
                            PlayerNumCard : integer);
```

```
  var
    Stand : boolean;
    Choice : char;

  begin {DoPlayersHand}
    Stand := false;
    while not (PlayerTotal >= 21) and not Stand do
      begin
        gotoxy(1, 23);
        write('                                                  ');
        gotoxy(1, 23);
        write('(H)it or (S)tand ? ');
        readln(Choice);
        case Choice of
          'H', 'h' : DealACard(DealerFirstCard, Deck, PlayerTotal,
                               PlayerNumCard, PlayerNumAce, false);
          'S', 's' : Stand := true
        end;
  end;

    if (PlayerTotal > 21)
      then
        begin
          gotoxy(1,23);
          write('BUST! BUST! BUST! BUST! BUST! BUST! BUST! BUST! BUST!')
        end;
    if (PlayerTotal = 21) and (PlayerNumCard = 2)
      then
        begin
          gotoxy(1,23);
          write('BLACKJACK! BLACKJACK! BLACKJACK! BLACKJACK! BLACKJACK!')
        end
  end; {DoPlayersHand}

procedure DoDealersHand(    DealerFirstCard : TypeDeck;
                        var Deck : TypeDeck;
                        var DealerTotal,
                            DealerNumAce,
                            DealerNumCard : integer);

  begin {DoDealersHand}
    while not (DealerTotal >= 16) do
      begin
        DealACard(DealerFirstCard, Deck, DealerTotal, DealerNumCard,
                  DealerNumAce, true);
        delay(2000)
      end;
    if (DealerTotal > 21)
      then
        begin
          gotoxy(1,11);
          write('BUST! BUST! BUST! BUST! BUST! BUST! BUST! BUST! BUST!')
        end;
    if (DealerTotal = 21) and (DealerNumCard = 2)
      then
```

```
        begin
          gotoxy(1,11);
          write('BLACKJACK! BLACKJACK! BLACKJACK! BLACKJACK! BLACKJACK!')
        end
  end; {DoDealersHand}

procedure UpdateMoney(var NumChips, BetAmount : integer;
                          PlayerTotal, DealerTotal : integer);
  begin {UpdateMoney}
    if ((PlayerTotal > DealerTotal) and (PlayerTotal <= 21)) or
       (DealerTotal > 21)
      then
        begin
          gotoxy(1,13);
          writeln('YOU WON ', BetAmount, ' CHIPS !!');
          NumChips := NumChips + BetAmount
        end
      else
        begin
          gotoxy(1,13);
          writeln('YOU LOST ', BetAmount, ' CHIPS !!');
          NumChips := NumChips - BetAmount
        end;
    delay(3000)
  end; {UpdateMoney}

begin {Blackjack}
  GameIsOver := false;
  GetNumChips(NumChips);
  PlaceBet(BetAmount, NumChips, GameIsOver);
  while not GameIsOver and (NumChips > 0) do
    begin
      SetupHand(DealerFirstCard, Deck, PlayerTotal, DealerTotal,
                PlayerNumAce, DealerNumAce, PlayerNumCard, DealerNumCard);
      if not (DealerTotal = 21)
        then
          DoPlayersHand(DealerFirstCard, Deck, PlayerTotal, PlayerNumAce,
                        PlayerNumCard);
      DrawCard(DealerFirstCard, 1, true, true);
      if not (PlayerTotal > 21) and
         not ((PlayerTotal = 21) and (PlayerNumCard = 2))
        then
          DoDealersHand(DealerFirstCard, Deck, DealerTotal, DealerNumAce,
                        DealerNumCard);
      UpdateMoney(NumChips, BetAmount, PlayerTotal, DealerTotal);
      if NumChips > 0
        then
          PlaceBet(BetAmount, NumChips, GameIsOver)
        else
          begin
            clrscr;
            write('YOU''RE BANKRUPT!!!');
            delay(4000)
          end
    end
end. {Blackjack}
```

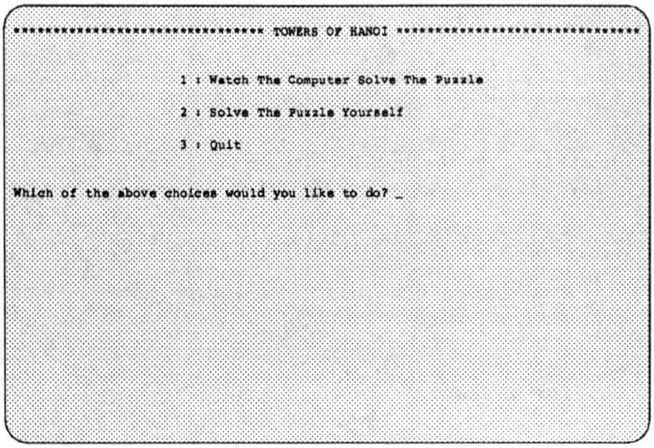

Figure 11.9. Towers of Hanoi menu

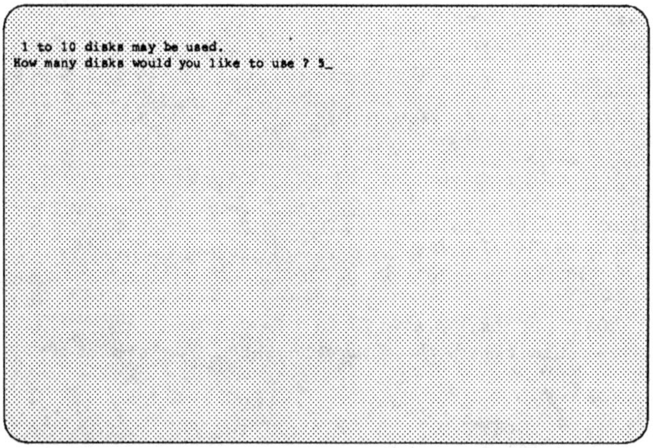

Figure 11.10. Selecting number of disks to use

The Towers of Hanoi

In this section, we present a program to play the game called `Towers of Hanoi`. The towers in question are towers of disks (or washers) on a peg. Proceeding from the bottom of the peg, the disks are in order of decreasing diameter. There are a total of three pegs. All disks are initially in a tower on the leftmost peg (the starting peg—see Figure 11.11). The idea is to restack the disks into a tower on the rightmost peg. You may move one peg at a time from the top of a tower to the top of some other tower. The completed configuration is shown in Figure 11.13.

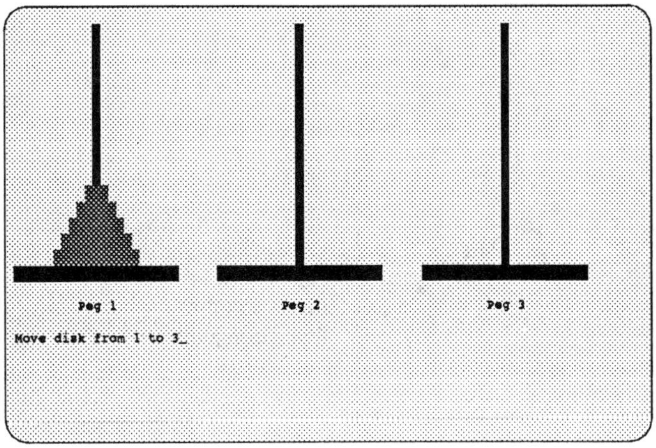

Figure 11.11. Initial configuration of disk

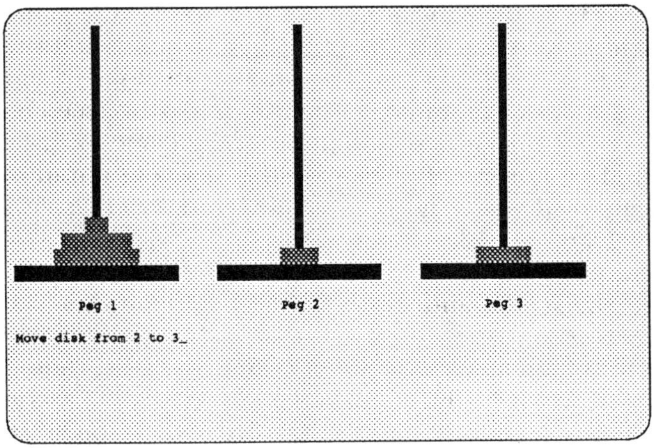

Figure 11.12. Redrawing the new configuration

In the figures, five disks are used. However, you may use any number to play the game. In the case of one or two disks, the game is very easy. However, once you get to a reasonable number of disks (say 7 or 8), the game is incredibly complex unless you look at it the right way, which is to introduce recursion! That is, solve the game for N disks in terms of the solution for N–1 disks. Here's how:

Play the game and arrange the top N–1 disks on the left into a tower on the right peg. Then remove the disks on the right, in order, onto the middle peg. Next, move the last disk on the left to the right. Then move the disks on the middle peg back over to the right peg. This completes the game for N disks! Simple, isn't it? Let's write a program which either allows you to play the game yourself or to play the game by itself.

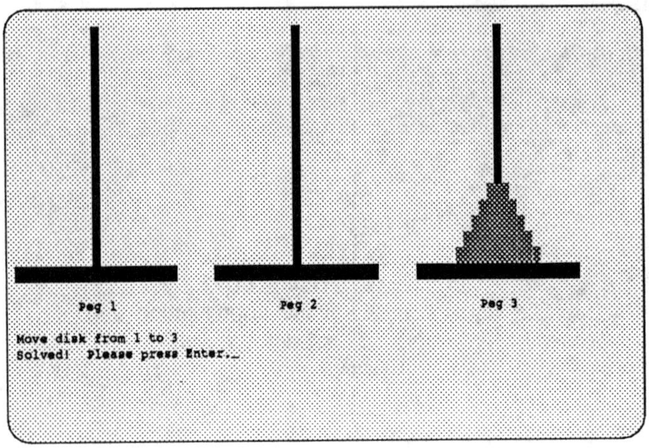
Peg 1
Peg 2
Peg 3
Move disk from 1 to 3
Solved! Please press Enter.

Figure 11.13. Displaying the final configurataion

When the program starts, it will ask you whether you wish to play the game or have the computer play it for you (see Figure 11.9). Let's assume that the computer plays the game. Then it will ask you the number of disks to use (see Figure 11.10). Then it will draw the initial configuration of disk (see Figure 11.11). Finally, it will execute the recursive solution of the game we have described above. After each disk movement, it redraws the new configuration and tells the movement being made (see Figure 11.12). Eventually, it displays the final configuration (see Figure 11.13).

If you play the game, the program asks you for your moves, in sequence. After each move, it redraws the screen and shows the new configuration. Of course, unless you solve the puzzle, you won't reach the final configuration.

The following code is pretty much self-explanatory. However, you should note the data abstraction used. We introduce a data type `TypeStackArray`, which is an array listing the numbers of the disks in the order they appear in a stack. The largest disk has the largest number. The arrays used are of size 10, so at most 10 disks may be used. Moreover, a `TypeStack` incorporates a `TypeStackArray` plus an integer `TopofStack` which equals the height of the stack. Finally, a data type `TypePeg` consists of a `TypeStack` plus an integer noting the peg number. (There are three stacks, one for each peg.)

The recursion takes place in the procedure `MoveDisks`. Note that this procedure calls itself. This is the recursive step.

Here is the code for the program.

Listing 11.6. Towers of Hanoi

```
program TowersOfHanoi;
{This program plays the game Towers of Hanoi.
This game asks you to rearrange a stack of N disks
of decreasing diameter (bottom to top) on a starting
peg to the same configuration on an ending peg. There
```

```
are three pegs for you to put the disks on: Starting
peg, ending peg, and auxiliary peg. You are allowed
to move the top disk on any peg to the top position on
any other peg as long as it remains the smallest disk
on top of the peg. An unlimited number of moves is
allowed. This implementation allows you to solve the
puzzle or allow the computer to solve the puzzle. You
may choose an initial configuration containing from 1
to 10 disks.}

  uses
    crt;

  const
    MaxItems = 10;
    Quit = 3;
    BaseLevel = 16;

  type
    TypeItem = integer;
    TypeStackArray = array[1..MaxItems] of TypeItem;
    TypeStack = record
                  StackArray : TypeStackArray;
                  TopOfStack : integer
                end;
    TypePeg = record
                Stack : TypeStack;
                PegNumber : integer
              end;

  var
    Choice : integer;

  {------------------------------------------------------}

  function EmptyStack(     Stack : TypeStack) : boolean;
  {Determines whether the specified stack is empty.}

    begin {EmptyStack}
      EmptyStack := (Stack.TopOfStack = 0)
    end; {EmptyStack}

  function FullStack( Stack : TypeStack) : boolean;
  {Determines whether the specified stack is full.}

    begin {FullStack}
      FullStack := (Stack.TopOfStack = MaxItems)
    end; {FullStack}

  procedure InitializeStack(var Stack : TypeStack);
  {pre-condition: Stack is undefined.
  post-condition: Stack is initialized and empty.}

    begin {InitializeStack}
      Stack.TopOfStack := 0
    end; {InitializeStack}

  procedure Push(var Stack : TypeStack;
                     Item : integer);
```

```
{pre-conditions: Item is the item to be pushed onto the stack.
                 Stack has been initialized and may be empty or
                 partially or completely filled.
 post-conditions: Item has been pushed onto the top of Stack.}
  begin {Push}
    if not FullStack(Stack)
      then
        with Stack do
          begin
            TopOfStack := (TopOfStack + 1);
            StackArray[TopOfStack] := Item
          end
  end; {Push}

procedure Pop (var Stack : TypeStack;
               var Item : integer);
{pre-conditions: Item may be undefined and stack has been initialized
                  and may be partially or completely filled (if not empty).
 post-conditions: The top item has been popped off Stack and stored
                  in Item.}
  begin {Pop}
    if not EmptyStack(Stack)
      then
        with Stack do
          begin
            Item := StackArray[TopOfStack];
            TopOfStack := (TopOfStack - 1)
          end
  end; {Pop}

{-----------------------------------------------------}

procedure ShowMenu;
{Writes the menu to the screen.}
  begin {ShowMenu}
    clrscr;
    write('*********************************');
    write(' TOWERS OF HANOI ');
    writeln('*********************************');
    writeln;
    writeln('1 : Watch The Computer Solve The Puzzle':60);
    writeln;
    writeln('2 : Solve The Puzzle Yourself':50);
    writeln;
    writeln('3 : Quit':29);
    writeln;
    writeln
  end; {ShowMenu}

procedure ShowMenuAndGetChoice(var Choice : integer);
{pre-condition: Choice is undefined.
 post-condition: Choice has been filled by the user's Choice.}
  begin {ShowMenuAndGetChoice}
    repeat
      ShowMenu;
```

```
      write('Which of the above choices would you like to do? ');
      readln(Choice)
    until (Choice in [1..3])
  end; {ShowMenuAndGetChoice}

{-------------------------------------------------------}

function NumberInStack( Stack : TypeStack) : integer;
{Recursively counts the number of items in Stack.}

  var
    Item : TypeItem;

  begin {NumberInStack}
    if not EmptyStack(Stack)
      then
        begin
          Pop(Stack, Item);
          NumberInStack := (NumberInStack(Stack) + 1)
        end
      else
        NumberInStack := 0
  end; {NumberInStack}

procedure InitializePeg(var Peg : TypePeg;
                           Number : integer);
{pre-conditions: Peg is undefined.
 post-condition: Peg is initialized and holds no disks.}

  begin {InitializePeg}
    with Peg do
      begin
        PegNumber := Number;
        InitializeStack(Stack)
      end
  end; {InitializePeg}

procedure InitializePegs (var StartPeg, AuxillaryPeg,
                              EndPeg : TypePeg);
{pre-conditions: All the pegs are undefined.
 post-conditions: All the pegs have been initialized.}

  begin {InitializePegs}
    InitializePeg(StartPeg, 1);
    InitializePeg(AuxillaryPeg, 2);
    InitializePeg(EndPeg, 3)
  end; {InitializePegs}

procedure GetNumberOfDisks(var NumberOfDisks : integer);
{pre-conditions: NumberOfDisks is undefined.
 post-conditions: NumberOfDisks has been filled by the number of disks
                  the player wants used.}

  begin {GetNumberOfDisks}
    repeat
      clrscr;
      writeln;
      writeln(' 1 to 10 disks may be used. ');
```

```
      write('How many disks would you like to use ? ');
      readln(NumberOfDisks)
    until (NumberOfDisks in [1..10])
  end; {GetNumberOfDisks}

procedure FillStartPeg(var StartPeg : TypePeg;
                           DiskNumber : integer);
{pre-conditions: The StartPeg has been initialized and the DiskNumber
                 contains the number of the disk being pushed.
 post-conditions: The StartPeg has one more disk placed on it.}
  begin {FillStartPeg}
    if (DiskNumber > 0)
      then
        begin
          Push(StartPeg.Stack, DiskNumber);
          FillStartPeg(StartPeg, DiskNumber - 1)
        end
  end; {FillStartPeg}

procedure WriteRepeatedChars(     CharacterToWrite : char;
                                  NumberToWrite : integer);
  var
    Counter : integer;

  begin {WriteRepeatedChars}
    for Counter := 1 to NumberToWrite do
      write(CharacterToWrite)
  end; {WriteRepeatedChars}

procedure WriteBase( Column : integer);

  begin {WriteBase}
    gotoXY(Column - 10, BaseLevel);
    WriteRepeatedChars('', 21)
  end; {WriteBase}

procedure LabelPeg(    PegNumber, Column : integer);

  begin {LabelPeg}
    gotoxy(Column - 2, BaseLevel + 2);
    writeln('Peg ', PegNumber)
  end; {LabelPeg}

procedure WriteStick(    Column : integer);

  var
    Counter : integer;

  begin {WriteStick}
    for Counter := 1 to (BaseLevel - 1) do
      begin
        gotoxy(Column, Counter);
        write('')
      end
  end; {WriteStick}

procedure WriteDisks(    Peg : TypePeg;
                         Column : integer);
```

```
  var
    Row, DiskNumber : integer;
    Item : TypeItem;

  begin {WriteDisks}
    with Peg do
      begin
        Row := (BaseLevel - 1);
        for DiskNumber := NumberInStack(Stack) downto 1 do
        begin
          textcolor(lightcyan);
          gotoxy(Column - DiskNumber, Row);
          WriteRepeatedChars('?', 1 + (DiskNumber * 2));
          Row := Row - 1;
          textcolor(lightgray)
        end
      end
  end; {WriteDisks}

procedure WritePeg( Peg : TypePeg);

  var
    Column, Row, Bottom : integer;

  begin {WritePeg}
    with Peg do
      begin
        Column := (11 + ((PegNumber - 1) * 26));
        WriteBase(Column);
        LabelPeg(PegNumber, Column);
        WriteStick(Column);
        WriteDisks(Peg, Column)
      end
  end; {WritePeg}

procedure WritePegs( StartPeg, AuxillaryPeg, EndPeg : TypePeg);

  begin {WritePegs}
    WritePeg(StartPeg);
    WritePeg(AuxillaryPeg);
    WritePeg(EndPeg)
  end; {WritePegs}

procedure SetUp (var StartPeg, AuxillaryPeg, EndPeg : TypePeg);

  var
    NumberOfDisks : integer;

  begin {SetUp}
    InitializePegs(StartPeg, AuxillaryPeg, EndPeg);
    GetNumberOfDisks(NumberOfDisks);
    FillStartPeg(StartPeg, NumberOfDisks);
    clrscr;
    WritePegs(StartPeg, AuxillaryPeg, EndPeg)
  end; {SetUp}

procedure SayMoveFrom(    FromDisk, ToDisk : integer);
```

```
  begin {SayMoveFrom}
    gotoxy(1, 20);
    write('                                      ');
    gotoxy(1, 20);
    write('Move disk from ', FromDisk, ' to ', ToDisk)
  end; {SayMoveFrom}

procedure SetCoordinates(var Peg : TypePeg;
                         var X, Y : integer);
  begin {SetCoordinates}
    case Peg.PegNumber of
      1 : X := 11;
      2 : X := 27;
      3 : X := 33
    end;
    Y := (MaxItems - NumberInStack(Peg.Stack))
  end; {SetCoordinates}

procedure EraseDisk(    Peg : TypePeg);

  var
    Row, Column : integer;

  begin {EraseDisk}
    Row := (BaseLevel - NumberInStack(Peg.Stack) - 1);
    Column := (1 + ((Peg.PegNumber - 1) * 26));
    gotoxy(Column, Row);
    WriteRepeatedChars(' ', 10);
    write('');
    WriteRepeatedChars(' ', 10)
  end; {EraseDisk}

procedure ReWriteDisk(    Peg : TypePeg;
                          Item : TypeItem);
  var
    Row, Column : integer;

  begin {ReWriteDisk}
    textcolor(lightcyan);
    Row := (BaseLevel - NumberInStack(Peg.Stack));
    Column := (11 + ((Peg.PegNumber - 1) * 26));
    gotoxy(Column - Item, Row);
    WriteRepeatedChars('?', 1 + (Item * 2));
    textcolor(lightgray)
  end; {ReWriteDisk}

procedure MoveDisks(var StartPeg, AuxiliaryPeg,
                        EndPeg : TypePeg;
                        Disks : integer);
  var
    Item : TypeItem;

  begin {MoveDisks}
    if (Disks > 0)
      then
        begin
          MoveDisks(StartPeg, EndPeg, AuxiliaryPeg, Disks - 1);
          SayMoveFrom(StartPeg.PegNumber, EndPeg.PegNumber);
```

```
        Pop(StartPeg.Stack, Item);
        Push(EndPeg.Stack, Item);
        delay(500);
        EraseDisk(StartPeg);
        ReWriteDisk(EndPeg, Item);
        MoveDisks(AuxiliaryPeg, StartPeg, EndPeg, (Disks - 1))
      end
  end; {MoveDisks}

procedure WatchPuzzle(    StartPeg, AuxillaryPeg,
                          EndPeg : TypePeg);
  var
    Disks : integer;

  begin {WatchPuzzle}
    Disks := NumberInStack(StartPeg.Stack);
    MoveDisks(StartPeg, AuxillaryPeg, EndPeg, Disks);
    gotoxy(1, 21);
    write('Solved! Please press Enter.');
    readln
  end; {WatchPuzzle}

procedure GetMove(var SourcePeg, TargetPeg : integer;
                  var Quit : boolean);

  procedure GetSourcePeg(var SourcePeg : integer;
                         var Quit : boolean);
    var
      Choice : char;

    begin {GetSourcePeg}
      Quit := false;
      repeat
        gotoxy(1, 20);
        WriteRepeatedChars(' ', 70);
        gotoxy(1, 20);
        write('Would you like to move from peg 1, 2, or 3 ');
        write('(Q=quit)? ');
        readln(Choice);
        case Choice of
          '1', '2', '3' : SourcePeg := (ord(Choice) - ord('1') + 1);
          'Q', 'q' : Quit := true
        end
      until (Choice in ['1', '2', '3', 'Q', 'q'])
    end; {GetSourcePeg}

  procedure GetTargetPeg(var TargetPeg : integer;
                         var Quit : boolean);
    var
      Choice : char;

    begin {GetTargetPeg}
        repeat
          gotoxy(1, 20);
          WriteRepeatedChars(' ', 70);
          gotoxy(1, 20);
          write('To which peg would you like to move the disk? ');
          readln(Choice);
```

```
          case Choice of
            '1', '2', '3' : TargetPeg := (ord(Choice) - ord('1') + 1);
            'Q', 'q' : Quit := true
          end
        until (Choice in ['1', '2', '3', 'Q', 'q'])
      end; {GetTargetPeg}

    begin {GetMove}
      GetSourcePeg(SourcePeg, Quit);
      if not Quit
        then
          GetTargetPeg(TargetPeg, Quit)
    end; {GetMove}

  procedure RemoveDisk(var StartPeg, AuxillaryPeg,
                           EndPeg : TypePeg;
                           SourcePeg : integer;
                       var Item : TypeItem);
    begin {RemoveDisk}
      case SourcePeg of
        1 : begin
              Pop(StartPeg.Stack, Item);
              EraseDisk(StartPeg)
            end;
        2 : begin
              Pop(AuxillaryPeg.Stack, Item);
              EraseDisk(AuxillaryPeg)
            end;
        3 : begin
              Pop(EndPeg.Stack, Item);
              EraseDisk(EndPeg)
            end
      end
    end; {RemoveDisk}

  procedure AddDisk(var StartPeg, AuxillaryPeg,
                        EndPeg : TypePeg;
                        TargetPeg : integer;
                        Item : TypeItem);
    begin {AddDisk}
      case TargetPeg of
        1 : begin
              Push(StartPeg.Stack, Item);
              ReWriteDisk(StartPeg, Item)
            end;
        2 : begin
              Push(AuxillaryPeg.Stack, Item);
              ReWriteDisk(AuxillaryPeg, Item)
            end;
        3 : begin
              Push(EndPeg.Stack, Item);
              ReWriteDisk(EndPeg, Item)
            end
      end
    end; {AddDisk}
```

```
function MoveOk(     StartPeg, AuxillaryPeg, EndPeg : TypePeg;
                     SourcePeg, TargetPeg : integer) : boolean;
  var
    SourceItem, TargetItem : TypeItem;

  function PegIsEmpty( PegNumber : integer) : boolean;

    begin {PegIsEmpty}
      case PegNumber of
        1 : PegIsEmpty := EmptyStack(StartPeg.Stack);
        2 : PegIsEmpty := EmptyStack(AuxillaryPeg.Stack);
        3 : PegIsEmpty := EmptyStack(EndPeg.Stack)
      end
    end; {PegIsEmpty}

  begin {MoveOk}
    if (SourcePeg = TargetPeg)
      then
        MoveOk := false
      else
        if PegIsEmpty(SourcePeg)
          then
            MoveOk := false
          else
            if PegIsEmpty(TargetPeg)
              then
                MoveOk := true
              else
                begin
                  RemoveDisk(StartPeg, AuxillaryPeg, EndPeg, SourcePeg,
                             SourceItem);
                  RemoveDisk(StartPeg, AuxillaryPeg, EndPeg, TargetPeg,
                             TargetItem);
                  MoveOk := (SourceItem < TargetItem);
                  AddDisk(StartPeg, AuxillaryPeg, EndPeg, SourcePeg,
                          SourceItem);
                  AddDisk(StartPeg, AuxillaryPeg, EndPeg, TargetPeg,
                          TargetItem)
                end
  end; {MoveOk}

procedure SolvePuzzle(     StartPeg, AuxillaryPeg,
                           EndPeg : TypePeg);

  var
    SourcePeg, TargetPeg : integer;
    Done : boolean;
    Item : TypeItem;

  begin {SolvePuzzle}
    GetMove(SourcePeg, TargetPeg, Done);
    while not Done do
      begin
        if MoveOk(StartPeg, AuxillaryPeg, EndPeg, SourcePeg, TargetPeg)
          then
            begin
              RemoveDisk(StartPeg, AuxillaryPeg, EndPeg, SourcePeg, Item);
              AddDisk(StartPeg, AuxillaryPeg, EndPeg, TargetPeg, Item);
```

```
            Done := EmptyStack(StartPeg.Stack) and
                    EmptyStack(AuxillaryPeg.Stack);

            if Done
              then
                begin
                  gotoxy(1, 21);
                  write('Congratulations! You solved it!');
                  readln
                end
          end
        else
          begin
            gotoXY(1, 21);
            write('Invalid move!');
            delay(1000);
            gotoxy(1, 21);
            write('              ')
          end;
        if not Done
          then
            GetMove(SourcePeg, TargetPeg, Done)
      end
  end; {SolvePuzzle}

procedure DoOption(     StartPeg, AuxillaryPeg,
                        EndPeg : TypePeg;
                        Choice : integer);

  begin {DoOption}
    case Choice of
      1 : WatchPuzzle(StartPeg, AuxillaryPeg, EndPeg);
      2 : SolvePuzzle(StartPeg, AuxillaryPeg, EndPeg)
    end
  end; {DoOption}

procedure PlayGame( Choice : integer);

  var
    StartPeg, AuxillaryPeg, EndPeg : TypePeg;

  begin {PlayGame}
    if (Choice < 3)
      then
        begin
          SetUp(StartPeg, AuxillaryPeg, EndPeg);
          DoOption(StartPeg, AuxillaryPeg, EndPeg, Choice)
        end
  end; {PlayGame}

{-----------------------------------------------------}

begin {TowersOfHanoi}
  repeat
    ShowMenuAndGetChoice(Choice);
    PlayGame(Choice)
  until (Choice = Quit)
end. {TowersOfHanoi}
```

12 Printer Programming

Until now, we have used the printer in a rather simple fashion for listing programs and for printing output. In this chapter, we discuss some of the fine points of printer usage, including:

- Printer command sequences.
- An introduction to printer graphics.
- A graphics screen dump that will print the contents of the screen in either of the two graphics modes.

Each printer is different. Printer capabilities and the techniques for accessing them vary widely among manufacturers and even among models by a single manufacturer. As an example, we have chosen to restrict this chapter to a discussion of one of the most common printer types, namely Epson-compatible 9-pin dot-matrix printers. Among the printers in this class are the Epson MX, FX, and LX series printers. Even if your dot matrix printer is not one of these, it is likely that it has a printing mode which is compatible. Check your printer manual. Even if your printer is not Epson-compatible, the fundamentals of printer programming are the same on all printers. As a result, this chapter can be taken as a model to use with the command set specified in your printer reference manual. Moreover, by using object-oriented programming, you can create printer objects and use inheritance to modify the object we create in order to have it access all the special features of your printer.

Printing Fundamentals

Printing by Dots

The Epson 9-pin dot-matrix printers accomplish printing by means of a printhead with nine wires arranged vertically. A character is sent to the printer as an ASCII code, which is an integer from 0 to 255. Some ASCII codes represent printable characters and some represent commands. In response to a printable ASCII character, the electronics of the printer cause the wires of the printhead to "fire" in particular combinations that have been preprogrammed. For a given character the print wires fire 12 times. After each firing, the printhead is advanced by 1/12 of a character (1/120 inch). The result is a set of dot patterns arranged within a rectangular grid nine dots high and 12 dots wide. For example, in Figure 12.1 we show the dot pattern corresponding to the letter A.

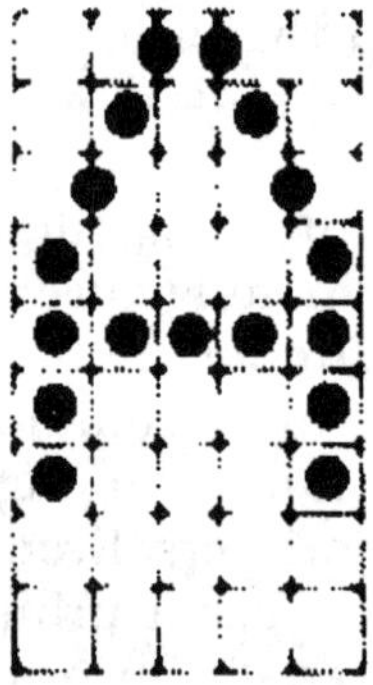

Figure 12.1. The letter A.

The above sequence of printhead firings happens extraordinarily fast; too fast, in fact, for the eye to observe. Because the printhead prints a set of dots within a rectangular matrix, this type of printer is called a dot-matrix printer.

Printer Communications

When you send data to the printer, here is what happens:

1. The data, in the form of a sequence of one-byte ASCII codes, are deposited in a section of the PC's memory called the *printer buffer.* This is a holding area for data awaiting transmission to the printer.

2. At intervals, the printer requests data. (Don't worry about how it does this.)
3. In response, the computer sends a number of bytes from the printer buffer, taking care to note which bytes were sent.
4. When the printer receives the bytes, it deposits them in its own buffer, to await printing.
5. Whenever the print mechanism needs a character to print, the printer looks to the buffer for a byte.
6. If the buffer is not empty, the printer takes the next byte in line.
7. The byte is decoded. It may correspond to a command or to a printable character.
8. The printer takes action on the byte. Either the command is executed or the character is printed.
9. Steps 5–8 are repeated until the printer's buffer becomes almost empty.
10. The printer then tells the computer to transmit more data and the process begins again with step 3.

The above procedure happens so quickly that you are unlikely to be aware of it. However, it is helpful to understand what is happening "under the hood" if you are to understand the operation (or nonoperation) of the printer commands.

Some Elementary Printer Commands

In using the printer from within Turbo Pascal, you should declare the `Printer` unit with a declaration of the form:

```
Uses Printer;
```

The `Printer` unit declares the printer to be the device `Lst`. As far as Pascal is concerned, `Lst` is a text file. Thus, you may use the procedures write and writeln to output data to it.

The most rudimentary printer command is the carriage return and line feed sequence. A carriage return is a command to return the print head to the leftmost end of the print line. A line feed advances the paper by one line. The carriage return–line feed sequence is used at the ends of most lines to reposition the print head for the beginning of the next line. In fact, the writeln statement automatically inserts the carriage return–line feed sequence after the text you specify.

A carriage return is indicated by ASCII code 13. A line feed is indicated by ASCII code 10. Therefore, a carriage return–line feed sequence should be generated by the string

```
chr(13)+chr(10)
```

You may generate either the carriage return or line feed separately by sending only one of these characters. For instance, to advance the paper one line without a carriage return, use the statement

```
write(Lst, chr(10));
```

You may use the carriage return without the line feed to produce some interesting print effects. For example, you may backspace and then overprint some characters. The backspace character is chr(8). Here is a program that prints the string Pascal, then backspaces to the beginning of the string and overprints each letter with a /.

```
write(Lst, 'Pascal');
for J :=1 to 6 do
  write(Lst, chr(8));
for J := 1 to 6 do
  write(Lst, '/').
```

Just as the line feed command allows you to advance the paper by one line, the form feed command allows you to advance the paper to the beginning of the next page. Form feed is indicated by ASCII code 12.

Printing Mailing Labels

You may use your printer to print mailing address labels; here's how. You can buy peel-off labels on continuous form backing. These labels are available in several layouts, including one and three labels across. Let's assume that we are dealing with labels three inches wide and 15/16 inches high, with a 1/16-inch vertical space between labels. At six lines to the inch vertical spacing, each label has room for five lines. The sixth line space is to the beginning of the next label. The layout of two consecutive labels is shown in Figure 12.2. (Of course, one or more of the lines can be blank.)

```
Line 1
Line 2
Line 3
Line 4
Line 5

Line 1
Line 2
Line 3
Line 4
Line 5
```

Figure 12.2.
Two consecutive labels.

I usually use labels three inches wide. Since the print on the printer is ten characters to the inch, this allows up to 30 characters per line. When I use labels that are packaged two across, the first label begins in print column 1, and the second begins in print column 50. (These numbers depend on the particular label.)

Below are two programs that do various label printing tasks. The first program allows printing multiple copies of a single label, using forms containing only one label across. The second program performs the same task for forms containing two labels across. I use these programs for generating address labels for people I communicate with often. I also use such labels when I travel. I address the labels to my home address and regularly mail papers home, rather than carry them with me for the duration of the trip.

Here are the programs:

Listing 12.1. Copies of a single label, one across

```
program Labels1;

  uses
    printer;

  var
    Label : array[1..6] of string;
    NumCopies, J, K : integer;

  begin
    writeln('Input number of copies.')
    readln(NumCopies);
    for J := 1 to 6 do
      begin
        writeln('Input label line', J);
        readln(Label[J]);
      end;
```

```
    for K := 1 to NumCopies do
      for J := 1 to 6 do
        writeln(Lst, Label[J])
  end.
```

Listing 12.2. Copies of a single label, two across

```
program Labels2;

  uses
    printer;

  var
    Label : array[1..6] of string;
    NumCopies, J, K : integer;

  begin
    writeln('Input number of copies.')
    readln(NumCopies);
    for J := 1 to 6 do
      begin
        writeln('Input label line', J);
        readln(Label[J]);
      end;
    for K := 1 to (NumCopies Div 2) do
      begin
        for J := 1 to 6 do
          write(Lst, Label[J]);
        write(chr(13)); {Carriage return, no line feed}
        for J := 1 to 49 do
          write(' '); {Move to column 50}
        for J := 1 to 6 do
          writeln(Lst, Label[J])
      end
  end.
```

Printer Command Sequences

Your printer is capable of a great many options with regard to type style, print spacing, page length, and so forth. This section presents an organized look at the various command sequences available to you.

Certain printer commands are given by means of a single ASCII code. For example, a carriage return is given with ASCII code 13. However, certain printer commands are given as a sequence of ASCII codes. For such commands, the sequence of codes begins with ASCII code 27 (Escape). This

ASCII code tells the printer that the following ASCII codes are to be interpreted as part of a command rather than as printable characters. For example, consider the sequence of ASCII codes: 27, 78, 3. It instructs the printer to skip three lines at the end of the page. This allows you to skip over the perforation between consecutive sheets of paper. You may communicate this sequence of ASCII codes to the printer as you would any other ASCII codes, using the statement

```
write(Lst, chr(27)+chr(78)+chr(3));
```

Line Spacing

The following commands are available for adjusting the vertical line spacing:

Action	Command Sequence
Set line spacing to 1/6 inch	27, 50
Set line spacing to 1/8 inch	27, 48
Set line spacing to 7/72 inch	27, 49
Set line spacing to n/72 inch	27, 65, n, 27, 50[1] 27, 65, n[2]
Set line spacing to n/216 inch[1]	27, 51, n
Executes one line feed of n/216 inch[1]	27, 74, n
Default setting: line spacing = 1/6 inch	

Figure 12.3 shows some samples of various vertical line spacings.

[1] IBM printers only.
[2] Non-IBM printers only.

```
Line Spacing8 /72 inches
Line Spacing10/72 inches
Line Spacing12/72 inches
Line Spacing14/72 inches
Line Spacing16/72 inches
Line Spacing18/72 inches
Line Spacing20/72 inches
Line Spacing22/72 inches
Line Spacing24/72 inches
```

Figure 12.3.
Examples of vertical line spacing.

Page Length and Layout

This group of commands allows you to set the length of the page and the amount of space to skip in order to avoid the perforations in continuous forms.

Set page length to n lines	27, 67, n
Set page length to n inches[3]	27, 67, 79, n
Leave n lines blank at bottom of page (skip perforation)[3]	27, 78, n
Cancel skip perforation[3]	27, 79

Notes:

1. You must set the page length before giving the Skip Perforation command.
2. The Skip Perforation command causes the number of printed lines to be decreased by the specified skip. For example, a skip of 10 lines and standard page length will cause pages to consist of 56 lines followed by 10 blank lines.
3. You may wish to adjust the paper so that any skip is evenly distributed between the bottom of a page and the top of the following one.

[3] Default setting: Page length = 66 lines = 11 inches

4. The beginning of the page is set when the printer is turned on. Any form feed commands make reference to the latest vertical line spacing and the latest page length information in spacing to the top of the next page.

Print Style

The Epson printers are capable of a number of print styles, including emphasized, double strike, double width, compressed, underlined, and subscript/superscript. We may group these attributes as follows:

Group A: Normal

Compressed

Emphasized

Group B: Double Strike

Subscript

Superscript

Group C: Double Width

Group D: Underline

You may combine attributes by selecting at most one attribute from each group. For example, you may select print that is simultaneously compressed, subscript, and double width. However, you may not select print simultaneously compressed and emphasized.

Figure 12.4 shows some samples of the various print styles possible with your printer.

```
This is the standard type font.
This line is emphasized.
This line is double-struck.
This line is double width.
This line is condensed.
This line is italics.
```

Figure 12.4. Various print styles.

Here are the print commands that govern the various print styles:

Emphasized print ON	27, 69
Emphasized print OFF	27, 70

Double strike ON	27, 71
Double strike OFF	27, 72
Subscript ON	27, 83, 1
Superscript ON	27, 83, 0
Subscript/Superscript OFF	27, 84
Compressed ON	15
Compressed OFF	18
Double-width ON (current line only)	14
Double-width OFF	20
Underline ON[4]	27, 45, 1
Underline OFF	27, 45, 0

Notes:

1. The double-width style prints five characters to the inch, but is the same height as standard print.
2. The compressed print style prints 132 characters per eight-inch line.

Tabs

Set horizontal tabs at columns n1,n2,...,nk	27, 68, n1, n2,...,nk,0
Horizontal tab	9
Cancel horizontal tabs	27, 68, 0
Set vertical tabs at columns n1,n2,...,nk	27, 66, n1, n2, ...,nk, 0
Vertical tab	11
Cancel vertical tabs	27, 66, 0

[4] Not available with the IBM dot-matrix printer or Epson MX/80.

Printer Graphics

In this section we will discuss the dot graphics capabilities of the Epson printers. As we have mentioned, the printhead has nine wires arranged vertically. In the graphics mode, only the top eight of these wires are used. Figure 12.5 shows the eight wires used in the graphics modes and numbers them, from bottom to top, with the numbers 0 through 7.

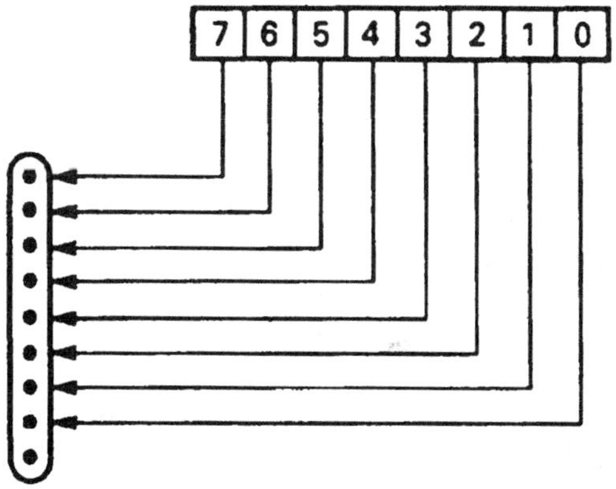

Figure 12.5.
The printhead wires.

Each print wire corresponds to a single printed dot. You may request the printhead to print any combination of dots corresponding to the eight wires used in graphics mode. Figure 12.6 shows a number of typical dot patterns.

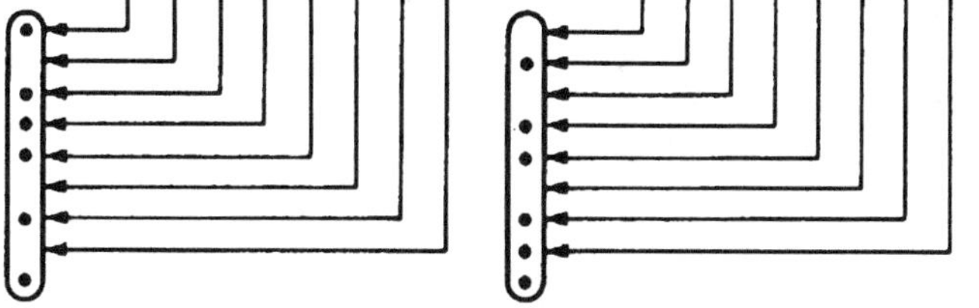

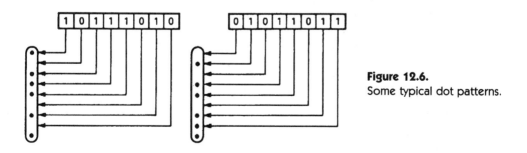

Figure 12.6.
Some typical dot patterns.

A dot pattern is specified as a single byte, with wire 0 corresponding to bit 0, wire 1 corresponding to bit 1, and so forth. The most significant bit corresponds to the top print wire. Figure 12.6 indicates the bytes corresponding to each of the given bit patterns.

Horizontal Dot Placement

There are three graphics modes, with the following horizontal dot densities:

Medium Resolution: 480 dots per eight-inch line

High Resolution: 960 dots per eight-inch line

Ultra High Resolution [5]: 1920 dots per eight-inch line

In medium resolution, adjacent dots have a noticeable horizontal space between them. In high resolution, this space is eliminated. In ultra high resolution, adjacent dots actually overlap. For each density, you may, in principle, print any eight-dot vertical pattern in each of the horizontal dot positions on a line (see below for an exception). For example, in medium-resolution mode, you may print 480 vertical eight-bit patterns per eight-inch line.

Actually, it is possible to mix graphics patterns with text. For example, you might print a line consisting of 50 standard printed characters (at ten characters to the inch = five inches), followed by 120 graphics patterns (at 60 per inch = two inches), followed by 10 standard printed characters.

As with most things in life, increasing the resolution comes at a price. If you wish to use high resolution without any restrictions in dot placement, you can print only at half the speed of medium resolution. A similar statement goes for ultra high resolution. If you wish to retain the speed, you must live with some restrictions in dot placement. In order for high resolution to run at full printer speed, you cannot print two dots that are horizontally adjacent to one another. In ultra high resolution, you can print dots only in every third horizontal dot position.

In order to initiate a printer graphics mode, it is necessary to give an escape sequence that tells the computer:

1. The graphics mode.
2. The speed.
3. The number of vertical eight-bit graphics patterns forthcoming.

These three data items are expressed by a four-byte code:

[5] IBM Graphics Printer.

```
27 42 m n1 n2
```

where m is a byte denoting the graphics mode/speed and n1 and n2 are bytes that, together, indicate the number of vertical eight-bit graphics patterns to come. Here are the meanings of m, n1, and n2:

m = 0 :	480 dots per eight-inch line
m = 1 :	960 dots per eight-inch line, half speed
m = 2 :	960 dots per eight-inch line, full speed, no adjacent dots
m = 3 :	1,920 dots per eight-inch line, full speed; can print only every third dot
n1 =	the remainder obtained when the number of graphics patterns is divided by 256
n2 =	the number of graphics patterns divided by 256 (integer part)

Thus, n1 and n2 satisfy this relationship:

```
<number of graphics patterns> = 256*n2 + n1
```

For example, suppose that you wish to print 400 graphics patterns in medium-resolution mode. Divide 400 by 256. The quotient is 1 and the remainder is 144. That is,

```
400 = 256*1 + 144
```

Therefore, n2 = 1 and n1 = 144. The command that specifies 400 graphics patterns in medium-resolution mode is then given by the sequence of bytes

```
27, 75, 144, 1
```

As a second example, suppose that we wish to print the letter A, given as the sequence of nine graphics patterns, as specified in the hexadecimal bytes

```
$1E    $20    $48    $80    $08    $80    $48    $20    $1E
```

Further, suppose that we wish to use low speed, high-resolution mode. Since 9 = 0*256 + 9, we have n1 = 9 and n2 = 0. We initiate the desired printing pattern with the sequence of bytes

```
27, 76, 9, 0
```

We follow these bytes with the bytes representing the nine graphics patterns. Here is a program that prints the desired nine graphics patterns:

Listing 12.3. Pattern

```
program Pattern;

  uses
    printer;

  begin
    write(Lst, chr(27)+chr(76)+chr(9)+chr(0));
    write(Lst, chr($1E)+chr($20)+chr($48)+chr($80));
    write(Lst, chr($8)+chr($80)+chr($48)+chr($20));
    write(Lst, chr($1E))
  end.
```

Note that we specified the graphics patterns in hexadecimal rather than decimal. This is done because it is easier to go from the actual dot pattern to hexadecimal. Translating the hexadecimal into decimal would provide room for errors. Finally, note that we sent each hexadecimal byte to the printer via a `chr` statement.

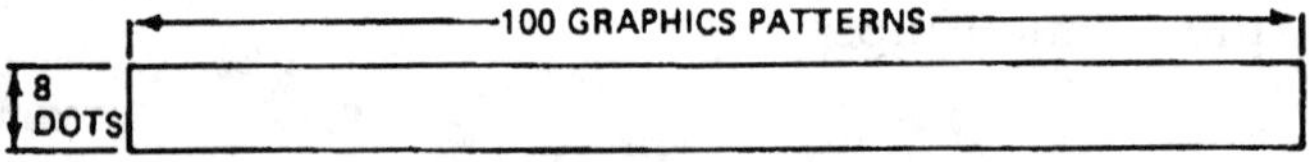

Figure 12.7.
High-resolution box.

As a further example, let's draw a box as shown in Figure 12.7. The box is 100 graphics patterns wide in high resolution. The bottom of the box is drawn by print wire 0 and the top by print wire 7. We may draw this box out of two graphics patterns, one consisting of all eight dots (for both ends) and a second consisting of only the top and bottom dot. The hexadecimal equivalents for these dots are, respectively, $FF and $81. (You should check this!) Here is a program that draws the box.

Listing 12.4. Box

```
program Box;

  uses
    printer;

  var
    Init, Side, Middle : string;
    J : integer;

  begin
    Init := chr(27) + chr(76) + chr(100) + chr(0);
    Side := chr($FF);
    Middle := chr($81);
    write(Lst, Init);
```

```
    write(Lst, Side);
    for J := 1 to 98 do
    write(Lst, Middle);
    writeln(Lst, Side)
  end.
```

Note that you may mix ordinary text and graphics. For example, let's print the phrase `WRITE YOUR ANSWER IN THE BOX.` immediately to the left of the box, and the phrase `STOP` immediately to the right. Our printed line should look like the one shown in Figure 12.8.

WRITE YOUR ANSWER IN THE BOX
STOP

Figure 12.8.
A printed line requesting user to write an answer in the box.

Here is a program to print this line:

Listing 12.5. Line

```
program Box;

  uses
    printer,
    crt;

  var
    Init, Side, Middle : string;
    J : integer;

  begin
    Init := chr(27)+chr(76)+chr(100)+chr(0);
    Side := chr($FF);
    Middle := chr($81);
    ClrScr;
    write(Lst, 'WRITE YOUR ANSWER IN THE BOX.');
    write(Lst, Init);
    write(Lst, Side);
    for J := 1 to 98 do
    write(Lst, Middle);
    write(Lst, Side);
    writeln(Lst, ' STOP')
  end.
```

This program prints the desired line and does a carriage return to the next line.

Note that the first `write` prints in ordinary text, the next 4 `writes` in high-resolution graphics mode. The final `writeln` returns to ordinary text. It is not necessary to give any special command to return to text mode. After the specified number of graphics patterns, the printer automatically reverts to ordinary text. Any special print modes (emphasized, subscript, compressed, etc.) in effect before entry into graphics mode remain in effect on return to text mode.

If you print two consecutive lines of graphics with default line spacing (1/8 inch), you will notice that there is a small blank area between them. You may eliminate this space, making a continuous graphics pattern. The secret is to use 8/72-inch spacing. (This corresponds to nine lines to the inch as opposed to the default eight lines per inch.) You may set this spacing using the command

```
write(Lst, chr(27)+chr(65)+chr(8));
```

You may print as many consecutive graphics lines as you wish. However, if you then wish to return to printing text, remember to reset the vertical line spacing.

13 Bit and Byte Manipulation

In this chapter, we will explore various topics related to manipulation of bits and bytes in Turbo Pascal. Our discussions include:

- The properties of the binary and hexadecimal number systems. Since binary and hexadecimal arithmetic has arisen throughout the book, we'll begin with a discussion of these important number systems.
- Bits, bytes, and memory addressing.
- Logical operations on bytes.
- Use of bits and bytes to describe line and paint styles.

Binary and Hexadecimal Numbers

Decimal Representation of Numbers

In grade school, we learned to perform arithmetic using the decimal number system. In this system, numbers are written as strings of digits chosen from among the ten numbers 0, 1, 2, 3, 4, 5, 6, 7, 8, 9. Here are some examples of these familiar numbers:

```
14312, -928372, 29831029831902938290
```

Such strings of digits are interpreted according to a system of place value. We proceed from right to left: The digit in the extreme right position represents the number of 1s, the next digit the number of 10s, the next digit the number of 100s, the next digit the number of 1,000s, and so forth. For example, the number 1935 stands for

```
1    1000s   1*1,000=   1,000
9     100s     9*100=     900
3      10s      3*10=      30
5       1s       5*1=       5
                         ____
                         1935
```

The values of the various digit positions, that is, the numbers 1, 10, 100, 1,000, ... are all powers of 10:

$1=10^0, \ 10=10^1, \ 100=10^2, \ 1000=10^3, \ ...$

Another way of expressing the number 1935 is

```
1*10^3 + 9*10^2 + 3*10^1 + 5*10^0
```

Note that we have arranged the digits in their usual order, which corresponds to decreasing powers of 10.

Binary Representation of Numbers

In the binary number system, numbers are represented by strings formed from the two digits 0 and 1. Here are some examples of binary numbers:

```
10, 01110000111, 100100100100
```

Just as the decimal number system is based on powers of 10, the binary number system is based on powers of 2, for example, the numbers

```
2^0=1, 2^1=2, 2^2=4, 2^3=8, 2^4=16,...
```

We interpret a binary number by examining the digits from right to left. The rightmost digit of a binary number corresponds to the number of 1s, the next digit to the number of 2s, the next digit to the number of 4s, and so forth. For example, the binary number 1101 represents

```
1    8s= 8
1    4s= 4
0    2s= 0
1    1s= 1
  1101= 13
```

Therefore, the binary number 1101 corresponds to the decimal number 13.

Converting from Decimal to Binary

As we have seen, every binary number has a decimal equivalent; however, the reverse is also true: Every decimal number has a binary equivalent. For example, consider the decimal number 61. Let's divide it by 2 to obtain a quotient 30 and remainder 1. Write these results in the form

```
61 = 30*2 + 1
```

There is a 2 present now. But the quotient 30 does not yet involve a 2, so we divide the 30 by 2 to obtain the quotient 15 and remainder 0. Write this result in the form

```
30 = 15*2 + 0
```

If we insert this expression for 30 into the expression for 61, we obtain the result

```
61 = (15*2+0)*2 + 1
   = 15*2^2 + 0*2 + 1
```

This is now closer to a representation of 61 by powers of 2, but the 15 does not yet involve 2, so let's now repeat the above procedure using the number 15 instead of 30. First, we divide by 2 to obtain a quotient of 7 and a remainder of 1. Next, we write the equation

```
15 = 7*2 + 1
```

and we substitute this equation into our preceding expression for 61:

```
61 = (7*2 + 1)*2^2 + 0*2 + 1
   = 7*2^3 + 1*2^2 + 0*2 + 1
```

This is a better representation of 61. To improve it, we repeat the procedure using the number 7:

```
7 = 3*2 + 1
61 = (3*2+1)*2^3 + 1*2^2 + 0*2 + 1
   = 3*2^4 + 1*2^3 + 1*2^2 + 0*2 + 1
```

Repeat the procedure using the number 3:

```
3 = 1*2 + 1
61 = (1*2+1)*2^4 + 1*2^3 + 1*2^2 + 0*2 + 1
   = 1*2^5 + 1*2^4 + 1*2^3 + 1*2^2 + 0*2 + 1
```

This last representation of 61 consists only of powers of 2. From this representation, we may read off the binary representation of 61 as the 1 or 0 coefficients of the powers of 2. Read from left to right. The representation is

```
61 (decimal) = 111101 (binary)
```

If you don't believe the computation, just proceed in reverse and convert 111101 to its corresponding decimal number. You will obtain 61 as the result.

A binary digit (0 or 1) is called a *bit*. The number 1,011 is four bits long whereas the number 10010011 is eight bits long.

There are four two-bit numbers, eight three-bit numbers, and 16 possible four-bit numbers:

```
0000, 0001, 0010, 0011, 0100, 0101, 0110, 0111
1000, 1001, 1010, 1011, 1100, 1101, 1110, 1111
```

It can be proven in a mathematics text that the number of possible N-bit numbers is equal to 2^N. This fact generalizes the particular cases (N = 2,3,4) observed above.

As we shall see, eight-bit and 16-bit binary numbers play a special role in the internal workings of the IBM PC. The number of eight-bit binary numbers is 2^8 = 256. They represent the numbers 0 through 255. Similarly, the number of 16-bit binary numbers is 2^16 = 65536. They represent the numbers 0 through 65,535.

The IBM PC and all other digital computers use the binary number system for their operation. It may appear as if the computer uses decimal numbers. However, all data must be converted into binary form if the computer is to process it. And this applies to text data and program statements as well as numerical data. Each type of information is translated into binary according to its own translation scheme (more about this later). Computer operations are performed only on binary numbers. When output is required, the computer translates from binary to either numeric or text format.

Hexadecimal Representation of Numbers

The hexadecimal number system is closely connected with the binary number system and is much easier to work with in many applications. There are 16 possible hexadecimal digits: 0, 1, 2, 3, 4, 5, 6, 7, 8, 9, A, B, C, D, E, F

The digits 0–9 have their usual numerical values and A, B, C, D, E, F have the respective values

10	11	12	13	14	15
A	B	C	D	E	F

A typical hexadecimal number is a string of hexadecimal digits, such as

```
A1EFF78A
```

The rightmost digit indicates the number of 1s, the next digit the number of 16s, the next digit the number of 256s (256 = 16^2), etc. For example, the above hexadecimal number corresponds to

```
10*16^7 + 1*16^6 + 14*16^5 + 15*16^4 + 15*16^3 + 7*16^2 + 8*16 + 10*1
```

The real advantage of hexadecimal is that it offers a shorthand way of writing numbers in binary. The 16 hexadecimal digits correspond to the following four-digit binary numbers:

Hexadecimal	Binary	Decimal
0	0000	0
1	0001	1
2	0010	2
3	0011	3
4	0100	4
5	0101	5
6	0110	6
7	0111	7
8	1000	8
9	1001	9
A	1010	10
B	1011	11
C	1100	12
D	1101	13
E	1110	14
F	1111	15

A binary number may be blocked off in groups of four digits and translated into hexadecimal according to the above table. For example, consider the 25-digit binary number

```
1 1111 0011 1001 0101 1110 0111
```

To convert it into hexadecimal, we first block it off into groups of four digits proceeding from right to left:

```
1 1111 0011 1001 0101 1110 0111
```

We complete the leftmost group by adding three zeros on the left:

```
0001 1111 0011 1001 0101 1110 0111
```

Finally, we translate each four-digit group into a hexadecimal digit:

```
0001 1111 0011 1001 0101 1110 0111
  1    F    3    9    5    E    7
```

Therefore, the hexadecimal equivalent of the binary number is 1F395E7. It is clearly simpler to work with the hexadecimal form rather than the binary form of the number.

Hexadecimal Numbers in Turbo Pascal

Hexadecimal numbers may be used in Turbo Pascal. To specify a number in hexadecimal, use $ as a prefix. For example, the hexadecimal number 1A2F is denoted $1A2F.

Bits, Bytes, and Memory

Our first application of the binary and hexadecimal number systems will be to describe the contents and the addressing scheme used in PC memory. At the same time, we will explore the contents of RAM and describe the various data present in RAM while you are using Pascal.

RAM is broken into a series of eight-bit binary numbers called bytes. The size of your RAM is measured in units of 1,024 bytes. One 1024-byte unit is called 1K (for Kilobyte), so a system with 32K of RAM contains 32 × 1024 or 32,768 bytes. A system with 64K contains 64 × 1024 or 65536 bytes. Your 8088-based IBM PC can address memory up to 1024K, while a 286- or 386-based PC can be expanded to contain as much as 16,372K (16 meg).

You should think of RAM as divided into a large number of cubbyholes with each cubbyhole containing a single byte. The cubbyholes of RAM are called *memory locations.* The contents of each memory location may be described by two hexadecimal digits (8 bits). For example, here are the contents of four memory locations:

```
7E 0F FF 81
```

The memory locations of a computer are numbered, usually beginning with 0. The number associated with each memory location is called its address. For example, in a simple computer system (not the PC) with 4K of RAM, the memory locations have addresses from 0 to 4,095 (decimal). At any particular moment, the contents of addresses 3,001–3,004 might be as follows:

```
Address    3001   3002   3003   3004
Contents   1A     B0     E8     F1
```

The computer makes use of addresses in its internal calculations and for this reason addresses are usually expressed in hexadecimal. Be careful not to confuse an address (a memory location number) with its contents (the data stored in that address).

We observed in the preceding section that 16-bit binary numbers correspond to the decimal numbers 0 through 65,535. On the other hand, 64K = 65,536. Thus, we see that the 16-bit binary numbers provide exactly enough addresses to handle a 64K memory. To address more memory than 64K requires binary numbers longer than 16 bits. Actually, the IBM PC is designed to economically handle 16-bit numbers, so that rather than use addresses consisting of, say, 24 or 32 bits, it uses pairs of 16-bit numbers. A typical address on the PC has the form (segment, offset) where segment and offset are 16-bit numbers with meanings that follow.

Bytes are numbered beginning with 0. The byte number corresponding to a particular address pair (segment, offset) is determined using the formula:

```
16*segment + offset
```

For example, consider the address pair (00FF,1F58). The segment portion, 00FF, equals 255 in decimal. The offset portion, 1F58, equals 8,024 in decimal. Therefore, this address pair corresponds to byte number 16*255+8024 = 12,104.

Suppose that we hold the segment portion of an address pair fixed and allow the offset portion to vary. The corresponding address pair runs over a set of 64K consecutive memory locations. Such a section of memory is called a 64K segment. In programming the 8088 chip (in machine language), such 64K segments play an important role.

The following notation is used to denote an address:

```
segment:offset
```

Then, in the above example, the address is:

```
00FF:1F58
```

Operations on Bytes

In many applications (we shall see a few shortly), it is necessary to perform operations directly on the bits of a byte. In this section, we will introduce you to these operations.

Shift and Truncate Operations

It is often required to move all the bits of a byte to the left or to the right. Such operations are called, respectively, a *left shift* and a *right shift.* For example, consider this byte:

```
1101 0110
```

If we apply a left shift, we obtain the byte

```
1010 1100
```

Note that the rightmost bit is a zero and the original leftmost bit has been "pushed off the end."

Similarly, a right shift applied to the original byte yields

```
0110 1011
```

Note that the leftmost bit is replaced by a zero and the original rightmost bit is "pushed off the end."

How can operations such as those just described be carried out in Turbo Pascal? Before we describe a method, let's remember that the binary number system is based on powers of two. If we multiply a decimal number by 10, we shift all the digits to the left one place. Similarly, in the binary number system, if we multiply a number by two, we shift the bits to the left one place. Moreover, if we divide a binary number by two (integer division), we then shift the digits to the right by one bit.

In the case of multiplication by two, there may be a bit shifted into bit position nine. We may rid ourselves of this bit by using `mod 256`. (The remainder of division by 256 is exactly the rightmost eight bits.)

Here is how to perform shifts on the value of the integer variable `A`:

```
Left Shift: Shl(A)
Right Shift: Shr(A)
```

The above use of the `mod` operation may be generalized. The remainder on dividing by `2^N` is precisely the rightmost `N` bits. The bits beyond `N` are replaced by zeros. This process is called *truncation.*

Logical Operations on Bytes and Words

Turbo Pascal has a number of built-in operations that you may perform on bytes (8-bit quantities) and words (16-bit quantities).

not

The `not` operation reverses all the bits of a number. For example, consider the word

```
not 0000 1010 1111 0101
```

We may compute this number by changing every 0 to a 1 and every 1 to a zero. The result is

```
1111 0101 0000 1010
```

We may apply the `not` operation to any integer, written in either decimal or hexadecimal form. The `not` operation converts the number to binary form, performs the above computation, and reconverts the number to decimal form. For example, let's compute `not 18`. We have

```
18 decimal = 0000 0000 0001 0010 binary
```

so that

```
not 18 = 1111 1111 1110 1101 binary
       = -19 decimal
```

and

The operation `A and B` produces a byte from the bytes `A` and `B`. More precisely,

```
A and B
```

is obtained as follows: Compare `A` and `B` bit by bit. For a given bit position, if both `A` and `B` have a one, then the corresponding bit of `A and B` is a one. If either `A` or `B` has a zero, the corresponding bit of `A and B` is a zero. For example, consider the words:

```
A = 1101 1011 1000 0000
B = 1001 0001 0011 1111
```

Then

```
A and B = 1001 0001 0000 0000
```

or

The operation `A or B` produces a byte from the two bytes `A` and `B`. More precisely,

```
A or B
```

is obtained as follows: Compare `A` and `B` bit by bit. For a given bit position, if either `A` or `B` have a one, then the corresponding bit of `A or B` is a one. If both `A` and `B` have a zero, the corresponding bit of `A or B` is a zero. For example, consider the words:

```
A = 1101 1011 1000 0000
B = 1001 0001 0011 1111
```

Then

```
A or B = 1101 1011 1011 1111
```

xor

The operation `A xor B` is called the *exclusive or of A and B.* The value of

```
A xor B
```

is obtained by comparing `A` and `B` bit by bit. For a given bit position, if `A` and `B` have different bits, then the corresponding bit of `A xor B` is a one. If `A` and `B` have the same bits, the corresponding bit of `A xor B` is a zero. For example, consider the words:

```
A = 1101 1011 1000 0000
B = 1001 0001 0011 1111
```

Then

```
A xor B = 0100 1010 1011 1111
```

Caution: Do not confuse the use of `and`, `not`, `or`, and `xor` within numerical operations and the use of the corresponding words to construct statements in conditional instructions. For example, note the use of `and` in the expression

```
(A>1) and (B<3)
```

In this case, the "and" serves as a logical connector. The statement given is true only if both of the statements `A>1` and `B<3` are true.

In a similar fashion, consider statements of the form:

```
not (A>1)
(A>1) or (B<3)
(A>1) xor (B<3)
```

The first of these statements is true provided that the statement `A>1` is not true. The second of the statements is true if either of the statements `A>1` or `B<3` is true. The third statement is true provided that the statements `A>1` and `B<3` are both false or true.

PutImage Options

In this section, we will apply some of what we have learned about binary numbers and bytes to the use of the `PutImage` procedure.

In Chapter 10 we introduced the `GetImage` and `PutImage` statements which can be used for storing and displaying rectangular images. Recall that `PutImage` has the following syntax:

```
PutImage(x,y:integer; var Bitmap; Application:word);
```

Here (x,y) is the upper left corner at which the image is to be place: `Bitmap` is an array containing the bit map containing the image. `Application` specifies the mode of application of the image to the screen. Application can have one of the following predeclared constant values:

```
CopyPut
XorPut
NotPut
AndPut
OrPut
```

Let's now explain the meaning of each of the five choices for Application. We have already dealt with CopyPut. This mode allows the image to be copied directly over the current contents of the target rectangle.

The choices XorPut, AndPut, and OrPut allow you to combine the image in the bit map with the current contents of the target rectangle by using xor, and, or, respectively. That is, each byte of the bit map is combined with the corresponding byte of the target rectangle using the respective operator.

The choice NotPut inverts the bitmap by applying the operator not to each byte. This produces an inverse image of the original bit map, which is copied onto the target rectangle.

Let's illustrate what happens when these various options are used in one of the 4-color CGA modes (CGA0–CGA3).

and Color Assignment

Current Color	**0**	**1**	**2**	**3**
Bit Image Color				
0	0	0	0	0
1	0	1	0	1
2	0	0	2	2
3	0	1	2	3

or Color Assignment

Current Color	0	1	2	3
Bit Image Color				
0	1	2	3	3
1	1	1	3	3
2	2	3	2	3
3	3	3	3	3

xor Color Assignment

Current Color	0	1	2	3
Bit Image Color				
0	0	1	2	3
1	1	0	3	2
2	2	3	0	1
3	3	2	1	0

Line Styles and Fill Patterns

In this section, we discuss the application of bit and byte manipulation to the creation of various line styles and fill patterns.

User-Defined Line Styles

Recall that in drawing lines, Turbo Pascal makes use of the parameters set by the procedure SetLineStyle, which has the syntax:

```
SetLineStyle(LineStyle:word; Pattern:word; Thickness:word);
```

As we previously discussed, there are a number of predefined line styles. However, you may define your own style by setting LineStyle equal to UserBitnLn and setting Pattern equal to a 16-bit pattern. For instance, to set a pattern of three pixels on and one off, you would set pattern equal to the hexadecimal equivalent of the word:

```
1110 1110 1110 1110
```

Since 1110 is equal to the hexadecimal letter E, the parameter pattern would be set equal to $EEEE.

For NormWidth, the specified pattern is used in a line one dot thick. For ThickWidth, the specified pattern is used in a line three dots thick.

As another example, here is a line that contains a long dash (11 pixels) followed by a one-pixel space, followed by a dot and another space.

```
Pattern = 11111111 11111010
hexadecimal Pattern = $HFFFA
```

User-Defined Fill Styles

As you will recall, you may fill a polygon or flood a region with a rectangular pattern. We have discussed a number of patterns you could use. In addition, you may use a bit pattern to represent a user-defined fill pattern. To define a user-defined fill pattern, use the SetFillPattern procedure which has the syntax:

```
SetFillPattern(Pattern:FillPatternType; Color:Word);
```

FillPatternType is an 8-byte array:

```
FillPatternType = array[1..8] of byte;
```

That is, a value of Pattern is an 8 × 8 pattern of bits, since each byte contains 8 bits. The zeros and ones in this pattern are translated into a pattern of pixels in the specified color.

The SetFillPattern has the effect of selecting the user-defined pattern for subsequent procedures which require a fill style. You can go back to one of the predefined fill patterns using the SetFillStyle procedure. This procedure can also be used to go back to the most recently defined user-defined fill pattern by specifying a fill style of UserFill.

14 Pointers and Dynamic Data Structures

Dynamic versus Static Data Structures

All of the data structures we have considered so far have been *static.* This means that Pascal allocates memory for them when it enters the block in which they are declared. These data structures occupy memory space throughout the execution of the block. In the case of data structures declared in the main block, they occupy memory throughout program execution.

Static memory allocation is simple to manage (from Pascal's point of view), but is rather inflexible. You feel this inflexibility, for example, when you declare arrays. You must tell Pascal how large an array you wish so that it can reserve the appropriate memory space.

In contrast to static data structures, Pascal includes provision for *dynamic* data structures. The memory for these data structures is allocated as the program proceeds. The size of a dynamic data structure can grow as needed. When part or all of a dynamic data structure is not needed, the memory it occupies can be released for use by other dynamic data structures.

Pointers

A *pointer* is a variable which points to a variable, that is, specifies the address of a variable in memory. To create a pointer, we first create a pointer type which specifies the type of data structure that the pointer is to point to. This is done using a declaration of the form:

```
type IntegerPointerType = ^integer;
```

The caret (^) when preceding a data type is read "pointer to" and indicates that the pointer type points to a variable of the indicated type, an integer variable.

Once a pointer type is declared, we may declare variables of that type in the usual way. Such variables are called pointers. For instance, here are declarations of two pointers of the type `IntegerPointerType`:

```
var AmountPtr, TotalPtr : IntegerPointerType
```

Here `AmountPtr` and `TotalPtr` are variables containing the addresses of variables of type integer.

In a similar fashion, we can define pointers to other types. For example, we may define:

```
type RealPointerType = ^real;
     BooleanPointerType = ^boolean;
     CharPointerType = ^char;
     IntegerArray = array[1..100] of integer;
     IntegerArrayPointerType = ^IntegerArray;

var RealPointer : RealPointerType;
    BooleanPointer : BooleanPointerType;
    CharPointer : CharPointerType;
    IntegerArrayPointer : IntegerArrayPointerType;
```

The variable pointed to by a pointer is indicated by placing a caret after the pointer identifier. For instance, in the first example above, `AmountPtr` points to the variable:

```
AmountPtr^
```

The variable `AmountPtr^` is said to be *referenced* by the pointer `AmountPtr`. A pointer variable is said to be of a *referent type* or a *pointer-type.*

A pointer is an indirect way of referencing a variable. By knowing the value of the pointer, you can obtain the value of the variable. Just read the value in the memory location indicated by the pointer.

The new Procedure

You create a pointer using a `var` declaration, just as you would to create any other variable. However, declaring a pointer does not create a variable for the pointer to point to. In order to create the variable, Pascal must set aside memory to store the value of the variable. This process is called *memory allocation* and is carried out using the procedure `new`. For example, to create an integer variable `AmountPointer^`, you use a statement of the form:

```
new(AmountPointer);
```

Having executed the above new statement, you may use the variable AmountPointer^ just like any other integer variable. For instance, you may assign it a value, as in the statements:

```
AmountPointer^ := 577;
readln(AmountPointer^);
```

Just by creating more pointers, you create more variables. For instance, you may create an array of 100 pointers as follows:

```
var PointerArray : array[1..100] of IntegerPointerType;
```

Then we may create variables corresponding to each of the pointers PointerArray[1],...,PointerArray[100] using a statement of the form:

```
for J := 1 to 100 do
  new(PointerArray[J]);
```

The variables are PointerArray[1]^,...,PointerArray[100]^.

As another example, consider the pointer IntegerArrayPointer. This pointer is a variable of type IntegerArray, that is array[1..100] of integer. In this case, the statement:

```
new(IntegerArrayPointer);
```

creates the variable IntegerArrayPointer^, which is of type IntegerArray.

The dispose Procedure

The new procedure is used to create a variable for a pointer to point to. You may dispose of this variable using the procedure dispose. For instance, the statement:

```
dispose(AmountPointer);
```

disposes of the variable AmountPointer^. After the execution of this statement, AmountPointer^ is undefined. The memory space which it formerly occupied is released for possible future assignment to some other dynamic variable.

Using a reference variable before it has been created by new or after it has been disposed of by dispose will produce unpredictable results (no error is generated).

At first glance, it may not seem that pointers are of much use. In fact, it probably seems like an awkward way to refer to a variable. And, for a beginner, perhaps this is the case. However, by using pointers, you can achieve incredible power of expression, since pointers allow you to create variables while a program is executing. Indeed, the new procedure allows you to define a variable which is not part of any var declaration. To put it another way, the procedure now allows you to create a dynamic variable. The procedure dispose allows you to destroy a dynamic variable. Using such variables, you can create dynamic data structures, which can grow or contract as the program proceeds.

Syntax Considerations

A definition of pointer type P has the syntax:

```
type P = ^T;
```

where T is a Pascal type, which must be declared in a later variable declaration (in the same block).

In addition, Turbo Pascal incorporates the generic pointer type Pointer which does not point to a specific data type. This pointer type can be used to point to a location within memory irrespective of how the memory is being used. This is especially useful in dealing with the heap (see below).

Pointer Operations

Pointer variables may be used in assignment and comparison operations. For instance, if ArrayPtr1 and ArrayPtr2 are two pointer variables of type IntegerArrayPointer, then you may make an assignment of the form:

```
ArrayPtr1 := ArrayPtr2;
```

This statement assigns the memory address stored in ArrayPtr2 to ArrayPtr1. In particular, as a result of this assignment, the values of ArrayPtr1^ and ArrayPtr2^ are equal. However, these latter identifiers remain distinct (as variables). They just happen to have the same value.

The predeclared pointer constant nil is the value that may be assigned to a pointer variable if the pointer is not pointing to anything. You may assign nil to a pointer in a statement, such as:

```
AmountPtr := nil;
```

Just as with any Pascal variables, pointer variables must be initialized. Using uninitialized pointers is an extremely common mistake, and one which may be difficult to catch, considering the indirect nature of pointers. At program initialization, the value of pointers are undefined (not `nil`). In practice, this means that a pointer's value is garbage until you assign it. If you wish a pointer variable not to point to anything, then you must assign it the value `nil`.

You may use a pointer in a comparison, such as:

```
if ArrayPtr1 <> ArrayPtr2
  then
    writeln('An error has occurred.');
```

In this statement, the memory addresses contained in `ArrayPtr1` and `ArrayPtr2` are compared to determine whether they are not equal.

Note, however, that you may not use pointer variables in any operation other than assignment and comparison.

Allocating Memory from the Heap

The procedure `new` creates a new variable referenced by a pointer. Pascal obtains the memory location for this variable from a memory reserve it maintains. This reserve is called the *heap*. The heap resides outside the memory space allocated to the program and its static variables and is used for a number of functions, the most common of which is as a memory supply for dynamically created variables.

The amount of memory in the heap depends on the amount of memory in your machine and the size of your program, as well as other factors, such as which memory-resident programs you are running.

Pascal keeps track of the amount and location of any memory in the heap at any given time during program execution. In designing a program which uses dynamic variables, you must pay close attention to how much heap memory you require. For if you create too many dynamic variables, you will create a heap overflow error.

Procedures for Allocating Memory

In many applications, you require a block of memory for temporary storage of data. You can grab such a block of memory from the heap using the procedure `GetMem`. The syntax of this procedure is:

```
GetMem(var P : Pointer; Size : word);
```

Here P is of generic type Pointer. The GetMem procedure allocates a block of memory of Size bytes from the heap and assigns the pointer P to point to this block. You can access this block using the referent variable P^.

To free a block of memory allocated on the heap, you may use the procedure FreeMem, which has the syntax

```
FreeMem(var P : Pointer; Size : word);
```

This procedure frees the block of memory of Size bytes pointed to by the pointer P. It is important to free exactly the same size block which was previously allocated.

As an example, let's consider the problem of storing a graphics image using the GetImage procedure. We previously stated that this procedure requires you to create a block of memory in which to store the image. The number of bytes in the image depends on your screen mode and video adapter and can be determined using a call of ImageSize. Here is a code fragment which gets the size of the image in the rectangle 10,15, 40, 75. A call to GetMem allocates a block of memory of the correct size in which to store the image and a pointer P to that block. The referent variable P^ can be used to store the image. Here is the code which stores the image in P^:

```
Size := ImageSize(10,15,40,75);
GetMem(P, Size);
GetImage(10,15,40,75, P^);
```

To put the image at location (100,100), you may use the statement:

```
PutImage(100,100, P^, NormalPut);
```

To free the memory block pointed to by P^, you may use the statement:

```
FreeMem(P, Size);
```

Linked Lists

Let's now illustrate the use of pointers in creating the most commonly used dynamic data structure, the *linked list.* In concept, a linked list is very simple. It consists of a sequence of records. Each record consists of two components. The first component is a data entry of every type you declare. For simplicity, let's consider a linked list of strings. Then the first field of the record is a string variable. The second field of the record is a pointer which points to the next record. This sounds a little complicated, but it really isn't.

But to be very concrete, let's create a simple linked list whose data items are the words "cat," "dog," "bird." We start by declaring some data types:

```
type
  StringListPointerType = ^StringListEntry;
  StringListEntry = record
                      Animal : string;
                      Next : StringListPointerType
                    end;
```

The type `StringListPointerType` is a pointer to a variable of type `StringListEntry`. In turn, a string list entry is a record consisting of two fields. The field `Animal` is a string; the field `Next` is a pointer of type `StringListPointerType`, to point to the next record in the list. In terms of these data types, let's construct the linked list of animal names. We start by declaring three pointers:

```
var
  FirstEntryPointer,
  LastEntryPointer,
  CurrentEntryPointer : StringListPointerType
```

These pointers will point to the first record in the list, the last record of the list, and the current record of the list (the one we are currently doing work on). Initially, these variables don't point to anything. We add the first entry to the list by first creating a record variable for the entry using `new`. Then we set the `Animal` field of the record. Finally, we assign the remaining pointers. Here's the code:

```
new(CurrentEntryPointer);
CurrentEntryPointer^.Animal := 'cat';
CurrentEntryPointer^.Next := nil;
FirstEntryPointer := CurrentEntryPointer;
LastEntryPointer := CurrentEntryPointer;
```

Note that `FirstEntryPointer` and `CurrentEntryPointer` both now point to the record we have created. Moreover, the `Next` field has been set to `nil` to indicate that at the moment, there is no next record.

To create a second record, we use `new` a second time to create a new record for `CurrentEntryPointer` to point to. We then assign the `Animal` field. The pointer `LastEntryPointer` still points to the previous record. Use this pointer to set the `Next` field for the previous record to point to the record just created. Here is the code:

```
new(CurrentEntryPointer);
CurrentEntryPointer^.Animal := 'dog';
CurrentEntryPointer^.Next := nil;
LastEntryPointer^.Next := CurrentEntryPointer;
LastEntryPointer := CurrentEntryPointer;
```

To add the third record is just a repetition of the same code:

```
new(CurrentEntryPointer);
CurrentEntryPointer^.Animal  := 'bird';
CurrentEntryPointer^.Next  := nil;
LastEntryPointer^.Next  := CurrentEntryPointer;
LastEntryPointer  := CurrentEntryPointer;
```

That's it! We have just created a linked list of three records. The data fields of the three records are the given animal names. The first record `Next` field points to the second record; the second record `Next` field points to the third record; the third record `Next` field points to `nil`, indicating the end of the list. The three pointers `LastEntryPointer`, `FirstEntryPointer`, and `CurrentEntryPointer` are used to manipulate the linked list, as we shall soon see.

Creating a Linked List

It is very easy to abstract what we have done to create linked lists of other data types. Here is the general scheme. Use these data types:

```
type
  ListPointerType = ^ListEntry;
  ListEntry = record
                Data : type;
                Next : ListPointerType
              end;
```

We then declare three variables of `ListPointerType` to manipulate the list.

```
var
  FirstEntryPointer,
  LastEntryPointer,
  CurrentEntryPointer  :  ListPointerType
```

We initialize the list using the assignments:

```
new(CurrentEntryPointer);
CurrentEntryPointer^.Data  := dataitem;
CurrentEntryPointer^.Next  := nil;
FirstEntryPointer  := CurrentEntryPointer;
LastEntryPointer  := CurrentEntryPointer;
```

We then add successive records using the following code for each record added:

```
new(CurrentEntryPointer);
CurrentEntryPointer^.Data  := dataitem;
```

```
CurrentEntryPointer^.Next  := nil;
LastEntryPointer^.Next  := CurrentEntryPointer;
LastEntryPointer  := CurrentEntryPointer;
```

Note that it is not necessary to know the length of a linked list in advance. As long as the heap contains memory to be allocated via `new`, you can keep adding records to the list. Compare this with using an array to store the data items. In that case, it is necessary to declare the size of the array in advance. If you are conservative and use a very large array, you waste memory. If, however, you risk using a small array size, you may not be able to accommodate a list size that arises later.

Of course, a data structure isn't much good unless you can manipulate it. In the next few discussions, let's describe some of the manipulations of a linked list.

Displaying the Contents of a Linked List

You may access the entries of a linked list by using the pointers `FirstEntryPointer`, `CurrentEntryPointer`, and `LastEntryPointer`. For example, you may display the contents of the above linked list using the following loop:

```
CurrentEntryPointer  := FirstEntryPointer;
repeat
  writeln(CurrentEntryPointer^.Animal);
  CurrentEntryPointer  := CurrentEntryPointer^.Next
until CurrentEntryPointer  = nil;
```

It takes some practice to learn to manipulate pointers to do what you want to do, but it is well worth it to become a "pointer expert." Most linked list operations involve manipulations with pointers. For instance, the skeleton for a general procedure for displaying a linked list is shown below. This procedure is a generalization of the display example developed above. Of course, the portion of the procedure which actually displays the data will depend on the data structure used for the data and will vary with the application.

```
procedure DisplayList(var FirstEntryPointer  : ListPointerType);
{Display the linked list pointed to by FirstEntryPointer}

  var
    Entry  : ListPointerType;

  begin
    Entry  := FirstEntryPointer;
    repeat
      {Display Entry^.Data}
      Entry  := Entry^.Next
```

```
    until Entry = nil
  end;
```

Remember that the entries in a linked list are not identified by individual identifiers. The only way to get at these entries is by using pointers. You will often need to obtain the nth entry in a list whose initial pointer is `List`. This is most conveniently done by creating a pointer `Entry` which will reference the entry. Here is a procedure for doing this:

```
procedure FindEntry(var FirstEntryPointer, Entry : ListPointerType;
                        N : integer);
  {Return a pointer Entry to the Nth entry in List.
   If there is no such entry, Entry is nil}

  var
    PtrCounter : integer;

  begin {FindEntry}
    Entry := FirstEntryPointer;
    for PtrCounter := 1 to N-1 do
      Entry := Entry^.Next
  end; {FindEntry}
```

Adding an Entry to a Linked List

Suppose that we wish to add a record to a linked list. We need to know where the addition is to be made and the data to be added to the data field of the new record. Suppose that we are given the place the addition is to be made in the form of a pointer `AdditionPointer` which points to the record just before the one you wish to add. Suppose, further, that `NewData` contains the new data to be added. Here is how to make the addition.

1. Declare pointers `Ptr1` and `Ptr2` of type `ListPointerType`.
2. Make the assignments:

   ```
   Ptr1 := AdditionPointer;
   Ptr2 :=Ptr1^.Next;
   ```

   This makes `Ptr1` reference the entry that precedes the location of the new record, and `Ptr2` references the entry that follows the location of the new record.
3. Execute the statement

   ```
   new(AdditionPointer);
   ```

   to create a new list entry referenced by `AdditionPointer`.

4. Assign values to the record fields of the new entry, that is, to the components of AdditionPointer^.

```
AdditionPointer^.Data := NewData;
AdditionPointer^.Next := Ptr2;
```

5. Insert the new entry into the list by making the pointer assignment:

```
Ptr1^.Next := AdditionPointer;
```

The Next pointer field of the preceding record (Ptr1) points to the new record (AdditionPointer) and the pointer field of the new record points to the following record (Ptr2).

Deleting an Entry from a Linked List

In many applications, it is necessary to delete an entry from a linked list. With an appropriate use of pointers, this is a very simple task. Now we need to know the location of the record that precedes the record to be deleted. The Next pointer field of this record references the record to be deleted. Suppose that the pointer DeletePointer references the entry just before the list entry to be deleted.

Note that DeletePointer^.Next points to the entry to be deleted. To make the deletion, we adjust the value of this pointer. If the entry to be deleted is the last entry of the list, then DeletePointer^.Next is set to nil. Otherwise, we let the pointer DeletePointer^.Next point to the entry after the deleted one. That is, we set DeletePointer^.Next equal to (DeletePointer^.Next)^.Next.

The deletion operation may then be accomplished with the code:

```
Ptr := DeletePointer^.Next
if DeletePointer^.Next = LastEntryPointer
  then
    begin
      DeletePointer^.Next := nil;
      LastEntryPointer := DeletePointer;
    end
  else
    DeletePointer^.Next := (DeletePointer^.Next)^.Next;
dispose(Ptr);
```

Sorting a Linked List

Suppose that we are given a linked list of real numbers. Let's write a procedure to sort the linked list into increasing numerical order.

For sorting, we will use a modification of the selection sort. Let's recall how this sort works on a list of integers. We maintain a pointer to the list. In successive passes, the pointer advances from the first to the last entry in the list. A pass consists of making successive comparisons between the referenced entry and the entries to the right, to determine the smallest among the compared entries. At the end of the pass, the referenced entry is swapped with the smallest entry.

We have deliberately described this sort using the terminology of pointers to make it easy to translate into code. To point at the list, we use the pointer `SortPtr`. To point at the smallest entry in a pass, we use the pointer `SmallestPtr`. Finally, to make the successive comparisons within a pass, we use the pointer `PosPtr` to indicate the position which is currently being compared with the amount referenced by `SmallestPtr`. Here is the code for the procedure `SelectSort`.

```
procedure SelectSort(var NumbersPointer : ListPointerType);
  {Implementation of selection sort for linked lists.
  The list pointed to by NumbersPointer is sorted into
  increasing order of the Data field}

  var
    SmallestPtr, SortPtr, PosPtr : ListPointerType;
    {SmallestPtr points to the entry with the least amount
    field.
    SortPtr points to the entry being currently sorted.
    PosPtr points to the entry being currently compared.}

  procedure Swap(var X, Y : real);
  {Swap the values of variables X and Y}
    var
      Temp : real;
    begin
      Temp := X;
      X := Y;
      Y := Temp
    end;

  begin {SelectSort}
    SortPtr := NumbersPointer;          {Begin at start of list}
      while SortPtr <> nil do
        begin
          SmallestPtr := SortPtr;
          PosPtr := SortPtr^.Next;
          {In the entries from SortPtr on, find the
          smallest amount field}
          while PosPtr <> nil do
            begin
              if (PosPtr^.Data < SmallestPtr^.Data)
                then
                  SmallestPtr := PosPtr;
              PosPtr := PosPtr^.Next
```

```
          end;
        {Bring smallest amount field into SortPtr
         position}
        Swap(SmallestPtr^.Data, SortPtr^.Data);
        {Move to next position in list}
        SortPtr := SortPtr^.Next
      end
  end; {SelectSort}
```

Queues, Stacks, and Trees

In the preceding section, we introduced the concept of a linked list, a dynamic data structure useful in many applications. Linked lists are not the only dynamic data structures which are useful. In this section and the next, we introduce several others.

Queues

A *queue* (pronounced like the letter "q") is a dynamic data structure consisting of a sequence of linked data entries. A queue grows by inserting new entries at one end (the rear of the queue) and shrinks by deleting new entries from the other end (the front of the queue). An example of a queue is the waiting line at the doctor's office. Patients are added at the end of the queue and deleted from the beginning. A queue operates on a "First In First Out" (or *FIFO*) basis. The early entries in a queue leave before later entries. It is this method of operation, which conforms to data structures in many applications, which give queues their importance.

For the sake of simplicity, let's consider queues of integers. The following discussion can easily be modified to include queues of other data structures.

A queue has a front and a back. We require two pointers `FrontPointer` and `BackPointer` to point to these entries. The queue entries themselves are records similar to those we used in connection with linked lists, in which one or more fields store the entry data and one field stores a pointer referencing the next entry.

Here are the declarations we require to declare a queue:

```
type
  QueuePointerType : ^QueueEntry;
  QueueEntry : record
                 Data : integer;
                 Next : QueuePointerType
               end;
```

```
var
  FrontPointer,
  BackPointer,
  EntryPointer  :  QueuePointerType;
```

It is an easy exercise in pointer manipulation to insert an entry into a queue. If the queue is empty, then both `FrontPointer` and `BackPointer` must point to the entry added. If the queue is not empty, `BackPointer` must point to the element added, but no modification of the value of `FrontPointer` is necessary. Here is a procedure for adding `EntryPointer` to a queue defined by the pointers `FrontPointer` and `BackPointer`.

```
procedure QueueInsert(var FrontPointer,
                          BackPointer  :  QueuePointerType;
                          Value  :  integer);
{Insert a new Value at the end of a queue.}

  var
    EntryPointer  :  QueuePointerType;

  begin {QueueInsert}
    new(EntryPointer);
    EntryPointer^.Data  :=  Value;
    EntryPointer^.Next  :=  nil;
    if BackPointer  :=  nil {Empty queue}
      then
        begin
          BackPointer  :=  EntryPointer;
          FrontPointer  :=  EntryPointer
        end
      else
        begin
          BackPointer^.Next  :=  EntryPointer;
          BackPointer  :=  EntryPointer
        end
  end; {QueueInsert}
```

Deleting an entry from a queue is even simpler. We just need to adjust the pointer `FrontPointer`. However, we must take care of the case where the queue is empty (`FrontPointer = nil`), in which case there is no `EntryPointer` to delete. Here is a procedure which deletes an entry from a queue. Note that the procedure returns the value of the entry deleted in the variable `Value`. If `BackPointer` is `nil`, then the queue was empty and there is no value passed back. (In this case, the `Value` in `EntryPointer` is garbage.)

```
procedure QueueDelete(var FrontPointer,
                          BackPointer  :  QueuePtr;
```

```
var
  Value : integer;

begin {QueueDelete}
  if BackPointer <> nil then
    begin
      Value := FrontPointer^.Data;
      FrontPointer := FrontPointer^.Next
    end
end; {QueueDelete}
```

Stacks

A *stack* is a dynamic data structure in which data items are linked together in a list. New entries are added to the current front (or top) of a stack and entries are deleted also from the current top of the stack. You should think of a stack as a pile of plates. You add plates by stacking them on top of the ones already there. You remove plates from the top of the pile.

A stack operates on the principle of "Last In First Out" or *LIFO*. There are many applications which require a data structure in which LIFO is the governing method of addition and deletion. Such data structures are modeled using stacks. It is extremely easy to add and delete entries from a stack. This accounts for the widespread use of stacks for storing intermediate results of computations which will be needed for further processing in a very short time. All computers use stacks to store data from the CPU's registers while the registers are required for other tasks. When required, the data can be restored rapidly from the stack to the registers.

For the sake of simplicity, let's consider stacks of integers. The following discussion can easily be modified to include stacks of other data structures.

A stack has only one end that we need to be concerned about. This end is customarily called the `Top` of the stack. We create a pointer `Top` to point to the top of the stack. The entries of stack are records linked together in the same fashion as in a linked list.

Here are the declarations we require to declare a stack:

```
type
  StackPointerType : ^StackEntry;
  StackEntry : record
                 Data : integer;
                 Next : StackPointerType
               end;

var
  TopPointer,
  NewEntryPointer : StackPointerType;
```

The procedure for adding an entry to a stack is called *Push*, and the procedure for removing an entry is called *Pop*. These names are universal and you will see Push and Pop instructions built into the instruction sets of most microprocessors. Here is the code for a Push procedure:

```
procedure Push(var TopPointer : StackPointerType;
                   Entry : integer);
{Place an entry on the top of the stack.}

  var
    NewEntry : StackEntry;

begin {Push}
    new(NewEntry); {Create new variable}
    NewEntry^.Data := Entry; {Assign data field}
    NewEntry^.Next := TopPointer; {Point to current Top}
    TopPointer := NewEntry {Define new Top}
  end; {Push}
```

Pop is equally simple to write. However, it is very important to first make sure that the stack is non-empty before applying Pop, or there will be an error called *stack underflow*. To guard against it, we use a parameter Error, which is set equal to true if Pop is called and the stack is empty. Otherwise Error is set to false.

```
procedure Pop(var TopPointer : StackPointerType;
              var Value : integer
              var Error : Boolean);
{Remove an entry from the top of the stack.}

  var
    Ptr : StackPointerType;

  begin {Pop}
    if TopPointer = nil
      then
        begin
          Error := true;
          writeln('Stack underflow')
        end
      else
        begin
          Ptr := TopPointer;
          Value := TopPointer^.Data;
          TopPointer := TopPointer^.Next;
          dispose(Ptr);
          Error := false
        end
  end; {Pop}
```

15 Dynamic Objects

Just as ordinary data structures may be static or dynamic, the same applies to objects. In this chapter, we will discuss the use of dynamic objects and provide a detailed application of objects in the form of a windowing package.

Dynamic Objects

Our previous discussion of objects was confined to objects which are created by a `var` declaration of an instance of the object. Such objects, like all variables declared in a `var` declaration, are allocated fixed memory space. However, you can create dynamic objects whose memory is allocated on the heap. The memory for instances of such objects is allocated during program execution by the procedure `new` and the instances are accessed via pointers.

Allocating Memory for Dynamic Objects

You can define pointer types to objects just as you define other pointers. For instance, we will introduce a windowing package in the next section. In this package one of the object types defined will be `TypeWinObj`, a window object. A pointer type for this object is declared by the type declaration:

```
type TypeWinPtr = ^TypeWinObj;
```

We declare pointers of this type using a declaration of the form:

```
var VanWindow : TypeWinPtr;
```

(As we shall see, `VanWindow` is a window object used to display a van.) To create an instance of `TypeWinObj` for `VanWindow` to point to, we use the `new` procedure:

```
new(VanWindow);
```

The window object itself is accessed through the referent variable `VanWindow^`. For instance, to execute the method `Init`, use the statement:

```
VanWindow^.Init;
```

You may pass the pointer `VanWindow` to procedures using the standard parameter passing techniques. For instance, here are several statements from the program VanView which we will discuss below.

```
SetCoordSys(VanWindow);
AddBody(VanWindow);
AddWheels(VanWindow)
```

Extension to New

In using `new` with objects, there is a variation on the syntax which allows you to allocate memory and perform the constructor at the same time. For instance, `Init` is the constructor for `TypeWinObj`. To allocate memory to `VanWindow` and perform the constructor initialization, we may use the statement:

```
new(VanWindow, Init);
```

Deallocating Dynamic Objects

You may deallocate memory allocated to dynamic objects using the procedure `dispose`. In deallocation of memory for a dynamic object, it is safest to define a method called a *destructor*, which takes care of any cleaning up prior to memory deallocation. Even if no cleaning up is necessary, you should declare a destructor with no body. Here is the syntax of a destructor declaration:

```
destructor Done; virtual;
```

To deallocate the memory associated with a dynamic object, you call the destructor for the object as part of `dispose`. For instance, to deallocate the memory for `VanWindow`, we would use the statement:

```
dispose(VanWindow, Done);
```

The destructor method automatically determines the size of the dynamic object and deallocates the correct number of bytes.

Windowing Package

The WinPack Unit

As a detailed example of an object package which incorporates everything we have discussed, let's consider a unit called WinPack, which is a window management package. This package defines two sorts of object, windows and the graphics object within a window. The objective is to create a form of window which will make resizing and moving windows easy and at the same time will easily allow for redefining a coordinate system within a window.

As a start, we define a TypeCoordSys which consists of (X1,Y1,X2,Y2). Variables of this type can be used either to describe a window—where the entries, in that case, give pixel coordinates—or to give a window a new coordinate system. A TypeCoord is a point of real numbers (X,Y) used to specify a point.

The most comprehensive object in the unit is a TypeWinObj, which is a window type. Since windows can be created and disappear, we utilize pointers of type TypeWinPtr which point to TypeWinObj. A window object, first of all, consists of a variable Visible which is boolean and determines whether the window is currently showing. A window also has a GlobalCoordSys which is the pixel location of the window and a WinCoordSys which is the current coordinate system in the window. Also, TypeWinObj has a PointRoot, which is a pointer to the linked list of graphics objects that the window contains. There are assorted methods for setting and retrieving current TypeWinObj settings.

As for the objects within a window, there are points, lines, ellipses, and rectangles. TypePointPtr points to TypePointObj. One of the fields WinObj points to the window the point is contained in. A point has coordinate fields and a field to determine whether or not it is visible as well as its color. There is also a pointer to the next point in the window. There are assorted methods to manipulate the data fields. Note that the function Contents creates a string which is an amalgam of everything associated with the point. This is used in deciding whether or not two points are the same.

The objects TypeLineObj, TypeRectObj, and TypeEllipseObj are all descendants of TypeLineObj. Where necessary, we have introduced methods unique to these objects as well as redefinitions of methods used ancestrally. Where such redefinitions are involved, we have used virtual methods.

Listing 15.1. The WinPack object-oriented window package

```
unit WinPack;

interface

  type
    TypeCoordSys = record
                       X1, Y1, X2, Y2 : real
                     end;
    TypeCoord = record
                    X, Y : real
                  end;
    TypeWinPtr = ^TypeWinObj;
    TypePointPtr = ^TypePointObj;
    TypePointObj = object
                       WinObj : TypeWinPtr;
                       Visible : boolean;
                       Coord : TypeCoord;
                       Color : integer;
                       NextPoint : TypePointPtr;
                       constructor Init;
                       destructor Done; virtual;
                       procedure Show; virtual;
                       procedure Hide; virtual;
                       procedure SetCoord(    NewX, NewY : real);
                       procedure SetColor(    NewColor : integer);
                       function IsVisible : boolean;
                       function CurrentX : real;
                       function CurrentY : real;
                       function CurrentColor : integer;
                       function Contents : string; virtual;
                     end;
    TypeEllipsePtr = ^TypeEllipseObj;
    TypeEllipseObj = object
                         (TypePointObj)
                         Radius : TypeCoord;
                         constructor Init;
                         procedure Show; virtual;
                         procedure Hide; virtual;
                         procedure SetRadius(    NewXRadius,
                                                 NewYRadius : real); virtual;
                         procedure GetRadius(var XRadius,
                                                 YRadius : real); virtual;
                         function Contents : string; virtual;
                       end;
    TypeLinePtr = ^TypeLineObj;
    TypeLineObj = object
                      (TypePointObj)
                      Vector : TypeCoord;
                      constructor Init;
                      procedure Show; virtual;
```

```
                    procedure Hide; virtual;
                    procedure SetVector(    X, Y : real); virtual;
                    procedure GetVector(var X, Y : real); virtual;
                    function Contents : string; virtual;
                  end;
    TypeRectPtr = ^TypeRectObj;
    TypeRectObj = object
                    (TypeLineObj)
                    procedure Show; virtual;
                    procedure Hide; virtual;
                    function Contents : string; virtual;
                  end;
    TypeWinObj = object
                   Visible : boolean;
                   GlobalCoordSys,
                   WinCoordSys : TypeCoordSys;
                   PointRoot : TypePointPtr;
                   constructor Init;
                   destructor Done;
                   procedure Add(    Point : TypePointPtr);
                   procedure Remove(    Point : TypePointPtr);
                   function AdjustedX(    WinX : real) : integer;
                   function AdjustedY(    WinY : real) : integer;
                   procedure Show; virtual;
                   procedure Hide; virtual;
                   procedure SetCoordSys(    NewGlobalCoordSys,
                                             NewWinCoordSys : TypeCoordSys);
                   function IsVisible : boolean;
                   procedure GetCoordSys(var CurrentGlobal,
                                             CurrentWin : TypeCoordSys);
                 end;

implementation

  uses
    graph;

  {-------- TypePointObj methods --------}

  constructor TypePointObj.Init;
    begin
      WinObj := nil;
      Visible := false;
      Coord.X := 0;
      Coord.Y := 0;
      Color := 0;
      NextPoint := nil
    end;

  destructor TypePointObj.Done;
    begin
      Hide
    end;
```

```
procedure TypePointObj.Show;
  begin
    if not Visible
      then
        begin
          with WinObj^.GlobalCoordSys do
            setviewport(trunc(X1), trunc(Y1), trunc(X2), trunc(Y2), clipon);
          putpixel(WinObj^.AdjustedX(Coord.X), WinObj^.AdjustedY(Coord.Y),
                   Color);
          Visible := true
        end
  end;

procedure TypePointObj.Hide;
  begin
    if Visible
      then
        begin
          with WinObj^.GlobalCoordSys do
            setviewport(trunc(X1), trunc(Y1), trunc(X2), trunc(Y2), clipon);
          putpixel(WinObj^.AdjustedX(Coord.X), WinObj^.AdjustedY(Coord.Y),
                   getbkcolor);
          Visible := false
        end
  end;

procedure TypePointObj.SetCoord(    NewX, NewY : real);
  begin
    if Visible
      then
        begin
          Hide;
          Coord.X := NewX;
          Coord.Y := NewY;
          Show
        end
      else
        begin
          Coord.X := NewX;
          Coord.Y := NewY
        end
  end;

procedure TypePointObj.SetColor(    NewColor : integer);
  begin
    Color := NewColor;
    if Visible
      then
        Show
  end;

function TypePointObj.IsVisible : boolean;
  begin
    IsVisible := Visible
  end;
```

```
function TypePointObj.CurrentX : real;
  begin
    CurrentX := Coord.X
  end;

function TypePointObj.CurrentY : real;
  begin
    CurrentY := Coord.Y
  end;

function TypePointObj.CurrentColor : integer;
  begin
    CurrentColor := Color
  end;

function TypePointObj.Contents : string;
  var
    XStr, YStr, ColorStr : string;
  begin
    str(Coord.X, XStr);
    str(Coord.Y, YStr);
    str(Color, ColorStr);
    Contents := concat('POINT', XStr, YStr, ColorStr)
  end;

{-------- TypeEllipseObj methods --------}

constructor TypeEllipseObj.Init;
  begin
    TypePointObj.Init;
    Radius.X := 0;
    Radius.Y := 0
  end;

procedure TypeEllipseObj.Show;
  begin
    if not Visible
      then
        begin
          with WinObj^.GlobalCoordSys do
            setviewport(trunc(X1), trunc(Y1), trunc(X2), trunc(Y2), clipon);
          graph.setcolor(Color);
          ellipse(WinObj^.AdjustedX(Coord.X), WinObj^.AdjustedY(Coord.Y),
                  0, 360,
                  abs(WinObj^.AdjustedX(Radius.X) - WinObj^.AdjustedX(0)),
                  abs(WinObj^.AdjustedY(Radius.Y) - WinObj^.AdjustedY(0)));
          Visible := true
        end
  end;
```

```
procedure TypeEllipseObj.Hide;
  begin
    if Visible
      then
        begin
          with WinObj^.GlobalCoordSys do
            setviewport(trunc(X1), trunc(Y1), trunc(X2), trunc(Y2), clipon);
          graph.setcolor(getbkcolor);
          ellipse(WinObj^.AdjustedX(Coord.X), WinObj^.AdjustedY(Coord.Y),
                  0, 360,
                  abs(WinObj^.AdjustedX(Radius.X) - WinObj^.AdjustedX(0)),
                  abs(WinObj^.AdjustedY(Radius.Y) - WinObj^.AdjustedY(0)));
          Visible := false
        end
  end;

procedure TypeEllipseObj.SetRadius(     NewXRadius, NewYRadius : real);
  begin
    if Visible
      then
        begin
          Hide;
          Radius.X := NewXRadius;
          Radius.Y := NewYRadius;
          Show
        end
      else
        begin
          Radius.X := NewXRadius;
          Radius.Y := NewYRadius
        end
  end;

procedure TypeEllipseObj.GetRadius(var XRadius, YRadius : real);
  begin
    XRadius := Radius.X;
    YRadius := Radius.Y
  end;

function TypeEllipseObj.Contents : string;

  var
    WorkStr, TempStr : string;

  begin
    str(Coord.X, TempStr);
    WorkStr := concat('ELLIPSE', TempStr);
    str(Coord.Y, TempStr);
    WorkStr := concat(WorkStr, TempStr);
    str(Radius.X, TempStr);
    WorkStr := concat(WorkStr, TempStr);
    str(Radius.Y, TempStr);
    WorkStr := concat(WorkStr, TempStr);
    str(Color, TempStr);
    WorkStr := concat(WorkStr, TempStr);
```

```
    Contents := WorkStr
  end;

{-------- TypeLineObj methods --------}

constructor TypeLineObj.Init;
  begin
    TypePointObj.Init;
    Vector.X := 0;
    Vector.Y := 0
  end;

procedure TypeLineObj.Show;
  begin
    if not Visible
      then
        begin
          with WinObj^.GlobalCoordSys do
            setviewport(trunc(X1), trunc(Y1), trunc(X2), trunc(Y2), clipon);
          graph.setcolor(Color);
          line(WinObj^.AdjustedX(Coord.X), WinObj^.AdjustedY(Coord.Y),
              WinObj^.AdjustedX(Coord.X + Vector.X),
              WinObj^.AdjustedY(Coord.Y + Vector.Y));
          Visible := true
        end
  end;

procedure TypeLineObj.Hide;
  begin
    if Visible
      then
        begin
          with WinObj^.GlobalCoordSys do
            setviewport(trunc(X1), trunc(Y1), trunc(X2), trunc(Y2), clipon);
          graph.setcolor(getbkcolor);
          line(WinObj^.AdjustedX(Coord.X), WinObj^.AdjustedY(Coord.Y),
              WinObj^.AdjustedX(Coord.X + Vector.X),
              WinObj^.AdjustedY(Coord.Y + Vector.Y));
          Visible := false
        end
  end;

procedure TypeLineObj.SetVector(     X, Y : real);
  begin
    if Visible
      then
        begin
          Hide;
          Vector.X := X;
          Vector.Y := Y;
          Show
        end
      else
        begin
          Vector.X := X;
```

```
          Vector.Y := Y
        end
  end;

procedure TypeLineObj.GetVector(var X, Y : real);
  begin
    X := Vector.X;
    Y := Vector.Y
  end;

function TypeLineObj.Contents : string;

  var
    WorkStr, TempStr : string;

  begin
    str(Coord.X, TempStr);
    WorkStr := concat('LINE', TempStr);
    str(Coord.Y, TempStr);
    WorkStr := concat(WorkStr, TempStr);
    str(Vector.X, TempStr);
    WorkStr := concat(WorkStr, TempStr);
    str(Vector.Y, TempStr);
    WorkStr := concat(WorkStr, TempStr);
    str(Color, TempStr);
    WorkStr := concat(WorkStr, TempStr);
    Contents := WorkStr
  end;

{-------- TypeRectObj methods --------}

procedure TypeRectObj.Show;
  begin
    if not Visible
      then
        begin
          with WinObj^.GlobalCoordSys do
            setviewport (trunc (X1), trunc (Y1), trunc (X2), trunc (Y2),
                         ClipOn);
          graph.setcolor (Color);
          rectangle (WinObj^.AdjustedX (Coord.X),
                     WinObj^.AdjustedY (Coord.Y),
                     WinObj^.AdjustedX (Coord.X + Vector.X),
                     WinObj^.AdjustedY (Coord.Y + Vector.Y));
          Visible := true
        end
  end;

procedure TypeRectObj.Hide;
  begin
    if Visible
      then
        begin
          with WinObj^.GlobalCoordSys do
```

```
            setviewport (trunc (X1), trunc (Y1), trunc (X2), trunc (Y2),
                         ClipOn);
          graph.setcolor (getbkcolor);
          rectangle (WinObj^.AdjustedX (Coord.X),
                     WinObj^.AdjustedY (Coord.Y),
                     WinObj^.AdjustedX (Coord.X + Vector.X),
                     WinObj^.AdjustedY (Coord.Y + Vector.Y));
          Visible := false
        end
  end;

function TypeRectObj.Contents : string;

  var
    WorkStr, TempStr : string;

  begin
    str(Coord.X, TempStr);
    WorkStr := concat('RECT', TempStr);
    str(Coord.Y, TempStr);
    WorkStr := concat(WorkStr, TempStr);
    str(Vector.X, TempStr);
    WorkStr := concat(WorkStr, TempStr);
    str(Vector.Y, TempStr);
    WorkStr := concat(WorkStr, TempStr);
    str(Color, TempStr);
    WorkStr := concat(WorkStr, TempStr);
    Contents := WorkStr
  end;

{-------- TypeWinObj methods --------}

constructor TypeWinObj.Init;
  begin
    Visible := false;
    PointRoot := nil
  end;

destructor TypeWinObj.Done;
  begin
    Hide
  end;

procedure TypeWinObj.Add(    Point : TypePointPtr);
  var
    Temp : TypePointPtr;
  begin
    if (PointRoot = nil)
      then
        PointRoot := Point
      else
        begin
          Temp := PointRoot;
          while (Temp^.NextPoint <> nil) do
            Temp := Temp^.NextPoint;
```

```
          Temp^.NextPoint := Point
        end;

    with Point^ do
      begin
        NextPoint := nil;
        WinObj := addr(Self);
        if IsVisible
          then
            Show
      end
  end;

procedure TypeWinObj.Remove(     Point : TypePointPtr);

  var
    Temp, PointToDelete : TypePointPtr;

  function Equal(     Point1, Point2 : TypePointPtr) : boolean;
    begin
      Equal := (Point1^.Contents = Point2^.Contents)
    end;

  procedure DeleteFromList(var PointRoot : TypePointPtr;
                               PointToDelete : TypePointPtr);
    var
      PrevNode : TypePointPtr;

    procedure FindPrevNode(     PointRoot, PointToDelete : TypePointPtr;
                           var PrevNode : TypePointPtr);
      begin
        if (PointToDelete = PointRoot)
          then
            PrevNode := nil
          else
            begin
              PrevNode := PointRoot;
              while (PrevNode^.NextPoint <> PointToDelete) do
                PrevNode := PrevNode^.NextPoint
            end
      end;

    procedure KillNextNode(var PointRoot : TypePointPtr;
                               PointToDelete, PrevNode : TypePointPtr);
      begin
        if (PrevNode = nil)
          then
            PointRoot := PointToDelete^.NextPoint
          else
            PrevNode^.NextPoint := PointToDelete^.NextPoint;
        PointToDelete^.Done
      end;

    begin
      FindPrevNode(PointRoot, PointToDelete, PrevNode);
```

```
      KillNextNode(PointRoot, PointToDelete, PrevNode)
    end;

  begin
    Temp := PointRoot;
    while (Temp <> nil) do

      begin
        if Equal(Temp, Point)
          then
            begin
              PointToDelete := Temp;
              Temp := Temp^.NextPoint;
              DeleteFromList(PointRoot, PointToDelete)
            end
          else
            Temp := Temp^.NextPoint
      end
  end;

 function TypeWinObj.AdjustedX(    WinX : real) : integer;
  begin
    AdjustedX := trunc(((WinX - WinCoordSys.X1) /
                       (WinCoordSys.X2 - WinCoordSys.X1)) *
                       (GlobalCoordSys.X2 - GlobalCoordSys.X1))
  end;

function TypeWinObj.AdjustedY(    WinY : real) : integer;
  begin
    AdjustedY := trunc(((WinY - WinCoordSys.Y1) /
                       (WinCoordSys.Y2 - WinCoordSys.Y1)) *
                       (GlobalCoordSys.Y2 - GlobalCoordSys.Y1))
  end;

procedure TypeWinObj.Show;

  var
    Temp : TypePointPtr;

  begin
    Temp := PointRoot;
    while (Temp <> nil) do
      begin
        Temp^.Show;
        Temp := Temp^.NextPoint
      end;
    Visible := true
  end;

procedure TypeWinObj.Hide;

  var
    Temp : TypePointPtr;
```

```
    begin
      Temp := PointRoot;
      while (Temp <> nil) do
        begin
          Temp^.Hide;
          Temp := Temp^.NextPoint
        end;
      Visible := false
    end;

  procedure TypeWinObj.SetCoordSys(     NewGlobalCoordSys,
                                        NewWinCoordSys : TypeCoordSys);
    begin
      if Visible
        then
          begin
            Hide;
            GlobalCoordSys := NewGlobalCoordSys;
            WinCoordSys := NewWinCoordSys;
            Show
          end
        else
          begin
            GlobalCoordSys := NewGlobalCoordSys;
            WinCoordSys := NewWinCoordSys
          end
    end;

  function TypeWinObj.IsVisible : boolean;
    begin
      IsVisible := Visible
    end;

  procedure TypeWinObj.GetCoordSys(var CurrentGlobal,
                                        CurrentWin : TypeCoordSys);
    begin
      CurrentGlobal := GlobalCoordSys;
      CurrentWin := WinCoordSys
    end;

end.
```

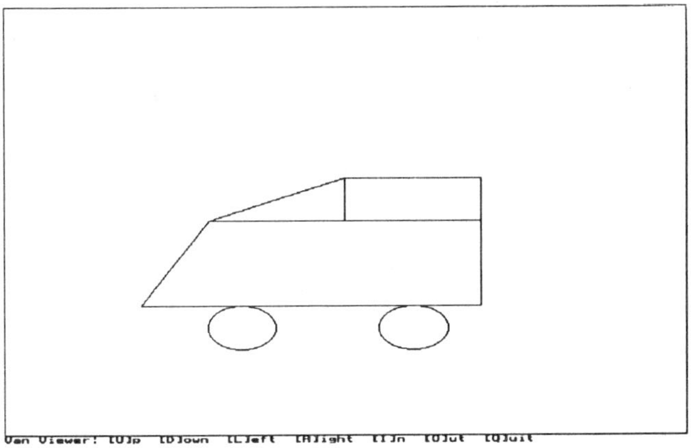

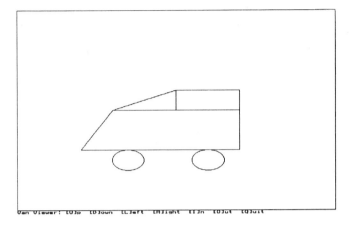

Figure 15.1.
Initial van screen.

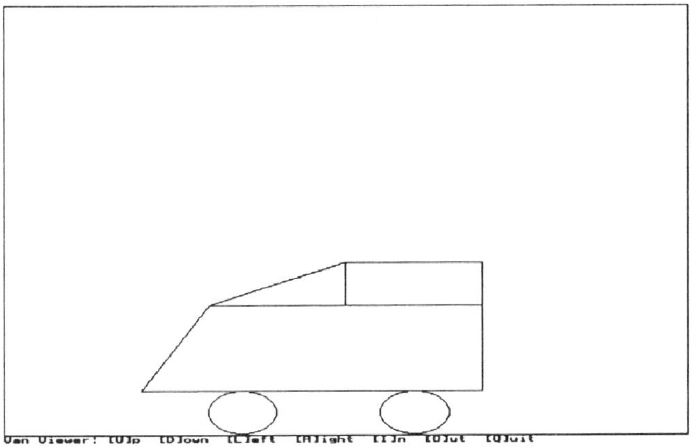

Figure 15.2.
Screen moved up.

Using WinPack

As an illustration of how the windowing package `WinPack` may be used, we offer the program VanView, which draws a picture of a van using the various graphic objects defined in `WinPack`. The program then uses the ability to redefine a window's coordinate system to move the van around the window, enlarge it, and shrink it.

When the program starts, you see the screen shown in Figure 15.1.

By pressing the keys R, L, U, D, you may move the window (not the van) right, left, up or down, respectively. By pressing the keys I and O, you

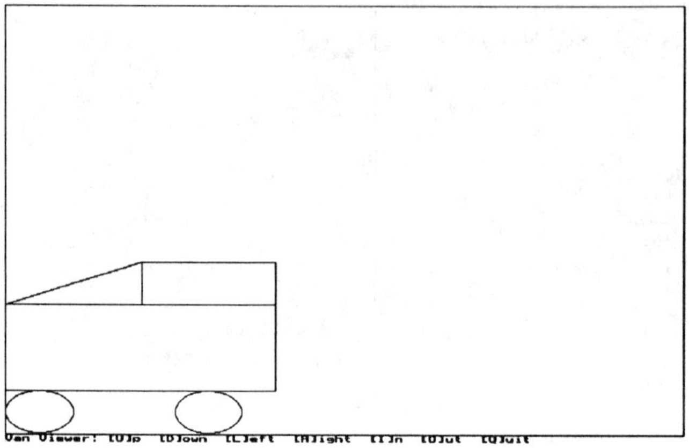

Figure 15.3.
Screen moved to the right.

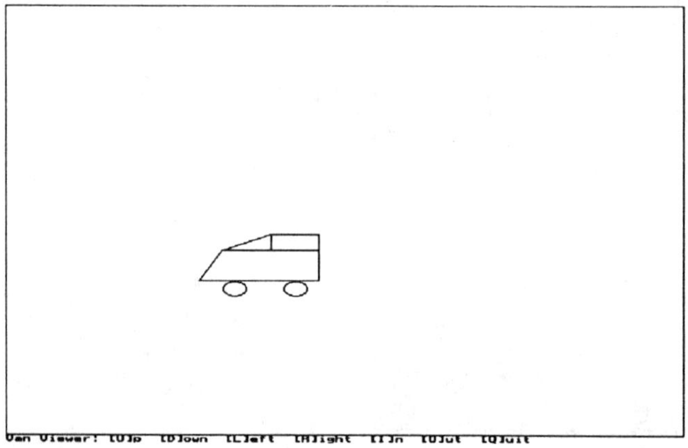

Figure 15.4.
Screen zoomed out.

may zoom the window in or out. Various combinations of keystrokes result in images like those shown in Figures 15.2., 15.3., and 15.4.

To quit the program, press Q.

You should study the code below to see how the redefinition of the coordinates in the window can achieve the various motions and transformations described above.

Listing 15.2. The VanView program

```
program VanView;

  uses
    crt,
    graph,
    WinPack;

  const
    ZoomIn = 'I';
    ZoomOut = 'O';
    Up = 'U';
    Down = 'D';
    Left = 'L';
    Right = 'R';
    Quit = 'Q';

  var
    VanWindow : TypeWinPtr;
    Command : char;

   procedure OpenGraph;

    var
      GraphDriver, GraphMode : integer;

    begin
      GraphDriver := detect;
      initgraph(GraphDriver, GraphMode, '');
      cleardevice
    end;

  procedure SetCoordSys(var VanWindow : TypeWinPtr);

    var
      Global, Win : TypeCoordSys;

    begin
      Global.X1 := 1;
      Global.Y1 := 1;
      Global.X2 := getmaxx - 1;
      Global.Y2 := getmaxy - 10;
      Win.X1 := -10;
      Win.Y1 := 10;
      Win.X2 := 10;
      Win.Y2 := -10;
      VanWindow^.SetCoordSys(Global, Win)
    end;

  procedure AddBody(var VanWindow : TypeWinPtr);

    var
      Body, Top : TypeRectPtr;
      Front1, Front2, Front3, Windshield : TypeLinePtr;
```

```
procedure CreateBody(var Body : TypeRectPtr);
  begin
    new(Body, Init);
    Body^.SetCoord(-4, -4);
    Body^.SetVector(8, 4);
    Body^.SetColor(white)
  end;

procedure CreateTop(var Top : TypeRectPtr);
  begin
    new(Top, Init);
    Top^.SetCoord(0, 0);
    Top^.SetVector(4, 2);
    Top^.SetColor(white)
  end;

procedure CreateFront(var Front1, Front2, Front3 : TypeLinePtr);
  begin
    new(Front1, Init);
    new(Front2, Init);
    new(Front3, Init);
    Front1^.SetCoord(-4, -4);
    Front2^.SetCoord(-6, -4);
    Front3^.SetCoord(-6, -4);
    Front1^.SetVector(0, 4);
    Front2^.SetVector(2, 0);
    Front3^.SetVector(2, 4);
    Front1^.SetColor(black);
    Front2^.SetColor(white);
    Front3^.SetColor(white)
  end;

procedure CreateWindshield(var Windshield : TypeLinePtr);
  begin
    new(Windshield, Init);
    Windshield^.SetCoord(-4, 0);
    Windshield^.SetVector(4, 2);
    Windshield^.SetColor(white)
  end;

begin
  CreateBody(Body);
  CreateTop(Top);
  CreateFront(Front1, Front2, Front3);
  CreateWindshield(Windshield);
  with VanWindow^ do
    begin
      Add(Body);
      Add(Top);
      Add(Front1);
      Add(Front2);
      Add(Front3);
      Add(Windshield)
    end
end;
```

```
procedure AddWheels(var VanWindow : TypeWinPtr);

  var
    FrontWheel, BackWheel : TypeEllipsePtr;

  begin
    new(FrontWheel, Init);
    new(BackWheel, Init);
    FrontWheel^.SetCoord(2, -5);
    BackWheel^.SetCoord(-3, -5);
    FrontWheel^.SetRadius(1, 1);
    BackWheel^.SetRadius(1, 1);
    FrontWheel^.SetColor(white);
    BackWheel^.SetColor(white);
    VanWindow^.Add(FrontWheel);
    VanWindow^.Add(BackWheel)
  end;

procedure CreateVanWindow(var VanWindow : TypeWinPtr);
  begin
    new(VanWindow, Init);
    SetCoordSys(VanWindow);
    AddBody(VanWindow);
    AddWheels(VanWindow)
  end;

procedure ShowMenu;
  begin
    setcolor(1);
    rectangle(0, 0, getmaxx, getmaxy - 9);
    moveto(0, getmaxy - 8);
    outtext('Van Viewer: [U]p [D]own [L]eft [R]ight [I]n [O]ut [Q]uit')
  end;

procedure GetCommand(var Command : char);
  begin
    repeat
      Command := upcase(readkey)
    until(Command in [ZoomIn, ZoomOut, Up, Down, Left, Right, Quit])
  end;

procedure DoCommand(     Command : char;
                     var VanWindow : TypeWinPtr);
  procedure ZoomWindowIn(var VanWindow : TypeWinPtr);

    var
      Global, Win : TypeCoordSys;

    begin
      VanWindow^.GetCoordSys(Global, Win);
      with Win do
        begin
          X1 := X1 + 1;
          X2 := X2 - 1;
          Y1 := Y1 - 1;
```

```
        Y2 := Y2 + 1
      end;
    VanWindow^.SetCoordSys(Global, Win)
  end;

procedure ZoomWindowOut(var VanWindow : TypeWinPtr);

  var
    Global, Win : TypeCoordSys;

  begin
    VanWindow^.GetCoordSys(Global, Win);
    with Win do
      begin
        X1 := X1 - 1;
        X2 := X2 + 1;
        Y1 := Y1 + 1;
        Y2 := Y2 - 1
      end;
    VanWindow^.SetCoordSys(Global, Win)
  end;

procedure RiseUp(var VanWindow : TypeWinPtr);

  var
    Global, Win : TypeCoordSys;

  begin
    VanWindow^.GetCoordSys(Global, Win);
    with Win do
      begin
        Y1 := Y1 + 1;
        Y2 := Y2 + 1
      end;
    VanWindow^.SetCoordSys(Global, Win)
  end;

procedure SinkDown(var VanWindow : TypeWinPtr);

  var
    Global, Win : TypeCoordSys;

  begin
    VanWindow^.GetCoordSys(Global, Win);
    with Win do
      begin
        Y1 := Y1 - 1;
        Y2 := Y2 - 1
      end;
    VanWindow^.SetCoordSys(Global, Win)
  end;

procedure PanLeft(var VanWindow : TypeWinPtr);

  var
    Global, Win : TypeCoordSys;

  begin
    VanWindow^.GetCoordSys(Global, Win);
    with Win do
```

```
        begin
          X1 := X1 - 1;
          X2 := X2 - 1
        end;
      VanWindow^.SetCoordSys(Global, Win)
    end;

  procedure PanRight(var VanWindow : TypeWinPtr);

    var
      Global, Win : TypeCoordSys;

  begin
      VanWindow^.GetCoordSys(Global, Win);
      with Win do
        begin
          X1 := X1 + 1;
          X2 := X2 + 1
        end;
      VanWindow^.SetCoordSys(Global, Win)
    end;

  begin
    case Command of
      ZoomIn : ZoomWindowIn(VanWindow);
      ZoomOut : ZoomWindowOut(VanWindow);
      Up : RiseUp(VanWindow);
      Down : SinkDown(VanWindow);
      Left : PanLeft(VanWindow);
      Right : PanRight(VanWindow);
      Quit : VanWindow^.Done
    end
  end;

begin
  OpenGraph;
  ShowMenu;
  CreateVanWindow(VanWindow);
  VanWindow^.Show;
  repeat
    GetCommand(Command);
    DoCommand(Command, VanWindow)
  until (Command = Quit);
  closegraph
end.
```

Turbo Vision

In our discussion of object-oriented programming, we introduced static and dynamic objects and have shown how they may be used in a number of example programs. However, one of the most significant aspects of objects is that you may create descendants of existing objects even if you don't have the source code for them. This means that you can make use of libraries of objects which perform all of the common tasks required by programs. Not only can you use the objects in the library, but you may modify their behavior by creating descendent objects.

In version 6.0 of Turbo Pascal, Borland has included an extensive object library called Turbo Vision. This library provides objects for including mouse applications, windows, menuing, dialog boxes, and many other common programming tasks. In addition, they provide the framework for creating object-oriented programs using these objects. By using Turbo Vision, you can simplify the creation of user interfaces for your programs. Moreover, by using objects from a single source, you can make all your interfaces consistent with one another.

This book has brought you to the point where you know enough to digest the Turbo Vision manual and learn about the large number of ready-made objects it provides. That should be your next choice for reading. Enjoy yourself, and good luck!

Index

G

H

I

J

K

L

M

Don't Waste Any Time!

Order the disk to accompany *Hands-On Turbo Pascal* by Larry Joel Goldstein.

Make learning to use *Hands-On Turbo Pascal* as fast and easy as possible. Avoid the tedium and potential errors of keying in the more than 100 programs that are included in the book.

To order the disk, clip or photocopy this page and fill in the coupon below. Send it with your check or money order for $20 (U.S. currency), or use your MasterCard or Visa. **(Maryland residents add 5% sales tax.)**

Send to:

Goldstein Software
21231 Georgia Avenue
Brookeville, MD 20833

Please send me ______ copies of the disk for *Hands-On Turbo Pascal* by Larry Joel Goldstein at $20 each.

Please indicate size of disk ______ 5¼" ______ 3½" $ ______ is enclosed.

Name ______________________ Charge my credit card

Address ______________________ ______ VISA ______ MasterCard

City ______________________ Account number ______________

State __________ Zip ______ Expiration Date ______________

Country ______________________ Signature ______________